Improving Staff Performance Through In-Service Education

Improving Staff Performance Through In-Service Education

BEN M. HARRIS
University of Texas at Austin

ALLYN AND BACON, INC.
Boston   London   Sydney   Toronto

Series Editor: David F. Pallai

Library of Congress Cataloging in Publication Data

Harris, Ben M
    Improving staff performance through in-service
education.

    Includes bibliographies and index.
    1. Teachers—In-service training—United States.
2. Teachers—In-service training—Law and legislation
—United States. I. Title.
LB1731.H27   371.1'46   79-22267
ISBN 0-205-06874-X

Printed in the United States of America

Contents

To mom, who knew very little of formal schooling, but who helped me to know about lifelong learning

Acknowledgments

To all of my colleagues and students who have encouraged and assisted me in so many ways, I owe continuing thanks. Their specific contributions are too numerous to recognize in detail. Professors Kenneth E. McIntyre and E. Wailand Bessent pioneered an earlier work with this author, which still influences me and is utilized in Chapter VIII. Maudean Sims and Scottie Littleton are but two of many students who have reviewed and criticized various chapters. A special set of contributions were made to Chapters I, II, and V by Drs. Jim Kidd, Jimmy Creekmur, Don Killough, and Dan McLendon as we worked together on a series of studies in Texas schools.

For unusually faithful and patient clerical and proofreading assistance, I owe special thanks to my wife, Mary Lee Harris, and to Cynthia Williams, Dottye Dement, and Barbara Kysor of Round Rock Texas.

Preface

This book is intended as a basic reference, source book, and text for those giving professional leadership to in-service training programs. The volume emphasizes practical approaches to planning, organizing, and directing training programs for professional staff personnel. Additionally, the book devotes much of its attention to the problems of designing training experiences for improving both acceptance levels and growth rates among participants. Both individualized and group training programs are included.

The focus of the book is upon the training of personnel in school and college settings with special emphasis on needs of the instructional staff. However, the basic principles and specific techniques presented may well apply to training needs of personnel in hospitals, business and governmental operations, and volunteer civic organizations.

The underlying assumptions utilized by the author are derived both from practical experience and study and from the theory and research relating to teaching, learning, change process, communications, and human relations. Planned programs of in-service education are emphasized in contrast with informal arrangements. Training for implementation of change processes, staff upgrading, as well as to assure accountability and quality control are emphasized throughout the book.

Distinctions among education, training, and staffing as components of staff development programs are developed to clarify operational requirements for each and interfacing possibilities.

This book is directed primarily at administrators, supervisors, training directors, and college personnel with responsibilities for policy development, planning, and program implementation. As a source book, it is essentially a practical guide to those practices most likely to be successful and includes case illustrations, forms, evaluation instruments, and sample training plans. However, a strong base of research and theory in the behavioral sciences is utilized to give readers professional-level understanding necessary for developing and maintaining in-service training programs of more effective and imaginative kinds.

The nine chapters of this volume are designed for use in at least three different ways. Chapter I is a rather lengthy introduction intended to provide the reader with considerable substantive information and to clearly delineate a point of view. Chapters IV and V are also largely informational and are intended to assist the reader in thinking about in-service education as professional leadership in the broader contexts of law, policy, and administrative organization.

In contrast to these informational chapters, all others attempt to assist the reader in practical ways. Specific procedures are illustrated and discussed; poor practices are noted; and alternatives are analyzed. The reader may sense some discontinuity in going from Chapter I, "The Nature of In-Service Education," to Chapters II and III on designing sessions and program planning, and then returning in Chapters IV and V to such broad concerns as law, policy, and organization. Users who wish to concentrate on the big ideas and problems may be well advised to bypass Chapters II and III temporarily. Those much more interested in the practical, technical aspects of design, planning, and implementation might want to bypass Chapters IV and V temporarily.

The Appendixes include a limited array of aids for the reader. Some provide greater detail on ideas or procedures previously presented. Appendix A provides the reader with a resource list that can be used in securing still additional practical aids.

Improving Staff Performance Through In-Service Education

1

The Nature of
In-Service Education

INTRODUCTION

In-service education (ISE), like any other kind of education, has to do with helping people grow, learn, improve, enjoy, think, and do (10:256). The title of this book gives a suggestion about the special place of in-service education in the larger arena of education. The phrase "improving staff performance" emphasizes the concern of this book for *staff* as people being served by in-service education. The term "performance" suggests the kind of educational outcomes that interest us most. These are but two of the important features of in-service education that set it apart from preservice education, but also from general education, vocational training, or career education, or adult education and even personal development, as important as all of these may be.

With no more careful definition than this, let's think about the tasks of helping people grow on the job! There are various approaches, of course, to improving performances of staff members. A tightly defined definition will be suggested later to help us keep on target. But first, why so much concern with people? The vignettes that follow depict diverse situations in schools, where modified performances may be in order. Each vignette depicts a unique individual or group facing ordinary but important problems of professional performance.

The New Teacher

Vignette 1 looks in on the new teacher at the end of his first year. He has performed reasonably well — his principal assures him that a new contract is forthcoming — but still he has ambivalent feelings about himself. He

---

Vignette 1. END OF THE FIRST YEAR

Bill Thompson has just completed his first year as middle school teacher of the "core" for sixth graders — English, reading, writing, spelling, social studies and advising, including career education. His principal has been talking with him about his new contract for next year with these words: "You've made good progress, Bill. I know you'll work harder next year to improve your teaching still more. I hope you'll start out with a much tighter rein on those kiddos. You know? Start out firm, make sure they know *your* rules. Clarify expectations. Set a no-nonsense tone to the classroom from the very first moment! You'll find that makes all the difference in the world."

As Bill left the principal's office, he felt relieved, he had a new contract and assurances of confidence in him from the principal, he thought. He walked down the hall to his empty room to straighten up and pack his things for the summer. Jack Martinez, eighth-grade math teacher was seen in the room across the hall. He was directing several students who were helping him clean and straighten things up. They were joking and laughing. Jack was seen sitting on a table, talking with a girl. Bill looked in and heard Jack saying, "I'll be back in town, Ellen, by August 2; so call me if you want a bit of help! Okay?"

Bill did not want to interrupt, so he paused just long enough to say, "See you next August, Jack, Mr. Martinez." He went to his room. As well as feeling relieved to know that he had a new contract and that the principal's evaluation reported no serious problems, he·was also glad the year was at an end. He packed the last of his personal belongings and walked into the hall. Jack could still be heard talking with students in the nearby classroom. Bill listened, curious about why Jack's students were staying around. Jack Martinez had been teaching five or six years. He wondered if he'd be better respected after a few years of experience, too!

The school was largely deserted. Report cards had been issued, and most students had gone for the summer. Bill felt a bit sad. Somehow, it hadn't been much fun! Oh, well, he thought, next year will be fine. The first year's the toughest!

---

senses that he is not yet competent, but he rationalizes that more experience is all that he lacks. His principal seems unaware of ways to help him grow. Valuable role models are close at hand, but still inaccessible without planning and facilitating. We will return to ways of helping Bill Thompson achieve excellence in later chapters as we describe individual growth planning, demonstrating, and diagnostic and clinical approaches.

Training for Leadership

Vignette 2 illustrates concerns for staff members other than classroom teachers. It is true, of course, that most in-service education focuses upon the growth needs of teachers, since they constitute the largest group of

---

Vignette 2.   THE NEW PRINCIPAL'S CRISIS

Jane Hunt had dreaded this moment. She had heard about such sticky problems and wondered what she'd do when faced with one. Now here she was in the middle of one. She was taking third grader Suzie by the hand down the hall. Her mother had come to the office to take her out of school. Jane had been principal of Airdale Elementary School for almost six months, and this was the first case of a mother asking to take her child out of the school when the father had expressly forbidden it *in writing*. Suzie was crying and pleading with Ms. Hunt, "I'm not s'posed to go with mommy! Daddy said not to let her take me away." Jane tried to be reassuring, "Well, she is your mother, so we must talk with her. Now no need to cry. We'll talk about it together in the office."

"I don't want to talk," Suzie screamed, pulling to release her hand from the principal's grip. Jane had to grab her to exercise her authority and found herself virtually dragging the child down the hall into the office.

Suzie's mother wanted to leave immediately with her daughter. She said, "We're leaving today. We must hurry or we'll miss the plane." Jane Hunt insisted they sit down and talk about the whole situation. Suzie was crying, her mother was irate. "I'm not going to talk with you about our family affairs," the mother blurted out. "It's none of the school's business. She's my flesh and blood, and we're leaving."

Jane was almost pleading for delay! Everything happened so fast. The secretary was out to lunch, so she couldn't even find the letter from the father. What had he said? she wondered. Were they legally separated or not? Was the father the legal guardian? Who registered the child — mother or father? Does that make any difference? What does the policy handbook say to do? Shall I call the superintendent? What will he think of me? Oh, why did I accept this job, anyway?

---

staff personnel in any school or college. However, Jane Hunt faces in the midst of crisis one of the many perplexing problems of effective leadership. That this is a crisis situation does not mask her need for opportunities to continue learning about the job of the principal. The legal, public relations, and child welfare ramifications of the situation she faces are numerous. The diversity of alternatives for action are not easily understood even by experienced administrators, because of changing conditions, new legal developments, and personal stylistic differences. Hence, only through continuing opportunities for in-service education can we hope to provide administrators and supervisors with deeper and broader understandings required of leaders. In a later chapter the use of simulations, in-basket exercises, and case materials is discussed as especially promising approaches.

A Team of Individual Needs

Vignette 3 focuses on the problems of a teaching team. Here we see illustrated the needs of well-experienced teachers for in-service education.

Vignette 3. CAUTION! A TEAM AT WORK

The team had been organized very carefully. Both experienced and inexperienced teachers were included among the five of them. They had a man on the team, well known as a good disciplinarian. He used to coach basketball and knew how to handle boys. Each team member had his or her own specialization. Helen was their grammarian; George was gung ho for American literature; and Jessie was interested in creative writing. Coach Mead was willing to work mostly on spelling, vocabulary drill, and punctuation, too. Ann was a bit of an oddball, some of her teammates had suggested privately. Her experience was mostly elementary and her major was library science, but she had a recent master's degree in reading and language development.

The team had operated all last year reasonably well. Swift High School was new; the team organization was new for Swiftown schools; and everyone seemed enthusiastic, did their own thing, and had gone along fairly well. At least, there were no big crises. Now it was late November of the second year! Parents had been asking questions about the English team. "Are the students getting a good program?" "Is it quiet enough in that large room with nearly a hundred students?" "What about college exams — will they be ready to pass them?"

The principal, too, was beginning to raise questions. Last week he had observed in the English team area twice for about fifty minutes each time. He left with some

Vignette 3 continued

concerns about what seemed to be happening. He asked to be invited to the next team planning meeting, but coach Mead, their team leader, replied that they would not have a formal meeting until after the Christmas holidays and asked, "Would that be okay?"

But the team was meeting *informally* this afternoon just before the Thanksgiving break. All were there except Ann, who had been released early to drive two other teachers to a workshop sponsored by the regional education service center in cooperation with the state unit of the International Reading Association. As the team members talked, they expressed concerns about many things: "Why has he [the principal] started observing in our area all of a sudden?" "What's he want to meet with us for?" "We know what we're doing!" "You know, this team thing may be for the birds after all." "I'm working harder than ever," Helen responded. "I'm afraid parents are getting up tight. Maybe we should begin to concentrate more on grammar and punctuation and vocabulary so they'll be ready for the SAT," proposed George. "The discipline problems just take so much time. If we could really concentrate on those who want to learn, we could get someplace!" offered Jessie.

Notice in this situation the common mistake of assuming that teachers could somehow learn to manage a team if they were turned loose. While the diverse needs of each individual on the team are emphasized, so too are the potential resources for promoting in-service growth suggested in that very diversity.

Never Too Late to Learn

The Elderly Matriarch represents a point of view about the importance of in-service education for all. The old-timers are all too often neglected both

---

Vignette 4.   ELDERLY MATRIARCH

She sat there in the lounge rocking away and drinking her tea. It seemed curious to Wayne Kennamer that only Loreen Cloran ever sat in that old-fashioned rocking chair in the teacher's lounge. He soon learned that she regarded it as personal property. Although no one knew for sure how that old chair got there, they did know it was "reserved" for Ms. Cloran, and she'd tell you "It's my chair" in no uncertain terms. Even the principal, Gordon Eckert, never challenged her right to the chair.

Vignette 4 continued

Ms. Cloran was the oldest teacher in town. No one knew how old she was because she wasn't telling, and no one else had been around long enough to remember. Wayne Kennamer, as the new curriculum director for Alpine Cove Schools, soon learned other interesting things about Loreen Cloran. She was the head of the sixth-grade teacher group. She prided herself in teaching "the good old-fashioned way" and made kids "toe the mark." She not only had a reputation for being tough but was highly regarded by many, if not most, parents as an excellent teacher. Furthermore, her test scores showed it. Of course, she insisted the principal give her plenty of the good students every year, and if any "boys acted up" she arranged to have them transferred to some other room.

Speaking of rooms, Ms. Cloran had had the same room for at least thirty years. She always refused to move, no matter what other changes took place. To Wayne's amazement, he also discovered that she had another rocking chair in her room. The kids said she used it a lot, too — taught from her chair.

Wayne Kennamer couldn't resist asking about Loreen Cloran. Principal Eckert advised him to ignore her as much as he could and try to get along with her. Wayne took that advice for about a year as he worked with teachers — observing in classrooms, arranging workshops, conducting demonstrations, leading curriculum development meetings. Ms. Cloran generally did not get involved with Wayne either. In fact, she failed to attend any of the activities he arranged unless it was part of a regular faculty meeting. They would chat in the lounge. He'd ask how she was, and she'd brag about her kids' progress or offer some negative feedback about one of his workshops in the form of hearsay! Still, they remained cordial with each other.

In the fall of the second year at Alpine Cove, Wayne was promoting more and better use of visual aids. Some teachers had expressed an interest in the use of 16 mm films now readily available from the regional service center, but blinds, screens, and projectors were not adequate for easy use of these aids. Wayne had secured money to remodel several classrooms over the summer; new projectors were purchased, screens were installed, and they had rolling carts designed so that even kindergarten children could roll the equipment in and out of the room.

To facilitate training, Wayne began to schedule "open clinics" in the teachers' lounge. He had a projector. Any interested teacher was welcome to come to the lounge anytime to get a demonstration and practice operating the new machines. Wayne spent as many hours as he could in the lounge each week to help out and promote the training.

It was predictable, of course! Ms. Loreen Cloran was not happy with all of this. Her lounge break was being disturbed. Those machines were a "nuisance." Having "boys" in the teachers' lounge was "just not right." "We teachers want a bit of privacy and relaxation when we get a break," she contended, obviously speaking for others as well as for herself!

Wayne Kennamer knew he was in trouble. He had to back down and shift his efforts elsewhere. But he also needed to save face. Ms. Cloran became his new challenge.

Wayne only had a short while to make up his mind. Teachers were talking. He decided to find a way to work with and through the "old matriarch." He

Vignette 4   continued

asked to visit her classroom. She said, "Sure, if you want to!" He did want to, and it gave him important insights. He found Ms. Cloran not nearly so tough as she pretended to be. In fact, she was well organized, systematic, friendly, helpful, and task oriented. She did teach from her rocking chair a good bit of the time, but the pointer she held was for pointing, not striking, as some had imagined. Her instruction was text dominated, chalkboard supplemented, and test oriented; but she differentiated assignments, guided learning on a personal basis, and even utilized supplementary materials some. She read stories, kept library books around, and used lots of pictorial material.

When she did get out of her rocking chair, she generally stayed up front, putting material on the chalkboard or pointing to and discussing writing and sketches prepared earlier.

As Wayne departed with a wave and a smile, Loreen Cloran hardly looked up. But a scheme began to develop in his mind. Ms. Cloran had made a comment that struck a spark. One of her students was holding a paper to show, and the teacher said, "You know I must save my legs for later. Don't make me get up! Come over here and show me!"

Wayne Kennamer began to put together *her* need to sit, *her* use of chalkboard and pictorial material, and *his* desire to get overhead projectors into use. He decided on a straightforward approach. He borrowed some of her pictures, made copies of them on transparencies, and showed her the results on the screen. He demonstrated the use of the film roll as a moving chalkboard, emphasizing that she could use simple grease pencils, sit in her rocking chair, and have full command of all the chalkboard she wished.

Only a few weeks later Wayne Kennamer was visiting in Loreen Cloran's room again. This time he had several other teachers with him. They were observing the use of the overhead projector but a lot more also. The old matriarch had become a better teacher, helping others grow on the job too. She and Wayne had worked together getting much of her regular material onto transparencies. She had developed a transparency file that reduced her use of the chalkboard, which students were now using more. She had a special stand that kept the overhead at the right level, right beside her rocking chair. She beamed as the other teachers watched her use the projector, first as a chalkboard, then for pictorial displays, and then to critique a sample of writing or reinforce a passage from the text.

---

as valuable human resources and as individuals who can grow and need opportunities to do so. This vignette also offers just a hint about the informal structures, traditions, and influence patterns that must not be ignored as in-service education is promoted as an essential aspect of the school operation.

The reader will be asked to refer to these four vignettes in connection with various ideas presented in subsequent chapters.

HELPING PEOPLE GROW ON THE JOB

Some will argue that "experience is the best teacher." If so, being on the job is nearly a guarantee of growth. Obviously, in the real world such formulas do not always hold true. For some, each year is a new and vital experience, and hence learning does occur with no special plan or arrangement. But for others many years are the same, except perhaps a bit duller, more boring, or more frustrating and confusing than those that went by before. For most of us the daily routines of the working assignment are neither panacea nor void but a mixed bag. Some on-the-job experiences do offer opportunities for learning, but the need for help in making the most of such experience is often crucially important. A chance to read, to see, to discuss, to analyze as one experiences can greatly enhance the learning process.

But then there is also the problem of assuring appropriate learnings. Experience teaches many things, and some of it is most *unfortunate*. Under certain conditions experience teaches us that so-called good practices won't work, or are too much work, or are impractical or too theoretical, despite their successful use right down the hall or across town.

Still another practical concern about helping people grow on the job rather than just hoping it will occur has to do with *timing*. Experience often doesn't offer what we need when we need it. Sometimes an experience is beyond our capabilities to absorb or analyze or adapt to our needs. At other times, we urgently need some enlightening experience, like that beautifully responsive youngster who makes a discussion click; but alas, there is no such person in the classroom today, so a chance for success is lost and we experience failure and disappointment. Or perhaps we try something new and promising and it just doesn't succeed. We need someone to critique the lesson, but neither the principal nor our supervisor was on hand to observe and help.

The new staff member is commonly inundated with experiences that tend to confuse and frustrate. Under such conditions learning rates may be reduced, and the person may adopt simplistic survival tactics. Such "successful" surviving may discourage further, later efforts to develop new skills and competencies; the survivor may not wish to take such risks again, let alone continually. Bill Thompson may well accept his principal's advice, and it may work, but how will he learn to function more like Jack Martinez?

Experienced personnel who have survived the trials and tribulations of being new on the job may receive little feedback on their performance they can use to assess the need for further growth. Under such conditions, the illusion may emerge in the mind of the isolated practitioner that his or her performance is quite satisfactory, highly successful, and adequate in all respects. Ms. Loreen Cloran may lose the opportunity to end a career feeling more competent than ever. To be sure, there are always problems, aggravations, even frustrations in the work life of the individual who is isolated in his or her endeavors. But these may be perceived, in the absence of feedback, as situational phenomena rather than as intrapersonal problems that might respond to changes in performance. Or, if the need for change is recognized, it may be sought in a random, rather unsystematic fashion, using only trial-and-error procedures. Furthermore, those changes in performance that ultimately seem to work may be only temporarily adopted if the perception guiding the search is one that holds the situation at fault.

Experience on the job is a good teacher if:

new experiences are provided
intellectual activity is related to the new experiences
negative outcomes are minimized
timing of experiences promotes learning in useful sequence
confusion and *frustration* are prevented
feedback for correcting faulty performance is available
choices of alternatives in performance are made in systematic ways

Assumptions about People

In-service education has no meaning at all except for the assumption that staff members can and will grow beyond minimum expectations of initial employment. As with other kinds of learners, it is often necessary to remind ourselves of such a fundamental assumption and be careful not to act as if it were not so, as Ms. Cloran's principal seemed to be doing. However, the utility of *raw* experience as in-service education has been called into question. One does learn as the result of the experiences he lives, and that learning continues throughout his active lifetime (69:5). If this were not so, people could not survive long in rapidly changing societies. However, raw experience may be woefully inadequate. The team members at Swift High School may well need in-service training to survive.

Exhibit 1–1 presents a set of assumptions that seem a sound basis for approaching the tasks of in-service education. We start, of course, by assuming that on-the-job learning will occur. However, the other assumptions are also stated explicitly and need to be more carefully analyzed if efforts to facilitate and promote in-service education are to be systematic.

The second assumption alluded to in Exhibit 1–1 holds that learning may be viewed as either appropriate or inappropriate to any given on-the-job situation. This is to say, all learning is not equally relevant to job per-

Exhibit 1–1.   ASSUMPTIONS SHAPING IN-SERVICE EDUCATION

1. People can and will learn on the job (48:380).
2. People tend to view each projected learning outcome as appropriate or inappropriate from an internal, personal frame of reference.
3. People experience satisfaction from learning that is clearly perceived as appropriate (69).
4. People need feedback on their own behavior to make efficient use of experiences for learning (12:5).
5. People need cognitive organizers (46) to make efficient use of feedback in guiding learning.
6. People need direct intervention in accomplishing *some* learning outcomes but not others.
7. People tend to want to learn some things, at some times, under certain conditions, at certain costs (but not all things, at all times, under all conditions and costs).
8. People are capable of learning (12:7) anything if the time, conditions, and motivations (rewards) are adequate (but not under any combination of these).
9. People learn best those things they perceive to be meaningful, purposeful, and satisfying.
10. People have developmental as well as situational and personal needs that learning can help to satisfy (48:55).
11. People's needs are met partially by learning, but never completely (they have other needs, too) (48:299–306).
12. People must learn in order to survive in the long run. But they do not have to learn to survive in the short run; instead, they can cope, resist, or endure.
13. People learn in active states under conditions of mild arousal, attentiveness, and stress (29:138).

formance expectations. Some learning may actually be detrimental to job performance expectations, but still other learnings may be highly relevant and helpful in meeting performance expectations on the job. This is *not* to say that all learning objectives contemplated for in-service education can be so nicely categorized, but it is to say that many can be. This point is expressed in terms of the learner in Exhibit 1–1. Equally important are these same considerations when decisions about the appropriateness of any given in-service objective are being made.

However, to reiterate, it seems essential to assume that many learning outcomes or training objectives can be clearly designated with substantial agreement as relevant or not to a job situation, and as positively or negatively related to desired changes in performance. Practically, such a classification permits in-service education program plans to concentrate on outcomes that are both relevant and performance related, while creating conditions that prevent the occurrence of other outcomes. Obviously, outcomes are less than fully desirable if they are not highly job related or are not concerned with performance change.

Using Vignette 1 (about Bill Thompson), useful objectives for his in-service education might call for learning that is related to students in more personal, friendly ways or learning to be more systematic and well organized. These could be valuable while not highly urgent performance changes. However, if this teacher learns to be even more distant from students, learns to create a very rigid and controlled classroom, or learns to be harsh and punitive in his response to student misbehavior, undesirable outcomes have resulted even though they are job relevant.

Assumptions about people's need for satisfaction, feedback, and cognitive organizers are closely related. Learning outcomes that are not perceived as appropriate are not viewed as potentially satisfying and hence are reluctantly pursued. However, less appropriate learnings once gained are less than truly satisfying and hence do not promote continuation of related kinds of learning activities. Feedback can help change the way people perceive reality and their perceptions of what is appropriate or inappropriate. Hence, it is not sufficient to say, "Well, if it's not appropriate to you, let's forget it." There may be a need for a more careful look at the data base being employed. Still, a further consideration involves the way the available data are organized to produce a particular perception. Different cognitive organizers may provide insights leading to new perceptions using the same data. For instance, in Vignette 2, had Jane Hunt, a principal, organized the erupting events in terms of the immediate emotional welfare of the child, she might have perceived it as quite inappropriate to bring the child to the office. Instead, she was using the legalistic frame of reference that demanded a different kind of response and may have prevented her from learning enough to make an informed decision. Similarly, the Swift High School English team (Vignette 3), suffering from lack of feedback, is suddenly reacting to its own uncertainty.

The assumption about direct intervention to produce learning is the focal point of many considerations in designing sessions, selecting strategies, and guiding in-service participation by staff members. The issue that arises in connection with this assumption is whether people can guide and direct their own learning as adults (71:244) or whether this may not usually be the case. Furthermore, if not all learning can be self-directed, how is the determination of the need for intervention to be made, by whom, and under what conditions? For example, did the principal at Swift High School intervene properly (Vignette 3)? Were the observations he has completed a form of intervention, or were they simply a response to his need to be informed? Did the principal err in not intervening earlier? Was it faulty to assume that learning to function as a team would be a natural outgrowth of sharing the same space and the same students over time?

The assumptions about people wanting to learn and being capable of learning are two sides of the same coin. Bloom's (12:76) concept of "mastery learning" has been widely misinterpreted to mean that anyone can learn anything. In a completely abstract, theoretical sense, this may be true. Operationally, however, the time required, the conditions for learning, the prerequisite skills, and the motivation required to persist in a learning task sometimes are too demanding. Similarly, it is true that all people undoubtedly seek to learn. But when, what, how, and at what cost?

Ann, the reading specialist on the Swift High School team, seems ready, willing, and able to learn a variety of things at the conference she is attending. But a three-day conference may not provide adequate time for her to learn what she seeks; the conditions found in a big conference setting may not be conducive to learning; or she may perceive the reactions of her teammates to be so discouraging that she may decide to enjoy the social festivities instead.

The last assumptions in Exhibit 1–1 fit no particular pattern. Each assumption seems important in its own right. Objectives are better attained when perceived to have not only meaning but purpose too, and satisfaction in the learning itself. Meaning and purpose are prerequisites of satisfaction in most instances. Satisfactions, however, are sometimes very personal; a sense of satisfaction is derived from having very personal needs met. Various situations demand certain performances and give satisfaction when they are forthcoming. Hence, the teacher who succeeds in enabling most of the students to pass the SAT in order to satisfy most parental expectations may feel satisfied. However, developmental needs are somewhat different. They change as we grow older; our values grow clearer, and life's circumstances may leave us more or less content with our lot in life. For most, the process of maturation (48) is one of identifying new needs that we seek to satisfy with new learning while old aspirations are left behind, realized or not. Ms. Cloran has no need to demonstrate her basic competence as a teacher, but Bill Thompson does. Ms. Cloran still has her sense of pride in her work and physical limitations of aging offer new problems to be faced.

The assumption that learning as such is sufficient to satisfy needs does not seem acceptable. Obviously, there are basic needs — food, shelter, security — that may be only indirectly related to in-service education. But, entertainment, social intercourse, sex, recognition, status, and other needs may compete with in-service education for time and attention. But they can also be made to serve. The Swift High School team could contribute to social and status needs and serve as a basis for in-service training, too. Bill Thompson feels lonely in his early efforts to learn to teach. Some personalized attention might serve both social and in-service purposes.

A Rationale for Staff Growth

In-service education is to the school operation what good eating habits and a balanced diet are to human growth and vitality.

Without substantial continuing growth in competence in personnel serving in our elementary and secondary schools and colleges, the entire concept of accountability has little meaning. The heavy reliance upon *people* to perform nearly all tasks required for building and maintaining quality educational programs is a reality that cannot be treated lightly. It is this reality that gives in-service education both its importance and its urgency. Were it possible to run schools with less dependence upon personnel, as in some industrial operations, in-service growth would be less essential. Were the competencies of school personnel less complex in nature, limited in-service training might suffice. If a ready manpower pool of highly competent people existed, improvements in education could be wrought by firings and replacements with less reliance upon in-service education. If few changes in the operation of the educational system were required in the near future, in-service education could be less of a concern. If the present certified personnel who are serving in our schools had all come through rigorous four- or five-year programs of *preservice preparation*, in-service preparation might be less urgent. If futurists could assure us that extensive retirements and withdrawals from teaching would permit much restaffing of our schools in the near future, then preservice rather than in-service education might be the more urgent need.

None of these conditions seems to prevail in the present or is likely to prevail in the foreseeable future. Significant improvement of education cannot be accomplished, it would seem, without a major programmatic effort at the in-service education of personnel in all elementary and secondary schools and colleges. This view is supported, whichever way we turn, when we ask how we can accomplish the improvement of education. The staff is the heart of the operation of schools. Money, materials, time, space, facilities, and curricula — all these are important, too. But initially, in process, and ultimately, the ability of the staff to perform is crucial. This is not always the case in certain other operations. Highly mechanized and programmed operations (e.g., a petroleum refinery) are heavily dependent upon people in the design and construction stages and become so again when rare malfunctions occur. However, such automated operations may operate for prolonged periods of time with little reliance on improving human behavior.*

By contrast with an automated operation, schools and colleges are heavily dependent upon human performance for nearly every aspect of their operation. Some might argue that schools are overly dependent on people and urge more efforts toward mechanical means to accomplish at least some of the high-cost operations of teaching. Hence, computer-assisted instruction, self-paced learning materials, and other approaches have been developed. However, these physical technologies have reduced dependence on people very little to date, and ultimately they may do more to rearrange or restructure people's responsibilities without much reduction in the overall reliance of schools and colleges on people.

So long as people make the crucial difference in the school operation, their in-service education will be a vital concern. Even if a fully qualified, ideally competent staff were available, *time* would gradually erode that competence as conditions change and old competencies become obsolescent. Even if new learnings could be gained from on-the-job experiences, staff turnover and the need to speed learning processes for some would still demand in-service education. The real problems confronting schools and colleges are enormous by comparison with any ideal conditions. The gap between what is known and what is in practice is enormous in nearly every school and college setting (67:1). The gap between what people can do and what they are capable of doing is also enormous for most staff members. Even the gap between what people are doing and what they want to do is very great for many staff members (69:5). Beyond such compelling needs there remains the long-recognized "obligation of all professional personnel to seek to improve themselves throughout their careers in education" (45:3).

Little has been said about *preservice* education as related to the need for in-service education. It would not be difficult to show the inadequacies of preservice programs for the preparation of teachers or counselors or supervisors. The literature abounds with such criticism. The contributions of preservice programs could also be lauded with references to significant improvements such as microteaching and competency-based training. Historically, excessive confidence in formal teacher preparation via college or university courses has had a negative effect on in-service education opportunities for school and college personnel (24:6). Phillip Jackson supports

---

* A curious and perplexing example of heavy reliance on *both* technological and human capabilities is to be found in the operations of modern airlines. Stockton (77) notes much concern among seasoned pilots that the National Transportation Safety Board tends to ignore the human factors in scheduling, regulating, and studying airline operations while attending in minute detail to the purely technical factors. And the near-tragedy at the nuclear power station at Three-Mile Island, Pennsylvania, has been reported more as a problem of human error than of technological defect.

this concern by noting that preservice training is "only the first stage of becoming a teacher" (42:38). Beginning teachers, administrators, librarians, and superintendents, are provided (hopefully) with survival skills, and the public is (hopefully) protected from "gross incompetence." The demonstration of competence in any complex job assignment is inevitably a matter of in-service education. Preservice education "is primarily an introduction to professional preparation" (36:3). These are the realities, too long ignored, that make in-service education the most important developmental task to which the schools and colleges of the nation must attend in the 1980s.

VARIOUS APPROACHES TO IMPROVEMENT

The improvement of instruction is the essential focus of in-service education. However, it is important to view this in perspective, to recognize the variety of approaches that can be utilized for improving instruction, for in-service education is not the only way. An initial distinction can be made between maintenance and change. The former consumes most of the time, personnel, and other resources allocated to school and college operations (35:21). The change function, in contrast to the maintenance function of the school operation, is often neglected. But neglected or not, changes can be wrought in diverse ways, each of which warrants special consideration; improving instruction means changing the ongoing operation in some way.

Changes can be *planned* or *unplanned*. In the former instance, we refer to them as developmental efforts or programs. In the instances of unplanned change, they tend to take the form of reactions, protective arrangements, coping mechanisms, and even organized resistance. The problems with unplanned change include the lack of predictability of outcomes and the high percentage of negative outcomes. Planned change offers no guarantee as a panacea, of course. However, when change goals are rationally selected, actions are controlled to assure reasonable change rates, and precautions are taken to assure minimum negative effect, the chances of improving learning opportunities for students are greatly enhanced.

Within the context of planned change, at least five rather different approaches to improvement are possible. Thinking more specifically about the improvement of instruction process, these approaches include:

1. improving instructional goals and objectives
2. improving instructional resources provided
3. improving the tools for instruction

4. improving the working conditions within which teaching and learning take place
5. improving staff performance

Obviously, the last listed approach relates directly to in-service education. The other four approaches are distinctly different, however, even though they might be utilized in concert with each other.

Improving Goals and Objectives

This approach to improving instruction tends to be most closely associated with curriculum development. It may well involve working with parents, staff, and students to secure changes in the school's instructional priorities. It might involve introducing new units, new lessons, or even new courses into the curriculum. While staff members will undoubtedly gain new knowledge and understanding as a result of working to change goals and objectives, the key outcomes tend to be substantially different. Changes in public perceptions, changes in students' expectations of themselves, changes in documents guiding teaching practices, and changes in content emphasized in classrooms are the direct, primary outcomes being sought in such operations. Concomitant changes in teacher performance are secondary, incidental, or indirect outcomes.

Because the school operation is so inevitably dominated by the people involved, it is virtually impossible to undertake changes in goals and objectives for instruction without also producing in-service growth, too. However, if goal setting is the purpose, in-service growth becomes a concomitant outcome. Furthermore, the in-service training required to assure that new goals and objectives will be fully utilized in skillful ways is essentially another matter. Hence, differentiation is important so that incidental in-service growth associated with curriculum development is not equated with the in-service education requirements for implementing new curricula.

There is another important distinction: whereas any curriculum development activity is surely going to be productive of in-service growth, the involvement of personnel will necessarily be selective, for all personnel can rarely be involved in all goal setting. However, when the primary objective is effective goal setting and restructuring of instructional objectives, the criteria for selective involvement will be quite different from those used when the primary objective is in-service education. Two quite different outcomes can derive from a single effort, but both are not likely to be optimally served.

At the risk of oversimplification, these distinctions can be illustrated. For instance, the school that seeks to secure public support for family life education in its middle school curriculum will need in-service education for the teachers involved. However, those faculty members working most closely with the parents' advisory committee to study the family life education proposals may need to be those requiring the *least* in-service education. Conversely, planned efforts to introduce career education as an integrated set of objectives throughout the curriculum may waste much time unless in-service education for the staff has been thorough and has preceded the work of introducing new objectives.

The emphasis on these distinctions and the inevitable relationships between improving goals and objectives and in-service education should not cause the reader to lose sight of the importance of each. Instructional improvements can be gained by improving goals and objectives in the absence of other efforts. Such changes inevitably produce others, but curriculum change can be a main effect.

Improving Resources

The resources provided for use in facilitating instruction can substantially and directly improve learning opportunities for students. Resources of directly instruction-related (29:4) kinds are diverse. Most obvious are fiscal and human resources. Within limits, fiscal resources can be converted into other kinds of resources that offer flexibility and variety in the ways that instruction can be improved. Human resources, while less flexibly employed, are obviously useful.

The use of funds for instructional improvement hardly needs to be illustrated. If money permits providing field trips, visiting lecturers, teacher aids, or other instructionally useful resources to be increased, there is at least some chance that student opportunities, too, will be enhanced. It is a common belief in educational circles that more money, less categorically budgeted, and earmarked for instructional purposes, will improve instruction. Such direct relationships do seem to exist. While money per se is not as powerful as is often thought, using money for instruction is quite obviously a way to stimulate improvements, quite apart from in-service education.

Human resources are a much-neglected resource. Obviously, more money can secure more human resources. But most often, increases in monies available have been utilized primarily to increase salaries. In so doing, increased or improved human resources are *not* assured, regardless of the worthiness of such expenditures for humanitarian, social, economic, or other reasons. The other side of this neglect is the failure to utilize human resources readily available for improving instruction with little or no money required (38). The wealth of human talent available through parents, students, and citizens has long been recognized but only nominally exploited. Peer tutoring, work-study programs, parental involvement, citizen advisory groups, and cooperative vocational programs are but a few of the numerous examples of efforts to utilize available human resources more fully. When skillfully used and properly coordinated, considerable increases in numbers and varieties of people functioning within the school operation can be attained. Distinct improvements in instruction can be provided in these ways with limited additional funding. In-service education will generally be required to assure efficient use of such human resources. However, the potential for change — for improvements — is essentially that of more people to serve students better.

Improving Instructional Tools

Anthropologists and archaeologists often consider the tools of a society as a crucial indicator of the society's development. Similarly, the tools employed give distinctiveness to each craft, trade, or profession and may well be an indicator of its developmental sophistication. If this is true, teaching in most schools and colleges is only gradually developing, but changes are clearly evident. The tools of nearly all classrooms a century ago would be extremely few and simple — a book or two, a slate, paper, and little more. Two generations ago the motion picture, the library, and the laboratory were added, but the older tools were still predominant. Only one generation has passed since tape recorders, television sets, kits, and games have become parts of the instructional scene.

The opportunities for improving instruction by improving the available tools for teaching and learning continue to be substantial. This seems not to be a neglected area, however. Expenditures in real dollars for instructional materials and equipment have increased enormously in recent decades. One could demonstrate that much of the tool kit for instruction tends to be underutilized. For instance, if one walked into nearly any school in the land at any instructional hour, one would observe a tiny percentage of students using the library. Notice the often locked doors of the language laboratory in many high schools. Notice the continued reliance on a single text in many classrooms, the limited and crude use of films, and the reluctance to employ simulations and games.

The neglect in this tools approach to improvement of instruction has been more in *utilization* than in provisioning. Hence, in-service education may well be an important missing ingredient. Nonetheless, many teachers can make better use of more and different tools. Television sets are still far too scarce in many elementary and secondary schools to facilitate in-classroom instruction (11). The single basal textbook still dominates some classrooms because school officials will not authorize the multiple adoptions many teachers need to use. If the tools of the teacher were regarded as more important, in-service program activities could better train teachers in their efficient use.

Improving Working Conditions

The condition under which the teaching/learning process is directed has many facets. The physical conditions usually receive the most attention, but other conditions may be even more important. Industrial operations have long attended to breaks, lighting, music, leaves, and other working conditions to improve morale to assure peak productive efficiency among workers. Morale in the school setting is also important, and it extends well beyond teacher morale to students and parents alike.

Many aspects of working conditions involve provisions for basic human needs: a place to rest and relax during off periods; toilet and first-aid facilities close at hand, clean and adequate for both emergency and normal uses; a place to eat without noise and burdensome responsibilities. Pioneers in industrial human relations have demonstrated the importance of people's feelings about their jobs and their place in the factory (33:50).

Yet schools and colleges often neglect to provide for the simplest of agreeable working conditions from both a humane and an efficiency point of view, in the name of economy, even while splurging on extraneous matters. A recently completed college facility costing $9 million had massive, expensive sliding glass doors throughout but no place to sit and eat in comfort, no telephone privacy, and not a single lounge for instructors or students. Open-space schools can be massive caverns with all the comforts of a factory building, or they can provide alcoves, corners, and special spaces to offer comfort and privacy as well as functionality.

Relating working conditions — physical or psychological — to the improvement of instruction is not easily accomplished. Physical conditions — open space, new equipment, special facilities — offer opportunities or limitations that may still rely on in-service education for productive utilization. The high school team of Vignette 3 is an illustration of unfulfilled teaming within a very modern arrangement of open spaces.

Improving Staff Performance

Improving instruction through change in staff performance can be thought of as virtually synonymous with in-service education. But no, it is not yet so simple. Given a staff group, without change, a fixed entity — then how else does one improve their performance? In-service education is the answer. But suppose people are retiring, resigning, being dismissed, being hired, being reassigned, or being promoted? Each of these conditions constitutes change in staff and is potentially an opportunity for improving instruction (38).

The performance of individual staff members tends to be most responsive to change and improvement via in-service education. But staff groups are a slightly different matter. When a third-grade teacher leaves Jane Hunt's Airdale Elementary School, an opportunity to improve instruction is created. When the Swift High School principal begins to search for ways to improve the English team operations, he may well consider reassignments of personnel as an approach right along with in-service education. When Loreen Cloran retires, her unique competencies will not be replaceable, but Wayne Kennamer and Gordon Eckert will have an opportunity for reassignment as well as a replacement. Bill Thompson and Jack Martinez need not work another year separated by a hall from each other; they could become partners, sharing problems and ideas.

In Exhibit 1–2, given in a later section of this chapter, the distinction between staff development through *training* and staff development through *staffing* is shown. The procedures suggested previously relate to staffing, but they have considerable promise for improving instruction.

DEFINING IN-SERVICE EDUCATION

Scholars and practitioners offer many variations of the definition of in-service education. But there is also a great deal of similarity in both concept and terminology used concerning this important developmental task. Both the similarities and the differences are important to recognize. Unfortunately, an extensive array of closely related terms has come into common use in referring to in-service education, and most of these terms are used without definitions. Accordingly, they tend to create confusion regarding possible similarities or variations in meaning.

Among the widely used terms that are used as if they were almost synonymous with the term *in-service education* are:

on-the-job training	continuing education
renewal	professional growth
staff development	professional development

Distinctions in meanings can and should be made among these terms. When they are used almost interchangeably, considerable uncertainty is created in the minds of many who are trying to communicate about in-service practices and concepts. Even some commonly used terms may take on special meaning. For instance, Nadler (55) attempts to differentiate the meaning of *training* as learning, which is job related from *education*, which is individual related, and from *development*, which is organization related. Obviously, such special meanings attached to commonly used words are very difficult to convey without reiteration, but these distinctions do represent an effort to be more precise about the meanings of terms.

A Definition

Throughout this book, the term "in-service education" is used to mean: *any planned program of learning opportunities afforded staff members of schools, colleges, or other educational agencies for purposes of improving the performance of the individual in already assigned positions.** This definition is intended to be broadly inclusive in certain ways while restricting the operations it embraces in other ways. For instance, no restrictions are implied on the kinds of activities to be provided. However, the purposes of in-service education are clearly restricted to learning outcomes related to the improvement of performances. The use of the term "staff" is unrestrictive, allowing for either broad or narrow application of in-service plans to various staff groups.

The essential terms utilized in this definition set some limits on the nature of in-service education as a task of the school or college operation.

A planned program is specified, eliminating a wide variety of events that accidentally or incidentally contribute to the purposes of in-service education. In prescribing in-service education as planned and programmatic, the emphasis is placed on designing learning experiences, assessing needs, projecting expectations, budgeting, assigning responsibilities, and evaluating.

Learning opportunities suggest the uniquely educational character of in-service education, distinguishing this task from curriculum development, staffing, public relations, and other tasks that may well be educative but that have quite different goals and objectives. For instance, engaging a staff group in the revision of a scope and sequence chart, selecting new text material, or working with the community to set instructional priorities are all developmental, valuable, and may produce learning outcomes. However, insofar as the primary objectives of these activities are other than the learning of the staff, they are not included as in-service education under this definition.

---

* This definition is adapted from one developed by the author in cooperation with staff members of the Texas Education Agency and representative school districts and education service centers in the fall and spring of 1976–77.

Staff members are specified as the persons for whom in-service education activities are planned. The reference to "teachers" is purposely omitted in this definition. In school and college settings, most in-service education should be targeted to teacher improvement because teachers are the bulk of the personnel employed. However, even in schools and colleges in-service education for administrators, aides, volunteers, supervisors, and board members cannot wisely be neglected. Of course, in agencies other than schools and colleges, in-service education is properly targeted to any staff group that is crucial to the effective operation of that agency (41:9).

Purposes of improving performance is a phrase with substantial hidden meaning. Improving rather than maintaining is implied, which in turn emphasizes the change process and eliminates monitoring activities. The term "performance" is utilized to emphasize job relatedness and practice. A narrow interpretation of this term would emphasize training activities and skill development. However, knowledge and attitude development are not excluded in this definition so long as they are clearly associated with job performance. Hence, a postobservation conference with a teacher that only reinforces current practice is not in-service education; if such a conference leads to the discussion of possible modifications of existing practice it is in-service education; however, creating a concern about the adequacy of certain observed practices may also be related to improved performance in the sense that cognitive dissonance is produced.

Still another omission is the term "instruction." To be sure, one could argue that in-service education should improve instruction. However, in-service education for noninstructional personnel is included within this definition, even though instructional improvement performances are obviously among the most important ones needed in school and college settings.

The individual is designated as the focus of in-service education in this definition. Obviously, only individuals can learn. However, the specification of individual performance as the focus for improvement emphasizes the concern for personal development within the school organization. The importance of needs assessment on a personalized basis is suggested. Furthermore, the implications of an individual focus are extensive when we come to consider planning procedures, the proper involvement of participants, and the array of learning alternatives that need to be afforded.

Already assigned positions is a restrictive phrase in this definition of in-service education. This is an essentially arbitrary restriction, which simply excludes a variety of training operations that are directed toward changes in personnel assignments rather than toward improvements in present assignments. Arbitrary as this distinction is, it has the effect of giving emphasis to improving performance in assignment without running the risk of in-service activities being directed toward promotions to new positions or even out-migration from the field or agency being serviced (22). In an era of rapid growth, with many new positions being created and urgent needs to reassign personnel, the limitations of the phrase "already assigned positions" would not be justifiable. The relatively stable character of staff in schools and colleges in the United States during the 1980s seems, however, to justify this restriction.

DIFFERENTIATING STAFF DEVELOPMENT

In a previous section, in-service education has been defined to include only limited aspects of supervision of instruction and program development. Similarly, various aspects of staff development and an array of terms in common use need to be more carefully defined. Throughout this book, staff development is seen as embracing much more than in-service education. Although general agreement does not exist on the meaning of these two terms, it serves educators well to become more precise in their meaning as used.

A Variety of Terms

The variety of basic titles or terms in current use to refer to in-service education is bewildering. Some are so general in meaning or so broad in scope of meaning that they cannot be useful when referring to in-service education. "Continuing education" undoubtedly is useful as a term referring to a great unspecified diversity of educational endeavor beyond the usual sequences of schools and colleges. "Professional growth" is likewise a term that may be useful in making reference to a very broad unspecified set of events. Neither of these terms can add anything but confusion, however, if utilized as synonyms for in-service education. "Renewal" appears to be one of those curious euphemisms so widely used by some, in an effort to avoid an unfortunate connotation. Unfortunately, these terms offer confusing niceties in place of precision in meaning.

Howsam (41:10) supports a very precise definition of in-service training and proposes to distinguish three widely used terms: preservice education, in-service education, and continuing education. Yarger (84) has developed a more detailed five-stage model for describing the time sequence for professional training. The term "continuing professional development" is being utilized in Oregon (62) as an overarching concept referring to a variety of kinds of training. These various individuals and groups have developed terms that reflect concepts largely associated with teacher certification. When the focus is on the formally organized schools with clearly designated staff groups to be served, a somewhat different perspective seems more useful.

Staff Development

The focus on school operations is important in giving emphasis to the context within which the staff works; the purposes toward which they direct their energies and talents; and the relationships among staff development, in-service education, and other operations. Exhibit 1–2 emphasizes only one side of the school operation — *the change function*. Ignoring unplanned change, five distinctly different approaches to planned change are recognized. Only one of these is *staff development*.

Within this framework, two distinct aspects of staff development are suggested in this exhibit. One aspect of staff development is referred to as "staffing" because it involves an array of endeavors that determines who serves, where, and when. The staffing task is concerned with having the best person in the appropriate assignment at the right time (38). Change involves group composition as far as staffing is concerned.

The other side of staff development includes at least two kinds of training. *In-service education* involves training of the kinds defined previously. *Advanced preparation* involves training, too, but is quite different in numerous ways. This kind of staff development involves preparation for new, advanced, different job assignments. It is a very important aspect of staff development because it relates to manpower planning.

Advanced preparation differs from in-service education in deriving its goals and objectives from projected or anticipated future needs and alternative job assignments, creating a whole array of relationships between trainee and trainer that are distinctly different from those involved with in-service education. Manpower projections, selective admissions to training, transfers, promotions, and reassignment are a few of the special problems that come into view for advanced preparation approaches to staff development. Important as this approach is, especially in growth situations, it is not in-service education.

EVOLVING CONCEPTS

The definition of in-service education provided in the previous section is consistent, to a large extent, with current practices (54) and concepts presented in the literature of supervision of instruction, teacher education (49), and personnel administration (38). The essential character of the in-service education task as defined has a long tradition in both theory and practice,

Exhibit 1–2. IN-SERVICE EDUCATION AS A PART OF STAFF DEVELOPMENT

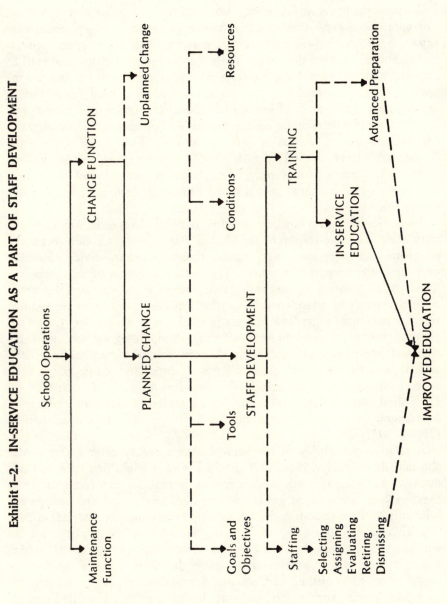

Adapted from *In-Service Education: A Guide to Better Practice* by Ben M. Harris, E. Wailand Bessent and Kenneth E. McIntyre.

even though the concepts have been evolving and the terminology is currently in disarray.

Historically, in-service education has been reactive rather than proactive. The continuous expansion of the school systems and colleges of an ever expanding nation has necessitated hiring any available person and providing additional training thereafter. The constant loss of well-trained staff to industry and family rearing has created added pressures for the use of "homegrown" personnel with full recognition of their need for in-service development. The growth of normal schools for preservice training was followed by rapidly developing college preparation programs, but the demand for teachers always seemed to outstrip the capacity of these institutions. The decade of the Great Depression (1929–39) provided one of the few opportunities for teacher supply to catch up to demand. But the World War II era quickly created new shortages that lasted for some thirty years (1940–70).

In-service education has been reactive to other changes in American society, too. The urbanization of the United States brought about vocational education and other curricular changes that required in-service education even of "fully prepared" teachers. The industrialization of our economy, along with legislation against child labor, moved schools toward universal, compulsory school attendance, which in turn demanded in-service education for personnel regardless of past preparation or experience. Other social and economic developments — immigration, desegregation, women's rights, depression, suburbanization, divorce, war, the automobile — have each influenced the schools and colleges in direct and subtle ways. Each such change has made in-service education less a matter of compensation for limited preservice education and more a matter of continuing education to respond better to the changing character of the school in society (51; 52; 61).

A relative oversupply of teachers became a reality after a thirty-year shortage in the early 1970s. This shocked teacher-educators, who had understandably come to think of shortages as normal. As they recovered from the shock of unemployed graduates and declining school and college enrollments, teacher-educators discovered in-service education (22; 25; 40; 49; 79). This sudden turn of events also triggered a new interest in in-service education on the part of militant teacher associations (46:32, 56–61) which began to seek more control over personnel decisions and attempted to respond to concerns of their constituents. Simultaneously, school administrators, local boards, supervisors, and state legislatures have exhibited new interest in in-service education as a clear necessity in assuring responsiveness to the demands of the society for better education.

The new, emergent interests in in-service education theory, practice, concept, control, and legislation are rewarding to those who have long maintained that this was indeed a crucial task that deserved much more attention than it had received (34:67–97). However, achieving perspective on the evolving concepts and practices of the past is essential if we are to avoid wasteful reinventions, or worse, repeating old mistakes.

The encyclopedic work of Barr, Burton, and Brueckner (6) was the most influential writing of the 1940s dealing with in-service education as an essential aspect of instructional supervision. These writers emphasized a vast array of "improvement devices" (6:326). This emphasis on process, procedure, and techniques was magnified by the extensive efforts of social psychologists and educators responding to post-World War II demands for in-service methodology. This was the "group process" era in which Cantor (15) and Bass (7) analyzed discussion leading, Bales (5) described the evolution of the work group, group therapy was applied to faculty groups (9), role playing became exciting (73), brainstorming (63) and buzz group techniques were lauded (17:87), workshops replaced institutes, and action research (4) and consultation became well-conceived ways of working. All of this had to do with in-service education, even when that term was not explicitly used.

Toward the end of this era of *techniques* in in-service, the National Education Association's publication, *The Teaching Profession Grows In Service* (1949) (50), stressed the importance of "planned program(s) designed to make the individual a more effective teacher" (57:9). This was one of a number of reactions against group dynamics for its own sake. Spears (76) published his unique work on *Curriculum Planning through In-Service Education* in 1957 in an effort to give clarity of purpose to in-service education activities that were seemingly without direction.

By the late 1950s in-service education had gained sufficient recognition as a distinctive operation in school programs that the National Society for the Study of Education (19) devoted one of its yearbooks to the topic. Edmonds, Ogletree, and Wear (24) were among a small group who were pioneering studies of in-service education with financing from the Fund for the Advancement of Education. Unlike earlier efforts that stressed either helping teachers survive or improving human relations within the school, Edmonds stressed "professional growth" (26:6), echoing the earlier pronouncements from the National Education Association (NEA). These writers further emphasized "the reality of the environment in which [the teacher] teaches" as the basis for in-service experience, clearly breaking with earlier notions about teacher preparation as course work and degree seeking. They also departed from earlier concepts in stressing "continuous and constant effort" criticizing "erratic, occasional activities" (24:6). In these respects, these writers of the early 1960s were well ahead of the practices of that era.

The National Society for the Study of Education published a yearbook in 1962 on education for the professions (59). This book ignored in-service education for the most part, noting that little was in evidence in most professions. "Continuing professional education" was briefly acknowledged in this yearbook as related to efforts in medical education (59:24).

The postsputnik era was one of new interest in in-service education related to curriculum revision. The National Science Foundation (NSF) institutes became the fad, with $30 million spent in 1959 and $40 million in 1962, despite growing evidence of the severe limitations of this simplistic approach (22:18). In response to growing dissatisfaction with NSF programs, the Congress amended the National Defense Education Act in 1964 to allow for institutes to be funded for both elementary and secondary school teachers in a broad array of content fields. Even so, these developments were regressive in the sense that a single approach and only content learnings were emphasized to the near exclusion of any other concepts or strategies.

The era of institutes and curriculum reform is still with us to some degree, but the War on Poverty programs of President Lyndon B. Johnson gave educators an opportunity to begin to emphasize program development, innovative programming, organizational restructuring for learning, materials development, and new staffing patterns. All of these developmental efforts were stimulated by various federal programs, including the Education Professions Development Act and the Elementary and Secondary Education Act with various amendments. Curiously, these acts initiated many changes in instructional programs in schools and colleges and greatly stimulated in-service education activities for facilitating these specific planned changes in existing programs. However, the emphasis was on program change, not on the needs of personnel for learning and growth as professional practitioners.

The concurrent efforts of Harris (1963) (34) to conceptualize educational change process as coordinated application of the various tasks of supervision had little effect. Even so, many federal programs began to serve in-service education needs at local levels. Even though such in-service programs were often distorted by compliance with guidelines of funding agencies, there were opportunities and money for attempting to design new and more imaginative in-service education programs.

The ferment caused by extensive efforts at instructional innovations in schools and colleges began to place emphasis upon the concept of design. What had tended to be only fragments of change — a guide, an institute, a learning packet—in the late 1950s and early 1960s became increasingly programmatic in the late 1960s. Individually Prescribed Instruction (IPI), a set of materials, gave way to Individually Guided Education (IGE), an approach to restructuring operations. Team teaching, an organizational arrangement, gave way to open education involving teaming and much more.

Similarly, in-service design began to have meaning in the literature. Bessent edited a monograph in 1967 emphasizing concepts of in-service design. In this document, Michael P. Thomas, Jr., developed a rationale for "organizational learning" as an essential outcome of in-service education where program change is desired (78). This is but one of a whole host of efforts to *design* for in-service education utilizing gaming and simulations, (82), laboratory approaches (50) and assessment/intervention systems (26), among many others.

This chronicle of in-service education as an evolving set of concepts and methodologies from 1940 to 1975 is hardly reassuring. Despite a long history of recognition as an essential part of the ongoing operation of the school program, in-service education seems constantly ensnared or diverted by less fundamental, but seemingly more urgent, development efforts. Nonetheless, a clearer notion about the unique character of in-service education as a developmental task of school organizations is emerging. This, in turn, is promoting fuller recognition of the fundamental importance of in-service education to the welfare of all concerned. Translating these new concepts into in-service education operations of better kinds is the substance of this entire book.

CURRENT STATUS OF IN-SERVICE EDUCATION

In-service education as defined and discussed in this chapter may be unique as a developmental task in our schools more by virtue of being widely neglected than because of its obvious importance. The publication of the fifty-sixth yearbook by the National Society for the Study of Education (19) on in-service education, published over twenty years ago, was clearly in recognition of a serious, growing problem of inadequate teacher training and selection in an era of growth in school enrollments. No gift of superior vision was required to predict increases in serious deficiencies in staff performances across the United States in the 1960s and beyond as a result of the baby boom following World War II. Obvious, too, was the growing urgency for in-service education, for the rapidly expanding corps of young, inexperienced, minimally trained, unselected teachers in public and nonpublic schools alike.

An Era of Neglect

Even though the problem was an urgent one and the needs were easily identified, the approach nationwide tended to be casual or sporadic. Many local school officials were highly preoccupied with school building programs and recruitment of new personnel from 1950 to 1960; in-service education received little serious attention in policy, little funding, and equally little time and attention of personnel. Colleges and universities were highly preoccupied with preservice preparation, as the demand for new teachers expanded steadily during this same period (40:6). Much of the service colleges had traditionally offered in the form of institutes, short courses, summer workshops, and extension work (82) continued but failed to expand and change to keep pace with enormously growing needs (22:5).

Federal agencies were among those that did begin to respond to the needs for in-service education in schools and colleges. The National Defense Education Act focused on improving teaching, as did the National Science Foundation through its teacher institutes. While these were clearly recognized responses to a serious problem, they tended to be poorly conceived, narrow in purpose, and rarely responsive to either local school problems or those of individuals.

Nearly every new federal education program has given some attention to in-service education over the years. Science, foreign languages, reading, mathematics, individually prescribed instruction, bilingual, early childhood, migrant, career, and special education have all been the targets of federally funded programs. All have given some large or small attention to in-service education. The results have been fragmentation of local efforts, sporadic thrusts with little continuity, and duplication of objectives and staff; rarely did an effective programmatic operation emerge offering either individual staff members or schools or colleges an opportunity for balanced growth and development.

After a decade of chaotic federal and local efforts to build responsive in-service education programs, many leaders began urging new approaches. Don Davies in testimony before the U.S. Senate Subcommittee on Education in 1967 said:

> Inservice teacher education is the slum of American education . . . disadvantaged, poverty stricken, neglected, psychologically isolated, whittled with exploitation and broken promises. (21)

This eloquent appeal has been reinforced by statements of grave concern numerous times in the ensuing decade. The extreme position that inservice education "has been neither functional nor useful" (70:506) is nearly echoed by some spokesmen for the NEA. A most outspoken critic argues that "inservice education is in a sad state," that it is "infamous" and "has no legitimacy in the structure of education at the state level" (22:24). Joyce expresses similar concerns in more analytical but still sweeping terms in asserting that "what is needed is not a pasting up of the old machine, but a building of a new one. There is something wrong with too many of the major dimensions of inservice education as it is presently being practiced" (43).

Nicholson (60) is among others who points out that the literature of in-service education has reflected and contributed to the neglect of good practice. He reports on an extensive survey of the literature to the effect that it "is voluminous . . . and as haphazard . . . as the programs it describes. . . . [T]here is only a handful of works that deal with inservice in any sort of comprehensive manner" (60:4).

One of the outstanding efforts of the era in behalf of in-service training was the Education Professions Development Act (EDPA) of 1964. This appeared to many to represent a commitment at the national level to support personnel development, to reduce fragmentation of efforts, and to view the improvement of education process as one of building staff capabilities at all levels in all programs. Unfortunately, both the legislative and executive branches of government failed to support this legislation. A report to the president by the National Advisory Council on Education Professions Development (39), dated October 4, 1969, warned that "Everywhere the mood appears to be one of cutting back — withdrawing — seeing how little we can get along with; in short, a steady retreat from the bold plans the nation launched several years ago" (39:1). This council referred to U.S. Department of Health, Education and Welfare (HEW) proposals as "timid and token" (39:6). These warnings were ignored, and the exciting promise of a "federal partnership" in building staff for local schools (rather than imposing new programs) was doomed to extinction. The EPDA expired some years later. The same council that had raised its voice in early warnings wrote in its final report in the form of a bitter criticism of both the president and the Congress.

A Brighter Side of Practice

All is not, critics to the contrary, in utter disarray. Most criticisms of in-service education as currently practiced (or not practiced) are justifiable, at least in part. But there is danger in failing to recognize the strengths while giving undue voice to weaknesses. Fortunately, in-service education takes many forms and has many sponsors and a long tradition. The roots of good practices go deep and remain healthy even when the tree is sickly, its blossoms few, and the quality of the fruit disappointing.

State and regional developments are growing out of the enormous flurry of interest, criticism, writing, questioning, and proposing in recent years. There appears to be a nationwide movement building. The federal efforts in promoting "teacher centers," a Teacher Corps, and special education objectives may be diverting and confusing, but they are not retarding the development of numerous other organizational arrangements for providing in-service education. Regional education service centers have been developed in state after state in the past ten years with legal mandates and funding to assist local schools with in-service education (3). Staff groups have been organized in hundreds of school systems to focus upon in-service education. State legislation and funding has emerged where nothing existed in many states in previous years.

A study by James T. Carthel (16) of documents from twelve selected state education agencies shows every one of them enacting legislation, establishing policy, or adding funding and staff for in-service education in the early 1970s. Another survey (62:3) of twenty-three states reports statewide action in fourteen of these relating in-service education to renewal of certificates. Similarly, these states had developed systems for approval of in-service programs, while sixteen had developed guidelines for use by local districts.

Professional associations offer still other evidence that in-service education is alive and developing. The numerous claims of various educational associations to some kind of proprietorship in in-service programming is striking. The NEA is clearly on record as wanting to be involved "in the formulation of policies related to inservice education" (47:469) and to negotiate and bargain collectively for the in-service education teacher groups may want. The Missouri State Teachers Association undertook a national survey (1976) focusing on legal requirements for in-service education to provide a basis for collective action (64). The United Federation of Teachers (UFT) has also demonstrated its interest by creating at least one "totally teacher controlled" (18:3) teacher center. The American Association of Colleges of Teacher Education (49) has been aggressive in its efforts to guide colleges of education toward a more active role in in-service education, sponsoring a survey of "competency-based inservice" programs (2) and a national institute for leaders in the field. Accrediting associations, such as the Southern Association of Colleges and Schools, have added to or strengthened their statements of policy on in-service education as an essential part of the school operation (75).

A study of effectiveness of nearly a hundred in-service programs is one of the more comprehensive studies of in-service education practices. This study offers some assurances that much technical competence is at work in school situations in offering in-service education of high quality. Gordon Lawrence (44) reported on over ninety selected evaluations of in-service education programs or projects. Only this limited number of programs was analyzed because his purpose was to assess "patterns of effective inservice education," and only carefully evaluated programs were included. The conclusions from this study of studies are not startling in terms of new knowledge. Much that has long been advocated was reaffirmed: teacher positive attitudes, active participation, self-instruction, differentiated experiences, personalized or clinical approaches, continuous programmatic efforts, and freedom of choice are all consistently associated with effective in-service education. More exciting is Lawrence's conclusion that the studies show a remarkable success rate, with 80 percent of the studies showing *significant* changes in teacher behavior. He further concludes that "differences in materials, procedures and design are associated with differences in effectiveness of inservice education" (44:7–8).

The Lawrence study throws some light indirectly upon the state of the nation with respect to in-service education. The critics have been very noisy, but the presence in the literature of nearly one hundred carefully evaluated studies is an important fact. Nearly all of these studies were dated between 1968 and 1973, a five-year period. Over half were dated between 1970 and 1974. Many reports of in-service programs were ignored by Lawrence simply because they were not well evaluated. However sound this might be for the researchers' purposes, it leaves us wondering about the number of case reports of fine programs excluded, and even more about the outstanding efforts scattered throughout fifteen thousand school systems in the United States (37). Recent studies in one state, reporting on many different local school district programs for in-service education, shows that many of the well-organized, ongoing programs of local schools are *not* well evaluated (20). This leads cautiously to a speculation that many times the number of effective programs studied by Lawrence are in fact in operation. Even more highly speculative is the expectation that the promising programs studies prior to 1974 are multiplying under the impetus of professional interest and concern.

The Florida program of "educational improvement for all . . . children" (28) deserves special attention as a recent beacon light for state-level leadership to improve in-service education. As early as 1968, the program known as EIE, educational improvement expense, became part of the Minimum Foundation Program in Florida. Each instruction unit (twenty-seven students) was given an appropriation of $1,720, for a total of $101 million for the entire state. These funds were utilized in various ways by different local (county) systems, but each submitted a carefully developed plan for the use of the funds. More than thirty different kinds of in-service activities were utilized by the sixty-seven counties of the state. Not a single county failed to make in-service education a planned part of its overall improvement plan. In subsequent years, Florida has continued to refine its statewide efforts at in-service education (49:26). Districts formulate five-year master plans (27:3–6) that are reviewed at the state level. Some "intensive or in-depth study" is required of all personnel sometime during the five-year period to guard against superficial programming. A record-keeping system has been developed to provide flexibility in allowing for travel, col-

lege courses, and other activities to be counted as part of the in-service requirement for each individual. Certificate renewal is also tied to this record
of in-service participation.

The funding pattern, in concert with master planning, remain the striking features of the Florida effort, in contrast with piecemeal approaches of
some other states. Funds are allocated specifically for in-service education;
hence, the commitment to the in-service level is clearly maintained. More
recent developments of less comprehensive kinds of Georgia, Texas (20),
Alabama (49:25–27), Oregon, North Carolina, and Wisconsin (16) support
the contention that some latent responsibilities are being assumed (30).

Six school districts were the focus of an intensive study by Sealey and
Dillon, under the sponsorship of the Ford Foundation (72). This set of six
case studies provides a better balanced view of the current status of in-
service education than most reports. Since the six districts were all medium
to large cities with 28,000 to 122,000 students enrolled, not all kinds of
situations were included. Nonetheless, quite a variety of situations were
studied, ranging from West Coast San Diego to Baltimore, Maryland, and
from Madison, Wisconsin, to Tampa, Florida; Austin, Texas; and Worces-
ter, Massachusetts. As might be expected, the findings from this set of
studies suggest a very mixed pattern of practices and arrangements.

Budget allocations are always an interesting indication of the commitment to and status of in-service education. One district studied had no
budget for in-service education, but all others had clearly budgeted items
ranging from a total of nearly $10.00 per student to a low of $1.23.

All districts studied had some kind of a director and office for staff development. All had been created rather recently. Rarely were these offices
directly related to others dealing with supervision and curriculum development, however. With only a single exception, "almost everybody agreed
that a high priority was accorded staff development" (77:19) and that it
could not be regarded as the responsibility of colleges. However, financial
and staff resources were not often reflective of this priority. None of the
administrators of these programs was at the superintendent's cabinet level.

These interviewers found no lack of responsiveness to in-service education among teachers. "There was no substantial feeling among teachers that
demand stemmed from the push for accountability" (77:20). Programs
tended to suffer from an overabundance of one-shot activities, but at least
there was evidence of tendencies toward workshops and hands-on experiences in a wide variety of formats (72:30) in contrast to the stereotyped
meetings so often referred to by critics.

Teachers expressed many desires for improvement but did not reject
in-service education. "It was generally agreed that classroom observations
for the purpose of helping teachers . . . were an important aspect of staff
development, but that they seldom took place (11). Needs assessment ac-

tivities in some of these districts were elaborate but largely subjective and unsystematic. Even so, teachers expressed to these researchers "a desire to have advisory help in their classrooms" (77:32). But the proportion of time spent responding to teachers' everyday needs was minimal.

This study of six school systems and their currently operating programs of in-service education clearly shows problems, efforts to respond, and priorities being assigned, but it also shows that much improvement is still needed.

A statewide survey of local district practices in Texas provides still another view of current in-service education (20). One hundred and sixty-nine local districts were surveyed, representing a full array of size and geographic categories within the huge state. While the study utilized only questionnaire data with a small sample of follow-up interviews by telephone, certain status findings seemed to be consistent enough to represent reality. For instance, only one district in four reported any kind of in-service planning committee or council with teachers serving on them. Interestingly, those districts using teachers on the planning committees tended to be larger districts. However, 84 percent of the districts indicated "some" involvement of teachers in planning in-service education. Even greater involvement of teachers in *evaluation* of in-service activities was reported, but an analysis of evaluation efforts indicates that evaluation design is one of the more severe weaknesses in current practice.

Another encouraging finding has to do with authorizing released time for teachers to participate in in-service education. Estimates indicate that over 30 percent of the teachers are provided with some released time over and above the seven days required by state policy.

The focus on *generic teaching* skills as well as on special problems of different subjects and levels was clearly indicated in most of these districts. While larger districts reported more attention to special problems, smaller ones reported that their in-service program time was approximately equally divided between the two kinds of objectives. The amount of in-service training provided each teacher ranged in this study from thirty hours to over sixty hours, with an average of forty-two hours for all districts.

Among the serious weaknesses revealed in this study was the lack of clearly budgeted funds, short-range planning, and superficial evaluation in many of the districts.

What Teachers Think

It is not possible to know with any certainty what teachers think about in-service education. Nonetheless, the question is often asked and needs to be responded to objectively. Unfortunately, critics often use statements concerning teachers' negative responses in extremely misleading, propagandistic ways. Rarely do some very outspoken critics specify whom the negative opinions represent or what in-service education experiences they are using as their frame of reference. Fortunately, there are numerous surveys of teacher opinion that can be useful. Interestingly, few of these surveys are overwhelmingly negative in their findings.

A statewide survey in Pennsylvania (66) in 1975 reported on over 500 teachers in 280 school districts concerning 360 in-service programs attended in the current year. They were largely experienced teachers with permanent certification. Nearly all of these teachers were *on their own time*. Simple ratings were used to secure teacher opinions. Instructors were rated "excellent" by 90 percent of the teachers. Approximately 90 percent rated the activities "overall" highly positively. Similarly high positive ratings were reported for "achievement" of competencies and relevance of activities. This study reports a high level of acceptance, even enthusiasm, for a broad array of in-service offerings. The lack of released time might have been expected to reduce acceptance, but apparently it did not. Simple rating scale responses do not warrant excessive confidence, but these responses are sufficiently uniform to call for some attention.

Another study of teachers' opinions utilized a statewide sample in Texas and compared teachers' responses to those of administrators and supervisors (51). In this instance, opinions were sought about a set of proposed *principles* of in-service education rather than actual practices.

McLendon utilized a modified form of the Delphi technique, in which respondents were asked to rate their acceptance of thirty "principles" of in-service education. The researcher hypothesized that teachers would be less accepting of the principles and *more* united in their expressions than other respondent groups — principals, supervisors, and others. Surprisingly, he found teachers highly accepting of these principles and neither more nor less unified than any other group.

This study, with completely random selection of classroom teacher respondents, cannot be presumed to reflect teacher opinions everywhere. However, differences in teacher responses by geographical regions — big city, highly urban, rural, and so on — were not markedly different. It appears from this limited evidence that teachers are highly accepting of in-service programs when they reflect some of the best-known and widely advocated principles of good practice.

A Tennessee study not unrelated to the one discussed above involved 646 teacher respondents sampled from every school district in the state (13). The focus of this study was attitudes of teachers toward current practices in their districts as well as some general opinions about in-service education. Highly positive (agreeing) responses were received to items having to do with freedom of selection (89 percent), recognition of different interests

(96 percent), involvement of teachers in planning (93 percent), released time (86 percent), and emphasis on performance objectives (90 percent). These were examples of things teachers *believed* about in-service education. In responding to items about current realities, teachers reported that most in-service activities "do not appear relevant" (73 percent), "do not like to attend" (63 percent), "are not well planned" (44 percent), and "are virtually useless" (31 percent). These are certainly indications that improvements are in order. They further criticized the activities in terms of lack of specificity of objectives, inadequate follow-up, and lack of planning (13:522).

Decisional participation by classroom teachers is widely advocated as important to teacher acceptance and program quality. For some, this notion seems to have become a fetish with the emphasis on control of decisions (18:3), school-based training, simplistic use of needs assessments, and subjective evaluations (71:244). A study by Belasco and Alutto (8) represents a body of knowledge that can help give perspective to the issues involved in questions of control and responsibility for in-service education. Building on a base of numerous studies on participation in decision making in organizations, these researchers studied teacher satisfaction with their jobs in two school districts in New York State. Over four hundred teachers were involved. They confirmed that teachers feeling the need for more participation in decisions that affect them also feel less job satisfaction than those more fully satisfied with their participation. That is, "Those teachers with lower satisfaction levels participate in fewer decisions *than desired*" (8:51). However, it was also found that the *most* satisfied teachers tend to be older, female, and elementary; and they are indeed most "saturated" with decision-making opportunities. Furthermore, satisfaction level is *not* closely related to amount of decision making but rather to the perception of the individual regarding *adequacy* of participation.

That participation in decisions is important for teachers and that job satisfaction can be enhanced are factors too important to ignore. However, this study supports others in showing wide individual variations in the need for participation. Furthermore, the greatest dissatisfaction with current participation tends to exist where organizational complexities offer the most serious restrictions.

The current status of in-service education is obviously not fully understood, yet it seems full of diversity from every objective perspective. What may be more important than *status* is the *ferment* that promises a nationwide movement toward higher quality in-service education. Rubin reports that "teachers, as a whole, are remarkably open to new methodology — even hungry for it" (69:5). He is not just expressing an opinion but is basing his conclusion on a study of substantial scope. Other studies seem to support this view.

What the many in-service events of the 1970s seem to portend is a breakthrough in understanding, by parents and classroom teachers on one hand, to administrators boards, legislators, and associations on the other. Understanding is growing that improvement in education must be pursued and can result only from improvement in the people operating the schools (68:3). Convictions emerge that in-service education is the primary vehicle for such people improving (14:310) and that we must become serious about building new programs (41). The technical know-how for developing in-service programs that are highly effective is available, in large measure. Obviously, there is much left to learn, but the knowledge base is quite adequate for designing to meet a large array of urgent, obvious in-service needs.

SUMMARY OF ESSENTIAL TASKS

This chapter has presented an introduction to in-service education as an approach to improving instruction in school and college settings. Tasks to be accomplished in mounting high-quality in-service education programs have been suggested but not analyzed in any detail. Much of this chapter has been focused on clarifying ideas, defining terms, looking at issues, and reviewing practices. The vignettes presented earlier were intended to give focus to the people who are in need of in-service learning opportunities. Assumptions about how people grow were briefly presented to provide a rational base for program planning. The different approaches to instructional improvements in schools were presented as a reminder that they are often associated with in-service efforts, yet must be clearly distinguished.

In rather carefully defining in-service education as a limited aspect of staff development, the writer seeks to give realistic, practical focus to all other chapters. There is a great need for better ways of conceptualizing the whole of staff development in education. Manpower planning, career development, selective recruitment, creative assignment, and productive personnel evaluation are all sadly neglected areas of *both* thought and practice in education. However, the focus of this book is not on any of these, because in-service education is more promising than any other aspect of staff development. More important, perhaps, it appears to be a cause whose time has come!

The tasks of building quality in-service programs are given detailed attention in subsequent chapters. Policies and other structural arrangements must be put into place at various levels — national, state, local, and individual. Strategies must be developed that can be responsive to a variety of problems, needs, and situations. There need to be program plans for implementing and maintaining ongoing operations offering learning experience of quality, but with strategic importance and continuity clearly recognized. The core of any program will always be the *session*, and the quality of the design for learning cannot be treated lightly. The training of leadership personnel to conceptualize, plan, implement, train, and evaluate for in-service education is perhaps a more serious concern than a chapter of this book can adequately reflect. The evaluation of in-service is a task that must be carefully provided for in order to assure both continuity and improvement in these operations.

Several chapters deal less with distinct tasks of in-service program development and are more illustrative in nature. Case studies, illustrations of instruments, plans, and training materials are provided in several chapters as well as in the Appendixes. It is hoped that these will serve as resource materials from which practitioners will wish to borrow.

REFERENCES

1. Allen, Dwight and Keven Ryan. *Micro-Teaching*. Reading, Mass.: Addison-Wesley, 1969. 151 pp.
2. American Association of Colleges of Teacher Education. "Report of Survey on Competency-Based Inservice Education." A report sponsored by the Performance-Based Education Committee. Washington, D.C.: Association for the Accreditation of Teacher Education, August 15, 1976 (mimeo).
3. American Association of School Administrators. *Regionalism: Past, Present and Future*. Executive Handbook, Series No. 10, by E. Robert Stephens. Arlington, Va.: American Association of School Administrators, 1977.
4. Association for Supervision and Curriculum Development. *Action Research: A Case Study*. Washington, D.C.: Association for Supervision and Curriculum Development, 1957.
5. Bales, Robert F. *Interaction Process Analysis — A Method for the Study of Small Groups*. Reading, Mass.: Addison-Wesley, 1950.
6. Barr, A. S., W. H. Burton, and Leo J. Brueckner. *Supervision, Democratic Leadership in Improving Learning*. 2d ed. New York: Appleton-Century-Crofts, 1938.
7. Bass, B. M. and F. T. M. Norton. "Group Size and Leaderless Discussions." *Journal of Applied Psychology* 35 (1951): 397–400.
*8. Belasco, James A. and Joseph A. Alutto. "Decisional Participation and Teacher Satisfaction." *Educational Administration Quarterly* 44–58.
9. Berman, Leo. "Mental Hygiene for Educators: Report on an Experiment Using Combined Seminar and Group Therapy Approach." *Psychoanalytic Review* 40 (October 1953): 319–32.
10. Berman, Louise. "Curriculum Leadership: That All May Feel, Value, and Grow." Chapter 11 in *Feeling, Valuing, and the Art of Growing: Insights into the Affective* (L. M. Berman and Jessie A. Roderick, editors). Wash-

* Suggested for further reading.

ington, D.C.: Association for Supervision and Curriculum Development, 1977.

11. Bessent, E. W., B. M. Harris, and M. P. Thomas. *Adoption and Utilization of Instructional Television.* Austin, Tex.: University of Texas, 1968.

*12. Bloom, Benjamin S. *Human Characteristics and School Learning.* New York: McGraw-Hill, 1976.

*13. Brimm, Jack L. and Daniel J. Tollett. "How Do Teachers Feel About In-Service Education?" *Educational Leadership* 31, no. 6 (March 1974): 521–24.

14. Calhoun, Thomas. "Throwaway Teachers?" *Educational Leadership* 32, no. 5 (February 1975): 310–16.

15. Cantor, Nathaniel. *Dynamics of Learning.* Buffalo, N.Y.: Foster and Stewart, 1946.

16. Carthel, James T. "An Analysis of Documents Reporting on Selected In-service Programs." A report to the Texas Education Agency. Austin, Tex.: Department of Educational Administration, University of Texas, May 1977 (mimeo).

17. Cook, Lloyd and Elaine Cook. *School Problems in Human Relations.* New York: McGraw-Hill, 1957.

*18. Cooper, Myrna. "Inservice Training Projects of the United Federation of Teachers." *NCSIE Inservice.* National Council of States on Inservice Education. Syracuse, N.Y.: Syracuse University, College of Education (November 1977): 3, 8–9.

*19. Corey, Stephan M. (chairman). *In-Service Education for Teachers, Supervisors and Administrators.* 56th Yearbook. Part I (Nelson B. Henry, editor). Chicago: National Society for the Study of Education, 1957.

*20. Creekmur, Jimmie L. "A Descriptive Analysis of Inservice Education Programs of Selected Texas School Systems Utilizing Operational Criteria." Doctoral dissertation, University of Texas at Austin, 1977.

21. Davies, Don. Notes and working papers prepared for the Senate Committee on Education, April 1967.

22. Edelfeldt, Roy A. "Can Competency-Based Teacher Education be Applied to Inservice Education? Should It Be?" A draft manuscript prepared for the Association for the Accreditation of Teacher Education, July 1976 (mimeo).

*23. Edelfeldt, Roy A. and Margo Johnson (editors). *Rethinking In-Service Education.* Washington, D.C.: National Education Association, 1975.

*24. Edmonds, Fred, James R. Ogletree, and Pat W. Wear. *In-Service Teacher Education: A Conceptual Framework* A theoretical base for the second phase of teacher education. *Bulletin of the Bureau of School Service* 36, no. 2 (December 1963). College of Education, University of Kentucky, Lexington, Ky.

25. Edson, William H. "Linking Schools and Colleges to Develop Continuing Education Programs for School Personnel." Minneapolis: University of Minnesota, College of Education, April 1974.

26. Evans, M. C., Ben M. Harris, and Richard L. Palmer. *A Diagnostic Assessment System for Professional Supervisory Competencies.* Document no. 11.

* Suggested for further reading.

Austin, Tex.: Special Education Supervisory Training Project, University of Texas, 1975.

27. Florida State Department of Education. *Criteria for Designing, Developing and Approving a District Master Plan for Inservice Education.* Tallahassee, Fla.: State Department of Education, n.d. [1975].

28. Florida State Department of Education. *EIE: Educational Improvement for All Florida Children. Plan Narrative and Statistics. 1968–1969.* Tallahassee, Fla.: State Department of Education, February 1969.

29. Fuir, Charles M. "The Reluctant Student: Perspectives on Feeling States and Motivation." Chapter 6 in *Feeling, Valuing, and the Art of Growing: Insights into the Affective* (L. M. Berman and Jessie A. Roderick, editors). Washington, D.C.: Association for Supervision and Curriculum Development, 1977.

30. Gage, N. L. *The Scientific Basis of the Art of Teaching.* New York: Teachers College Press, Teachers College, Columbia University, 1978.

31. Geffert, H. N. et al. *State Legislation Affecting Inservice Staff Development in Public Education.* Model Legislation Project. Washington, D.C.: Lawyers' Committee for Civil Rights Under Law, March 1976.

32. Group for Human Development. *Faculty Development in a Time of Retrenchment.* New Rochelle, N.Y.: Change Magazine Press, 1974.

33. Gyllenhammar, Pehr G. *People at Work.* Reading, Mass.: Addison-Wesley, 1977.

34. Harris, Ben M. *Supervisory Behavior in Education.* Englewood Cliffs, N.J.: Prentice-Hall, Inc., 1963.

35. Harris, Ben M. *Supervisory Behavior in Education.* 2d ed. Englewood Cliffs, N.J.: Prentice-Hall, Inc., 1975.

36. Harris, Ben M., E. W. Bessent, and Kenneth E. McIntyre. *Inservice Education: A Guide to Better Practice.* Englewood Cliffs, N.J.: Prentice-Hall, Inc., 1969.

37. Harris, Ben M. and William Hartgraves. "Supervisor Effectiveness: A Research Résumé." *Educational Leadership* 30, no. 1 (October 1972): 73–79.

38. Harris, Ben M., K. E. McIntyre, Vance Littleton, and Dan Long. *Personnel Administration in Education.* Boston: Allyn and Bacon, Inc., 1979.

39. Haskew, Laurence D. (chairman). "Leadership and the Educational Needs of the Nation." Report of the National Advisory Council on Education Professions Development to the President and the Congress of the United States, October 1969.

40. Hite, Herbert. "Three Scenarios for Inservice Education." A paper prepared for the Committee on Performance-Based Teacher Education. Washington, D.C.: American Association of Colleges for Teacher Education, October 1976 (mimeo).

41. Howsam, Robert B. "The Profession of Teaching." In *Issues in Inservice Education: State Action for Inservice.* Syracuse, N.Y.: National Council of States on Inservice Education, Syracuse University, College of Education, November 1977, pp. 9–13.

42. Jackson, Philip W. "On Becoming a Teacher." *Today's Education* 63, no. 2 (March–April 1974): 37–38.

43. Joyce, Bruce R. "Structural Imagination and Professional Staff Development." *NCSIE Inservice.* National Council of States on Inservice Education. Syracuse, N.Y.: Syracuse University, College of Education (March 1977): 3.

*44. Lawrence, Gordon, Dennis Baker, Patricia Elzie, and Barbara Hansen. *Patterns of Effective Inservice Education.* Prepared under contract for the State of Florida, Department of Education. Gainesville, Fla.: University of Florida, College of Education, December 1974.

45. Lindsey, Margaret (editor). *New Horizons in Teacher Education and Professional Standards.* A preliminary report, major recommendations and proposals for action. Washington, D.C.: National Commission on Teacher Education and Professional Standards, National Education Association, 1960.

46. Lohman, Ernest E. "Differential Effects of Training on the Verbal Behavior of Student Teachers — Theory and Implications." A paper presented to the American Educational Research Association, New York, February 16–18, 1967.

*47. Luke, Robert A. "Collective Bargaining and Inservice Education." *Phi Delta Kappan* 57, no. 7 (March 1976): 468–70.

48. Maslow, Abraham H. *The Farther Reaches of Human Nature.* New York: Viking Press, 1971.

49. Massanari, Karl (editor). *Higher Education's Role in Inservice Education.* Highlights of a Leadership Training Institute in Atlanta, Georgia, December 1–3, 1976. Washington, D.C.: American Association of Colleges of Teacher Education, January 1977.

*50. McIntyre, Kenneth E. "The Laboratory Approach." In *Designs for Inservice Education* (E. W. Bessent, editor). Austin, Tex.: Research and Development Center for Teacher Education, University of Texas, February, 1967.

*51. McLendon, Dan Proctor. "A Delphi Study of Agreement and Consensus Among Selected Educator Groups in Texas Regarding Principles Underlying Effective Inservice Education." Doctoral dissertation, University of Texas, August 1977.

*52. McPherson, R. Bruce. "Three Priorities for In-Service Education." *Instructor Development* 1, no. 4 (January 1970): 2.

53. Miller, George E. "Medicine." Chapter 5 in *Education for the Professions.* 61st Yearbook. Part II (Nelson B. Henry, editor). National Society for the Study of Education. Chicago: University of Chicago Press, 1962.

54. Miller, William C. "Inservice Education — New Strategies and New Priorities." *The School Administrator* (June 1974): 18–19.

55. Nadler, Leonard. "Implications of the HRD Concept." *Training and Development Journal* 28, no. 5 (May 1974).

56. National Council of States on Inservice Education. *Issues in Inservice Education: State Action for Inservice.* Syracuse, N.Y.: National Council of States on Inservice Education, Syracuse University, College of Education, November 1976.

* Suggested for further reading.

*57. National Education Association. *The Teaching Profession Grows In Service*. National Commission on Teacher Education and Professional Standards, Washington, D.C.: National Education Association, 1949.

58. National School Public Relations Association. "The School Volunteer." *It Starts in the Classroom*, April 1977, p. 1.

59. Nelson, B. Henry (editor). *Education for the Professions*. 61st Yearbook. Part II. National Society for the Study of Education. Chicago: University of Chicago Press, 192.

*60. Nicholson, Alexander M., Bruce R. Joyce, D. W. Parker, and Floyd T. Waterman. *The Literature on Inservice Teacher Education. An Analytic Review*. Report no. 3. Palo Alto, Calif.: Stanford Center for Research and Development in Teaching, 1976.

61. Oliva, Peter F. "Inservice Program Component Log of Collier County [Florida] Public Schools." In Appendix B, *Supervision for Today's Schools*. New York: Thomas Y. Crowell, 1975.

62. Oregon Teacher Standards and Practices Commission. "Continuing Professional Development: A Discussion Paper." Prepared by the Committee on Professional Growth. Salem, Ore.: The Commission, September 10, 1977 (mimeo).

63. Osborn, A. F. *Applied Imagination: Principles and Procedures of Creative Thinking*. New York: Charles Scribner's Sons, 1957.

64. Ray, William K. "Required School Attendance for Public School Students." Columbia, Mo.: Missouri State Teachers Association, Research Division, December 1977 (mimeo).

65. Rea, Robert E. and Robert H. Arnspiger. *Professional Development Programs — Education: II Instructional Personnel*. St. Louis, Mo.: University of Missouri at St. Louis, School of Education, February 1970.

66. Reardon, Francis J. "Participant Survey of Pennsylvania Inservice." *NCSIE Inservice*. National Council of States on Inservice Education. Syracuse, N.Y.: Syracuse University, College of Education (November 1977): 9–10.

67. Rogers, Everett N. "Discussion of Change Processes in Education: Some Functional and Structural Implications." A paper presented at the American Educational Research Association meeting. Chicago, April 7, 1972 (mimeo).

*68. Rubin, Louis J. "A Study on the Continuing Education of Teachers." Part I. *Instructor Development* (General Learning Corporation), 1, no. 6 (March 1970): 1, 3, 6.

69. Rubin, Louis J. "A Study on the Continuing Education of Teachers." *Instructor Development* (General Learning Corporation), 1, no. 8 (May 1970): 5–6.

70. Ruff, Thomas P. "How to Use the Consultant." *Educational Leadership* 31, no. 6 (March 1975): 506–8.

71. Saylor, Galen. "Three Essentials in Determining the Quality of Education." Editorial in *Educational Leadership* 34, no. 4 (January 1977): 243–45.

*72. Sealey, Leonard and Elizabeth Dillon. *Staff Development: A Study of Six*

* Suggested for further reading.

School Systems. A report to the Ford Foundation. New York: The Ford Foundation, 1976.

73. Shaftel, George and R. Fannie. *Role Playing the Problem Story.* An Inter-Group Education Pamphlet. New York: National Conference of Christians and Jews, 1952.

*74. Slagle, Allen T. "In-Service Education." In *A Candid Discussion of the Issues in Education* (J. M. Lipham, editor). Madison, Wis.: Wisconsin Department of Public Instruction, 1975.

75. Southern Association of Colleges and Schools, Commission on Elementary Schools. "Standards for Early Childhood Centers and Kindergartens." Area F, Standard 21. Atlanta, Ga.: The Association, April 1977, p. 5.

76. Spears, Harold. *Curriculum Planning Through Inservice Programs.* Englewood Cliffs, N.J.: Prentice-Hall, Inc., 1957.

77. Stockton, William. "Your Pilot Could Be an Accident Waiting to Happen." New York Times News Service. *Austin American-Statesman*, April 17, 1977, pp. C–1, 4.

*78. Thomas, Michael P., Jr. "Inservice Programs as Organizational Learning." In *Designs for Inservice Education* (E. W. Bessent, editor). Austin, Tex.: Research and Development Center for Teacher Education, University of Texas, 1967, pp. 59–73.

79. Thompson, James L. and Nancy C. Johnson. "Inservice Education: New Directions for Colleges of Education," (1975), 7 pp. ERIC ED 109 088.

*80. Toole, James. *Work, Learning and the American Future.* San Francisco: Jossey-Bass, Inc., 1977.

*81. Tyler, Ralph W. "Inservice Education of Teachers: A Look at the Past and Future." In *Improving Inservice Education: Proposals and Perspectives for Change* (Louis J. Rubin, editor). Englewood Cliffs, N.J.: Prentice-Hall, Inc., 1974.

82. University Council. *Rationale and Uses of UCEA Monroe City Simulation.* Columbus, Ohio: University Council on Educational Administration, n.d.

83. Wagoner, William H. *Staff Development: An Emerging Function for Schools.* Washington, D.C.: Department of Rural Education, National Education Association, 1964.

84. Yarger, Sam J. and Sally K. Mertens. "About the Education of Teachers — A Letter to Virginia." In *Issues in Inservice Education: State Action for Inservice.* National Council of States on Inservice Education. Syracuse, N.Y.: Syracuse University, College of Education, November 1976, pp. 35–40.

* Suggested for further reading.

II

Designing Training Sessions

INTRODUCTION

Sooner or later, in-service education takes the form of a *training session* in which one or more individuals engage in activities for purposes of improving individual performance. A session may be part of a larger program; it may be of short or long duration; or it may involve an individual, a small group, or a mass. It may be highly structured with carefully detailed activity sequences, or it may be fairly freewheeling. Whatever its form, certain preplanning and instructional designing are essential to success.

THE CONCEPT OF SESSION

The session is a basic unit of training in several respects. A designated client or group, one or more objectives, and a time frame are the essential minimum requirements for planning and designing. Without at least some solid information regarding each of these three factors, a design for instruction is not feasible. Other kinds of planning are undertaken for in-service education when clients are only nebulously defined (i.e., teachers, staff, aides), but session planning that provides some assurance of an effective learning experience for clients requires information about their numbers, their past experiences, their perceptions of need, their job responsibilities, and the like. These data provide the designer with at least a starting base upon which to determine objectives for training, specify an appropriate time frame, and proceed to develop a session plan.

A Time Frame

A time frame is a specified period of time, designated as to date and time, during which a given client or client group engages in planned activities, for specified purposes, without significant interruption. Ordinarily, a time frame for training will be no less than thirty minutes and not exceed four hours in length. The specified minimum length of a session is based on the belief that shorter time frames are not likely to be productive of discernible outcomes. The specified upper limit for a time frame is based simply on the physiological need for food and rest. Obviously, it is conceivable that an effective session of shorter or longer duration could be designed under special circumstances. However, the more important design problem is that of tailoring objectives and activities to time available and adapting time allocations to essential requirements of selected activities and objectives.

Objectives and Client Needs

The focus of a session plan upon objectives that are explicit and directed toward needs of a specified client or group, however determined, gives a unity to the learning experiences that result. A session is designed, therefore, to assure the accomplishment of the objective(s) for the client(s) at the conclusion of the designated time frame. Still another session might follow, of course, utilizing another time frame. Similarly, other objectives might be pursued with the same client(s), or with a different client or group.

The importance of the *session* as a distinct and basic unit of training is that it assures a focus on the who, what, and when in planning for in-service education. Still other important design considerations remain, but clients, objectives, and time are the minimum essential bases upon which to begin designing for learning. Once these are clearly known, activities can be selected, objectives refined, events sequenced, described materials developed, and logistical arrangements made.

Planning Distinctions

A set of distinctions in terms will assist the reader in understanding the details to be presented in this chapter regarding designing in-service training sessions. One of these distinctions is that of *a session* versus *a session plan*. A second distinction is that of a *plan* versus *planning*. Finally, let's distinguish between *design* and *plan*. A session is an operating reality. It involves real people, using time, engaging in activities for purposes of learning. In contrast, a session plan is a physical thing, a document or set of materials that precedes a session and guides the events of the session.* Elizabeth Wilson cautions against confusing these: "the thing in-action never really looks like the plan" (53:27).

This thing referred to as a session plan may be developed and utilized in a variety of ways, and the planning process is often regarded as of great importance (38:8, 6:19, 26). This chapter is not primarily concerned with planning processes, as important as these are. Design is our concern here. A design can be distinguished from a plan only with considerable difficulty. A plan is a physical thing while a design is a quality or set of qualities reflected in the plan. Even Webster's dictionary is not very helpful in clarifying the concept of design, but two definitions come close:

> an underlying scheme that governs functioning, developing, and unfolding; an arrangement of elements that make up a work of art, a machine, or *other* man made object. [italics added] (51:224)

In studies of innovative programs closely associated with in-service education, Berman and McLaughlin (6:19) reported that the "*amount* of planning was not . . . related to project outcomes." However, they found that "the quality" of the planning was important. In part, at least, the concept of the *quality* of a plan is one of process. We hold, however, that a grand and glorious process that lacks design will not suffice. The frequently observed, teacher-planned, grade-level meetings tend to be rather poor in-service education even when participants report positively about them. Planning process that leads to a high-quality design for in-service education is essential. In this chapter, our concern will be with such design.

DETERMINING GOALS AND OBJECTIVES

A session plan always has goals and objectives. They may be explicit or not; they may be realistic or not; they may be important or not. Ordinarily,

---

* We sometimes talk about a plan as a set of ideas about procedures that are in a person's mind. This meaning has special implications of its own, but then our use of the term is never this.

explicit, realistic (18:496), important objectives related to intermediate-range or long-range goals are advocated (36;44). However, the objectives must also be *related* to the client(s) to be served and other in-service education or program development efforts in logical ways.

There is a great deal of agreement among teachers, administrators, trainers, planners, and others that objectives for training must be relevant and reasonably explicit (18; 10; 8). Bessent (7:6) proposed as one of his "three commandments": "Thou shalt not commit inservice programs unrelated to the genuine needs of staff participants." However, this thoughtful observer also cautioned against the "superficial" needs assessment survey as a way of determining in-service objectives. Teachers strongly express preferences for "very concrete . . . 'how-to-do-it' workshops given by local personnel" (6:19). Fortunately, these are the kinds of objectives that are most easily specified but are not so easily designed for or evaluated. Furthermore, even when such "needs" are translated into objectives for training, it is still a matter of great concern that attention to such easily identified needs may neglect more fundamental problems, may be preoccupied with the technology of professional practices, and may serve the clients' need for personal assistance without adequate attention to needs for improving effectiveness or efficiency in practice (12). Rather rigorous needs assessment procedures have been developed. A kit developed in California (13) illustrates one approach that gives some assurances that superficial needs do not become dominant.

Making Objectives Explicit

Training objectives should be as explicitly stated as possible, both for purposes of validating them against the needs they are intended to serve and to guide the selection of activities and other design considerations. Mager (36) has developed a very useful guide to the writing of performance objectives. He argues that objectives are well stated, explicit, and convey maximum meaning with least uncertainty when they clearly express three things: (1) the *performance* sought in behavioral terms; (2) the *conditions* under which the behavior will be demonstrated; and (3) the *standard* of acceptability of the performance. These guidelines for writing performance objectives are certainly useful in session planning. However, they have limitations that must be recognized:

1. Certain learning outcomes (performances) cannot be so clearly specified in advance.
2. Such explicit statements of outcomes tend to encourage preoccupation with fragments of a larger, more complex performance.

3. Such statements tend to give importance to those outcomes that are most easily observable and undervalue those that are difficult to detect.

Elsewhere, the need to relate goals and objectives to each other is discussed. This is, of course, one approach to overcoming the limitations of performance objectives. A useful technique is to make explicit the goal-objective relationships at three or more levels of specificity, as follows:

Goal statements
    Major or general objectives
    Performance objectives

A more detailed breakdown of goals and objectives is often necessary to assure that long-range goals or complex program developments are addressed by the very explicit performance objectives selected for a training session.

Exhibit 2–1 illustrates schematically the relationships between goals and objectives for a faculty group in a senior high school.

In this exhibit, it is important to recognize that only a single goal and a *selected* array of objectives are shown in relation to each other. This is the *product* of a planning process in which many goals and objectives were discussed in terms of priorities for the school, needs of individuals, and practical realities. The objectives finally agreed upon were still too general for session-planning purposes. However, the schematic illustrated here is a document that reflects a set of agreements and understandings about what the various sessions will seek to accomplish.

Based on one of the objectives in Exhibit 2–1, a specific set of performance objectives for one or more in-service sessions is shown as follows:

1.2. To communicate better with students.
    1.22. To ask open-ended questions. (The teacher will make use of open-ended questions in talking with students on a one-to-one basis or in small informal groups).
        1.221. To differentiate open-ended from closed questions, given a teaching episode containing questions not clearly identified.
        2.222. To identify both open-ended and closed questions on tape recordings of one's own teaching.
        2.223. To revise closed questions into open-ended questions.
        2.224. To role-play informal conferences with students using predominantly open-ended questions.

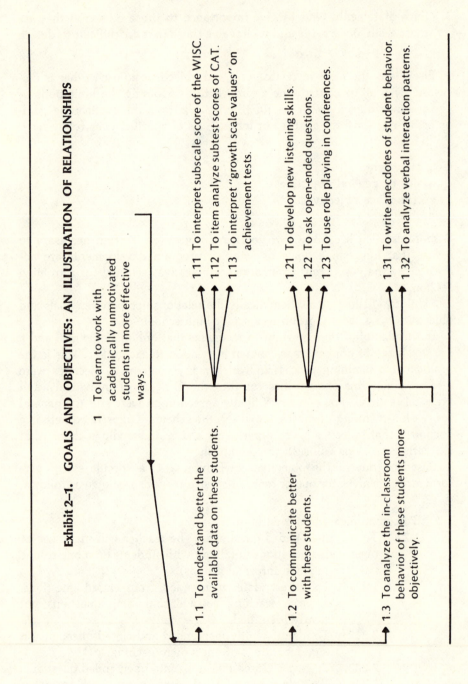

Exhibit 2–1. GOALS AND OBJECTIVES: AN ILLUSTRATION OF RELATIONSHIPS

1   To learn to work with academically unmotivated students in more effective ways.

1.1 To understand better the available data on these students.

1.11 To interpret subscale score of the WISC.
1.12 To item analyze subtest scores of CAT.
1.13 To interpret "growth scale values" on achievement tests.

1.2 To communicate better with these students.

1.21 To develop new listening skills.
1.22 To ask open-ended questions.
1.23 To use role playing in conferences.

1.3 To analyze the in-classroom behavior of these students more objectively.

1.31 To write anecdotes of student behavior.
1.32 To analyze verbal interaction patterns.

2.225. To utilize open-ended questions in an actual classroom situation, avoiding closed questions more than
one third of the time.

Defining Realistic Objectives

The problem of assuring that objectives are realistic as well as relevant
cannot be overestimated. It is easy to be overly ambitious, to specify
idealized outcomes that cannot possibly be accomplished within a given
time frame or with available clients, materials, leadership capability, or resources. It is often necessary to complete a preliminary session plan before the realistic character of the objectives can be determined. Specifically,
once a set of objectives is specified, one or more activities are selected and
associated with each objective, materials, facilities, and personnel are designated, and events are sequenced (see Exhibit 2–2). Then the following questions need to be asked:

1. Do all activities as sequenced (including consideration of procedures
   required) fit into a realistic time frame?
2. Does each activity or set of activities associated with each objective
   seem thoroughly adequate for accomplishing that performance for
   nearly all of the participants?

Exhibit 2–2. ILLUSTRATION OF A SEQUENCE OF ACTIVITIES RELATED TO OBJECTIVES

General Objective		
1.22	To ask open-ended ques-tions.	

Time Objective	Activity Description	Materials/ Arrangements
(min.)		
0 1.2	Visualized Lecture. Present via a transparency a re-view of the several con-cerns expressed (i.e., communicating with stu-dents, understanding test	Overhead projector, screen. Extension cord. Three-pronged male adapter. Transparencies 1 and 2.
1.22	data, and analyzing class-	

Exhibit 2–2   continued

Time Objective	Activity Description	Materials/ Arrangements
(min.)		
3	room behavior). Identify communicating with students and open-ended questioning as focus of session.	
1.221 4	Reading. Distribute a teaching episode. Ask participants to read it quickly.	Teaching episode reproduced for all. Leaders copy of episode already analyzed. Transparency 3.
6	Guided Practice. Present on screen via transparency the first question from the episode. Ask, "Is it an open or closed question?" Say, "It is closed if the student response is restricted in some way. It is open if the student has a variety of optional ways	
7	of answering."	
	Present on the screen the next question from the	Transparency 4.
8	episode. Repeat the question: "Is this open or closed?"	
	Reading. Direct participants to study each question and mark each on "open" or "closed" in the margin. Circulate about the room to give individual assist-	Allow silence.
12	ance as needed.	
14	Buzz Groups. Ask each group of 5 to 11 participants to discuss their decisions and see if all	
35	can agree.	
	Visual Lecture. Call participants to attention. Present a key via transparency,	Use natural groupings at library tables, or have every other row turn

Exhibit 2–2 continued

Time Objective	Activity Description	Materials/ Arrangements
(min.)		
	allowing each to check his or her decisions. Ask "How many agreed 100 percent?" Count hands raised. Praise. Ask if there are disagreements. "Do we need to discuss some?" Respond to questions with clarifying points. In any case, review. (1) Open-ended questions give students response options — optional content and optional format for response. (2) Closed questions tend to restrict *both* content and form of response.	about to face the one behind. Transparency 5. Overhead projector.
40 1.222	Tape Listening. Ask participants to see if they can differentiate open-ended from closed questions when listening to a tape; start recorder. Stop after first question and student response. "Bill, do you think this is an example of stereotyping?" Student: "No, I don't think so." Guided practice. Repeat the question. Ask participants, "Open or closed?" Reinforce: "Yes — closed. The yes-or-no response was dictated and the 'I don't think so' was about as much as was asked for." Tape Listening. Proceed to	Tape recorder, tape of classroom dialogue. Preanalyzed examples of questions.

Exhibit 2–2   continued

Time Objective	Activity Description	Materials/ Arrangements
(min.)		
	play another tape segment. Stop after one question. Guided Practice. Repeat above. Tape Listening. Proceed to repeat several times until no problems seem evident. Stop before interest begins to wane.	
60	Lecture. Suggest next steps. Ask each participant to prepare a 10 to 30 minute recording of his or her talking with students using questions, etc.	
	Adjourn.	

3. Can we secure the materials, facilities, personnel, and time as specified in the plan?
4. Are the personnel we can secure to lead participants in these activities competent to do so?
5. Are the participants as we know them going to participate in these activities willingly?

If *any one* of these questions is answered with a no, then changes in objectives may be in order from the point of view of feasibility. Of course, these questions may help in identifying other weaknesses in the selection of activities, materials, and so on. However, a logically developed session plan emerges from its objectives; hence, any weaknesses in these statements of intended purposes must be detected as soon as possible to assure a well-developed plan.

In answering question 1 in the list presented near the beginning of this section, those developing the session plan must mentally "walk through" the procedures for each activity proposed for each activity. A time estimate must be made for each activity with allowances made for passing materials, late arrivals, answering unanticipated questions, and special difficulties.

The more experienced trainer-designer knows how to estimate the time consumed by any given activity within close tolerances. The inexperienced will have to allow for errors in estimates. When a new or unfamiliar activity or set of materials or situation is involved, it may be wise to be more cautious, allowing more than a minimum amount of time. A trial run of an activity is always helpful, of course. When time estimates are summed for an entire series of activities for a session, the planners can readily see whether the total amount of time exceeds that available in the time frame provided. If the time required exceeds the length of the available frame, alternatives are open for corrections: (1) extend the time frame; (2) eliminate certain activities; (3) change the objectives. It is this latter alternative that needs very serious consideration in the *early stages* of planning.

Too many objectives, or objectives that are too complex, cannot be adequately dealt with by a longer session or by abbreviating activity sequences. To resort to these solutions courts failure. It is important to look at objectives with a critical, realistic eye and to revise them as drastically as necessary before the plan becomes fully developed. The cardinal principle here might be: *better do a little well than a lot poorly!*

Selecting the Important Objectives

When objectives have been selected for relevance by relating them to larger goals and needs, specified clearly, and tested for feasibility, they may still *not* be very important. The rigorous processes of narrowing, limiting, selecting, and specifying can lead to choosing the least important ones of all. This is not likely, given a thoughtful set of sequences as suggested above, but it surely can happen. How does one avoid this?

A simple technique for testing the importance of a carefully selected objective is to allow a few days to pass before finalizing decisions about objectives for a session. Still another technique is to compare and contrast selected objectives with a representative group of those objectives that were cast aside in the planning process. A still more elaborate but very promising technique involves asking participants and others concerned to review and react to a set of proposed objectives.*

---

* Bishop (8) is one of many who present rather elaborate schemes for student needs and system priorities determination as ways of determining objectives. These have merit, of course, but may be much too costly for practical application. Obviously, if elaborate assessment systems are in operation and such data and priorities have been generated, then they become useful sources for at least preliminary selection of objectives. Still, many of the validation problems present here will need to be applied when a particular client or group and a specific session are in focus.

To illustrate this problem and the need for validation of objectives in terms of criteria of importance, consider the efforts of a curriculum development project team.* Exhibit 2–3 schematically indicates the flow of events related to the team's efforts in developing new curricula and field testing their materials. They began to recognize the need to train teachers in using the materials prior to testing. As this was analyzed, it became apparent that while specialized competencies required were minimal, an array of very basic competencies was essential, and many teachers included in field tests did not have a full repertoire of these competencies at their disposal. Skills in giving positive reinforcements and in stimulating verbal interactions among students were missing or at a low level in most teachers associated with the project. The field tests were not valid and could not be used to demonstrate the effectiveness of the curriculum materials so long as prerequisite teaching competencies were missing.

This project team turned to the task of planning in-service training sessions for teachers based on this assessment of needs. Referring to Exhibit 2–3 again, five general objectives and related specific objectives for each are shown below in abbreviated form:

II. Positive Reinforcement
    A.   To avoid negative reinforcers.
        1.   To avoid any of the negatively loaded terms specified in nine out of ten episodes selected from three lessons.
        2.   To avoid any comments on papers returned or posted which are negatively loaded for three months.
    B.   To increase verbal reinforcers.
        3.   To increase the variety of praising terms used three or more times during a lesson so that at least seven different terms are employed on an average in a sample of three lessons.
        4.   To increase the length of praising phrases or expressions so that 60 percent are more than five words long.
    C.   To increase nonverbal reinforcers.
        5.   To increase broad smiles.
III. Verbal Interaction
    A.   To reduce teacher talk.
    B.   To increase pupil-to-pupil interactions.

As might be expected, training activities could most readily be planned to focus on the objectives relating to reducing teacher talk. This was a most enticing starting point. This could hardly be accepted, however, as a

* Based on the author's work with the Multi-cultural Social Education Project, Southwest Educational Development Laboratory, Dr. Dell Felder, Director, 1969–70.

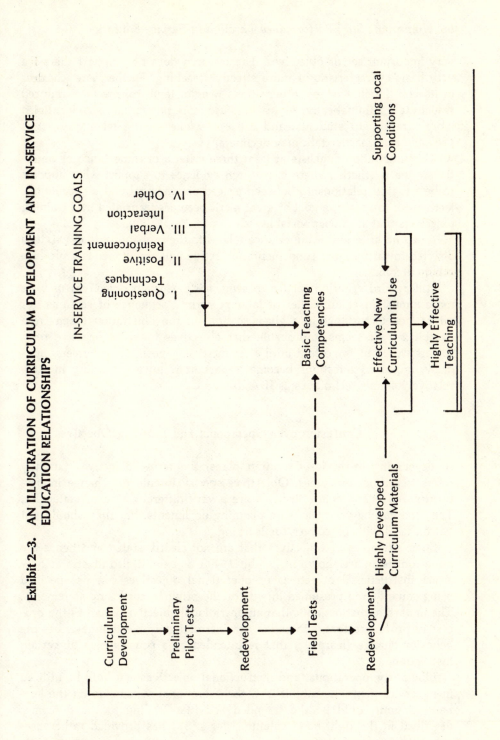

Exhibit 2–3. AN ILLUSTRATION OF CURRICULUM DEVELOPMENT AND IN-SERVICE EDUCATION RELATIONSHIPS

IN-SERVICE TRAINING GOALS

I. Questioning Techniques
II. Positive Reinforcement
III. Verbal Interaction
IV. Other

Basic Teaching Competencies

Effective New Curriculum in Use

Highly Effective Teaching

Supporting Local Conditions

Curriculum Development

Preliminary Pilot Tests

Redevelopment

Field Tests

Redevelopment

Highly Developed Curriculum Materials

very important set of objectives. The research does not support this as a very basic characteristic of more effective teaching. Furthermore, changes in teaching behavior of other kinds would tend to produce reduced teacher talk automatically. As teachers use more nonverbal behavior, listen more carefully to students, and use better questioning techniques, it is probable that teacher talk may decline anyway.

This illustration suggests at least three criteria of importance of objectives. One is whether there is research evidence to support what appears to be a logical relationship between a need and/or goal and a specific objective. All too often, a goal of great merit becomes translated into training objectives that are unsupportable.

A second criterion of importance relates to the probability that activities directed toward a more fundamental objective will simultaneously produce other outcomes.

Still a third criterion relates to sequencing. Certain objectives may be more important at an earlier or later point in a sequence of sessions but might lack importance in a given session. In the illustration taken from Exhibit 2–3, it seems improbable that objectives to avoid negative reinforcers would be important until after increasing positive reinforcers. Similarly, improved questions become important following training in such relatively simple techniques as II A, B, and C.

Confusion over Operational and Learning Obectives

In developing in-service education plans, the term "objectives" usually refers to learner outcomes. Objectives specify intents for change in performances. *Operational* objectives are a very different kind of statement. They too can be very useful in planning documents, but they should not be confused with objectives for learning.

Some examples of objectives that are not clearly stated and hence are quite confusing are shown in Exhibit 2–4. This exhibit also illustrates how either instructional objectives or operational objectives can be specified using some of the presumed intents of the original, confusing statements. The important distinction is that an operational objective describes the process or procedure that is intended. An instructional objective describes the behavior change (learning) that is intended as a consequence of certain instruction.

Obviously, operational and instructional objectives can *both* be utilized in in-service plans. In Exhibit 2–4, the operational statements on the left-hand column could be the intended activities leading to the outcomes described in the right-hand column. Mager (36) has provided rather useful guidelines for using operational objectives in planning instruction. Gen-

Exhibit 2–4. EXAMPLES OF OPERATIONAL AND
INSTRUCTIONAL OBJECTIVES

Revised as Operational Objective	*Confused, Unclear Statement*	*Revised as Instructional Objective*
To verbalize personal experiences connected with readiness problems. To write a set of anecdotes, briefly reporting experiences. To use a list of readiness principles and concepts as the basis for discussing anecdotes.	"To analyze a personal experience as a basis for discussing readiness."	Given a set of readiness principles or concepts, will analyze anecdotes to match principles and concepts to events described, to concur with peers 85 percent of the time.
To meet with a specialist following a lesson that is tape-recorded to apply guidelines and check agreements.	"To evaluate own performance during a lesson applying guidelines."	To analyze a tape-recorded lesson applying performance guidelines so as to agree with a specialist on 80 percent of the items.

erally, they seem to be more widely used in specifying project operations of noninstructional kinds.

In evading responsibility for being rather explicit about the intended outcomes of a session or program, some planners resort to an array of vague and curious phrases. For instance:

"Specifically, this conference aims to provide opportunities to study the way in which . . ."

". . . the focus is on an exploration of how attitudes . . . influence and the ways in which men and women exercise authority and leadership."

The training planning document from which these vagaries were taken also assures participants that their several days and hundreds of dollars will not include an "attempt to prescribe what anyone shall learn. The focus, however, is upon the problems encountered in the exercise of authority and leadership" (1:4). This dedication to lack of prescriptiveness is likely to be more appreciated than the lack of specificity about what might be taught. Plans such as these, without objectives, cannot be criticized so long as participants are willing, recognize that no specific learning outcomes have been designed for, and have pretty explicit information about the character of the activities planned. These conditions don't often hold in training situations. Participants have needs and interests, and the designers have a responsibility for trying to arrange relevant experiences. If objectives cannot be specified, how do we validate the experiences? The foregoing quotation, along with many years of experience with such group relations sessions, leads this author to conclude that the objectives are, in fact, clearly specified but not shared with the participants. That possibility raises many new issues!

Withheld Objectives

The illustrations given of confusing, vague, and even evasive statements of objectives may bring to the mind of the reader questions about discovery approaches where the design calls for participants, in effect, to discover what the objective was. Certainly, this is a legitimate approach. It represents one of a number of circumstances that justifies either withholding objectives (even though they have been made explicit in the plan) or even failing to specify objectives at all.

In those instances when the design is such that a carefully sequenced series of activities is planned to lead the participant to discover, deduce, or synthesize, the objectives must still be clearly specified. They are withheld from participants to heighten curiosity, maximize initiative, stimulate creativity, challenge for involvement, and the like. Similarly, the objectives are used at a later point in the sequence as a way of helping participants check their accomplishments and organize the learning.

In-service sessions involving cases (16), simulations and games (30), or the laboratory approach (39) often call for withholding objectives. They rely instead on the stimulating nature of the activity itself, the face validity of the material, and the confidence or trust in the trainer to motivate participants and make the session meaningful from the beginning.

There are, of course, experiences that are so real, so involving, so satisfying *in the doing*, and so potentially productive of a broad range of learning outcomes that they can be utilized without carefully specified objectives. Examples of such in-service activities include demonstrations of teaching, visits to other classrooms, field trips, internships, a powerful dramatic production, or a social-recreational event. Unfortunately, the outcomes from such experiences tend to be more potential than assured. To be sure, all of these experiences have been productive for some individuals under some sets of conditions, but when they are quite expensive in terms of time and other costs, their use without specified objectives must be questioned. In fact, using these same experiences with carefully formulated objectives, even if general, seems to add to their effectiveness.

THE SESSION PLAN

The *plan* referred to here is a document or set of documents and materials that guides the implementation of session activities in operation. Session plans are sometimes retained in the head of the person in charge, but this is not a *plan* as referred to here because of the serious defects associated with such tangible planning. While it is conceivable that an individual with great skill and experience can direct an effective in-service session with no planning document in existence, such is highly unlikely in most instances. Carefully detailed plans are important (4) in order to assure the following:

1. That the best possible design has been developed.
2. That all materials and arrangements have been provided for.
3. That the design can be communicated to others who need to be involved.
4. That the session leaders will be guided to implement the session designed.
5. That the design can be reused with minor variations with another client or group.

A session plan may be a relatively simple document when only a few activities or persons are involved or when the design is highly standardized, as in the case of programmed materials. As a greater variety of materials, activities, and persons become actively involved in the session events, the planning document and support materials are necessarily more elaborate. A plan in its most simple format may consist of a two- or three-page outline, is shown as Appendix C. This outline provides details regarding the theme or topic, date(s), place, phone contact, sponsoring organization, characteristics of participant group. A major goal and specific objectives are specified. A detailed agenda includes a timetable for activities as sequenced. Activities are described and keyed to an objective. Responsibilities are designated. A checklist of equipment and materials needed is detailed and responsibility designated.

Basic Parts of a Plan

Much more elaborate plans are most often required, because the limited detail provided in the above outline leaves too much for further development. Exhibit 2–5 outlines eight parts of a more complete session plan.

Exhibit 2–5. GUIDELINES FOR PREPARING AN IN-SERVICE SESSION PLAN

I. *Statement of the Problem*
   A. The educational problem to which the session is related is clearly identified.
   B. The problem is described in concrete terms related to real situations. The problem is documented as real and its importance to the organization made clear.
   C. The problem is defined in terms that make it at least partially responsive to in-service education or training, as distinguished from curriculum development, staffing, funding, and so on.
   D. The problem is translated into needs for improved performance of staff members.

II. *Client Specified*
   E. The individuals or groups toward which the activities will be directed are clearly specified. Clients are described in terms of background of training, experience, prior involvement with the problem, and the like.
   F. The relationship of these clients to the problem is indicated. Similarities and differences in attitudes, skills, and knowledges related to the problem are described or estimated.
   G. The rationale for focusing upon these clients instead of others is presented.

III. *Goals and Objectives*
   H. The major outcome(s) anticipated from the session(s) is (are) specified. Major outcomes specified are clearly in observable terms. Major outcomes specified are related directly to the problem and needs described in item I. Portions of the problems or needs *not* addressed are clearly designated.
   I. The specific objectives anticipated as outcomes are specified. Specific objectives are each clearly designated as relating to a major

Exhibit 2–5 continued

outcome. Specific objectives are expressed in performance terms. Specific objectives reflect differentiated needs of participants.

- J. The goals and objectives selected are the most i portant as well as realistic ones. Specific objectives are selected to deal with the problem in a truly significant way.

IV. *Schedule of Events*

- K. A master calendar of events indicates dates for preplanning, implementing, and follow-up.
- L. An agenda for the session clearly indicates the timetable of activities. Carefui, realistic allocations of time are designated for each activity.
- M. Sequences, allocations, activities, and relationships among them are shown.

V. *Description of Procedures*

- N. Each activity specified in the session agenda (item L) is fully described, as to what happens, the objective(s) in focus, the sequence, the materials used, the special arrangements, persons involved, simultaneous events, and special problems to consider.
- O. The selection of each activity is justified in terms of the specific objective focus, and special conditions limiting activity selection.
- P. Illustrations of materials, displays, room arrangements, and so on are included to clarify procedures of special kinds.
- Q. Alternative procedures or variations that might be required are described.

VI. *Evaluation*

- R. A set of evaluation procedures is clearly described. Evaluation of outcomes related to objectives is provided for. Evaluation of affective, skill and cognitive outcomes is included where appropriate. Processes as well as outcomes are evaluated.
- S. Carefully developed instruments are selected and/or prepared for each aspect of the evaluation. Instruments are objective, pretested, appropriate to objectives and activities. Instruments are simple enough for practical administration.
- T. Analytical procedures to be used in the evaluation are clearly shown. Tables to be used are prestructured. Analytical procedures are described.

VII. *Follow-up Plans*

- U. Follow-up plans are outlined and/or described in sufficient detail to show continuity toward full resolution of the problem.
- V. Immediate *next steps* are carefully detailed to guide *both* clients and leaders.

VIII. *Exhibits*

- W. Materials to be used in the session are illustrated. Handouts, advanced information, name tags, tests, work sheets, tapes, transparencies, questionnaires, instruments, bibliographies, and lists of materials are included.

Exhibit 2–5   continued

X. Equipment and special physical facilities arrangements are listed with sources clearly designated.
Y. Resource persons are clearly designated including all pertinent communications relating to each; curriculum vitae, address, phone, letters of invitation and follow-up letters, assignment sheets, and so on.
Z. A budget is prepared showing all expenses and clearly detailing cash outlay costs.

Each part presents essential information for assuring a well-designed, readily implementable in-service session.

The various parts of the plan will take different forms dictated by the need for each part to guide the implementation process readily. Hence, the statement of the problem and need may be just a written narrative, but it may also include tables, charts, or graphs to communicate more vividly. Similarly, the client group and goals and objectives may be described in both narrative and graphic forms. Goals and objectives may need to be clearly prioritized or categorized to show their relevance to certain clients and needs. The schedule of events is often just a simple schedule, detailing time allocations and sequences. However, it may be important for more complex designs to be depicted, using flowcharts and a PERT (Program Evaluation and Review Technique) (15) network as well as simple schedules.

An often neglected portion of a session plan is the description of procedures. When the session leader is also the designer, the process of carefully describing, in narrative form, the detailed procedures to be used helps to detect flaws and refine other portions of the plan. When the leader and designer are different people, then details of procedures are truly indispensable for communicating about intended events. The dangers in assuming that a few sketchy notes on procedures will suffice are very great. Notice the difference of the following procedures:

Abbreviated Procedures
Introduce the session briefly. Have communicator describe the message (Form A). Instruct receivers to estimate their confidence.

Fully Described Procedures
Introduce the session by telling the group that they are going to take part in a demonstration concerning communicating with people. Specifically, announce that "We will focus on how to have your directions understood."

Introduce the communicator and say, "There has been no coaching of our communicator, he has been instructed in the rules we are all to follow. You

are to receive the message; he will communicate. Here's how it works: . . ."
(Rules explained. Procedures presented. Materials distributed.)

As the communicator begins, the group leader reminds him to record the time. The session continues without interruption until the communicator is finished. If necessary, remind the group of any rules not being followed.

When the communicator has finished, participants are instructed as follows: "Estimate the number of items you *think* you got correct." The leader circulates among the participants, assisting them if they need help. "Record your estimate of the number you think are correct in the space designated for your C score."

While this is going on, the communicator can relax. He is then given the new set of directions to study.

Evaluation plans need to go well beyond the preparation of some kind of instrument. Questions to be answered need to be selected and specified. Product and process questions both need attention. Instrumentation needs to be pretested, and analytical procedures should be worked out in advance. Although more careful attention is given to procedures for evaluating in-service sessions in Chapter IX, it is important to recognize here that evaluation can rarely be successful as an afterthought. Planning for evaluating must be a part of session planning.

A session plan is called upon to give at least passing attention to follow-up activities. A session planned without considering necessary follow-up events is very likely to be unrealistic in trying to accomplish too much. Furthermore, the realities associated with possible follow-up events may influence the very nature of the session plan. In any event, follow-up is nearly always desirable, if not essential, and should be reflected in the plan itself.

A unique and most practical part of a plan is the collection of exhibits. These are detailed in Exhibit 2–5. The plan at this point may take the form of a box, suitcase, or even a trunk as each item of material (or a facsimile) is prepared or selected and physically made a part of the plan.

The Planning Documents

The character of the plan under discussion and outlined in detail in Exhibit 2–5 makes it clear that a variety of documents will be contained in any well-developed plan. Curiously, few documents have become *standard*. Only in the instance of independent, self-instructional modules has any standardizing of format been accepted. It may well be that the great variety of potential forms of in-service training sessions defies any effort to adopt common forms of documentation. The experienced observer, however, noticing the almost complete absence of formal plans for in-service sessions, is inclined to suspect that the art of planmaking is simply quite primitive among most school and college staffs.

Certainly, a few basic documents are clearly suggested by Exhibit 2–5 that go beyond efforts at narrative presentation. These *basic* documents include:

1. *A Session Agenda.* This supplies basic supporting information on the time, place, group, and materials needed (see Appendix C).
2. *A Checklist of Presession Arrangements.* A working instrument for use during planning and final preparations phases to assure that no detail is overlooked (see Exhibit 2–5).
3. *A Flowchart of Events or a PERT Network.* This provides a graphic overview of events, their sequences and relationships (see Exhibits 2–6 and 2–7).
4. *A Checklist of Material.* The checklist indicates each item of material and equipment in the sequence in which it will be utilized.
5. *One or More Evaluation Instruments.* Refer to Chapter IX for illustrations.

Flow-charting Events

One document that has special utility when a session plan is rather complex and involves subgroups and a diversity of activities is the flowchart. Flowcharts can be rather simple, giving only limited information, but they can also be more detailed, using an array of symbols for easy visual communications. Exhibit 2–6 illustrates a flowchart with an array of details for a teaching demonstration session. This flowchart depicts three simultaneous sets of events that were planned to provide groups of forty to sixty viewers to see carefully planned demonstrations of exemplary teaching practices on closed-circuit television screens.*

Three strands of events are shown. The topmost series depicts the sequence of events planned with teacher and students. This series constitutes not just the demonstration but prior and subsequent events that are crucial to the demonstration and related activities for viewers. The second sequence of events is numbered from 2 through 8. These represent the actual experiences of the participants from arrival at the demonstration center to follow-up. The third strand or sequence of events simply indicates technical

---

* These demonstrations were conducted as part of an in-service education program by the author for the South Park School District, Beaumont, Texas. This flowchart is based on a case report in E. W. Bessent, ed., *Designs for Inservice Education* (Austin, Tex.: Research and Development Center, University of Texas, February 1967), chap. IV, pp. 41–56.

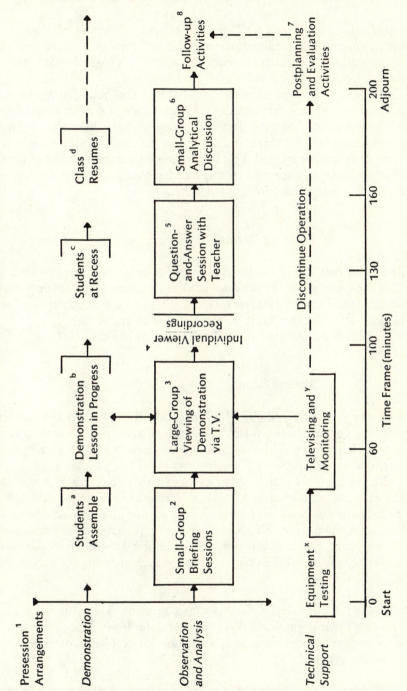

Exhibit 2–6. ILLUSTRATION OF A FLOWCHART FOR AN IN-SERVICE SESSION

Presession [1] Arrangements

Demonstration

Observation and Analysis

Technical Support

Students [a] Assemble

Demonstration [b] Lesson in Progress

Class [d] Resumes

Students [c] at Recess

Follow-up [8] Activities

Small-Group [2] Briefing Sessions

Large-Group [3] Viewing of Demonstration via T.V.

Individual Viewer [4] Recordings

Question- [5] and-Answer Session with Teacher

Small-Group [6] Analytical Discussion

Postplanning [7] and Evaluation Activities

Equipment [x] Testing

Televising and [y] Monitoring

Discontinue Operation

Time Frame (minutes)

Start   0   60   100   130   160   200   Adjourn

67

support activities x and y. These are related to the use of closed-circuit television, multiple monitors, remote-operated cameras, and various sound equipment, the proper and coordinated operation of which was essential to the session.

While each of these three *strands* of events was quite distinct from each other, they illustrate dramatically the importance of coordination of events during a session. The flowchart shows approximate time relationships between events in the three strands. More detailed plans for each strand were, of course, developed. This illustration suggests the utility of the flowchart in showing such relationships and providing an overall view of all essential events while avoiding minor details.

PERTing Events

The PERT network is another document for inclusion in an in-service plan. This document generally provides more detail about specific events than the flowchart and concentrates on careful timing and the coordination of simultaneous activities that must be associated with each other.

Exhibit 2–7 illustrates a PERT network that depicts events.

Pacing Events

Both the flowchart and the PERT network, illustrated in the exhibits as planning documents for in-service education, give special attention to time-event relationships. They can also be employed so as to give systematic attention to the problems of pacing events.

Pacing involves planning for events so that activities as sequenced in the plan are completed in a reasonable amount of time, so that idle time periods are not needlessly lengthy, and so that the next scheduled event follows without delay. Of course, such pacing requires that planned events be sequenced, but it also requires that the time required for each event be accurately estimated. The big problems in such planning for pacing involve the following:

allowing for individual differences in completion rates of participants
allowing for interruptions, diversions, or unforeseen difficulties
allowing for reasonable amounts of time for rest and contemplation between events

The problems of pacing that relate to individual differences can be dealt with in part by allowing the fast workers to take extra time to relax and

Exhibit 2–7. ILLUSTRATION OF A PERT NETWORK FOR AN IN-SERVICE SESSION

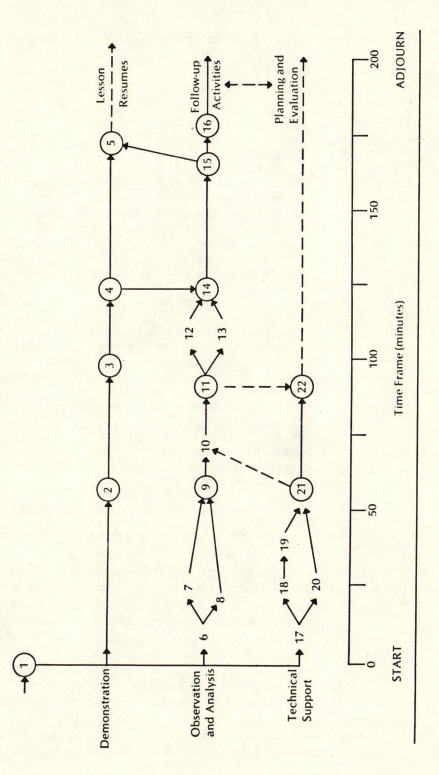

Exhibit 2–7 continued

(Time)		Description of Events
(0)	1.	All arrangements completed.
(60)	2.	Students, aide, and teacher all assembled ready for lesson to begin.
(110)	3.	Demonstration lesson terminated.
(120)	4.	Students leave for recess with aide. Teacher goes to demonstration viewing center.
(160)	5.	Teacher returns to classroom; students return from recess.
(15)	6.	Viewers arrive at designated briefing session rooms.
(35)	7.	Materials distributed.
(40)	8.	Coffee serving ended.
(55)	9.	End of briefing session for teacher viewers.
(60)	10.	Viewers assemble in viewing room.
(110)	11.	End of observation for viewers.
(111)	12.	Lights turned on.
(112)	13.	Viewers reminded of recording procedures.
(125)	14.	Completion of writing period during which teacher viewers complete observation and evaluation reports.
(155)	15.	End of question-and-answer period with demonstrating teacher.
(200)	16.	End of discussion of observed demonstration and recorded notations.
(15)	17.	Power switch on.
(35)	18.	Camera testing completed.
(4)	19.	Sound testing completed.
(45)	20.	Television monitor testing completed.
(50)	21.	Coordinator notified of technical readiness.
(115)	22.	Television system turned off. Operations discontinued.

contemplate the implications of the activity. In this way, the first problem can help alleviate the third one. However, for the slower participants, the pacing problem is severe. If the session is planned for an individual, of course, a simple change in time frame may suffice. Thus, another use may be found for the fast workers in group sessions; they may be utilized as tutors to move slower ones along. Activities may be planned to allow for more and less involvement of participants, depending on the rate of progress of individuals. Whatever the specific approaches selected are, this first problem of pacing is crucial and must be given careful planning consideration.

The problem of allowing for interruptions, diversions, and unexpected difficulties cannot be planned for so much as handled *in progress*. If plans provide too much slack to allow for the unexpected, then other pacing problems are aggravated. More promising is to alert and caution session leaders regarding the sources of such problems within the design, and leave it to those leaders to make adjustments. For instance, an activity that is likely to generate a great deal of chatter or confusion among some (e.g., the nonmathematical) can be scheduled with only minimum time allowances for these diversions. However, the schedule of events can allow for shortening a discussion or buzz session to allow for errors in such allowances.

Time for rest, relaxation, or contemplation is partially provided for when some finish ahead of schedule. However, the slower participants may be neglected if this is the only opportunity provided. Short *stretch breaks* can be planned to allow relaxation without losing the pace of events. Short *buzz sessions* can be scheduled to assure opportunities for sharing. Coffee breaks are scheduled, of course, at appropriate intervals, and these must be timed to offer rest and relaxation without destroying continuity of activity. The use of such formal breaks — coffee, lunch, adjournment, and the like — scheduled on the basis of "take a break when you are finished" can greatly assist in dealing with the fast-working participants previously discussed.

SELECTING RELEVANT ACTIVITIES

Activities are the building blocks of the training session (26). Much has been written about activities for training — brainstorming (50), discussing (25;28), role playing (47), demonstrating (14; 40:358). Harris has developed and refined on several occasions lists of activities and detailed descriptions of their unique characteristics (26; 27;28). While it is not possible to exhaust the possibilities open to selection by in-service designers, those presented in Exhibit 2–10 are relatively comprehensive.

The design problems to be resolved when selecting activities for an in-service education session include:

1. What activity or activities are most likely to stimulate learning toward the objective(s)?
2. Will more than one activity be required? If so, which ones?
3. What sequence of activities is likely to be most effective?
4. How feasible are the chosen activities, given the time frame, size and composition of the client group, leadership competencies, materials, and other resources available?

Each of these questions needs to be carefully answered for an effective design to emerge. If any cannot be answered with reasonable certainty, then the probable effectiveness of the session *in operation* must be questioned. In fact, of course, the designer is always faced with uncertainty and hence must be both creative and analytical in approach (41).

Activity-Impact Relationships

Every activity in use is presumed to have some influence for learning. The influence potential of an activity as distinguished from the actual influence of an experience on an individual has been the focus of interest for in-service designers as well as researchers for many years (23:153–81). Activity selection has tended to be a by-product of other interests rather than the central focus of concern for design. Hence, learning theory has dictated interest in drill, sequence, task analysis, reinforcement, and other principles (22). The various technological developments of photography, electronics, and computers have each emphasized unique applications of machines to training (35;11). Psychiatry and clinical counseling are examples of other specialized fields of inquiry that have spawned methodologies, which in turn have been advocated for adaptation to training (1; 45; 54). The influence of Rogers and many others, emphasizing non-directiveness in relationships among staff personnel, is widely represented in the literature on in-service education by persistent references to teacher involvement (1), self-renewal (29), joint decision-making outcomes (42), self-evaluation (45), free choices from among many alternatives (54), respect for preferences (55), and even "staff liberation" (5). Whatever the merits of this thrust toward client-centered in-service education may be, it leaves questions about selection of activities in the design of training experiences confused and uninformed.

The consequences for the designer of training sessions are an over-abundance of alternative activities offered by advocates of various kinds, a dangerous tendency to rely on uninformed preferences (12), and little guidance available to assist in making rational choices. The yearbook of the National Society for the Study of Education (1976) dealing with teaching methods is interesting in the emphasis its writers give to *basic* activities — lecturing, discussion, tutoring, games, simulations, films — but with almost no attention to design. Harris (26) was among the first to attempt to inventory and describe differentially the various kinds of activities then in use. He listed twenty-six "distinctive" activities and suggested a way of analyzing each to estimate its "level of experience impact" (26:72). As crude as this effort was, it offered at least a limited way of thinking about activities as distinctive kinds of experiences with different amounts of potential impact for learning. Harris, Bessent, and McIntyre (28) built upon many of the ideas of earlier writers in developing their *in-service design grid* as a way of relating experience impact, type of activity, and type of objectives to each other so as to identify three different design categories. These are shown in Exhibit 2–8.*

The type of objectives shown on this design grid are based on Bloom's (9) taxonomy of educational objectives. The specific training objective, if clearly specified, can usually be located along the horizontal dimension of the grid; when objectives are specified, they can be designated as appropriately belonging in one or more columns of the grid. As activities are selected for any given objective, an intersection between type of objective and activity is produced. A cell, in effect, is designated by the relationship between activity and objective.

Exhibit 2–8.   IN-SERVICE DESIGN GRID

Type of Activity (Examples)	Level Experience Impact*	Type of Objective					
		Knowledge	Comprehension	Applications	Synthesis	Values	Adjustment
Lecture	7	Design					
Demonstration	12	I					
Observation	13	Cognitive					
Interviewing		Outcomes					
Problem				Design			
Solving	14			III			
Brainstorming	12			A Broad Spectrum			
Discussion	10			of			
Buzz Session	14			Outcomes			
Role Playing						Design	
(Structured)	15					II	
Guided						Affective	
Practice	19					Outcomes	

*Based on estimates of potential influence for learning inferred from specific criteria.

* Several writers have adapted these ideas in more recent years for special purposes. An analysis of activities by type of skills to be learned was developed by Lloyd E. McCleary and K. E. McIntyre (37). Stone and Bickimer related Harris's experience impact idea to cost factors in training (49). Allen (2) related types of media to type of objectives in a chart that varies only slightly from a 1963 version by Harris.

Such intersections, on inspection, can be determined to fall within or outside the shaded area on the grid. When within the shaded area, appropriateness of match can be inferred between activity and objectivity. When *outside* the shaded area, inappropriateness of match can be inferred and the selection of activities reexamined.

To illustrate the utility of this simple procedure for selecting activities, the situation described in Exhibit 2–3 above might be useful. If the objectives specified include those shown below, both appropriate and inappropriate activity selections can be designated.

Chosen Specified Objectives	*Alternate Activity Selections*	*Appropriateness and Reason*
IIB, 3. "To increase the variety of praising terms used three or more times during a lesson."		
3a. To recall from memory at least ten *praising* terms.	Lecture Demonstration Role playing	Yes Yes No
3b. To substitute for commonly used terms one of the others, when editing a lesson transcript or tape.	Interviewing Group discussion Lecture	Yes Yes No
3c. To use spontaneously at least seven different *praising* terms in a practice session.	Role playing Guided practice Lecture	Yes Yes No

The table illustrates three objectives at each of three levels of outcome: knowledge, comprehension, and application. While lecture or demonstration activities might have sufficient experience impact to produce the recall of terms, higher levels of impact are needed when comprehension involving substituting one term for another is required. However, at the application level, higher impact activity is required such as that provided by role playing or guided practice.

It should be noted that while the lecture is completely inappropriate for objectives 3b and 3c specified above, role playing is not so completely inappropriate for objective 3a. In fact, role playing might indeed be utilized to assist participants in recalling *praising* terms. The rejection of this activity is based on the criterion of inefficiency. That is, there are more efficient (less elaborate and/or more direct) ways of accomplishing this simple knowledge-type objective. Even demonstration activity might be criticized as needlessly elaborate for presenting a set of *praising* terms that could form the basis for demonstrating knowledge. Reading a list, underlining such terms in a typescript, or writing such terms as observed in use are relatively direct, simple activities for accomplishing objective 3a.

This illustration of the in-service design grid as a useful tool for selecting activities is based on the assumption that the designer is aware of the numerous in-service activities and their *levels of experience impact*. Only a few examples of activities are shown in Exhibit 2–8, and they are already arranged in order of impact from lowest to highest. A more detailed analysis of a more complete list of activities is shown in Exhibit 2–10 and is discussed later in this chapter.

More about Experience Impact

This notion that an activity, by its very nature, has either more or less potential to influence learning of various kinds needs to be considered carefully. First of all, it is important to realize that the *quality of use* of the activity is not involved in this concept of experience impact. Obviously, an activity of any kind that is poorly utilized, improperly implemented, disrupted, or distorted cannot be expected to have a positive influence for learning toward any kind of objective. However, when a distinctive set of events referred to as an *activity* is utilized with reasonable procedures, skillful leadership, and appropriate conditions, *only* certain types of outcomes are likely to emerge. A lecture, no matter how skillfully delivered, is highly unlikely to produce new skills in listeners (20:81). A demonstration, if well organized, planned, and presented is more likely to help participant-observers comprehend relationships between teaching materials and techniques for their use than reading about them will do. Role playing is more likely to give one a sense of spontaneous application of skills and knowledge to a given context than a writing exercise about such applications.

The critical dimension we refer to as experience impact seems to be one associated with each distinctive activity type, making each one more or less appropriate for use in accomplishing objectives. The characteristics of an activity that seem associated with experience impact are not surprising. Since activities vary widely on a number of characteristics that make a difference in impact, it is not surprising that impact levels are also quite different. At least some of these are listed as follows:

1. *Senses involved:* extent of involvement of the various senses called upon.

2. *Interactions multiple:* extent to which communication flow is two-way or three-way or multichanneled.
3. *Controlled experience:* extent to which character of the experience is under control — has structure.
4. *Focus:* extent to which the experience is given a focus, has unity, internal consistency.
5. *Activeness:* extent to which the experience calls for active use of inputs.
6. *Originality:* extent to which inputs are original in content, form, or relationships.
7. *Reality:* extent to which realities rather than abstractions are utilized as frames of reference.

A few highly contrasting activities will serve to illustrate the distinct differences in experience impact among them, based on these seven characteristics. Exhibit 2–9 shows impact estimations based on ratings applied to each of the activities for each of the seven characteristics listed. Using an arbitrary three-point scale, the highest impact level would be twenty-one while the very lowest would be seven. Harris (27) previously made similar estimates for a set of twenty-four activities, using a more limited number of characteristics. In chapter 9, these impact-level estimates are used in evaluating session plans.

Other Features of Activities

The designer of training sessions cannot overlook the fact that selection of activity considerations may extend beyond experience impact. As important as this concept might be, other possibilities should not be ignored. Mc-Cleary and McIntyre (37) distinguished types of skills to be learned. They indicated that activities may be differentially appropriate for technical, conceptual, and human skills. Their scheme involved relevance to these three types of skills.

Another important way of thinking about activities and their usefulness in a training session involves relating type of outcome to type of involvement. Verbal involvement may well generate verbal learning; psychomotor involvement is most likely to generate psychomotor learning; emotional involvement may be essential to attitudinal and value changes. This is such a simple, self-evident way of viewing designs for learning that it seems needless to develop in detail. However, the practice of ignoring such simple guidelines is all too common. We are tempted to settle for a simple discussion in hope that skills will emerge, rather than plan the more complex activities needed. Conversely, having decided to settle for the simple-to-implement activity, it is tempting to revise our objectives to conform to the simple outcomes that can be expected.

Faced with the need to train for complex patterns of performance, the designer cannot seek comfort in inappropriate activities or in unimportant objectives. A variety of activities must be selected and put together as a sequence of experiences, much as a tailor puts together different garments for different clients and purposes. The basic problems of design are always present, but the fabrics must be carefully chosen to fit each unique garment.

An Array of Activities

Selecting activities for inclusion and sequencing in a training session relies heavily upon the designer's understanding of each of the many activities at his or her disposal. Exhibit 2–10 provides a list of activities described and differentiated with respect to sensory involvement, experience impact, type of objectives to be served, and special features.

Ideally, designers should have firsthand experience with each of these activities in order to use them discriminatingly in designing sessions. The preoccupation of individuals with a pet activity, previously criticized, does often offer the advantage of producing numerous descriptions in books, monographs, and journal articles regarding these techniques. Hence, the designer of training sessions will do well to turn to the references provided here and elsewhere to read about each of the many activities available.

The principle of variety provides the designer with a highly trustworthy if not very sophisticated way of approaching the problem of activity selection. When all is said and done, any session is likely to be better with activities of a substantial variety than with only a single activity or two that are very much alike. This principle of variety, simply stated, holds that a variety of activities, other things being equal, is likely to be more effective than any given activity. Unfortunately, the danger in applying this principle lies in selecting for variety while ignoring the question of appropriateness. Inappropriate activities will not produce results, no matter how diverse. However, less *efficient* activities can often be included in a session to add variety and strengthen impact characteristics of the experience, even if such activities may be more costly than necessary.

The selected descriptors shown in Exhibit 2–10 for each activity listed are more carefully defined here:

(1) *Sensory involvement* refers to the physiological senses utilized by the participant. Only those clearly used in the activity are included. Each of the senses is listed in order of importance for learning. For instance,

Exhibit 2–9. EXPERIENCE IMPACT ESTIMATES FOR FOUR SELECTED ACTIVITIES *

Selected Activities	1 Senses Involved	2 Multiple Inter-actions	3 Experi-ence Control	4 Focus	5 Active-ness	6 Origi-nality	7 Reality	Impact Total
Demonstration (A presentation of a prearranged series of events to a group for their observation.)	1	1	3	1	1	2	3	12
Brainstorming (A structured inventory of ideas orally expressed in a group setting so as to stimulate maximum numbers of ideas and contributes by all.)	1	1	3	2	1	2	2	12
Buzz Session (A small-group verbal interaction session, limited to a particular time, topic, and	2	3	2	1	2	2	2	14

purpose to assure
maximum verbal
interaction with
full involvement.)

Guided Practice
(A guided individual-
ized experience in
a real situation
modified only by
closely directed.)

| 3 | 3 | 2 | 3 | 3 | 2 | 3 | 19 |

* Rating criteria: 1 = low; 3 = high.

Exhibit 2–10.   BASIC ACTIVITIES FOR IN-SERVICE EDUCATION SESSION DESIGN

Activity	Sensory Involvement	Group Size	Experience Impact	Type of Objective
(1) Analyzing and calculating	Visual, kinesthetic	Ind.	16	Cognitive
(2) Brainstorming	Audio, visual, oral	Med.	13	Cognitive
(3) Buzz session	Audio, oral	Sml.	14	Cognitive, affective
(4) Demonstrating	Visual, audio	Med.	12	Cognitive
(5) Discussing, leaderless	Audio, oral, visual	Sml.	10	Cognitive
(6) Discussing, leader facilitated	Audio, oral, visual	Ind.	11	Cognitive, affective
(7) Film, television, filmstrip viewing	Visual, audio	Med.	10	Cognitive, affective
(8) Firsthand experience	Audio, oral, visual, kinesthetic	Ind.	21	Skill, cognitive, affective
(9) Group therapy	Audio, oral, visual	Sml.	16	Affective
(10) Guided practice	Kinesthetic, visual, audio	Ind.	19	Skill, cognitive
(11) Interviewing, informative	Audio, oral	Ind.	9	Cognitive
(12) Interviewing, problem solving	Audio, visual, oral, kinesthetic	Ind.	15	Cognitive
(13) Interviewing, therapeutic	Audio, oral, visual	Ind.	17	Affective
(14) Lecturing	Audio	Lrg.	7	Cognitive
(15) Material, equipment viewing	Visual, kinesthetic	Med.	12	Cognitive
(16) Meditating	Kinesthetic	Ind.	12	Affective, cognitive
(17) Microteaching	Audio, visual, oral	Sml.	18	Skill, affective
(18) Observing systematically in classroom	Visual, audio	Sml.	13	Cognitive, affective
(19) Panel presenting	Audio, visual	Lrg.	8	Cognitive
(20) Reading	Visual	Ind.	14	Cognitive, affective
(21) Role playing, spontaneous	Audio, visual, oral	Sml.	16	Affective

Exhibit 2–10 **continued**

	Activity	Sensory Involvement	Group Size	Experience Impact	Type of Objective
(22)	Role playing, structured	Audio, visual, oral	Sml.	18	Cognitive, skill
(23)	Social interaction	Audio, visual, oral	Sml.–Med.	13	Affective, cognitive
(24)	Tape, radio, record listening	Audio	Lrg.	7	Cognitive, affective
(25)	Testing	Audio, kinesthetic	Med.	16	Cognitive
(26)	Videotaping or photographing	Visual, kinesthetic	Ind.	16	Cognitive
(27)	Visualizing	Visual	Lrg.	9	Cognitive
(28)	Writing or drawing	Visual, kinesthetic	Ind.	12	Cognitive

This activities list is adapted from Ben M. Harris, *Supervisory Behavior in Education,* 2d ed. (Englewood Cliffs, N.J.: Prentice-Hall, Inc., 1975), p. 73. Detailed descriptions of each activity are found in Harris's work, pp. 72–87.

"3 Panel Presenting — Audio, visual" indicates listening is most important, while visual involvement with the several panelists is less important for participant learning.

(2) *Group size* indicates the group that probably represents optimum use of the activity. For many activities, *both* larger and small groups are feasible, but effectiveness may be sacrificed or special arrangements may be required.

(3) *Experience impact* is estimated for each activity, utilizing the scale of assigned values illustrated with selected activities in Exhibit 2–9.

(4) *Type of objective* refers to the outcomes that are most probable and clearly possible under normal conditions of use of the activity (37). Other objectives are always *potentially* possible, of course. For instance, a lecture could be so dramatically presented as to have affective outcomes. Testing could be employed under special circumstances to produce affective outcomes. The interview could relate to problem solving in ways that model and hence produce problem-solving skills.

Group Size-Activity Relationships

The number of participants involved in a particular session has a bearing on the kinds of activities selected. The characteristics of each activity impose some limits on group size, ranging from those activities that are essentially individual in nature to those that are capable of accommodating large masses of participants. Some activities can be used with various-sized groups, depending upon special arrangements.

Exhibit 2–10 indicates for each of the activities listed a single group size. This is designated as the size that is most appropriate, offering optimum conditions for each activity to be well utilized. Generally, low experience impact activities — for example, lecture, visualization, panel presentation — have unique advantages in that large groups can be accommodated. However, these can readily be adapted for use in much smaller group situations. Middle-range experience impact activities tend to be most readily useful with small or medium-sized groups. Hence, discussing and buzz session activities are often utilized in groups ranging from five or six to a dozen or more persons. Obviously, somewhat larger numbers of participants can be accommodated by procedures that provide for multiples of the buzz groups or discussion groups in operation simultaneously. Demonstrations and classroom observations represent middle-range experience impact activities that can accommodate larger groups only with special logistics but can readily be utilized on an individual or small-group bases. Obviously, their use on an individual basis would be rather costly.

Exhibit 2–11 provides a graphic view of the relationships among the group size, experience impact, and complexity of objectives in any session design situation. These three variables enter into selection of activity decisions as shown. Lower experience impact activities can be chosen as less complex outcomes are sought, and larger groups can be utilized. As objectives become increasingly complex, increased experience impact is required of selected activities, and small groups must be utilized. High experience impact activities selected for less complex outcomes with smaller groups lead to inefficiency. Low experience impact activities directed toward more complex outcomes with larger groups lead to ineffectiveness.

The unshaded areas on each side of the group-size diagonal indicate *zones of marginality* where activity selection to serve a range of objectives and group sizes is possible without undue loss in effectiveness or efficiency. It is important to note, however, the rather narrow zone of marginal effectiveness compared with that for marginal efficiency. This implies that considerable latitude is allowed a designer in using higher impact activities than necessary. Costs are just increased. However, less latitude is allowed in using lower impact activities for more complex objectives because of the risk of having no resulting outcomes or even negative consequences.

Similarly, it is important to note the narrowing of *both* zones of marginality as the group size is increased. In practical terms, this means that the designer must select lower experience impact activities as the group size increases and hence must be very hardheaded about the complexity of objectives to be served in such groups by such activities.

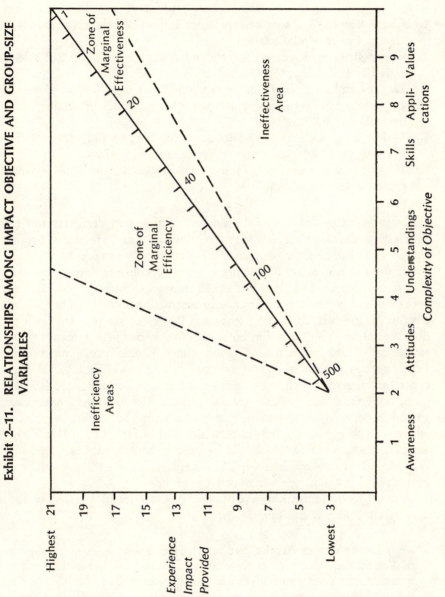

Exhibit 2-11. RELATIONSHIPS AMONG IMPACT OBJECTIVE AND GROUP-SIZE VARIABLES

The general principles governing the selection of activities as related to group size and experience impact can be stated as follows:

1. Group size can increase as experience impact of selected activities decreases (inverse relationship).
2. Group size can decrease independent of experience impact of selected activities (independent relationship).
3. Larger numbers of participants can sometimes be served by higher experience impact activities by arranging for multiples of smaller groups operating simultaneously.
4. Middle-range experience impact activities tend to provide most flexibility in being adapted to a wide range of group sizes.
5. Highest levels of experience impact are persistently provided by small-group or individual activities.

These principles offer useful guidelines for session designers not only in selecting activities but also in making logistical and procedural arrangements. The ideal sequence or pattern of session activities provides precisely the amount of experience impact needed to accomplish each objective at the lowest possible cost in time and other resources. Such an ideal is rarely realized, because the art and science of instructional design is not yet very advanced. However, in seeking to design in-service sessions that will produce optimum conditions for both *effective* and *efficient* learning, consideration of the relationships noted above should prove most useful. Larger groups *should*, of course, be used to increase efficiency, but higher experience impact activities should *not* be rejected to accommodate large groups if objectives require greater impact. Conversely, the efficiency gained in serving larger numbers of participants should *not* be sacrificed whenever low experience impact activities will in fact suffice. Finally, high experience impact activities should be utilized as needed, but larger numbers of participants can be served, if necessary, by adapting activities and procedures for handling medium or large groups.

A case illustration making use of some of the principles discussed above may be clarifying at this point.

An in-service session was designed for teachers involving cognitive objectives relating to the importance of two-way communications rather than one-way communications with students, faculty, and parents. The objectives were at the comprehension and applications level (see Exhibit 2–8) and hence required some middle-range experience impact activities.

A laboratory-type training session was designed, utilizing a simulated communications problem in which all participants were to engage actively and individually in trying to show accurate reception of a message being delivered orally to all.* The sequence of activities was as follows:

1. *Lecture.* A very brief introductory statement was followed by an *oral, no-feedback* message, to which all participants were asked to react by listening.
   1a. *Writing and drawing.* A work sheet was used to determine participants' understanding of the message.
2. *Lecture.* The procedures above were repeated except that a new message was used and procedures changed so participants could
   2a. *discuss* the information being presented, ask for clarification, react, and reinterpret.
   2b. *write and draw* on a second work sheet simultaneously with listening and discussion activities.
3. *Analyzing and calculating.* Participants were guided in scoring their two work sheets on accuracy of perception of the messages.
   3a. *visualizing* the correction key that participants were to use was presented on two transparencies, along with oral directions.
4. *Social Interaction.* Coffee break.
5. *Visualization.* During the break, a team of tabulators proceeded to collect and tabulate scores for individual participants. Transparencies were prepared and presented at this time showing comparisons between *no feedback* and *free feedback* in communication.
6. *Brainstorming.* Participants were asked to use data presented showing that a message presented with verbal interaction (free feedback) from presenter to receiver was more accurately received, better understood, and more confidently understood. Ideas from brainstorming were to be focused on "implications of these data for our practices in school."

Session ended with indications of follow-up activities for individual faculty groups.

The session just described could readily be utilized with a group of ten to fifteen participants. All activities selected were appropriate for small- or medium-sized groups (see Exhibit 2–10) *except* writing or drawing and analyzing and calculating. These are individual activities. However, any group can be restructured so as to become a set of individuals. In this instance, an individual work sheet on which to write and draw and a structured scoring procedure allowing each individual to score his or her own work sheet facilitates use of individual activities. Without such logistical arrangements, participants might or might *not* function as individual

---

* The laboratory exercise referred to here is described in detail in *InService Education: A Guide to Better Practice* by Ben M. Harris, E. W. Bessent, and K. E. McIntyre (Englewood Cliffs, N.J.: Prentice-Hall, Inc., 1969).

writers and *analyzers*. If they failed to do so, much of the impact of the activity could be lost and the integrity of the whole session jeopardized.

What about utilizing this laboratory session with a large group? This writer has, in fact, followed almost identical procedures with a group of over five hundred participants from many different schools. But adaptations and special arrangements were essential for *discussion, analyzing*, and *calculating*, and *brainstorming* activities. In such a large mass situation, discussing was feasible only because the session leader had five assistants, each with a microphone on a long cable, who circulated among participants. As questions or comments were to be expressed by participants, an assistant passed the microphone to each individual so that all could hear. The message presenter was also equipped with a microphone so that his or her words were clearly heard by all. A similar arrangement permitted brainstorming comments to be expressed by over one hundred individuals, and heard by all. Three recorders using separate screens and overhead projectors permitted all participants a ready view of ideas generated in the brainstorming.

The above case illustrates logistical problems associated with the use of small-group and individual activities with large numbers of participants. Structuring of individual activities to assure that they will be actively experienced as intended, even within the context of a mass situation, was essential. Providing special sound and video equipment to assure that a large group could hear, speak, and see was prerequisite. Having a carefully coordinated team of leaders handling different aspects of the session was facilitating. As the total number of participants to be served increases, logistical requirements become increasingly complex. Therein lies the danger! Larger numbers to be served tend to promote large-group activity selection regardless of the experience impact required. The replication of a session designed for small- or medium-sized groups is not always feasible. The alternative illustrated previously involves the very careful adaptation of a session involving small-group and individual activities to larger numbers of participants.

LOGISTICAL ARRANGEMENTS

Much of what needs to be done to assure an effective in-service training session amounts to good communication and careful organization. These are matters of logistics rather than design, but they influence the character of the plan that emerges and cannot be kept completely separate. Physical facilities are among the most important arrangements that directly influence design. Under conditions where people have to come and go from one place to another during a session, transportation schedules and communications among all of those involved become critical elements of the plan.

Physical Facilities

The right spaces, furnished properly and with necessary special equipment, are all crucial to the success of an in-service education session. Such simple arrangements as reserving a room large enough to accommodate all participants seated at tables when writing or manipulative activities are planned assures comfort for participants and makes certain activities feasible. If the appropriate space or the tables were not available, changes in the session plan would be required.

Consider the foolishness of planning for the use of a colored 16 mm film in a room with trilateral lighting and no drapes. Even plans to utilize the overhead projector can be full of frustration for want of a three-prong adapter for the power cable or an extension cord. But much more subtle influences of physical facilities need attention during the time planning is in progress.

Space for subgroups. Any session, regardless of the number of participants, may call for subdividing into several smaller groups. Role playing may require simultaneous involvement by several two- or three-person teams. Buzz sessions or discussions may require subgroupings. Being sure that appropriate physical spaces are available is essential to the success of such subgroups. If a very large room is available, each of the four corners can serve for a subgroup, but tables, chairs, screens, chalkboards, and other necessary equipment need to be arranged in advance so that movement from total group to subgroup can take place without waste of time and without confusion. The noise from one subgroup may distract another, so such problems need to be anticipated in advance and separate rooms provided nearby.

Materials distribution with ease, speed, and a minimum of confusion becomes a problem when groups become large. A schedule of distributions should be developed if numerous handouts are involved. Generally, handouts should be passed directly to each individual, *not* passed along from one person to another. However, in auditorium situations, rows may be too narrow to allow for passing handouts to each person individually. This situation requires careful counting of materials for each row and, if possible, passing from *both* ends of the row.

Obviously, if the group exceeds a very small number or more than a few handouts are involved, the leader should make advance arrangements for participants to assist with distributions, and the procedures they employ should be planned prior to the beginning of the session. In addition to expediting distributions, arranging for handouts to be timed properly is very important. Materials should not be allowed to distract from the focus of attention on a presenter, nor should they disrupt participant activity.

Seating arrangements must vary for different activities. Changes in seating can be time-consuming and confusing, however, unless advanced arrangements are carefully planned. Brainstorming, films, visual presentations, panel presentations, and lectures all require an auditorium arrangement in the sense that participants must be facing in a specific direction to focus on the screen or presenter(s). This is a simple arrangement, but if such activities are preceded or followed by buzz groups, role playing, discussing, writing, interviewing, and the like, then changes in facilities are demanded. One approach is to have alternate spaces as mentioned above, so that participants simply leave the "audience" setting and go to another location. Another approach involves a "conference arrangement," with rows of tables instead of just chairs. This permits regrouping *around* tables with only limited movements of furniture. Buzz groups are sometimes organized by having every other row of participants turn their chairs about to face those behind them.

Assigning participants to subgroups can be arranged well in advance to avoid confusion and loss of time. This is especially desirable when participants will frequently form subgroups, when a variety of regroupings is required, and when control is needed over who is assigned to which group. On-the-spot assignments can be made, of course, but this can be time-consuming. Name tags or plaques that are prepared in advance for participants can include assignment information to buzz groups, teams, rooms, and so on.

Transportation and Schedules

Participants as well as leaders of in-service sessions need to be well informed in advance regarding the schedule of events. When people come from great distances, transportation becomes a factor in planning the starting and adjournment times. Furthermore, if the site selected for the session is not thoroughly familiar to all, special instructions are in order.

Provide everyone with an advance schedule of events, even if all the details are not included. Suggest early arrival times if hotel registrations, travel from an air terminal, or just walking distances are likely to be time-consuming. If the time for adjournment is set to allow for some uncertainty in scheduled activities, be sure that the session will not extend beyond the specified time.

Transportation grows increasingly costly and always requires some special arrangements. When several participants are coming from the same school or town, aiding them in sharing a ride can be helpful, and it can also pay dividends in learning outcomes as they share ideas in follow-up travel.

Visiting consultants often need more assistance with travel arrangements than local participants do. Such visitors are often appreciative of information about airline schedules and bus, limousine, or taxi service; and they often need a map or a guide to assure that they find the location of the session without problems.

Communications and Clearances

Any in-service training session that has more than routine activities built into it will demand close attention to be sure that all who need to be involved and informed are. As various individuals share responsibilities for physical arrangements, refreshments, name tags, presentations, equipment, materials reproduction, or any other part of the operation, someone needs to assure that they are all fully informed. Appendix C shows a basic planning document that helps to assure that the person in charge has communicated well. However, those who share responsibility need general information; they need specific guidelines; and they need personal contact to provide them opportunities for questions, counterproposals, reassurance, and reinforcement. While the person in charge is well advised to put in writing his or her directions to each responsible person, this hardly takes the place of face-to-face contacts.

Miscellaneous Arrangements

It goes without saying that certain other arrangements should be made. Name tags should be provided if even a few participants do not know each other. Place cards with names indicated in large letters are especially important when verbal interaction of any kind is desired. Serving refreshments at a break in the session activities has become so universal in practice that it seems unwise to omit arrangements to do this.

Flow pens and extra acetate sheets, marking pencils, a cloth for cleaning, and a pointer should all be standard equipment, along with an overhead projector, screen, and prepared transparencies. When any kind of audiovisual equipment is to be used, extension cords, extra projector lamps, and three-prong adapters will save many a session plan from early disaster.

Even if pencils, notepads, and drinking water are not provided for every participant, it is a good idea to have them on hand for those who need them.

SUMMARY

This has been a lengthy chapter attempting to develop the concept of session as the basic training unit. The design of sessions has been stressed in an effort to be both practical and challenging. The relationship of objectives to goals and to activities was developed in an effort to promote design of sessions that are related to larger programs of in-service education and yet to attend to specific needs for learning. Considerable attention was devoted to the concept of experience impact as the main tool for design. The selection of activities does not follow directly from a consideration of either objectives or group size, as important as they are. Hence, experience impact considerations have been emphasized to promote *both* efficient and effective designs for sessions.

This chapter has presented numerous illustrations for use in assisting with session planning. It is the planning process that counts most, of course, and the design concepts are central to that. However, a carefully developed planning document has been proposed and illustrated as a prerequisite to effective implementation.

REFERENCES

1. A. K. Rice Institute. "Group Relation: A Residential Conference on Male-Female Work Relations in Group and Organizational Settings." Washington, D.C.: A. K. Rice Institute, January 1976.
*2. Allen, William B. "Instructional Media Stimulus Relationship to Learning Objectives." *Audiovisual Instruction* 12, no. 1 (January 1967): 28.
*3. Armstrong, Robert J., R. E. Kraner, T. D. Cornell, and E. W. Roberson (editors). *Developing and Writing Behavioral Objectives*. Tucson, Ariz.: Educational Innovators Press, 1968.
4. Barrera, Rebecca Maria. *Catching the Kinks in Staff Development Programs*. San Antonio, Tex.: Inter-Cultural Development Research Association, March 1976.
5. Beegle, Charles W. and Roy A. Edelfelt. *Staff Development: Staff Liberation*. Report of a conference jointly sponsored by ASCD and the Department of Administration and Supervision, School of Education, University of Virginia. Washington, D.C.: Association for Supervision of Curriculum Development, 1977.
6. Berman, Paul and M. W. McLaughlin. *Federal Programs Supporting Edu-*

* Suggested for further reading.

cational Change. Vol. 4. *The Findings in Review.* Santa Monica, Calif.: The Rand Corporation, April 1975.

7. Bessent, E. Wailand. "Inservice Education — A Point of View." In *Designs for Inservice Education* (E. W. Bessent, editor). Austin, Tex.: Research and Development Center for Teacher Education, February 1967.

8. Bishop, Leslee. "Visualizing a Staff Development Plan." In *Staff Development: Staff Liberation* (C. W. Beegle and Roy A. Edelfelt, editors). Washington, D.C.: Association for Supervision of Curriculum Development, 1977.

*9. Bloom, Benjamin S. et al. Taxonomy of Educational Objectives, *Handbook I: Cognitive Domain.* New York: David McKay, 1956.

10. Brimm, Jack L. and D. J. Jolle Hy. "How Do Teachers Feel About Inservice Education?" *Educational Leadership* 31, no. 6 (March 1974): 521–25.

*11. Bunderson, Victor C. and Gerald W. Faust. "Programmed and Computer-Assisted Instruction." *The Psychology of Teaching Methods.* 75th Yearbook. Part I (N. L. Gage, editor). Chicago: National Society for the Study of Education, 1976, pp. 44–90.

12. Burrell, David. "The Teachers Centre: A Critical Analysis." *Educational Leadership* 33, no. 6 (March 1976): 422–27.

13. California State Department of Education. *A Kit of Materials for Needs Assessment and Evaluation.* Sacramento, Calif.: Bureau of Inter-Group Relations, October 1974.

14. Coody, Betty. "A Study of the Impact of Demonstration Teaching on Experienced and Inexperienced Teachers Under Various Supervisory Conditions." Doctoral dissertation, University of Texas, 1967.

*15. Cook, Desmond. *Program Evaluation and Review Technique: Applications in Education.* Washington, D.C.: U.S. Department of Health, Education, and Welfare, U.S. Government Printing Office, 1966.

16. Culbertson, Jack A., Paul B. Jacobson, and T. L. Reller. *A Casebook.* Englewood Cliffs, N.J.: Prentice-Hall, Inc., 1960.

17. Davison, Ronald. "How Are You Using Your Inservice Consultants?" *High School Journal* 56, no. 8 (May 1973): 370–73.

18. Ernst, William. "What Makes a Workshop Jell?" *Educational Leadership* 31, no. 6 (March 1974): 496–98.

19. Fleming, Robert S. "Action Research for School Improvement." In *Staff Development: Staff Liberation* (C. W. Beegle and Roy A. Edelfelt, editors). Washington, D.C.: Association for Supervision of Curriculum Development, 1977, pp. 46–51.

20. Flocke, Lynne. "Retirement: For Some It's Only Temporary." *Austin American Statesman,* November 11, 1976, p. B1.

*21. Gagne, Robert M. *The Conditions of Learning.* 2d ed. New York: Holt, Rinehart and Winston, 1970.

22. Gagne, Robert M. "Military Training and Principles of Learning." *American Psychologist* 17 (February 1962): 83–91.

*23. Glaser, Robert. "Implications of Training Research in Education." *Theories*

* Suggested for further reading.

of Learning and Instruction. 63d Yearbook. Part I (Ernest R. Hilgard, editor). Chicago: National Society for the Study of Education, 1964, pp. 153–81.

24. Goodlad, John I. and M. Frances Klein. *Behind the Classroom Door.* Worthington, Ohio: Charles A. Jones Publishing Corp., 1970.

*25. Hall, D. M. *Dynamics of Group Discussion.* Danville, Ill.: The Interstate Painters and Publishers, Inc., 1963.

26. Harris, Ben M. *Supervisory Behavior in Education.* Englewood Cliffs, N.J.: Prentice-Hall, Inc., 1963.

*27. Harris, Ben M. *Supervisory Behavior in Education.* 2d ed. Englewood Cliffs, N.J.: Prentice-Hall, Inc., 1975.

*28. Harris, Ben M., E. W. Bessent, and Kenneth E. McIntyre. *Inservice Education: Guide to Better Practice.* Englewood Cliffs, N.J.: Prentice-Hall, Inc., 1969.

29. Hart, Helen A. "Self-Renewal: A Model." *Educational Leadership* 31, no. 6 (March 1974): 499–501.

30. Heyman, Mark. *Simulation Games for the Classroom.* Bloomington, Ind.: Phi Delta Kappa Educational Foundation, 1975.

31. Killough, Don P. "Inservice Education Practices of Regional Education Service Centers in Texas." Doctoral dissertation, University of Texas at Austin, August 1977.

32. Lash, Kenneth. "To Know a Lemon Brings Inner Richness." *Christian Science Monitor,* November 8, 1976, p. B7

*33. Lawrence, Gordon. *Patterns of Effective Inservice Education: A State of the Art Summary of Research on Materials and Procedures for Changing Teacher Behaviors in Inservice Education.* Tallahassee Fla.: State Department of Education, December 1974.

34. Lawrence, Gordon et al. "Patterns of Effective Inservice Education." *NCSIE Inservice.* National Council of States on Inservice Education. Syracuse, N.Y.: Syracuse University, College of Education (February 1977): 1–3, 8.

*35. Lumsdaine, A. A. "Instruments and Media of Instruction." In *Handbook of Research on Teaching* (N. L. Gage, editor). Chicago: Rand McNally, 1963.

*36. Mager, Robert F. *Preparing Instructional Objectives.* Palo Alto, Calif.: Fearon Publishers, 1962.

37. McCleary, Lloyd E. and Kenneth E. McIntyre. "Competency Development and University Methodology." *National Association of Secondary School Principals Bulletin* 56, no. 362 (March 1972): 53–68.

38. McDonald, Frederick J. "Criteria and Methods for Evaluating Inservice Programs." *NCSIE Inservice.* National Council of States on Inservice Education. Syracuse, N.Y.: Syracuse University, College of Education (March 1977).

39. McIntyre, Kenneth E. "The Laboratory Approach." In *Designs for Inservice Education* (E. W. Bessent, editor). Austin, Tex.: Research and Development Center for Teacher Education, 1967, pp. 13–26.

40. Miles, Matthew B. and A. Harry Passow. "Training in the Skills Needed

* Suggested for further reading.

for In-Service Education Programs." Chapter 14 in *In-Service Education for Teachers, Supervisor and Administrators.* 56th Yearbook (M. B. Henry, editor). Chicago: National Society for the Study of Education, 1957.

41. National Institute of Education. "Decision Making in Educational Organizations." Report of a conference. Cambridge, Mass.: National Institute of Education, May 8–10, 1975.

42. *Outcomes,* "Project on Utilization of Inservice Education R. and D. Outcomes," 1, no. 1 (December 1976). Washington, D.C.: National Education Association.

*43. Pharis, William L. *Inservice Education of Elementary School Principals.* Washington, D.C.: Department of Elementary School Principals, National Education Association, April 1966.

44. Popham, W. James and Eva L. Baker. *Establishing Instructional Goals.* Englewood Cliffs, N.J.: Prentice-Hall, Inc., 1970.

45. Reavis, Charles A. "Clinical Supervision: A Timely Approach." *Educational Leadership* 33, no. 5 (February 1976): 360–63.

46. Rule, Flossie. "Models for In-Service Education in East Tennessee." *Instructor Development* (General Learning Corporation), 1, no. 8 (May 1970): 2.

*47. Shaftel, Fannie and George R. Shaftel. *Role-Playing for Social Values. Decision Making in Social Studies.* Englewood Cliffs, N.J.: Prentice-Hall, Inc., 1967.

48. Slagle, Allen T. "Inservice Education." In *A Candid Discussion of the Issues in Education* (James M. Lipham, editor). Madison, Wis.: Wisconsin Department of Public Instruction, 1975.

49. Stone, James C. and David A. Bickimer. "A Protocol Continuum." *Instructor Development* (General Learning Corporation), 1, no. 6 (March 1970):5.

50. Taylor, Donald W., Paul C. Berry, and C. H. Block. "Does Group Participation When Using Brainstorming Facilitate or Inhibit Creative Thinking?" *Administrative Science Quarterly* 3, no. 23 (June 1958): 57.

51. *Webster's Seventh New Collegiate Dictionary.* Springfield, Mass.: G. and C. Merriam Company, Publishers, 1970, p. 224.

52. Wiles, David K. *Monroe City's Educational Program.* The Monroe City Materials, Urban Simulation. Columbus, Ohio: University Council for Educational Administration, n.d.

53. Wilson, Elizabeth C. *Needed: A New Kind of Teacher.* Bloomington, Ind.: Phi Delta Kappa Educational Foundation, 1973.

54. Yeatts, Edward H. "Staff Development: A Teacher-Centered Inservice Design," 33, no. 6 (March 1976): 417–24.

55. Zigarmi, Patricia, L. Betz, and D. Jensen. "Teachers' Preferences in and Perceptions of Inservice Education." *Educational Leadership* 34, no. 7 (April 1977): 545–51.

* Suggested for further reading.

III

Planning Programs

INTRODUCTION

When more than a single person is involved in any operation, some means of communication about what is to occur becomes important. If only a few individuals are involved, the operation is a simple set of routines, and the individuals can interact about the operation face to face, no further medium of communication may be needed. Why, then, are plans required? They are media of communications, guides to actions and their coordination. Plans also provide reference materials for monitoring and evaluating operations. For in-service education (ISE), as with virtually all human operations, plans are indispensable under the following condition or conditions:

1. Operations are to continue over sustained time periods or are periodic rather than continuous.
2. An array of persons are involved in nonroutine, differentiated ways.
3. When face-to-face communications cannot be consistently provided before and during the operation.
4. Events comprising the operation must be sequenced and coordinated with others.

5. Approvals, allocations, or commitments of resources are required that are not routinely available.
6. Creative, original, unique contributions of individuals are desired as part of the operation.
7. Evaluation of the operation and/or its products is an important undertaking.

Plans are media for communication about future intended operations. They take some physical form — written document, graphic display, mathematical formula, or visualization. As media of communications, they are best when multisensory in nature. As communications, they must take differentiated forms, depending upon the persons who are to use them and the purposes for which they are intended.

Plans are guides to actions and the coordination of such actions. As such, a plan should clearly indicate what people should do; what they should do it with; when, where, in what sequence; and in what ways. These are simple requirements for a plan, but they become elaborate when many persons are involved or a variety of whats, whens, and wheres makes for great complexity.

Plans are reference works for use in implementing, monitoring, and evaluating operations. As such the who, what, when, where, and how provisions of the plan must be sufficiently specific that all concerned may know when compliance and deviations are occurring. For evaluation of outcomes, the plan must be explicit about goals and objectives. But for more comprehensive evaluation purposes, the plan must indicate relationships among resources, operational events, and anticipated outcomes.

This chapter will concern itself primarily with intermediate- and long-range ISE plans. Other chapters focus on short-range session plans and the logistics directly associated with these. Furthermore, the vast literature on planning process, especially as it relates to interpersonal relations in planning, argues against still more attention to planning as basic human affairs. Instead, this chapter deals with planmaking as a technical-creative problem. It further attends to the use of a variety of approaches to documenting a plan and some of the common problems in making such documents (physical entities) effective instruments of communication. Finally, this chapter describes several different media for planmaking.

PLANMAKING

Planning is essential to all efforts at directing organizational endeavors in a goal-oriented fashion. Many views of planning as process have been developed stressing sequence (5, 9), resources (20, 12), and interpersonal dynamics (2, 7, 11). Nearly all approaches to planning presume that a plan of some kind will be the product of planning as process. Furthermore, it is often assumed that either the process of planning, the product (the plan), or both will somehow guide and facilitate implementation and evaluation of actual operations. In fact, this latter assumption might well be challenged. The emergence of "management systems" or techniques such as systems analysis (21) PERTing (9) and Gantt (5) chart analysis and program budgeting (20) all direct attention, in part, toward the fact that "the best-laid plans" are often not realized in operation.

Systematic Planning

Despite the serious problems inherent in operationalizing or implementing any plan, its existence is a prerequisite for ordered change, and the physical character of the plan as well as the processes employed probably make a difference in the consequences likely to follow. Haskew* utilizes the term "planmaking" to refer to a systematic planning operation with a set of clearly delineated tasks with a plan as a tangible end product. He conceptualizes a set of technical procedures utilized to produce an operations design in the form of a plan. While not a sequence of events, such procedures can be viewed as two sets in relation to each other (see Exhibit 3–1). These sets of procedures in planmaking do no more than suggest what needs doing to produce a plan and how the various procedures relate to each other. The upper set all tend to involve choice making growing out of logical, analytical, interactive processes. The lower set of procedures all tend to involve information processing essential to choice making that is realistic. Communications among related subsystems assures that the planning process makes use of available resources, secures needed information, and assures that the larger organization is aware of the intents of the emerging ISE plan.

Two procedures of highly creative kinds are required as outgrowths of choice making, information processing, and communicating. One of these involves *synthesizing an operational design*. The other is *transforming the operational design* into tangible materials that can facilitate communications about intents in the form of a plan. In the real world of planmaking for in-service education, operational designing and plan producing are closely interrelated. They overlap one another in sequence and evolve as a paper representation of future operational reality that does not yet exist.

* Adapted from lecture notes developed by L. D. Haskew and utilized in his teaching of planmaking at the University of Texas at Austin, 1976–78.

Exhibit 3–1. PLANMAKING AS INFORMED CHOOSING, COMMUNICATING, AND DESIGNING

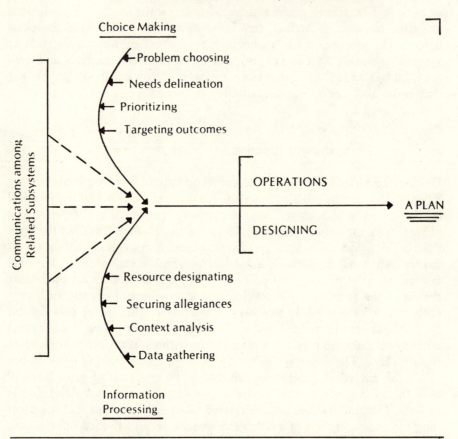

Hence, operational designing is largely a conceptualizing, imagining process. As the planners complete the choice making, information processing and interacting, the *creative tasks* are undertaken in an effort to imagine what the new training operation will be like if fully implemented and what the various events will be like. To the extent that the planners have vivid and detailed images of these new operations, they can be transferred to paper in the form of performance statements, operational descriptions, scenarios, vignettes, systems diagrams (32), PERT networks (9), program budgets (20), and illustrations.

Planmaking Problems

Several potential problems face ISE planners in utilizing these ideas. The necessary information for making sound choices may be lacking or go unused. The available data may be inadequately processed or utilized so that the really important implications are not recognized. A third problem often encountered involves a failure to explore alternatives fully without carefully estimating advantages and disadvantages before choices are finally made regarding the outcomes to be targeted.

The tendency to *substitute* planning documents for operational designing may be the most common and most serious flaw in planmaking. We often find plans that consist largely of long lists of objectives, detailed schedules, and budgets with little description of events. This derives from the inability to conceptualize, to create mental images of alternative forms of training. This is a very difficult part of planmaking, of course; but it is also an absolutely essential part, unless a plan is to be merely a description of current operations and hence not a plan at all. Planmaking as discussed here involves actions undertaken in response to some kind of discrepancy between what is and what ought to be. If already known and currently operating systems were adequate to respond to the problem, then planning, of this kind at least, would not be called for.

In bypassing *operational designing*, with all of its difficulties and intangible processes, the planner focuses on known procedures, implemented by known combinations of people, time, space, and material. The result is not a plan, but a prescription for maintaining the status quo with illusory new outcomes predicted. An example of such stereotyping of the design process is reported below:

> A colleague of mine had a wonderfully efficient approach to planning a workshop or conference. He had a standard format or operational design. No matter what the problem, outcomes desired, resources available, expectation, or prior experiences happened to be; the basic structure was the same. (1) Start with an opening address by a prestigious individual broadly focused on the problem. (2) Divide the total group into discussion groups to interact, presumably in terms of ideas presented. (3) Reassemble the total group and have discussion group recorders report on their discussions. (4) Adjourn or turn to the next problem (topic) repeating the same format.

If the case description of events above sounds familiar it may be because many workshops throughout the country function on this stereotyped format or some slight variation of it. This may be a useful format for certain purposes and under certain conditions, but the planning involved is of a very different order than that we are trying to describe.

Planning for Different Kinds and Levels of Operations

One of the sources of confusion about the kind of planning needed for operationalizing high-quality in-service education is the failure to clearly define different kinds of operations being planned for and the different operational levels at which planning is required. In Chapter II the designing and the planning of training sessions are considered in considerable detail. The operations in focus are called sessions and the planning level is clearly at the *level of direct delivery of training services.* However, planning as discussed in this chapter is at a more remote level, at least one planning stage away from session-training plans. At least three levels of planning are needed in most school districts: (1) the overall or master plan (2) the project or program plan, and (3) the session plan. We need to be explicit in differentiating direct training plans from indirect plans even though they have much in common. Conrad (8:5) refers to "strategic," "tactical," and "operational" planning as three such levels of plans.

The kind of operation being planned for is also important to distinguish. In Exhibit 1–3 in Chapter I the distinction between maintenance operations and change operations is presented. Harris (17:21–24) develops in greater detail elsewhere the notion that operations can range from being highly *tractive* to highly *dynamic* in their orientations. From a planmaking point of view, only the more clearly dynamic in-service education operations require detailed, creative planning with an elaborate plan as the product. Conversely, dynamic efforts to improve, depart, upgrade, and innovate cannot be realistic if routine, standard operating procedures are used as a substitute for planmaking. Exhibit 3–2 attempts to show relationships among three different kinds of operations and four different types of planning that need to be considered.

Continuous operations are those that, once implemented, or if already in operation, are expected to continue without interruption or change. Such continuous operations include classroom teaching, providing supporting services, purchasing, bookkeeping, and so on. They are not continuous in the sense of being twenty-four-hour-a-day operations but in the sense that during each normal working day they do resume; there is continuity of activity from day to day; and the goals, objectives, resources, personnel, and time and space allocations are relatively constant.

Intermittent operations are most common for ISE. Direct training operations are rarely continuous in the on-the-job context. At the more indirect levels of program or project planning, implementing, monitoring, and coordinating the operations become more nearly continuous but are still really intermittent. An intermittent operation is one that recurs regularly but with rather lengthy time periods between each operation during which staff are

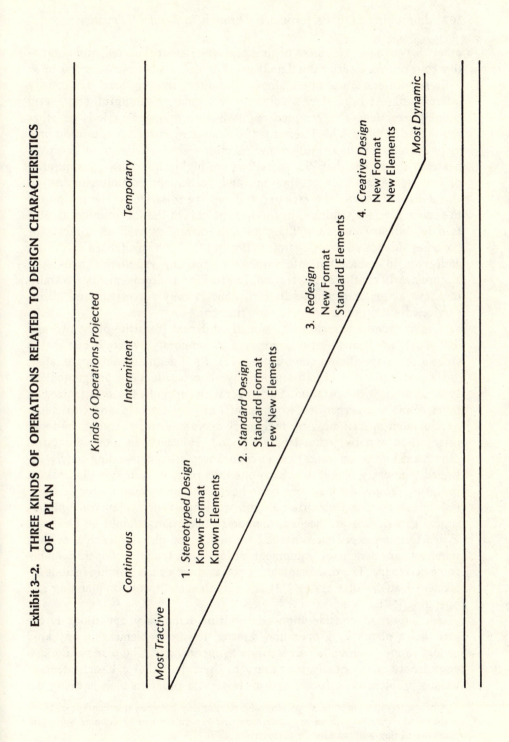

Exhibit 3–2. THREE KINDS OF OPERATIONS RELATED TO DESIGN CHARACTERISTICS
OF A PLAN

Kinds of Operations Projected

Continuous   Intermittent   Temporary

Most Tractive

1. *Stereotyped Design*
   Known Format
   Known Elements

2. *Standard Design*
   Standard Format
   Few New Elements

3. *Redesign*
   New Format
   Standard Elements

4. *Creative Design*
   New Format
   New Elements

Most Dynamic

otherwise engaged, resources of time and space are reallocated, and alternative (but not necessarily unrelated) goals and objectives are attended to.

In-service education operations at the direct training level are usually intermittent. At best, they involve fairly regular, meaningful, short-term training experiences interrupted regularly by prolonged periods of other job-related activity. This intermittent character of in-service education provides both its unique definition and its most serious challenge to effectiveness. To the extent that ISE operations are highly intermittent, continuity of experience, transfer of training, and participant commitment are all threatened. However, the fact that trainees are *in service* is the reason for in-service forms of training in the first place. On-the-job training as utilized in industry and in military establishments, as well as clinical approaches advocated by Cogan (6), Boyan (3), Wilhelms (38) and others, endeavors to reduce the intermittence of training experience, making it a more nearly continuous operation. Internships as arrangements for training have a similar rationale. In fact, none is fully successful, and all in-service education remains highly intermittent.*

The temporary operation is distinctly different from the other two and less widely used for in-service purposes. A temporary system is one that is created for a specific unique purpose (16). Its time, materials, space, staff, goals, and objectives are all temporarily allocated. It has a designated life span as a distinct operation. Such operations include those organized in times of major emergencies, experimental or pilot projects, and curriculum development operations. Any temporary operation can, of course, be replicated when and if circumstances demand. However, in most situations, "the hand moves on" and new circumstances arise demanding newly designed temporary operations. Each one thus presents a unique planmaking problem. Temporary ISE operations have enormous potential for addressing unique and/or stubborn training problems. When intensive, uninterrupted experiences are needed, temporary operations should be designed. When training experiences needed are highly complex, expensive, or they require scarce personnel, equipment, or locations, temporary operations become necessary. The disadvantages associated with such training include inefficient transfer of training (33) and large expenditures for planning and operating (37).

An important consideration emphasizing temporary operations is the fact that a planmaking operation directed toward implementing any kind of innovative program is necessarily a *temporary* one. The planmaking discussed here is essentially temporary to the extent that a clearly defined, unique problem is in focus, and an in-service program plan is being de-

---

* It is interesting to note, in passing, the relationship between this concept of intermittence and the widely held misconception that experience can be equated with continuous learning as discussed in Chapter I.

veloped to address the problem creatively. The in-service training that follows from such planning could, of course, be intermittent or temporary or both. The plan, once developed, could be utilized intermittently to guide other programs in operation.

Design Formats and Elements

Operations designing can be conceptualized as a two-dimensional problem. Exhibit 3–2 suggests that a plan for an ISE operation has both a format and a set of elements. The more tractive, less dynamic designs require little operations designing because standard (well-known and accepted) formats are utilized, and the elements are equally well known. The highly dynamic designs require much more elaborate and detailed planmaking because new formats and elements are being put together in a creative process. A new and different, unfamiliar operating reality is being projected for implentation. This involves more elaborate planning procedures for choosing, information processing, and designing. It also involves attending to the very difficult problems of communicating about the image of operations that has emerged to those not involved in its creation. Obviously, a broad base of involvement and continuous communications in the process of such planning would be well advised.

A format is a structure for operating that clearly indicates sequences, responsibilities, and groupings as well as space, time, and material utilization. The overly stereotyped format for a workshop described earlier in the chapter clearly illustrates a very simple format. The "clinical supervision" cycles of Cogan (6) and others (3) are a bit more elaborate but nonetheless illustrate a standard design. Such a format often calls for the following:

1. *Preconference.* The teacher and supervisor confer to establish rapport, discuss concerns, and agree to an observation with appropriate, limited focus.
2. *Teaching and Classroom Observation.* The supervisor observes and records according to the agreed-upon focus. The teacher strives to teach as well as possible.
3. *Postobservation Analysis.* The supervisor analyzes observed and recorded data to provide more easily understood information for interpretation.
4. *Postobservation Conference.* The teacher and the supervisor confer. They study the analyzed observation data. They discuss possible interpretations. The teacher is encouraged to draw conclusions regarding the successful and not so successful elements in his or her teaching performance as observed.

5. *Replanning Session.* The teacher does this alone or meets with the supervisor again for teaching to secure further improvements. They agree on changes to be attempted as the focus for further observation.
6. *Reteaching and Observation.* New elements are introduced in terms of special concerns of the individual teacher, the unique set of interpersonal relationships involved between clinician and teacher, and situational elements within the context of the school. However, the format is standardized and requires little imaginative effort for its design. A training kit to facilitate widespread use of this as a standard operation has recently become available (4).

Microteaching as described by Allen (1) and others offers another illustration of a format for in-service education that is not unlike that used for clinical supervision. The highly standard format includes use of mini-lessons, focused on a specific technique, videotape recording and collaborative observation and analysis of the lesson via the replay of the videotape. Even though objectives, content, and interpersonal elements may be unique in every situation, this too is a highly standard operation for in-service education. (See Chapter VI for more detail on clinical and other individualized designs.)

Still a different format for in-service training is illustrated by what I call cafeteria-type programs. Variations are found in school systems as far ranging as Portland, Oregon (31), Philadelphia (25) and Victoria, Texas (36). The format is usually sequenced and specified as follows:

1. A large diverse target population is designated.
2. A survey of interests in training topics, objectives, or activities is conducted.
3. An array of discrete training sessions is planned to match the most frequently identified interests.
4. The training sessions are scheduled, publicized, and arranged.
5. Individuals within the target population elect to attend and participate in one or more of the sessions.
6. The sequence is repeated periodically.

All the formats outlined above are cyclical in nature. They provide for a sequence that is relatively easy to replicate. Hence, if such training programs seem effective, replications permit serving other needs or increasing the size of the operation with only minor variations in plans. The simplicity and replicability of such standard cyclical formats undoubtedly accounts for their popularity. Unfortunately, such simplistic designs also may account for the ineffectiveness of many ISE programs, especially when used repetitively and indiscriminatingly for all kinds of purposes.

The elements of design are all of the numerous materials, activities, time frames, spaces, group arrangements, locations, facilities, and people that are brought together within a format to give character to the operation. An analogy from architectural design would distinguish the structural character of a house from the surface materials, appliances, and special features that make a house functionally what it is.

The format outlined for cafeteria programs retains the same structural features regardless of many elements that might greatly affect the quality of training experiences produced. For instance, outstanding leaders directing many of the sessions in contrast with amateurs' show-and-tell presentations would make a major difference. Many sessions linked to each other to provide for a set of skills in progression with schedules that promote the selection and use of such a training series would make for a different quality operation (19:40). Sufficient numbers of appropriate sessions to assure small groups when needed could make a difference in quality. A diagnostically powerful needs assessment process with incentives provided to encourage participants to select sessions in terms of carefully prioritized needs would enhance the productivity of the operation. Even a timing element that would assure session activities within the morning hours of a regular workday rather than in afternoons, evenings, or Saturdays when participants are tired or inconvenienced can substantially influence program quality.

The design of in-service education programs goes beyond the normal procedures of planning. Design involves creating structural formats that set the stage for more meaningful, purposeful, and satisfying experiences for participants. But attention to structure alone is rarely adequate. The creative, selective use of an array of elements — time, people, materials, groupings, spaces — that provide the best set of conditions for session activity is also essential.

Standardizing the Innovative Plan

The arguments for careful planmaking that give special attention to *operational designing* procedures are also strengthened at times by arguments for standardized practices. A plan that has been well developed, implemented, and evaluated can be *adapted* for use in other situations or on similar occasions. The heavy expenditures required for high-quality planmaking with creative designs are much more readily justified when the plan itself is so carefully developed as a set of documents and materials that others can use it for replicating the in-service programs without undertaking such extensive planning.

Simulations and games provide some of the best examples of detailed, carefully designed planning documents. In these particular kinds of training programs, a format is often developed that is extremely complex. Furthermore, elements in the form of playing materials, visuals, tests, scorecards, and many others are often developed with highly specialized purposes in mind. The whole game or simulation represents a creative endeavor that should be preserved and reemployed by many others. To facilitate such diffusion of plans, carefully developed manuals are provided along with a full array of materials for implementation.

Hence, the most exciting planmaking can contribute best, perhaps, to implementation of in-service programs in somewhat standardized ways. (See Chapter VII for more detail on simulations and games.)

Self-instructional packets and other well-designed training kits are becoming increasingly common as products of special programs or projects. Like well-designed simulations and games, these packets and kits usually contain materials for participants to use that are of a variety of kinds — films, tapes, transparencies, and tests, for instance. These richly varied, often professionally produced elements are an integral part of a larger format of procedures and sequences carefully detailed in manuals or guides. Such kits offer opportunities for extended use of predesigned program plans with formats and elements that could not be readily developed in most school settings.

The formats of two widely used stereotyped or standardized training program plans may serve as a caution with regard to the severe limitations inherent in any single format or set of elements. These two designs take the form of the *textbook* and the *college course*. Both of these are commonly used for in-service training purposes. Both utilize standardized formats with only limited variations. Both have serious limitations in the kind and variety of elements that are generally included. Accordingly, they tend to be program plans of the *stereotyped design* type. At best, they are standard designs. They serve well for continuous operations, but more creative alternatives are generally available for intermittent and purely temporary in-service training operations.

There appears to be a growing pattern of use of courses for ISE programming. With growing demands for a variety of experiences, more freedom of choice and some kind of certificate renewal programs are emerging that are characterized as "cafeterias of courses." This is not a new development, but it appears to be growing rapidly. Philadelphia's In-Service Council (25) is reported to have enrolled eighteen hundred teachers in fifty-eight courses in the spring of 1977. In Texas (10, 36) extensive offerings of topical sessions ranging from one and one half to eight hours are published by local school districts and regional service centers with teachers encouraged to make free choices based on interests. Portland, Oregon (31), schools have developed a rather elaborate system of approved in-service classes offered to facilitate meeting the "Professional Growth Salary/In-Service Requirement" of the district.

Forey (15:197) refers to programs of this type as "a supermarket" and critically notes that "exposure to new approaches are of little use if teaching in the classroom and supervision remain exactly as before." Of course, the advocates for such *standardized* or *stereotyped* designs would argue that they can affect classroom practice. Great reliance is placed on the quality of a specific class or course or topic; the quality of choices being made; the appropriateness of the timing of the experience; and the supportiveness of conditions for implementation at home. Obviously, these are not all likely to be facilitating.

DOCUMENTATION

The physical forms and the essential parts of a program plan cannot be well represented in printed form. Unfortunately, any effort to illustrate a plan of complexity requires not only many pages but also numerous visual displays. Portions of an incomplete plan are included in this chapter and in Appendix E. In the pages that follow, some planning documents will be described in greater detail and illustrated, but the reader is cautioned that full understanding is likely to develop only as a result of participating in and using plans that have been developed by others. Unfortunately, only the commercially distributed kits, packets, games, and simulations are generally available. The other work of many creative designer-planners is not often reproduced.

The Physical Forms of a Plan

Most plans contain a narrative document including the usual list of objectives, schedules, budgets, and staffing plans. When they are master plans or strategic plans (8:5), the documentation may be devoted largely to defining goals, specifying operational components, designating responsibilities, indicating strategies to be implemented, specifying target populations, setting schedules, and estimating costs in terms of time and money. Tactical (8) or program plans usually include the same kind of narrative and tabular material. However, considerable additional detail is usually provided in terms of specifying objectives related to goals, describing the operating events, and detailing anticipated expenditures.

Both strategic and tactical plans specify some arrangements for evaluation. Again, the master plan of long-range character should clearly specify the outcomes to be used for evaluation and may leave details of instrumentation and data handling to be planned by others. Program plans, on the other hand, should clearly indicate outcomes and processes that are to be evaluated. Furthermore, at least a general description of instrumentation, data-gathering procedures, and feedback schedules should be included.

Depending on the specific format, the array of elements included, and the comprehensiveness of a plan, the physical document can vary from a small pamphlet to an enormous box of materials.

The Essential Parts

Most writers describe the essential steps of a planning process in such ways as to at least suggest the documentation. Bishop's (2:55) list of steps or phases of planning is fairly typical: (1) identify needs; (2) determine specific target(s); (3) determine basic resources; (4) determine effective grouping or format; (5) present specific program plans; (6) complete preparation activities; (7) perform implementation; and (8) conduct evaluation. The first three of these eight steps can be translated fairly readily into a list of needs; a description of participants to be served; and some kind of tabulations or listings of time, space, staff, equipment, and money required. The specific forms in which the other steps are to appear in a plan is not so easily recognized.

Conrad, Brooks, and Fischer (8:7) propose "phases" for planning that do suggest some additional forms for documentation. They stress developing the data needed, which suggests that data displays showing needs-targets-objectives relationships might be useful. They suggest both establishing goals and clearly describing plans for achieving goals.

Certainly, the minimum essential features of a document representing a plan for in-service education should include the following:

a statement of the reason for undertaking the training (the problem or the need)

a description of the specific goal(s) and objectives selected as outcomes

a detailing of the participants to be served and how or why they (groups or individuals) are related to goals and objectives

a calendar of major events showing their relationship to objectives and participants

a designation of the responsible person or group assigned to each major event

a description of the operating characteristics — format and elements or strategy or approach — that is anticipated for each major event

a list of resource requirements for each major event and one for overall
coordination

a description of the procedures for evaluating the plan providing timely
feedback on the operation

a schedule and list of procedures for monitoring the total program

The challenge in documentation is not in getting these nine kinds of decisions made or ideas developed but in getting them on paper, chart, or other
form so that the total plan clearly communicates, guides, and facilitates. An
extensive narrative may be necessary to make certain parts of the plan explicit and clear, but such narratives tend not to be much used in the implementing. Outlines, charts, graphs, tables, checklists, and other graphics
with sufficient narration to assure clarity of meaning and intended use are
often desirable.

Special Features

The graphic displays mentioned above can often be included in a plan
using 8 1/2 by 11 inch paper. But often such print media are unduly con-
fining. Wall charts not only facilitate the presentation of graphic or illustrative material; they may also facilitate periodic referral to such material by personnel involved in implementation. Similarly, visuals, PERT
charts, Gantt charts, flowcharts, films, videotapes, sound recordings, tests,
and even objects and exhibits may be important special features to include
in a documented plan for in-service education.

When many group leaders are to be utilized in a program, the training
of these individuals may require a separate training session plan with a
film or a filmstrip and visuals for use on the overhead projector with handouts. All of these materials should be included as part of the larger plan if
they are essential to successful implementation. When certain major components of a larger operation are to be delegated to different individuals,
effective coordination may require materials that clearly depict relationships among those components at every stage in the operation. Hence, a
PERT network such as illustrated in Chapter II and/or a Gantt chart may
be devised and maintained for monitoring purposes. When different components must operate with considerable conformity to design requirements, manuals, illustrative materials, a procedural checklist, and other specific aids may need to be provided as part of the plan.

The following is a brief description of the contents in a very simple
program plan in the form of a kit:

CONTENTS OF A SECONDARY STAFF DEVELOPMENT PROGRAM KIT *

This program plan is referred to as a "self-study kit." An introductory section of fewer than four pages provides "an overview," "relationship of kit to crime prevention and drug education," a brief description of each of the four modules included, directions for using the modules in "study clusters of three or four teachers," a description of the "process" or sequence participants are to pursue for each module, a statement of responsibilities of the "Cluster Leader," and a list of filmstrips, cassette tapes, and study materials available for each module in the Facilitator Kit.

Following the brief introductory section, each module is presented, with "handouts" attached. Each module deals with a specific objective and only two to five pages are utilized to direct the study activities estimated to last about two hours.

Module II is called "Positive Reinforcement." The basic format or structure of activity is overviewed and then utilized as a sequence of specific directions.

"Objective. Upon completion you should be able to use positive reinforcement. . . ."

"Rationale." (A brief explanation provided.)

"Pre-Assessment. Self-administer and score the pretest on positive reinforcement (Handout 2.1)."

"Content. Individually read Handout 2.2, 'Positive Reinforcement.' "

"Interaction. Meet with your cluster members and complete the following activities: (1) Using discussion questions in Handout 2.3, . . . (2) Listen to the tape. . . . (3) Brainstorm and record . . . reinforcers. . . . Review. . . . Plan to add these to your reinforcement repertoire. (4) Optional activity. . . . Follow directions in Handout 2.6."

"Self-Reflection. Read and respond to questions . . . (Handout 2.7). This is strictly personal. . . ."

"Practicum . . . an opportunity for each teacher to assess her/his present level . . . , set goals for improvement, and to begin working toward these goals." Detailed instructions are provided for taping a lesson and analyzing it.

"Debriefing. After all cluster members have completed the practicum, meet in clusters and discuss. . . ." Suggestions for discussion foci are provided.

Handouts for this module include a pre-assessment test, a six-page reading on positive reinforcement, discussion questions, a response sheet for use with a prerecorded tape, a form for recording brainstorming responses, and worksheets for use in Practicum exercises with illustrations of procedures to use.

---

* This program plan, entitled *The Greening of Students*, by Scottie Littleton and Jim Miller was developed as a self-contained packet. (Austin, Tex.: Region XIII, Education Service Center, n.d.)

The kit described above is illustrative, in a very simple format, of many of the ideas being presented in this chapter. Brevity and ease in use are assured by a format that is consistently followed in all four modules. The basic strategy calls for independent study, small-peer-group interaction, and application of new skills to individual classroom situations.

The kit is in two parts. One is a complete user's guide including orientation, procedures, and materials needed by all. The other part, a facilitators kit, provides more details for organizing, coordinating, and planning while also containing all of the tapes and nonconsumable materials to be shared by participants.

Because this training program plan is presumably for self-study it does *not* include many provisions for guiding and facilitating the implementation process that might well be essential! A facilitator is designated as being needed; but of course, in a fully developed plan one might be needed in each of several schools, programs, or departments; and an overall program coordinator might be needed. A component plan for getting facilitators appointed or otherwise designated and providing them with time, materials, and training would be needed. Budget estimates with designated sources of funds should be included to assure adequate supplies of materials, released time, and other resources. Finally, to qualify as a fully developed plan, some kind of evaluation process would need to be indicated.

Dilemma: Too Much or Too Little Structure

An alert reader might easily react to the ideas and illustrations presented here as calling for too much structure. Still another alert reader might complain of too little specific detail. Both concerns are real and legitimate. To be sure, most planning documentation suffers from one or both of these ailments. Within the same plan, objectives may be specified with almost ridiculous detail, while staff assignments, activity descriptions, or grouping arrangements are nebulous or nonexistent. Planners tend, of course, to present vividly what they know best and to neglect other details. Unfortunately, this often leads to plans that are not very useful.

Robert F. Mager (26) is well known for making complex things simple to learn. He suggests that a plan needs to answer only three questions (26:vii):

1. Where are we going?
2. How shall we get there?
3. How will we know we've arrived?

Obviously, these are the very *core* questions a plan must address, but they are only a beginning.

Kaufman (21), Silvern (32), and others (including this author) are inclined to present systems diagrams in plans with elaborate sequences of rectangles representing neatly labeled "steps" (21:17), including: 1.0, identify problem; 2.0, determine alternatives; 3.0, select strategy; 4.0, implement; and so on. Each of these rectangles is logically related to every other one. But the dilemma for the planner-designer-user is that little detail is provided regarding *within rectangle* events. Fortunately, considerable assistance on specific procedures for needs assessing (21:28–51) and specifying objectives (26) is available from various sources. Even HEW rules and regulations tend to give much emphasis to planning that clearly specifies needs, how determined, how utilized, and how selected (34).* Perhaps it is fortunate that program design and implementation strategies are neglected in at least some federal legislation.

Interestingly enough, the rules and regulations for in-service training under the Education of the Handicapped Act (Public Law 94–142) offer some useful descriptors of content that might well be included in in-service education program plans of both long- and intermediate-range kinds. Some of these are explicit requirements of the plan:

"insures that ongoing inservice training is available to all personnel. . . ."
"include . . . use of incentives which insure participation. . . ."
"The involvement of local staff. . . ."
"The use of innovative practices. . . ."
"Identify the areas in which training is needed. . . ."
"Specify the groups requiring training. . . ."
"Describe the content and nature of training for each area. . . ."
"Describe how the training will be provided in terms of . . . geographical scope . . . and . . . source. . . ."
"Specify . . . funding sources to be used, and . . . the time frame for providing it. . . ."
"Specify procedures for effective evaluation. . . ."

Planning for in-service education as conceived by this set of federal regulations gives credence to the view that plans should be somewhat detailed. Certainly, it is possible to become so prescriptive that there is little latitude for creative implementation. Furthermore, the uncertainties about future conditions make rigidly conceived plans less likely to fit real needs.

---

* Public Law 94–142 on education for handicapped children provides for in-service training. Regulations make repeated reference to specifying needs with terms like "annual needs assessment," "based on assessed needs," "results of needs assessment," "broken out by need," "process used in determining needs," and "areas in which training is needed." However, only one reference to "content and nature of the program" is included is a highly detailed document.

Hence, the longer the time frame and the more macroscopic the operation, the less wisdom there is in highly prescriptive planning documents. However, these circumstances also pose dangers that demand rigorous planning nonetheless. It is the very long-range plan that deals with highly demanding persistent performance problems, and powerful imaginative designs are required. It is the large, unwieldy program operation that fails from inadequate implementation and coordination. It is the truly sophisticated design that requires careful timing, competent trainers, and elaborate logistical support.

There appears to this writer to be no acceptable substitute for *maximizing detail*. The details should avoid verbosity. Flexibility should be provided for by detailing alternatives and backup systems. The awesomeness of a bulky, voluminous document with a variety of media and separate component plans can be overcome by properly structured introductory material. When plans are sketchy, there is reason to believe that the process was not fully accomplished.

Sociologist James G. March (27) has suggested two areas of difficulty in planning that seem to be applicable to the dilemma posed here. He notes that:

> the prime problem . . . is the problem of discovering alternatives, of generating alternatives. (27:123)

This is, of course, the design process in part. He further announces Gresham's law of planning as follows:

> routine drives out planning, routine drives out thinking. (27:123)

Two unfortunate corollaries might be:

1. Having dispensed with thinking and planning, routine makes it unnecessary to produce carefully detailed planning documents.

Therefore:

2. In-service education simply evolves unplanned, but it does not prosper!

Those leading the planning process must resist the tendency to make it a routine. It must be creative, imaginative, rigorous, logical, systematic, and even laborious and stimulating. What it should not be allowed to be is a routine task.

Bridging from Plan to Operations

Implementation is widely viewed as so simple and so automatic that it will follow from planning without being planned. Kaufman comments:

Implementation is what educators do best, since we have been rewarded most of our lives for doing things. . . . (21:134)

His point is valid, but only if we assume rather routine "doing" operations. Such is rarely the case with high-quality in-service education. As we deal with the implementation of plans for creating highly stimulating learning experiences for mature personnel, that is no routine affair.

A well-developed in-service education plan will clearly and explicitly guide implementation. This is a notion closely related to the problem of *teaching for transfer*. We cannot assume that new knowledge and skill learned in one context will transfer to another. Similarly, we cannot assume that a carefully detailed set of abstract representations of training will in fact become translated into operating reality. The intellectual power that is applied to create images of events that might be tends to blind planners to the fact that images are not reality. Translations are required.

A planning document must include very specific suggestions and/or directions on who is to do what, with whom, using what procedures or materials in what sequence, and within what time frame. The PERT procedures applied to education by Cook (9) have great utility in this portion of the plan. The Gantt (5) chart is one of the oldest management tools for guiding implementations of programs. It is illustrated in Exhibit 3–5. It is of special utility when time allocations are critical and an array of related components need coordination.

The more fascinating management tools should not blind planners to the indispensable use of a master schedule with carefully determined target dates. For in-service planning purposes, the kind of schedule that reflects time, space, and personnel relationships can be especially useful to avoid confusion and assure the smooth flow of activities over time, with flexibility for participants to make individual decisions.

Flowcharts are sometimes utilized to graphically depict the flow of major events (37:67). Since they lack time-line designations, flowcharts are not too helpful in monitoring. For example, a rather detailed, thirty-event flowchart of an in-service and preservice Teacher Corps program gives all events for a single year on a time line (13:117). However, the time frames tend to be distorted. Furthermore, events are generally described for actual use in facilitating implementation. Most flowcharts are a simple series of rectangles and arrows that show sequences of major events but little more. They look impressive to the neophyte, but they add little detail. They may assist with communication in an overview fashion. (See Exhibit 3–4.)

Plans for implementation can include more than detailed assignments, schedules, and graphic aids. Specific provisions for monitoring ongoing events should be included in plans for implementation. Such a monitoring plan should identify *critical events* associated with each major goal or objective and/or training components. Such critical events can become the basis for constructing a checklist for observers to use in monitoring. Furthermore, these critical events can be focused upon as items in process evaluation instruments for use during the operation of a program.

The *checklist for plan review* shown in Exhibit 3–3 provides a con-

---

Exhibit 3–3. CHECKLIST FOR REVIEWING AN IN-SERVICE EDUCATION PROGRAM PLAN

I. *Goal Specification*
- _____ A. A problem of importance is clearly described.
- _____ B. A need for training is clearly designated.
- _____ C. Long-range outcomes are defined.
- _____ D. Specific goals and related major objectives are specified.

II. *Strategy*
- _____ E. The overall training strategy is clearly developed.
- _____ F. Influences or conditions conducive to (or inhibiting) the strategy are indicated.
- _____ G. Cautions and limitations of the strategy are made explicit.

III. *Design*
- _____ H. A series of clearly designated sessions is sequenced.
- _____ I. The various sessions are clearly related to specific goals and/or major objectives.
- _____ J. The various sessions are related to clients to differentiate experiences.
- _____ K. Resources required for each session are designated.
- _____ L. Logistics relating time, space, people, and materials to each other have been described.

IV. *Implementation*
- _____ M. Responsibilities for each major component of the program have been assigned.
- _____ N. Schedules of events and their coordinate relationships have been carefully detailed.
- _____ O. Procedures for monitoring and providing corrective feedback are described.
- _____ P. Provisions have been made for detailed planning, training, and orientation activities for leadership personnel.
- _____ Q. Communications have been prepared to use in informing all persons involved.

V. *Evaluation*
- _____ R. Instrumentation and procedures for gathering data on the program in operation are available.
- _____ S. Analytical procedures have been described for processing data.
- _____ T. Procedures for utilizing evaluation findings are designated.

Exhibit 3–3   continued

VI. *Material*

——————— U.   Materials to be utilized throughout the program are fully developed and ready for use.

——————— V.   Facilities and equipment to be required are listed and/or described.

———————W.   Resource lists of materials and equipment that might be useful are provided.

——————— X.   Facilities arrangements that are to be required (or are desirable) are described.

VII. *Other*

——————— Y.

——————— Z.

venient listing of important components of a plan. When properly documented, in whatever form, the formal plan should provide clear evidence that each kind of information is included. Such a checklist can be useful as a guide in reviewing a plan prior to final preparation. It can also be useful as a guide to planners in the preparation process. Such detailed analysis might be especially important when plans are being selected on a competitive basis. However, for those attempting to refine their skill in planmaking, the more detailed criteria can be used diagnostically as well.

ILLUSTRATIONS OF PLANNING DISPLAYS

The Gantt chart, the flowchart, and schedules in various forms have been mentioned as graphic displays for making plans more fully useful. It is always hazardous to isolate a few techniques or procedures and exclude others; but these three, while being employed to some extent, need more careful consideration in order to be utilized in forms that assure a real contribution.

The Flowchart

An illustrative flowchart is included here as Exhibit 3–4. It belongs as a part of one of the displays in the *Comprehensive Plan* provided as Appendix E. This is a flowchart for a single major component of a larger in-service plan. It represents only one year of a five-year plan.

This chart reads from top to bottom. Some charts read from left to right.

Exhibit 3–4. FLOWCHART FOR COMPONENT I: IN-SERVICE EDUCATION FOR OBSERVING AND ANALYZING CLASSROOM PRACTICES

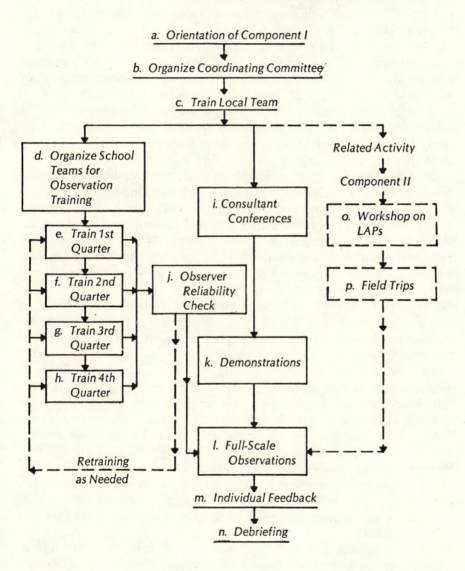

* Learning activity packets.

The events or classes of events are shown as rectangles and are roughly sequenced from top to bottom as shown by the connecting arrows. The approximate sequence of events is further emphasized by the letters assigned to each rectangle. Actually, the letters add to the chart primarily by providing a symbol to identify each rectangle of events.

Parallel rectangles indicate simultaneous classes or sets of events. For instance, while d, e, f, g, and h follow each other, i, j, k, and p are clearly shown as events or sets of events that are in progress during the same time span. Arrows from i to k, from j to l, and from i to p all denote sequential relationships even though the timing is only crudely indicated on the chart and the specific character of the relationship is not indicated.

A series of *arrows* as shown from e, f, g and h to j can be interpreted in various ways. It is intended to mean that the reliability checking of trainees (j) occurs following each of the other four sets of events. It could, of course, mean that j is continuously in operation, but that was not intended.

Dotted lines are used on this flowchart to indicate two different relationships, so they are labeled for explanatory purposes. Dotted lines from j to e, and f, g and h indicate that the reliability check may lead to retraining or more training that would dictate repeated or continued events in the training rectangles (e through h). Dotted lines leading to o and p are used to indicate that these are events that are associated with, or related to, another in-service component but are significantly related to this one and hence are being shown.

A flowchart of this type is quite informative. It does indicate the main sets or classes of events that are to be implemented. It indicates the sequences and some of the relationships planned. What such a flowchart *does not* communicate is also important to consider. Sequences are roughly shown, but specific time frames or target dates are *not* shown. Relationships between classes of events (rectangles) are only suggested; they are not clearly specified. For instance, an arrow from e to j, if specified more explicitly, is intended to mean that only after a full series of training activities should the first group of trainees be checked for interobserver reliability. However, the arrow from i to k means something quite different. Reference to the details of the plans reveals that this arrow simply means that pre- and post-observation conferences with observer trainees and those being observed is desirable at an early stage in the operation so that ideas from those conferences can be used to plan and guide field trips and demonstrations.

As the foregoing explanations of meanings of arrows indicates, a flowchart's greatest limitation is its lack of specificity about the relationships, sequences, and events within rectangles. This is a limitation of all flowcharts and also of systems diagrams as used, for instance, in Chapter IV. If the planmaker tries to add details, include a time line, and show sequences more precisely, what emerges is a very complex chart that loses its graphic simplicity. If we try to extend a chart like this to include a second or third year, it becomes a large display and requires special handling as a wall chart or foldout exhibit.

The distinctions between a flowchart and a *systems diagram* should be carefully *noted*. The two look much alike and are sometimes confused with each other. In fact, a most confusing practice is to corrupt a systems diagram so it is not clearly in either form. Systems diagrams employ very explicit symbols and rules regarding arrows, lines, and rectangle placements. Silvern offers the reader a very useful guide to these techniques (32). These rules do not apply to flowcharts; hence, the latter is a less precise tool in some ways but is perhaps more useful in providing a vivid overview of major events in an operation, especially when sequencing is important.

The Gantt Chart

One of the early graphic display tools for planning was developed for industrial production operations. In a rather old book, Wallace Clark (5) reviews the origins of the Gantt chart, named after its originator, and provides detailed illustrations for using the chart in business and industry. In educational planning, the Gantt chart has had a rebirth of use, but in a corrupted form that greatly limits the utility of the technique.

In Exhibit 3–5, a Gantt chart is presented from the *Comprehensive Plan* in Appendix E. The Gantt illustrates the careful plan for sequencing and timing each of an array of specific operations. While only two out of four components of a total in-service education plan are shown, the utility and the unique character of the Gantt chart can be appreciated if the reader will study this exhibit carefully.

Clark (5:59) reminds the Gantt chart user that it "is not a record of what *was* done; it . . . is usually thrown away after the . . . programme has been completed." The main purposes have to do with making a plan and guiding actions for implementation. Every distinctive operation is represented as a planned and explicit time frame. Each operation appears as a simple bracket on a time line. Since all brackets are shown on the same chart with the same time line, a set of time relationships between all operations is graphically and precisely shown. In studying Exhibit 3–5, the planmaker begins to appreciate the unique and explicit contributions the Gantt chart can make both to planmaking and to implementing.

The symbols for the Gantt chart are very important. The simple bracket is the basic symbol. It shows the time frame for each operation, indicating start-and-stop times *according to plan*. A symbol is superimposed on the

Exhibit 3–5.   GANTT CHART FOR IN-SERVICE EDUCATION: INDIVIDUALIZING INSTRUCTION PROGRAM

Rock Meadows Public Schools   1975–76   Office of In-Service Education

Components of Program	Aug.	Sept.	Oct.	Nov.	Dec.	Jan.	Feb.	Mar.	Apr.	May	June
I. *Observation of Classroom Practice*											
A. Orientation of staff, etc.		(1)									
B. Training local personnel	(2)										
C. Reliability checks			(3)								
D. Full-scale observations and feedback				(4)							
E. Pre- and post-conference											
II. *Learning Activity Packets*											
A. Orientation and organization											
B. Field trips				(5)							
C. Workshops					(6)						
D. Demonstrations				(5)							

Dates: 20 1 15 30 15 30 15 30 15 30 15 30 15 28 15 30 15 30 15 30 15

SYMBOLS

End time—actual

Present point in time (checkpoint)

Scheduled time frame

Progress toward completion

Start time—actual

bracket to show when the operation *actually* started. *Progress* toward completion of the operation is shown by a heavy line along the top of each bracket. This heavy line is simply extended periodically to show progress at any given *checkpoint* along the time line. The *termination* of an operation is shown by a special symbol superimposed on the bracket at the point on the time line when the operation *actually ended.*

To illustrate the communications power of the Gantt chart, the numbered reference points on Exhibit 3–5 have been added. Notice the bracket on line ID opposite the operation "Full-scale observations and feedback." This is the original plan for a time frame for this operation. It indicates a starting date of March 10 and an ending date of April 25. Notice now the (1) below the bracket for operation IA. This bracket has been darkened to show starting on time in August, continuing in operation through to about September 20, somewhat past the September 15 date planned for completion.

Another interpretation is illustrated by reference (2). Notice that the planned start was about August 25, but the actual start was delayed until September 1. A similar delay is shown by reference (3) and a longer delay by reference (4). In contrast, notice that operation IIA started and ended right on schedule. But look at IIC; reference (6) indicates that this operation began on time and ended *early*, ahead of plan. Conversely, operation IID started ahead of schedule.

The uniqueness of the Gantt chart for use in implementing operations according to plan is emphasized by the use of symbols that clearly show progress toward scheduled target dates. Implementation is also emphasized by this technique because the chart is developed as part of the plan, but then must be utilized periodically *during* implementation. In effect, it is a monitoring device and encourages *action* related to plans, but it also encourages use of the plan to guide and coordinate different operations. The fact that all brackets are unchanged from December 15 forward simply means that the last periodic review was on that date, shown by the last triangle at the bottom on the time line.

Relationships among operations are shown by the display of all symbols on a single time line. Relationships are shown only with respect to time, however. Staff relationships, shared resources, or other interdependencies are clearly not shown. In this respect, the Gantt chart fails to offer one advantage the PERT network provides as shown in Chapter II. Because only time-sequence relationships are shown by the Gantt, it has its greatest utility when several operations (1) are highly independent of each other, (2) need to be sequenced in relation to each other, and (3) are in need of very careful timing. Such conditions do not prevail in all in-service program-planning situations. The Gantt chart may not be superior to a carefully developed schedule if only sequencing is a concern. The PERT network has advantages over Gantt if completion dates are most crucial and interdependencies are more numerous among operations.

Time and timing are always critical considerations in in-service education program planning. Therefore, the Gantt chart has potential as one of several kinds of displays. For instance, in a training series in which participants are sequenced from one session and space to another and staff have shared responsibilities, plans for careful timing and sequencing are so important that the Gantt chart could be most helpful. (See Harris's [18] description of a program of teaching demonstrations for an example of such a program [Exhibit 3–3].)

Schedules

Charts, graphs, and outlines all have in common the intent to provide an overview or quick reference to a complex array of events. They strive to provide a gestalt, communicating meaning about a complex program while providing some detail, too, if desired. Schedules are still another form of information display. Unlike flowcharts, they generally give much more detail. Like the Gantt chart, they emphasize sequence and timing but offer a greater variety of detail; yet schedules are not particularly useful for monitoring progress unless they are quite detailed.

Schedules take many forms; in their most traditional form they are, in effect, a list of events, sequenced and dated or timed for starting and stopping. As such, they are of little help in showing relationships between events. In other forms, schedules become more graphic, showing time, place, and other relationships that can be a rich source of quickly available information. Of all the display or exhibit forms for use in plans, the schedule is the most commonly used, perhaps because of its flexibility and adaptability to many situations.

The simple schedule of listed events is well known and often looks something like this:

Schedule of In-Service Events: Preschool Workshop Planning, August 1978

Monday, February 6	Preparation of proposed seminars completed.
Monday, March 31–	Proposed seminar plans submitted.
Friday, April 7	Additions, deletions, changes made to proposed seminars.
Monday, July 31	Schedules and materials for registration sent to teachers.
Wednesday–Friday	
August 16–18	Preschool Workshops
Monday, August 28	Workshop evaluations and attendance reports submitted.
Friday, October 13	Evaluation analysis completed.

This simple schedule, like any schedule, could be expanded by a more precise, detailed listing of events and dates. Similarly, it could be simplified even more by presenting a more limited array of events. How detailed such a listing becomes depends on what the intended users need to know. If the schedule is to be used for monitoring, then detailed sequences of events should be listed. Similarly, if other portions of plans are being prepared in great detail, schedules can and should reflect this detail. However, if planning detail is being delegated, or delayed for later planning, then schedules can be simplified.

Considerable detail can be added, if desired, without departing too much from the basic listing format for a schedule. For instance, the excerpts below from a countywide schedule of workshops showing not only the dates, events, and sequence but also the objectives, competency reference numbers, times, places, and consultants.

County COOP In-Service
August 22, 23, 24, 19—
Date/Time/Place/Topic/Objective/Competency/Consultant

August 22 9:00–12:00 noon Premont Elementary School	1.	Television as an instructional medium to plan for effective use of TV as an instructional medium (2.02, 2.05, 3.02).	Ms. Jerry Kroloff, Channel 16
August 22 1:30–4:30 Kingsville J. E. Conner Museum	2.	Using your museum to plan for the use of a museum as an instructional facility (3.02, 2.05, 2.10, 3.02).	J. Picquet, J. E. Conner Museum
August 24 9:00–4:00 Riviera High School	19.	Individualization in the secondary math program. To develop strategies for improving math skills. To select and modify instructional aids for math (2.03, 3.02, 5.01).	Dr. Herbert K. Heager, University of Texas at San Antonio

Adapted from documents provided by Ms. Marion Czaja in connection with her work as a consultant for Region II, Education Service Center, Corpus Christi, Texas, in 1978.

A schedule like this one is still essentially a listing. Since it is intended primarily to inform implementers and participants about the various offerings, more detail is provided to guide specific actions for implementation. Participants can make choices knowing what, when, where, and who the consultant will be. Principals and their teachers can plan together in terms of competency needs, matching needs with competency designations that refer to a set of specified competencies that had been developed for this purpose. This kind of schedule is not a particularly useful tool for monitoring these various operations, however.

An interesting variation in scheduling is represented in the illustration below, which combines a simple listing with a time line of sorts:

Planning Schedule: Staff Development Program, April 5–7, 19——

Page 2			Times Frames								
			Monday 4/5			Tuesday 4/6			Wednesday 4/7		
Session No.	Computer No.	Topic	1	2	3	4	5	6	7	8	9
38	945	Motivating the reluctant reader	x	x	x	x	x	x	x	x	x
39	947	Visual literary	x	x	x						
45	959	Facing inter- personal problems		x	x		x	x			

This tool was designed by Dr. Dan McLendon, Deputy Superintendent, Richardson Schools, Richardson, Texas.

This schedule, while quite simple in form, provides a great deal of information. With many different events being planned for a single three-day period, modular scheduling provides for up to three modules each day. Some topics are scheduled for the full three days with all nine modules being utilized. Others are scheduled in a single day, on two days, on mornings only, and so on. The uses of this schedule are more important for planning than monitoring. It is especially useful to participants in making choices involving careful use of the time available. For monitoring purposes, each event is assigned two numbers. One identifies the topic or session that might be repeated subsequently. The computer number is a unique number that is not repeated, because it represents the specifics of this particular program event and is the basis for accounting and provides access to data for evaluating specific events.

A cyclical series of events calls for a schedule that reflect the cycles. For example:

1st Mondays. Submit logs reporting on prior activities of prior weeks.
1st Fridays. Assemble staff for problems review.

2d Fridays. Individual conferences with principals on their efforts in growth planning with teachers.

3d Mondays. Meet with districtwide advisory council for ISE.

These repetitive events that need to be scheduled are often displayed on a calendar as well as listed, to avoid other events from being planned that interfere.

Another modification of a schedule form is one that shows a series of events, some of which are replicated.

Monthly Activity Schedule

Time/Date	10th	15th	22d	29th
9–12	Group Dynamics by Dr. Martha Williams and Mr. Louis Tomaino	High school only. Overview of Regional Center ESC staff	Jr. col. only. Same as previous week	Review and summary (morning only)
1–3	Laboratory Method	High school only. Practicum in Innovative Practices by Robert Sloan	Same as previous week	no activity
	First Week	Second Week	Third Week	Fourth Week

Developed by Dr. Herbert Overfield while working with the diffusion of innovative practices projects. *The Diffusion of Educational Practices—A Prototype In-Service Training Program Involving Selected Junior College and Public School Faculties in Central Texas* (Waco, Tex.: Region XII, Education Service Center and Extension Teaching and Field Service Bureau, University of Texas, 1968–69.

Still a further variation on the periodic schedule shown above is one that details the use of time and dates by *type of activity.*

Time	8/24	9/13	9/22	10/2	11/14	12/2	2/11
				Dates			
8–9	A	—	A	—	A	—	A
9–10	C	B	F	B	D	CorF	CorF
10–11	D	E	D	B	D	E	D
11–12	E	E	D	B	D	D	D
afternoon	B	B	B	B	—	B	—

A — Breakfast meeting   D — Buzz groups or T groups
B — Individual conferences   E — Role playing
C — Demonstrations   F — Films or videotapes

This type of schedule is especially useful in planning as a way of assuring balance, sequence, and variety in activities as discussed earlier in relation to session design. (See Chapter II.)

The illustrations of schedules, flowcharts, the Gantt chart, along with the PERT network and systems diagrams shown in other chapters should assist in-service education planners in selecting a variety of graphic displays. A plan must, of course, contain narrations depicting needs, objectives, activities, people, and other resources. Even extended narratives in the form of scenarios are often quite useful. But graphic displays are especially useful in allowing for alternative ways of conveying meaning to planners, implementers, participants, and evaluators alike. Obviously, no one display can do a complete job. An array of displays is often advisable, and using different kinds is undoubtedly to be desired.

SUMMARY

This chapter has focused on the processes and products for planning in-service education programs. Planmaking rather than planning process has been our major concern, even though they are closely interrelated. The basic position taken here is that planmaking combines both technical skill and creative processes. However approached, whoever is to be involved, ISE planning must be systematic, emphasize design, and generate a set of materials called *the plan*.

By emphasizing planmaking and the product of that activity as a physical thing called a plan, we do not ignore the fact that plans can be in the mind only! Or they can be disorganized things, partially in the mind of one or more persons, partially in a planning document, and partially scattered about in files and folders. We doubt that these latter forms of planmaking are likely to lead to the highest-quality in-service education. Nonetheless, some might argue that the detail and rigor of documentation called for in this chapter is unrealistic. Possibly these are ideals we should consider, knowing full well that we must aim high if even less ambitious targets are to be attained.

REFERENCES

*1. Allen, Dwight and Keven Ryan. *Micro-Teaching*. Reading, Mass.: Addison-Wesley, 1969.

*2. Bishop, Leslee J. *Staff Development and Instructional Improvement: Plans and Procedures*. Boston: Allyn and Bacon, Inc., 1976.

 * Suggested for further reading.

3. Boyan, Norman J. et al. "Final Report: 1972–73. The instructional Supervision Training Program." Project no. 141155. Santa Barbara, Calif.: Graduate School of Education, University of California, September 1973 (mimeo).

*4. Boyan, Norman. J. and Willis D. Copeland. *Instructional Supervision Training Program.* Columbus, Ohio: Charles E. Merrill, 1978.

*5. Clark, Wallace. *The Gantt Chart: A Working Tool of Management.* 3d ed. London: Sir Isaac Pitman and Sons, Ltd., 1952.

6. Cogan, Morris L. *Clinical Supervision.* Boston: Houghton Mifflin Company, 1973.

7. Coleman, James. "Comment." In *Planned Variation in Education* (Alice Rivlin and P. M. Timpane, editors). Washington, D.C.: The Brookings Institution, 1975.

*8. Conrad, M. J., Kenneth Brooks, and George Fischer. "A Model for Comprehensive Planning." *Planning and Changing* 4, no. 1 (Spring 1973): 3–14.

*9. Cook, Desmond L. *PERT: Applications in Education,* OE-1214, Cooperative Research Monograph no. 17. Washington, D.C.: U.S. Government Printing Office, 1966.

10. Corpus Christi Schools. *Staff Development, 1977–78. Equivalency Time Program.* Corpus Christi, Tex.: Office of Staff Development, Corpus Christi Independent School District, 1977.

11. Creekmur, Jimmie L. "A Descriptive Analysis of Inservice Education Programs in Selected Texas School Systems Utilizing Operational Criteria." Doctoral dissertation, University of Texas at Austin, August 1977.

12. Drucker, Peter F. "What Results Should You Expect? A User's Guide to MBO." *Public Administration Review* 36, no. 1 (January–February 1976): 12–19.

13. Edelfelt, Roy A. (editor). *Inservice Education: Criteria for and Examples of Local Programs.* Bellingham, Wash.: Western Washington State College, 1977.

14. Florida State Department of Education. *Criteria for Designing, Developing and Approving a District Master Plan for Inservice Education.* Tallahassee, Fla.: State Department of Education, n.d.

15. Forey, Ambrose J., Jr. "Participation and Personal Growth: Keys to Staff Development." In *The In-Service Education of Teachers. Trends, Processes and Prescriptions* (Louis Rubin, editor). Boston: Allyn and Bacon, Inc., 1978, pp. 195–98.

16. Gant, Jack, Oron Smith, and John H. Hansen. *Temporary Systems.* Tallahasse, Fla., 1977.

*17. Harris, Ben M. *Supervisory Behavior in Education.* 2d ed. Englewood Cliffs, N.J.: Prentice-Hall, Inc., 1975, 21–24.

18. Harris, Ben M. "Teaching Demonstration Model." Chapter 4 in *Designs for Inservice Education* (E. W. Bessent, editor). Austin, Tex.: Research and Development Center for Teacher Education, University of Texas, February 1967.

* Suggested for further reading.

19. Harris, Ben M. and E. W. Bessent, and Kenneth E. McIntyre. *Inservice Education: A Guide to Better Practice.* Englewood Cliffs, N.J.: Prentice-Hall, Inc., 1969.

20. Hartley, Harry J. *Educational Planning, Programming, Budgeting — A Systems Approach.* Englewood Cliffs, N.J.: Prentice-Hall, Inc., 1968.

*21. Kaufman, Roger A. *Educational System Planning.* Englewood Cliffs, N.J.: Prentice-Hall, Inc., 1972.

*22. Knowles, Malcolm S. *The Adult Learner.* Houston, Tex.: Gulf Publishing Company, 1973.

23. Littleton, Scottie and Jim Miller. *The Greening of Students.* Austin, Tex.: Region XIII, Education Service Center, n.d.

24. Lutz, John E. "Inservice Personnel Development: A Systematic Approach to Program Planning" *Educational Technology* 16, no. 4 (April 1976): 44–47.

25. Lytle, James H. "Pennsylvania's Pioneering Program of Inservice Education." *Phi Delta Kappan* 59, no. 4 (December 1977): 267–68.

26. Mager, Robert F. *Developing Attitude Toward Learning.* Palo Alto, Calif.: Fearon Publishers, 1968.

27. March, James G. "Organizational Factors in Supervision." In *The Supervisor: Agent for Change in Teaching* (James Raths and Robert R. Leeper, editors). Washington, D.C.: Association for Supervision and Curriculum Development, 1966, pp. 107–24.

28. Nadler, Leonard. "Support Systems for Training." *Training and Development Journal* 25, no. 10 (October 1971): 2–7.

29. Ohme, Herman. "Ohme's Law of Institutional Change." *Phi Delta Kappan* (December 1977): 263–65.

30. Overfield, Herbert. *The Diffusion of Educational Practices — A Prototype In-Service Training Program Involving Selected Junior College and Public School Faculties in Central Texas.* Waco, Tex.: Region XII, Education Service Center and Extension Teaching and Field Service Bureau, University of Texas, 1968–69.

31. Perko, Laura. "A Twelve-Point Guideline and Checklist for Conducting an Approved Inservice Class." Portland, Ore.: Portland Public Schools, January 1977.

*32. Silvern, Leonard Charles. *Systems Engineering Applied to Training.* Houston, Tex.: Gulf Publishing Company, 1972.

33. United Press International. "Seminar Organizer Avers Many of Them Prove to Be of Little Value." *Christian Science Monitor*, February 21, 1978, p. 18.

34. U.S. Office of Education, Department of Health, Education, and Welfare. "Education of Handicapped Children: Implementation of Part B of the Education of the Handicapped Act" *Federal Register* 42, no. 163 (August 23, 1977): 492.

35. University Council on Educational Administration. *Rationale and Uses of*

* Suggested for further reading.

UCEA Monroe City Simulation. Columbus, Ohio: University Council on Educational Administration, n.d.

36. Victoria Public Schools. "Option Inservice Program" Victoria, Tex.: Victoria Independent School District, November 3, 1977 (mimeo).

37. Waxahachie Independent School District. *Prescriptive Opportunities for Individual Needs Training.* A staff development model for funding under title IX, part C, P.L. 93–380. Waxahachie, Tex.: Waxahachie ISD, 1977.

38. Wilhelms, Fred. *Supervision in a New Key.* Washington, D.C.: Association for Supervision and Curriculum Development, 1973.

IV

Organizing and Directing Training Programs

INTRODUCTION

Every staff group, regardless of the individual needs identified, regardless of policies or programs in operation, will have continuing and changing requirements for in-service education over the years. Such diverse yet ongoing needs for training of many specific kinds could be responded to in an ad hoc fashion. But the needs are always too numerous to be fully served; the resources of time, money, and staff are always limited; hence, it is necessary to establish priorities and capitalize on programmatic planning to maximize training outcomes. Therefore, an organized and directed in-service education operation is generally required.

Any operating unit can be utilized as the focus for organizing, planning, and directing training programs. Individualized self-directed programs, school-based programs, and district- or college-wide programs are among those most commonly employed. Increasingly, specialized organizations are developing and being advocated. They include teacher centers of several kinds (3; 83), regional service centers (49;73), college-based extension centers (76), and even international efforts (53).

The session designing discussed and illustrated in Chapter II focused upon specific staff members as trainees and upon specific objectives as intended in-service outcomes. In this chapter, *programs* as distinguished from *sessions* are given close scrutiny, and they focus upon staff groups within operational units and changes in performance most appropriate for those units. Obviously, since we are still attending to training, individual learning and changes in performances are still in focus. However, the organizing, planning, and directing is aimed at initiating, facilitating, guiding, coordinating, and giving continuity to training operations rather than developing the specific plans for sessions.

Another way of viewing programs of in-service education in distinction from sessions for training is suggested in Exhibit 1–3 (Chapter I). That figure indicates a variety of developmental or instructional improvement task domains, all of which are important and all of which relate to *change* in the operations within schools or colleges. They all have potential for improving instruction in any school, college, or other educational setting. In-service training is only one part of staff development as shown on this prior exhibit; but these programs must be organized, planned, and directed within the context of the larger school operation, drawing upon other approaches to improving instruction when needed, and assuring coordination and continuity of multiple efforts (53; 70).

The operating unit to be served by in-service education programs may be large or small, or a diverse combination (38:18). The individual school with its many programs of instruction and diverse faculty groups (especially in secondary schools and colleges) may be used as the unit for program organization, planning, and directing. However, more typically the school district or college is the organizational unit employed. But smaller departmental or even teacher groups (teams) cannot be overlooked as possible operating units for in-service program directing.

Frequently, curriculum areas, such as science, art, or bilingual education, rather than operating units are selected as the basis for organizing and directing in-service programs (53;67). Some of the severe limitations of such arrangements were discussed in Chapter I in connection with federal funding and programming. Certainly, there are growing numbers and a proliferating variety of organizations that are being established for purposes of providing supporting services to schools and colleges of one kind or another. The regional education service centers (39; 57; 73), college and university extension divisions (8; 49), regional development laboratories (13), teacher centers (9; 25; 28; 40; 53), professional associations (19; 42), and a host of private business firms (22; 65; 72) are all increasing in numbers and playing important roles in providing in-service education. While attention will be given to these external delivery systems outside the normal operating jurisdictions of schools and colleges, this chapter will give primary attention to the organizing, planning, and directing of in-service programs as a regular part of school and college operations.

This author assumes that in-service education is too important and too clearly linked with instructional operations to be given anything less than a central position in the organizational structure of the educational system. This is not to suggest that *external* resources for in-service education programming are not enormously important. They are! Arranging for the selective use of such externally organized and planned services as supplements to those available within schools and colleges is one of the essential tasks of organizing, planning, and directing programs.

OPERATIONALIZING POLICY

In chapter V considerable detail is provided regarding formulating policy and allocating resources so that responsible personnel can organize, plan, and direct programs of the highest quality. Ideally, a clear mandate for in-service programs will be provided by state law; legal precedents; traditions; local policy statements; and implementing regulations, including contract provisions with individual staff members (and bargaining units, if such are officially recognized).

In addition to a clear mandate for in-service education as a part of the educational operation, resources should be clearly designated. Staff, money, and time for training are resources that need to be routinely provided as the basis for program organizing and directing (14). However, in many situations (66:45), such conditions do not prevail, and important tasks of organizing and directing involve policy developing, budget revising, and staffing for support of in-service programs.

Priority Setting

Several sources of information are utilized to provide clear guidelines for giving priority to in-service programs in a given situation. Assuming that all possible programs cannot be accommodated, selections must be made and priorities assigned. Sources of information include the following:

1. *Policy provisions:* laws, court decisions, contract provisions, local board policy, and so on.
2. *Program evaluations:* accreditation reports, program analyses, testing data, public concerns, and so on.
3. *Individual evaluations:* classroom observation reports, personnel records, needs assessment, and so on.

4. *Program proposals:* new programs, changes in organizational arrange-
    ments, community changes.

The listings under each of the four types of information sources are
illustrative only. Many specific considerations are possible and desirable in
making priority decisions regarding in-service education. In actual situations, all of these kinds of information do tend to influence decisions about
priorities. Decision making often occurs very haphazardly, however. A
single report on an achievement survey may be given widespread publicity
or otherwise become magnified as a need for in-service education "to make
sure those scores are raised." Similarly, a special program — Right to Read
(Public Law 94–142) for handicapped children (2), career education, or
adult literacy (7) — may become the focus of concern by influential individuals who use money to entice officials to give undue attention to a
particular in-service education priority.

One of the major responsibilities related to program management involves organizing and implementing procedures whereby priorities for in-
service education are established in an orderly fashion. Much emphasis has
been given to the importance of *needs assessment* (11; 16; 37).

The term "needs assessment" has many connotations, ranging from
diagnosing individual staff members' needs to assure individually relevant
in-service activities (55) to community opinion analysis, student achievement testing, to selecting in-service objectives to be emphasized. For administrative and supervisory personnel responsible for in-service programs,
the key is *not* to be found in any single assessment system, review committee procedure, or survey of opinions of community or staff. A set of
procedures is developed in which a responsible and representative body
carefully reviews a variety of kinds of relevant information and selects
priorities that represent informed professional judgments about the best use
of limited resources for improving instruction. In the small-town setting
these procedures may be largely implemented by a single "Staff Development Council" with principals, teacher representatives, and special program directors comprising the group (59;82). In larger systems with more
diversity in programming, a staff development council may be supplemented by school-level committees (66:33), special advisory committees,
project teams, teacher center councils, regional service center boards, and
teacher association committees.

One of the problems besetting in-service education is posed by the mul-
titude of interest groups that are inevitably concerned. Under the strain
of the cross pressures from such groups, school officials face the dilemma of too little organization and staff to coordinate and balance these
interests in the form of rational priorities. Without such coordinated efforts,
priorities are simply never clearly identified and resources are wasted. A
Teacher Corps project, for instance (8), purports to serve on a countywide

basis in six different schools involving nearly two hundred school personnel of all kinds, "to provide individualized . . . support" with a coordinating staff of two part-time college professors with full teaching loads on
campus. Such a project is likely to be more a thing of paper than a training reality.

Identifying Major Programs

A clearly defined program created to respond to each major priority provides the basis for translating long-range goals into objectives, delegating
responsibilities, and operationalizing training in response to policy and
priority. The Houston School District plan developed in 1975 illustrates
this principle in clearly designating six programs and assigning a director
to each (35:3). Special projects often operate under such arrangements, but
when they emerge under the influence of outside funding, they tend to
reflect special interests better than prioritized needs and are often *not* a
part of a coordinated system for in-service education. Illustrating this growing tendency toward isolated project building at the expense of system
building are the nine "local programs" reported by Edelfelt as representing promising developments around the nation. Eight of the nine programs
were described as special projects, funded outside normal channels, focusing on a limited number of buildings, and without local policy support
(18: 29–30). Officials directing in-service operations for a system or a college need to struggle constantly to keep special-interest programming integrated into the overall plans, policies, and priorities of the larger organization.

A program can be defined in many ways. One way to think about and
clearly designate programs is to specify the following characteristics:

1. High-priority training goal(s) associated with ideals of the organization are clearly specified.
2. An extended time frame is designated to adequately provide a life span
   necessary for goal attainment.
3. A target group is identified whose on-the-job responsibilities make
   many of them likely participants for training related to the goals
   designated.
4. Staff member(s) are clearly designated as responsible for the training
   operations.
5. A plan of action for implementing training activities and evaluating
   outcomes is in evidence.
6. Resources are allocated for implementing the plan.

These six characteristics of *programs* are not unlike those specified to
define a *session*. Certain distinctions are important, however. A program

focuses on long-range or intermediate-range goals, not on specific objectives of a short-term character. Accordingly, the time frame tends to be quite long — weeks, months, or years — in contrast with only a few hours or a day for a session. The target population designated for training tends to be defined by responsibility to the organization primarily and by individual needs secondarily. The *converse* tends to be true for sessions. Planning characteristics at this level of programming tend to be strategic and logistical rather than tactical as in session plans. These terms are used here to distinguish between plans that must be given much more detailed expression by the individuals actually leading the training sessions from those plans that specify selected goals, relate them to target groups, identify strategies, arrange for scheduling and resource allocating, delegate further planning, and design for evaluating.

Programs, as discussed here, can be clearly differentiated from sessions. However, wide latitude is still provided for programs to be identified and structured on the basis of a very limited or a very extended operation. If a limited goal is defined, a short time frame provided, and a small target group designated, a program may well be little more than a series of sessions, as discussed in Chapter III. Such limited, or "special," programs are in fact often structured and may be quite appropriate ways of responding to certain needs. Unfortunately, when programs are repeatedly characterized in this way, it may reflect lack of effective leadership in planning and organizing. Such ad hoc programs tend to be numerous when priorities are not carefully established, when staff in charge are reactive rather than proactive, and when crises dictate operations.

At the other extreme, programs can be defined so broadly and with such long time frames that they become a bureaucratic unit within the larger organization. These become permanent organizations with their own staffs, traditions, resources, and policies. They manufacture their own priorities out of context with the larger operation. Since they have permanent staff members, traditions, clearly developed operating procedures, and evidence of past success, they can be strong advocates for self-perpetuation. New priorities have little chance of competing with such well-organized interest groups.

Organizing Programs

Programs should be structured to avoid the evils of both *ad hocracy* and *bureaucracy* (1). Every program should have clearly attainable, specific goals, not vague missions or ideals alone. A time frame of proper length for accomplishing goals should be clearly specified and staff resources allocated accordingly. In addition to normal monitoring of the operation from within and without the program, a full-scale review should be provided at least once during the designated life of each program. The review should be conducted to determine *when* the program should be terminated and how; *not if* it should be terminated. Obviously, by terminating programs, resources are released for reallocation to newly established or higher priorities.

These suggestions for maintaining flexibility in implementing in-service programs, so as to be responsive to needs and priorities, are based upon concepts of management by objective (MBO) or program budgeting (33). These concepts have their greatest validity in *temporary systems* as distinguished from *continuous systems*. When an organization and its staff is assigned responsibility for continuous response to inputs in efforts to produce a continuous flow of outcomes, a system is developed that has rather regularized procedures. In fact, such systems become so regularized and their procedures so standardized that traditions and habit patterns tend to dominate decision making. They become unresponsive to changing conditions that might warrant changes in procedures. Even so, when held responsible for continuous production, regularized procedures are essential, and continuous systems emerge.

In-service education shares with virtually all developmental operations (curriculum development, materials development, staffing, and evaluation) in schools and colleges the distinction of being a *discontinuous operation*. Gant (20) refers to them as "temporary systems."* Their virtue is found in being able to respond to changing priorities, to concentrate resources for short time periods on urgent or difficult problems, to avoid the constraints of traditions, to "borrow" human talents otherwise unavailable, and to attend to change rather than to maintenance. The price the organization must pay for these virtues is loss of *direct productivity* (32) from these resources allocated to change process. To be sure, these activities — in-service education and others — directed by such temporary programs will be *indirectly* productive. Students will learn more or more appropriately because teachers and others have learned to perform better. But in the short run, temporary systems are always under attack, being challenged and often deprived of resources (30) because they are not seen as directly productive.

Because continuous systems produce and temporary systems *seem* not to do so, the latter always face a precarious existence (30). The natural tendency is to become more permanent, less temporary! Herein lies the danger of losing all the special advantages of being temporary for the sake of greater security, more acceptance, and a sense of belonging. These tendencies are natural enough. The challenge to staff members in charge of in-service programs involves providing for those assigned to a program the

* This concept of temporary systems has been developed by Dean Jack Gant, College of Education, Florida State University.

satisfactions they need without corrupting the system. Harris (30) has conceptualized an approach to this in describing the "amplified team" approach to improving instructional programs. Others advocate extreme decentralization at the building (23; 34) and grade level to make in-service programs integral parts of the school operation. Others suggest elaborate means for isolating or insulating in-service education from the dominant influences of school governance (84). Some of these suggestions are reflected in advocacy for teacher centers (38: 19; 85) and professional control of in-service education (25; 42).

This writer sees the need for school districts and colleges to create their own structures for dealing with these organizational dilemmas, for they will not go away and are not restricted to in-service education. Every aspect of the operation of schools and colleges must face the challenges posed by internal conflict between the need for stability and the need for change. No less demanding are the centripetal forces threatening to rend the operating system into many small fragments. In-service education can be unusually helpful in dealing with each of these dilemmas. Programs must be spawn under the leadership of an organizational unit — office, department, division — that is directly associated with the larger school system or college structure at the highest administrative and policy-developing levels (66; 78). Such an office must be a *permanent* one for purposes of assessing needs, deploying staff, initiating programs, allocating resources, and coordinating efforts (47). However, major training programs can and should be developed as temporary systems.

RELATING GOALS AND PROGRAMS

In previous works, Harris, McIntyre, and Bessent (31:32) conceptualized program design for in-service as a matter of relating the ideals of the school to specific selected goals, which were in turn related to objectives and then training activities. This set of relationships is more helpful for session planning, however, than it is for organizing and directing complex sets of programs. Two systems diagrams of the educational operation may be helpful in visualizing the very complex set of operations with interlocking relationships (68) needed to assure effective, continuing program implementation (68).

A Complex Systems View

In-service education needs to be seen as one of a complex of interrelated systems. Both developmental and operational systems of various kinds are involved. Exhibit 4–1 shows such a complex schematically depicting the

Exhibit 4-1. A SYSTEMS VIEW OF THE TOTAL EDUCATIONAL OPERATION ASSOCIATED WITH ISE

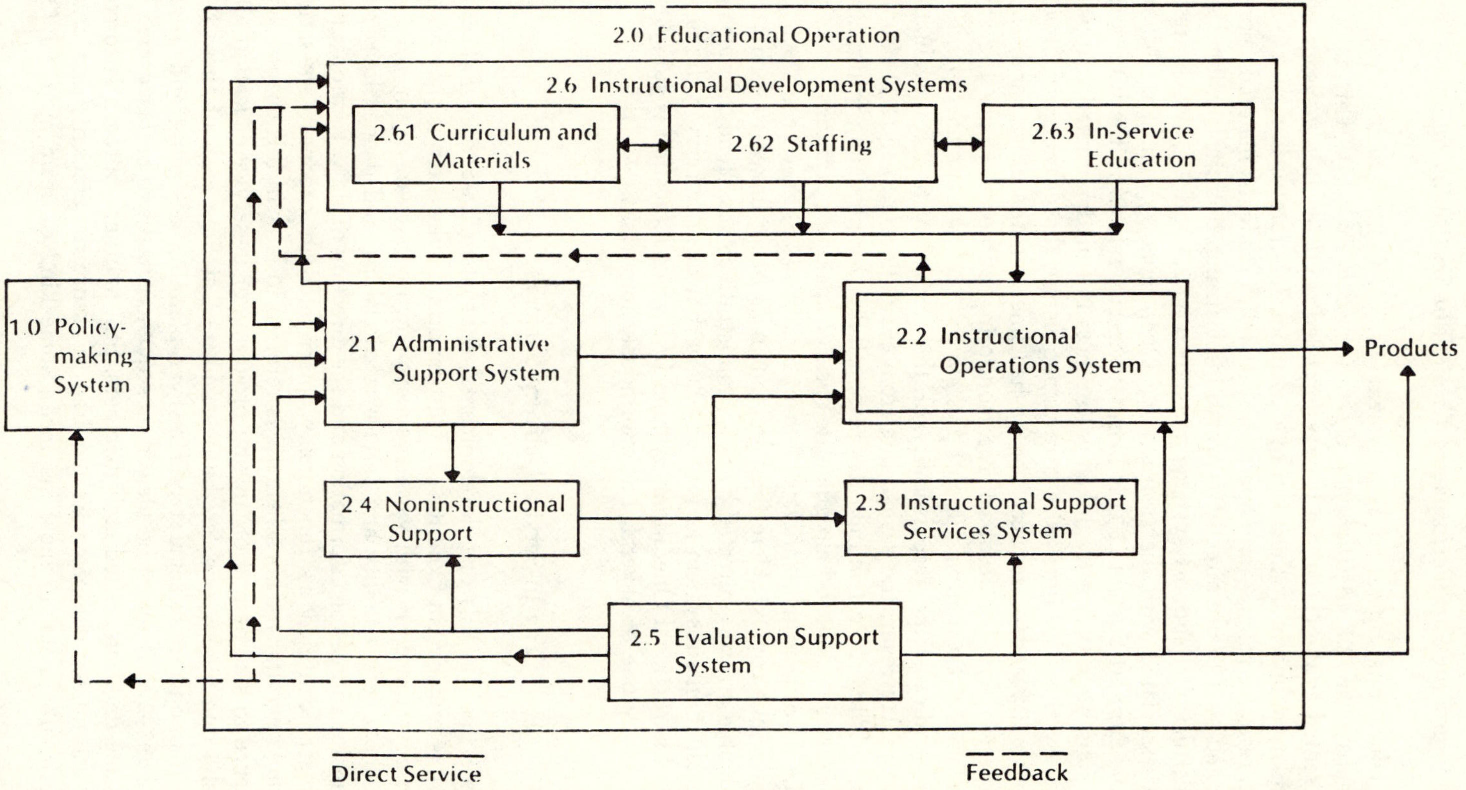

Ben M. Harris, *Supervisory Behavior in Education*, 2nd edition, © 1975, p. 53. Reprinted by permission of Prentice-Hall, Inc., Englewood Cliffs, New Jersey.

total educational operation as a system (30:53). Central to this system is the subsystem 2.2 *Instructional Operations System* (IO). This may be represented as the classroom if oversimplified. Actually it is a system that has many subparts in the form of classroom, laboratory, library, reading clinic, resource room — any operation that takes students, materials, space, time, and staff to use directly in promoting learning. Both instructional and noninstructional support systems are shown as 2.3 and 2.4, which are directly associated with the *Instructional Operations System*. The *Administrative Support System* (2.1) is likewise directly related to the IO system. Each subsystem is directly linked with others in functional relationships as shown by the solid lines with arrows suggesting the direction of flow of responsibility and/or service. The dashed lines, on the other hand, show information flow for feedback for monitoring purposes. Hence the solid line from 2.5 *Evaluation Support System* to 2.2 *Instructional Operations System* indicates the responsibility of the former system for evaluating the latter. However, the dashed line from evaluation (2.5) to (2.1) *Administrative Support System* indicates responsibility for providing information to the latter system to help guide its decision-making operations.

The set of *Instructional Development Systems* (2.6) have been discussed in a previous context. Here they are shown as being linked to each other (see double arrows), directed by the administrative subsystem, informed by the evaluation subsystem as well as others, but directly serving the needs of the Instructional Operations System. *In-Service Education* is subsystem 2.63 — only one of several, but enormously important.

The In-Service Delivery System

A closer look at this one developmental subsystem, *In-Service Education* (2.63), is provided in Exhibit 4–2. This important subsystem is shown here as an operating unit with various subsystems of its own. Again, solid arrows show responsibility and service relationships, and dashed lines suggest major sources of information and the direction of flow. Four operating units are identified as functionally interrelated in producing *in-service training operations*. This schematic is referred to later in this chapter with reference to staffing and organizing programs of in-service education. Obviously, one might consider the possibility of staffing each of these four subsystem operations separately. However, planning, designing, and operating (2.632–2.634) might be viewed as sequenced tasks to be performed by the same undifferentiated staff members. Still another approach is to consider the unique competencies required to assure the efficient functioning of each subsystem. In most instances, some kind of team approach (30:

Exhibit 4-2. IN-SERVICE EDUCATION AS A DELIVERY SYSTEM

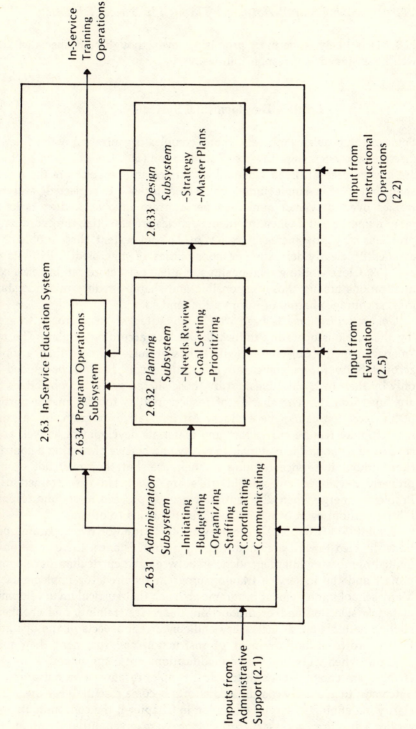

128–31) is likely to be most promising, even though staff specialists may well be assigned key responsibilities.

Relating Developmental Systems

Some of the problems inherent in any complex organization with somewhat discrete subsystems are those of coordination (68). Coordination problems are always present. Even when all aspects of an operation are the sole responsibility of a single individual, some tasks are neglected, and time frames overlap. When numerous persons are involved, when tasks are more numerous, and when interdependencies are essential, the coordination problems may grow increasingly severe. To some extent, these problems are avoided by clearly delegating responsibilities as suggested in Exhibits 4–1 and 4–2. Close working relationships in a team structure can increase communications among those responsible and thereby reduce misunderstandings, encourage sharing of information, and so on.

Goal specification has been widely advocated as an approach to assuring that various operating units will produce according to plan. The term "management by objectives" (MBO) has promise as more than a tool of accountability for outcomes (48; 62). Subsystems need to be guided not only by their own objectives but by those shared goals and objectives that are superordinate. The sharing of responsibilities for designated portions of an operation cannot be avoided. An innovative program, to be implemented, may require curriculum and materials development as well as in-service education. The materials may have no chance of making a contribution without in-service training in their use, but they may not even be properly developed unless field trials are conducted with trained users. Problems emerge when different staff groups proceed to assume responsibilities without even being aware of relationships to others.

Exhibit 2–3 (Chapter II) provides an illustration of two separate operations directed toward a common goal. In this instance, there were only a limited number of interdependencies between the curriculum development project and the in-service training program required for implementation. Many school improvement programs are such that curriculum development, materials selection and/or production, in-service training, and changes in staffing patterns are all necessary and concurrent aspects of the operation. When efforts at improvement of instruction call for more than minor changes; when truly innovative modifications are being undertaken; when changes are complex enough to affect people, resources, organization, and outcomes, then closely coordinated efforts become essential. For the sake of clarity in defining in-service education in Chapter I, the concomitants to in-service education necessary for change were given little attention. (See

Exhibit 1–3.) However, in-service education cannot be regarded as the solution to all problems, and simultaneous developmental efforts are nearly always required to assure the effectiveness of training.

Superordinate goals should be specified early in any planning for in-service education operation as a way of identifying the other developmental systems that need to be involved. To illustrate this approach using the high school English team vignette from Chapter I, suppose the faculty and principal, together with feedback from Ann, the librarian-reading specialist on the team, defines a training goal as follows:

> To develop competence in using individual educational plans with students to assure that diagnostic data will be translated into individually prescribed activities guided by programmed learning packets.

Such a goal could be seen as one involving a set of training objectives. Some of these might be the following:

1. To utilize at least one diagnostic instrument or procedure with an individual or small group to generate a reliable diagnostic profile.
2. To select from among an array of learning packets those that best relate to specific diagnostic needs.
3. To confer with individual students, using nondirective, positively reinforcing techniques, in planning a study sequence to assure that the student (a) accepts assigned tasks and (b) understands expectations.

Other objectives could be inferred as necessary or appropriate to the training outcome or goal. However, such training, no matter how carefully specified as a set of objectives or how well implemented as workshop, laboratory, or clinical experience, is likely to lack transfer capability for our team of English teachers at Swift High School. Where are these diagnostic instruments our trainees will be learning to use? Has preselection already been completed? Should these teachers get involved in defining the learning problems that need diagnosis? What about these learning packets? Do we have a good collection available for these English teachers to use? If not, can we get them, or will they need to be developed? In any case, will some curriculum planning need to precede training, or should we work on all fronts simultaneously?

To approach this problem in a slightly more systematic way, the specification of a superordinate goal might be useful. If the goal is stated as an *operational* outcome of a desired yet realistic kind, then logically related objectives of various kinds can be identified and their relationships recognized. Exhibit 4–3 tries to give some order to the concerns raised previously as an array of questions. By starting with an operationally defined goal, the focus of each developmental effort has something in common with

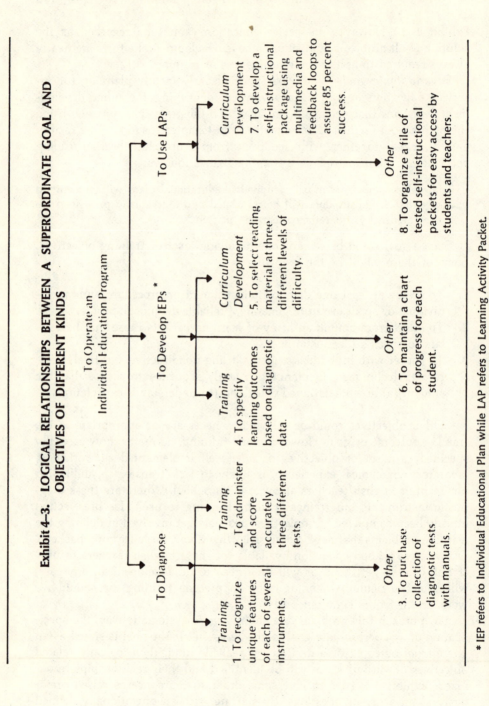

Exhibit 4–3. LOGICAL RELATIONSHIPS BETWEEN A SUPERORDINATE GOAL AND OBJECTIVES OF DIFFERENT KINDS

To Operate an Individual Education Program

To Diagnose

Training
1. To recognize unique features of each of several instruments.

Training
2. To administer and score accurately three different tests.

Other
3. To purchase collection of diagnostic tests with manuals.

To Develop IEPs *

Training
4. To specify learning outcomes based on diagnostic data.

Curriculum Development
5. To select reading material at three different levels of difficulty.

Other
6. To maintain a chart of progress for each student.

To Use LAPs

Curriculum Development
7. To develop a self-instructional package using multimedia and feedback loops to assure 85 percent success.

Other
8. To organize a file of tested self-instructional packets for easy access by students and teachers.

* IEP refers to Individual Educational Plan while LAP refers to Learning Activity Packet.

every other one. In-service training, curriculum and/or materials development, and other kinds of developmental efforts are given unique recognition to facilitate and direct the assigning of responsibilities. However, clusters of operationally related efforts are also clearly designated. This provides a basis for team efforts, for information and resource sharing.

STAFFING AND ORGANIZING

Any operational unit that is expected to maintain and develop in-service education offerings for school and college personnel has a large, complex responsibility. The best ways to staff and organize for the "delivery" of such in-service education opportunities are largely unknown at the present time. Proposals and current practices range widely from the sublime to the ridiculous. Even larger school districts have only recently developed offices (66:5) or departments for in-service education purposes, and these are a diverse and precarious array of arrangements. Colleges have grown increasingly interested in the development of staff, but well-organized programs reaching a substantial number of faculty members are still rare (10:47).

An enormous array of special programs and projects involving in-service education as referred to in Chapter I has given rise to the proliferation of diverse organizational arrangements with staffing patterns of similar diversity (50:71–77). While there may well be merit in such diversity, the impression an observer is likely to get is one of unbelievable chaos.

(1) Teacher centers as consortia of school systems, universities, and other agencies are being created under both federal and state sponsorship for in-service education purposes (80). New provisions of federal teacher center legislation require 51 percent of the members of the governing board to be classroom teachers (69) giving emphasis to demands for policy-level influence or control by classroom teacher groups (42; 85).

(2) Other teacher centers that are sometimes training facilities (74) are being developed under local district (80) university (43), regional service center (39; 40; 84), and other (8) auspices for numerous special purposes, ranging from early childhood education (15), to English education (67), to new teacher basic skills development (3; 9; 16).

(3) One state program (27) is reported with great enthusiasm as simply identifying outstanding "classroom teachers" who are trained "and then made available to all school districts in the state, free of charge" (27:1). The organization is described as so simple and uncomplicated that the unwary might be inclined to forget about planning and organizing. After all, these "resource agents" just respond to a phone call by interested teachers and then proceed "to set up a series of workshops . . . at their convenience."

(4) The training of "School-Based Teacher Educators" (81) is proposed by the University of Houston, among other colleges, on the assumption that a lone individual in every school will somehow make available all the in-service training needed. Unlike the Vermont Resource Agent Program (27), this SBTE would be extremely expensive, but perhaps also too simplistic. Thurber (77) reports on a so-called school-based in-service education program after a three-year trial in Florida. This report indicates that the concept is indeed too limiting as this district continues to extend district-level services. Gourley (25) reports on the "Portland Consortium Training Complex," an essentially school-based operation depending largely upon the teacher-dominated teacher education council with little apparent coordination beyond the school itself.

(5) Teacher Corps efforts proceed in the area of in-service education (69) providing extended five-year funding, hoping for longer-range planning, mandating a "community council . . . as an elected body" to assure a legitimate role for community involvement that goes beyond the limits of advice. The focus of these in-service program activities remains the individual school.

The United Federation of Teachers (12:38) proclaims a "unique role in teacher inservice training," with the establishment of "a teacher-run center *which is totally teacher controlled*." The program is described as follows: "Teachers tear out the form [from the newspaper] and sign up for whatever course they want to take and mail us $3. The union provides the facility, a room at our union's main building, where instruction is offered. . . . On Saturdays, we have offered more open types of workshops . . . to come in and make instructional materials."

Once again, the simplicity of this operation as described makes one pause to consider why there should be a whole book about in-service education. But it is reassuring to note that the UFT has not yet conquered all. "What we would like to do is to be able to respond more rapidly to all kinds of needs."

Other, less transient notions about organizing for the delivery of in-service education are being implemented and tested. The regional education service center movement has resulted in well-established service organizations in many states (47) with heavy responsibility for supplementing and supporting local school district in-service programming efforts (73). Colleges and universities have greatly expanded the core of directors and deans of faculty development as a clear indication that responsibility has been designated at college and departmental levels (10:47). Using the results of a survey of twenty-six hundred degree-granting colleges, Centra (10) estimates that 60 percent have "an organized program or set of practices for faculty development and improving instruction." Seventy-two percent of those colleges with programs or practices were able to clearly designate a person in charge with some time allocated.

On the assumption that in-service education will largely remain a responsibility of the local school district or college employee (75:21), organizational arrangements and staffing patterns will be discussed in the next section with these units of operation in mind. To be sure, other units will always be involved in various ways. Colleges, professional associations, state agencies, service centers, consortia, and private firms will undoubtedly provide manpower, materials, developmental efforts, technical support, and funding for in-service education. The challenges to the local school district or college are to retain control, respond to needs, and assure steady growth in quality of programs. This involves staffing and organizing for the orchestration of a very complex operation not unlike that described by Nelson (50:75–78) as the Montgomery County "systematic corporate model."

Competencies Needed

Every program is likely to have need for certain specific competencies in planning, organizing, designing, implementing, and evaluating training operations. Fairly routine activities directed toward simple basic generic skill development may be arranged by those with sophisticated teaching competencies. More complex problems or more elaborate in-service programs will certainly call for staff personnel with an extensive array of special competencies.

A competency-guided program for leadership training has identified five "critical" and a larger number of major competencies directly associated with in-service education. These were specified as minimally essential and not comprehensive at all. They included clinical, planning, conducting, coordinating, and leader-training competencies (71:73–75). The school-based teacher educator project mentioned earlier (81:11) specifies twenty competencies that are largely those expected in any teacher. Five of the twenty do suggest special skills and knowledge in evaluating instruction, individual growth planning, conferencing, making referrals, demonstrating, and facilitation of research.

William R. Tracy (79), in reference to industrial training programs, suggests a series of steps that imply competencies for those directing such programs. These include identifying training needs, analyzing job data, selecting and writing objectives, constructing instruments, selecting content, selecting training strategies, and selecting training aids. These tend to reflect the more specific operating needs of program implementation and do not prescribe a particular approach or organizational structure. Some of the competencies that might well be most important among the staff group giving regular direction to in-service education are described below:

Planning
1. To produce an assessment of needs for training that results in prioritizing in terms of various individuals, institutions, programs, and purposes.
2. To develop a master plan that provides clear guidelines for specific programs, identifies resources required, and designates strategies and time frames.
3. To write program or project proposals for responding to specific training priorities; detailing goals and objectives; and specifying activity sequences, schedules, costs, staff arrangements, materials, and evaluation criteria.
4. To assist teachers in the preparation of individual professional growth plans that include objectives, a schedule of experiences, with assigned staff responsibilities and criteria specified for evaluation (71:56).

Designing
5. To design or adopt a training session plan, specifying objectives, activities, procedures, materials, and methods of evaluation to assure participant interest, involvement, and learning (71:57).
6. To produce a self-instructional training packet employing multimedia, with carefully sequenced experiences presented, with outcome measures included in feedback provided periodically to assure successful completion of 85 percent of the intended users.
7. To lead a group in planning and designing a series of training sessions all of which relate to a superordinate goal, have differentiated objectives, provide for active involvement of participants, yet assure individuals opportunities for choices.

Implementing
8. To select a training plan, make arrangements, and lead participants through a sequence of meaningful learning activities (71:19).
9. To lead teachers through individually planned clinical cycles using preplanning, classroom observations, nondirective feedback techniques, and follow-up planning that produces change in classroom practices (71:55).
10. To train personnel in specific procedures for conducting in-service training sessions to assure that basic techniques for leading discussions, presenting visualizations, role playing, and brainstorming will be skillfully used.

Evaluating

11. To utilize systematic procedures instrumentation for observations in classrooms to produce objective analyses and interpretations of teacher performance.
12. To construct a questionnaire eliciting objective, reliable, discriminating responses from personnel or others for use in needs assessment or evaluation of training sessions.
13. To conduct an interview for gathering objective, reliable and discriminating data from personnel or others that have greater depth than questionnaire data.
14. To analyze data derived from more than one source, using several graphic techniques for drawing different interpretations.

Each kind of in-service program operation will tend to present requirements for staff competencies different from the requirements of other operations. The need for cooperative or participative decision making as well as other kinds of teacher involvement in many in-service education operations suggests the need for personnel who have competencies in group leadership (67; 56:1). Clinical supervision strategies for in-service education would tend to emphasize competence in face-to-face interpersonal communications. In contrast, a program that emphasizes use of independent study packets creates a heavy demand for staff competencies related to instructional design, materials development, programming, graphics, and test construction. Still different competencies will be needed in staffing for in-service programs that emphasize individual growth planning as utilized in the De Kalb County Schools project (16). Here diagnostic and supportive intervention teams must have competence in classroom observation, data analysis, demonstrating, and consulting.

Since the character of all programs should be different in response to differing needs of individuals, differing purposes, and changing conditions, it is usually unwise to develop a permanent staff on the basis of highly specialized competencies. Instead, rather basic competencies relating to planning, observing, working with groups, and working with individuals may be the ones most clearly required. The amplification of the permanent staff's competencies by creating ad hoc training teams for specific in-service education endeavors makes it feasible to utilize a great variety of competencies beyond those possessed by a small staff group. St. Landry Parish Schools describe such efforts in connection with their MBO Training Program (62).

Much emphasis has been given to teacher involvement in in-service education (6; 41; 61). Involvement of any person in decision making, in assessing needs, in evaluating, and in implementing in-service activities is, of course, desirable only to the extent that it contributes to the quality of the in-service education program. The emphasis on *teacher* involvement is appropriate, to be sure, because the teachers are so large a part of the reason for in-service education. However, viewed as a concern for full effective use of human resources (47:204), the emphasis shifts to involvement of staff, not just teachers. Furthermore, the emphasis can and should shift from involvement for representation purposes to involvement for purposes of assuring competencies needed.

Organizing for Collaborative Decisions

The highly personal nature of in-service education creates a demand for collaboration in all facets of program operations. Collaborative decisions involve more than just representation of interests. It requires that those to be affected and who have contributions to make shall be involved in decisions. This helps to assure that interests are balanced without loss in the quality of the program. In local school districts, such bodies as advisory councils (69), planning committees (82), in-service self-study committees (77:6), and other groups are being utilized more and more to oversee the planning, implementing, and evaluating of the in-service programs for the entire school district. These groups usually operate under the direction of the superintendent guided by local policy or district master plan. Such groups almost always include classroom teachers in substantial numbers as the most affected group in the system. Administrators, supervisors, school board members, and lay citizens or parents are also included. The size of the group may range from nine to fifteen persons without becoming unwieldy for effective action.

Colleges, too, are utilizing some form of faculty advisory group in growing numbers. These tend to be predominantly faculty representatives by departments within a college. An assistant dean is sometimes designated as the person in charge.

The use of collaborative decision-making groups can and often does extend outside the school system when teacher center consortia, educational service centers, or universities are organized to provide supplementary in-service training. Similarly, a central advisory council or committee rarely takes the place of similar decision-making groups on the level of the individual school (25).

Waxahachie, Texas (82), although a relatively small community, has impaneled both building- and district-level planning groups. Zenke (86:179), in reporting on teacher center legislation in Florida, raises concerns about excessive or inappropriate assigning of funds and responsibility for *ISE* to labor union leadership. Both Smith (69) and Gourley (25) emphasize the local school and community as units of control and decision. At even a more personal level, collaborative decision making is emphasized by

Olivero in the form of "a development plan prescribed by the individual educator, a growth plan unique to personal needs" yet formalized and guided by the use of a formal planning document (52:197).

Collaborative decision making involving a variety of groups and individuals at different levels of the organization can create problems unless responsibilities are rather carefully delineated. Each decision-making group needs a charter clearly indicating rights, responsibilities, and restrictions. A comprehensive master plan for in-service education can serve as a guide for decision by various groups (80). Plans review procedures, funds allocation controls, and board-approved priorities are a few of the various ways to assure delegation and involvement without creating chaos or waste.

Planned Variation

The search for an ideal approach or perfect model for organizing in-service education is surely fruitless. The school-based approach to in-service education as advocated by Goodlad (24), Thurber (77), Smith (69), and others may have strengths in the closeness of staff to decisions and funds, in the diversity of approaches stimulated, and in the freedom from bureaucratic controls. However, decentralized in-service education can become inflexible, too. School staffs can be unresponsive to needs defined through other eyes. Isolation of staff groups within self-contained schools can be as stultifying as isolation of individual teachers in self-contained classrooms has been. Teacher Corps director Bill Smith (69) may have sensed this problem in reference to the school-centered in-service education projects as he insists on "the community council" for each school with elected parent representatives. Goodlad's assertion that "the single school is the largest and the proper unit for educational change" (24:110–11) may not be true. Certainly, such immutable rules are likely to promote rigidities in our view of alternatives, and hence could lead to undesirable uniformity.

Thurber (77), in reporting on his experiences with school-based in-service education in a recent paper refers to "school-focused" in-service education, apparently suggesting some shift in emphasis in Palm Beach County schools over the years.

Planned variation may well be a more useful principle of organization than many others. Cohen contrasts variations in programs (58:170) as an alternative to experimental efforts. "Instead, these efforts are pilot studies of models forced into substantial use. Their merit lies in their exposing the difficulties of implementing . . . programs." In a field like ISE where a great deal of promising practice has been developed, the need for such pilots seems obvious.

Lawrence's (41) study of effective in-service education programs contrasted the school-based and the college-based programs, favoring the former. However, he found quite a variety of organizational variations to be effective. Portland, Oregon, Madison, Wisconsin, and Palm Beach County are all using arrangements whereby the districts promote peer teaching in one form or another, quite independent of building assignment (17:167). Yarger suggests seven "organizational types" (85:19–22) including the independent program, the almost independent program, the professional organization program, the single-unit program, the free partnership program, the free consortium program, and the legislative political program. These are admittedly not pure types. They do suggest an array of variations that might be encouraged and utilized. As Yarger defines these types, he sees all local school district operated programs as falling into the single-unit in-service program. This tends to obscure two important possibilities for planned variation: internal and external.

Within a school system, with whatever resources, an individual, a group of individuals, a school or a part of it, a district or a part of it can be organized in diverse ways to generate and consume in-service education. Clinical supervision, although essentially an individualized delivery system, can be utilized as a schoolwide operation, be limited to individuals in a school, or be available in many schools. The teacher center facility that serves as a place where staff personnel can engage in training encounters may serve a school, a project, a district, or a region. What is more basic, however, is the need to organize in response to real, high-priority training needs in effective and efficient ways. In so doing, a program plan should allow for a great variety of alternatives and combinations. The teacher being assisted today in his or her own classroom via clinical supervision may well want to be in a teacher-training facility for skill development a bit later. Furthermore, a regional service center or university or professional organization may or may not be involved with this teacher in various ways.

The Basic Staff Group

If the ideas of local school district as the responsible agency, competence as essential to staffing, collaborative decision making as crucial to involvement, and planned variation as the organizing principle are tenable, what kind of staff group can provide leadership for such an operation? It must be a staff group, assigned to top management (66). It must be a staff with an array of leadership competencies in planning, communicating, conceptualizing, designing, training, and evaluating. It must be a small group that works through other people. It must be composed of individuals whose self-perceptions are not easily shaken and whose positions are quite secure.

It must be a group that is imaginative, creative, and risk taking. Open-mindedness, with critical analytical abilities need to be in abundance.

Sealy and Dillon (66:33–34) suggest that the six cities included in their study were not yet fully realistic about "the Office of Staff Development." Teachers reported to these scholars the need for "a central facility," but the lack of "intermediaries" between the district and the classroom was often noted. Staff development offices are often very small indeed, even in fairly large cities. Only one of these cities studied by Sealy and Dillon had more than two persons assigned to the director of staff development. These researchers express concern that in no case was the office of staff development headed by a top-level administrator.

Exhibit 4–1 suggests a set of subfunctions or tasks to be performed at the central office level. It is probable that each subsystem of the in-service education delivery system will require a distinctive set of competencies to assure that the tasks are properly performed. Referring to Exhibit 4–2, the reader will recognize the various administrative, planning, designing, and program-operating tasks indicated. Evaluation tasks are shown as responsibilities of an external system and may not need to be performed by a member of the ISE delivery system staff if close working relationships are developed with those providing evaluation services.

A staff group of no less than four professionals is indicated by the character of the tasks to be performed. Obviously, a smaller task group may be able to function if part-time consultants or cooperative arrangements with other staff groups can be negotiated. Larger school systems will extend the basic staff group in various ways.

Exhibit 4–4 suggests traditional organization charts with three different patterns of staffing for in-service education at the school district level. Pattern A emphasizes in-service education as a part of program planning and development. Pattern B gives emphasis to human resource development with in-service education only a part of a larger operation. Pattern C gives full emphasis to in-service education as a major developmental concern of the school system. Any of these patterns gives in-service education the direct influence of a high-status administrator. Pattern A offers advantages for a school district intent upon major efforts of innovation in instruction. The inclusion of all of the developmental services within a single division provides some chance of insulation from the pressures of routine operations. Furthermore, the presence of staff with competencies in curriculum development, in-service education, personnel, and evaluation all within a single division provides resources that are crucial to success in innovative endeavors.

Patterns B and C have special advantages for school districts giving high priority to personnel development. Rapidly growing districts or those re-staffing in rather substantial ways because of high turnover and retirement

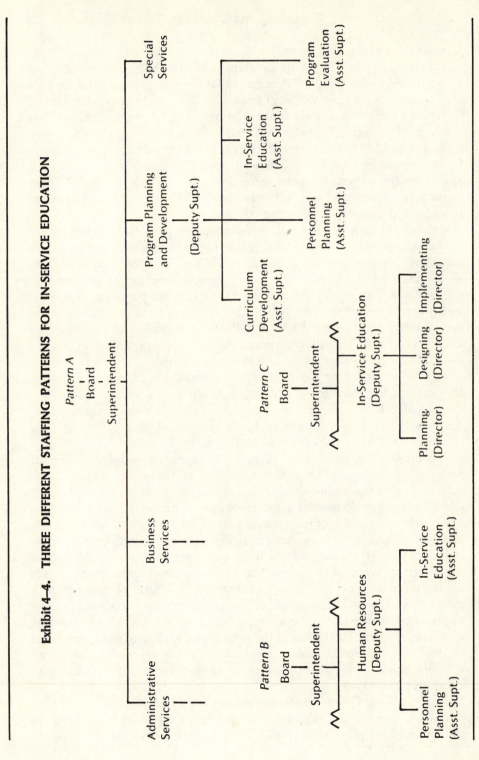

Exhibit 4–4. THREE DIFFERENT STAFFING PATTERNS FOR IN-SERVICE EDUCATION

rates may need to give the kind of emphasis to in-service education and related personnel-planning tasks that justify these patterns. Obviously, pattern C makes in-service education a top priority and provides for a kind of isolation from other developmental services that might be justified only temporarily.

Traditional staffing patterns at central office levels in local school districts rarely follow any of the three patterns shown in Exhibit 4–4. Commonly in-service education is not clearly assigned but is assumed to be the responsibility of some staff person. If there is an assistant superintendent for instruction that person may be, in effect, the director of staff development. When separate divisions of elementary and secondary education are provided, the directors or assistant superintendent in charge of each of these may be assigned in-service education responsibilities. As these districts respond to growing pressure for better in-service education, staff development specialists may be added to existing structures. Still another way of trying to organize in-service education staff is to assign someone in the personnel office to coordinate these programs. Separate staff development offices are also being created as satellites to the existing structure.

None of these approaches seems likely to be adequate either to provide the key staff group required or to become a significant influence on the quality of instruction. Special project groups, of course, offer still other approaches. So, too, do teacher centers, which in effect become a kind of intermediate service center for this one specialized kind of service. As useful as special projects and teacher centers may be as a way of organizing for in-service education services of some kinds, they do not eliminate the necessity for having some structure for relating in-service education to the various other developmental functions to be served and to assure that the services do in fact relate to, and are coordinated with, the ongoing instructional program. With due consideration of these needs for carefully linking these systems, the staffing suggested in pattern A seems quite promising.

Borrowing Staff Resources

The need to make fullest possible use of available competencies for planning, designing, and especially implementing in-service education programs has been mentioned in various sections in this chapter. In arguing for a fully assigned, responsible staff group at the central office level, a small group is also projected. This is possible, of course, only if the office or division responsible for in-service education has authority and resources for borrowing personnel.

Borrowing staff resources can and should take a variety of forms. Central staff personnel in all instructional development offices should be utilized. Hence, curriculum development specialists, program evaluation personnel, and special service personnel all have contributions to make toward in-service education. Arrangement for borrowing their services for specific assignments must be made. Conversely, of course, these staff members will often be directing in-service education programs within their own areas of responsibility, and their efforts will need support and coordination.

Classroom teachers are among the most promising staff members to be borrowed for in-service education. Not only is this a very large body of highly educated personnel with a great variety of competencies, but most classroom teachers need opportunities for experiences outside the confines of the classroom. As the recipients of most in-service education (61:297), they also need to be heavily involved in many aspects of planning, implementing, and evaluating. Borrowing teachers for in-service education may involve released time from classroom duties, overtime paid for as such, or an extended contract for additional days, weeks, or months beyond the regular contract year.

Previous references to teacher centers, educational service centers, and college extension services indicated still another kind of borrowing of personnel to staff in-service education programs. Whether these centers are governmental units or private institutions, when they have competent personnel who can contribute to the in-service education needs of a school or college, they should be seen as a potential resource. Recreation departments of municipalities, community college facilities, child guidance centers, and local industry all have personnel with contributions to make to in-service programs if proper arrangements and coordination of efforts are provided.

Perhaps the most widely neglected and potentially most promising human resource is to be found among the parents and other individual citizens of every school and college community (32). In stereotyping such people as laymen, we ignore the many kinds of expertise possessed by a large percentage of the public. The problem is one of identifying these talents and finding means for utilizing them in appropriate ways. Fortunately, most citizens, especially parents, are usually eager to contribute time to school program improvements of nearly any kind. Hence, a very inexpensive human talent pool is readily available.

GUIDING PRINCIPLES AND PURPOSES

Various writers have proposed sets of operating principles as guidelines for in-service planning. A surprising amount of similarity is found in the guidelines developed by Edelfelt (19) and Lawrence (41) and by McLaughlin

(45), McLendon (46), and Rubin (60), to mention only a few. Even so, the guidelines or statements of principle as proposed by various individuals tend to reflect different biases, interests, and perspectives. An effort has been made here to synthesize and generate a more comprehensive list than has previously been available. The list that follows is less than complete, however, and is restricted to operational and planning concerns that are larger than, and precursors of, those concerns to be faced when designing specific training sessions. Furthermore, the list that follows, while generally supportable by research and theory, is not likely to be the last word on this matter. Nicholson and Joyce (51) emphasize this still emerging character of in-service education practice in noting, "there is only a handful of works that deal with inservice in any sort of comprehensive way" (51:4).

A Set of Principles

Clients Served
1. All personnel within a designated target organization or operating unit should be provided opportunities for in-service education (18:25, 29; 60:295).
2. No client should be required to participate in a specific program or session simply because it serves the convenience of scheduling, planning, or funding (30).
3. Different client groups (or individuals) should be recognized within any given program of ISE (31:5).
4. Individuals or groups are designated as clients on the basis of rational and explicit relationships between individual needs and program goals (30:49, 51).
5. Groupings of clients are developed to facilitate optimum learning and assure transfer.

Timing Training
6. Time frames normally allocated for in-service education programs, for both client participation and planning, designing, and evaluating, are part of the normal work load and assignment schedule of personnel (18:19; 60:294).
7. Special events, requiring substantial variations in the normal work load and assignment of personnel, should be utilized sparingly and planned so as to provide reimbursement for overtime.
8. Time allocations allow for continuity of training experience.
9. Time allocations allow for flexible use of time as needed to design for an appropriate and necessary variety of activities.

Involvement
10. Clients should have opportunities to serve selectively in roles as planners, designers, managers, presenters, and evaluators of ISE programs or sessions as well as being trainees (18:19; 60:xi).
11. Clients should be provided with opportunities for making choices among alternatives within ISE program plans (46).
12. All personnel involvement should be by virtue of competence needed or offered rather than because of desire to control or serve self-interest (18:17; 46).
13. Client perceptions of needs in relation to job realities are among the various criteria for determining involvement.

Locale(s) for Training
14. The locations selected for training activities should be determined by training requirements rather than by arbitrary preferences of either trainees or administering officials.
15. The use of remote locations (regional centers, colleges, conferences, etc.) should be an open option for any in-service activity or program to be determined by cost/benefit analysis in comparison with local alternatives.
16. When resources needed for training are not available locally or can be more economically utilized at a remote location, program plans and regulations should facilitate their judicious use.
17. When remote locations are utilized, the plans should be clear about predeparture and reentry training activities that assure that full benefits will be derived (20).

Resources
18. Time should be provided for both client participation and planning and evaluation activities that are sufficient to meet urgent needs and adequate to assure quality programs.
19. Personnel, programs, materials, and other resources of various institutions (colleges, teachers' organizations, local school districts, regional service centers, commercial and community organizations) should be shared with each other in providing for ISE (18:19–20; 46).
20. Funds for in-service education should be budgeted through normal channels regardless of source (18:20; 45:193).
21. Costs associated with full participation in ISE should be fully defrayed without personal expense to clients.

Locus of Control and Decision
22. Those most directly affected should be the most completely involved in decisions regarding those portions of the operation that affected them (18:13).

23. Control over various operations should be retained as close to the people responsible as is commensurate with economy and efficiency (18:13; 45:193).
24. Decision making should involve all who have responsibility as well as a contribution to make.
25. Decisions should be guided by law, explicit policy statements, planning documents, and the dictates of research on good practice (18:23).

Scope of Planning
26. Program plans should be clearly related to larger efforts (larger organizational units, larger goals, longer timetables, etc.) (29:2–3).
27. Each school district, college, service center, or other legal entity should have a comprehensive plan for ISE within which subunits can plan their operations (46).
28. Program schedules and timetables should provide for continuity both within the program and *among* related programs or other operations (46).

Systematicness of Planning
29. Program planning should continue as implementation and process evaluation indicate needs for change refinements and additions (45:192).
30. Program plans should include statements of objectives that are specific in identifying kinds of performance changes anticipated (46).

Designing for Learning
31. The design of activity sequences and materials for use should provide for some differentiated experiences even when common goals, objectives, and needs are being served (18:22; 45:194).
32. The activities and materials should be designed to assure active, meaningful, and purposeful experiences as much as possible (46; 31).
33. A great variety of activities should be planned that are task oriented and reality based as much as possible (31; 46).

Content for Learning
34. Objectives should be selected to reflect *both* organizational development needs and those of individual clients (18:16–17).
35. Objectives for in-service programs should identify performance outcomes that are directly related to: (a) job realities, (b) the improvement of performances, and (c) only important performances (18:16; 45:192).

Incentives for Participation

36. Special incentives should be provided in the form of compensatory time, overtime pay, or special privileges when ISE participation extends beyond the normal work-load assignment schedule (45:194).

37. Negative incentives should be eliminated or counterbalanced to assure that all participation is positively encouraged (18:25).

Leadership

38. Responsibility for each major component of in-service program planning, implementing, coordinating, and evaluating should be clearly assigned to an individual or group.

39. Responsibilities for each major component of the program should be assigned on the basis of available time, expertise, commitment, and involvement (46).

Evaluation

40. A planned, systematic evaluation effort should be a part of any major ISE program.

41. Efforts to evaluate ISE should be focused primarily upon identifying strengths, weaknesses, and possible improvements.

42. Objective data, free of bias and sampling error, should be utilized for evaluation purposes as far as possible.

43. Both short-term and longer-range evaluation efforts should be planned whenever possible.

44. The scope and complexity of the evaluation design should be dictated by the extensiveness of the ISE program, the importance of goals, and the technical capability of the staff.

Policies

45. Policy statements should clearly indicate that ISE is both a right and a responsibility of all.

46. Policy should clearly provide for funding, staffing, and standard operating procedures for continuity of ISE.

47. Policy should provide for cooperative and collaborative relationships with colleges, service centers, and other selected agencies.

System relationships

48. Program and personnel evaluation data should be utilized as data bases for planning ISE programs.

49. The unique contribution of ISE to larger programs or projects should be clearly identified in planning documents (26:32–33).

50. Other developmental programs (curriculum, materials, staffing, evaluation, etc.) should be clearly designated when they are planned as coordinated parts of a larger project or program (18:16).

Essential Purposes to Be Served

Planning, organizing, and implementing in-service programs must be guided by differentiated individual purposes and needs as well as by fundamental guiding principles as previously stated. This focus on the individual can be promoted via overall operational plans that clearly reflect four different purposes:

basic, generic competency development
remediation of inappropriate performance patterns
specialized competency development
innovations-related competency development

Any individual staff member may need one or more kinds of in-service training, but any given training experience is *not* likely to serve more than a single purpose. Furthermore, programs of in-service education, planned with one or more of these four purposes in view, is likely to be more effective if each purpose is clearly designated and appropriate plans developed accordingly.

Basic, generic competency development. This refers to in-service education and training that relate to the preservice goals of the teaching profession. The development of a common core of generally accepted and widely employed competencies is the purpose. Such programs recognize the limited character of preservice programs; they seek to assure more than survival levels of competence and eliminate deficiencies (14).

Remediation of inappropriate performance patterns. This refers to the elimination of undesirable practices. The retraining or behavior-modifying approaches are called for. This is the aspect of in-service education that is necessarily most highly individualized. It is critically important both because of the difficulty of eliminating certain inappropriate behavior patterns that may have been developed over many years and also because these patterns often interfere with basic generic performances (66:44).

Specialized competency development. This refers to competencies that have importance to only a limited number of staff members because of unique position, role, or problem. Hence, they are sometimes advanced levels of competence of generic kinds or truly different competencies (66:28).

Innovations-related competency development. This refers to the special sequence of in-service education that must be associated with each systematic effort to introduce a significant change in the operation that also demands substantial changes in people as well as structures. In-service activities supporting systematic adoption of innovations involves awareness training and systematic trials with associated evaluation activities to determine feasibility and relative advantages (5:26; 26:32; 32:60; 60:xi).

For each purpose will be different for individual trainees who are appropriately involved. Preconditions and needs assessment procedures will be substantially different for each purpose. Furthermore, the staff assigned, the strategies employed, the locale selected, and the time frame utilized all may be affected by the realities of purpose.

To illustrate only a few of these differential implications of purpose for operations and planning, consider a program to implement individualized instructional practices in a given school system. For new teachers, the focus may be *basic, generic skill* development in organizing and operating classrooms with multiple-activity groups. For certain experienced teachers, the focus may be *remedial* in the sense that rigid achievement standards with undifferentiated objectives are eliminated and replaced with at least a limited variety and flexibility in expectations. For primary teachers, the focus may be upon developing *special* competence in the use of diagnostic testing procedures in determining reading deficiencies of selected students. For an entire team and their principal in one school, the focus may be upon the numerous changes in procedures, new knowledge of materials, and the team-planning competencies essential to operating as a team-teaching program in conjunction with a newly developing media resource center.

For each individual or group, the appropriate locale, staffing, and strategy may be quite different. The new teachers may need highly individual assistance with in-class guidance as new room arrangements and lesson plans are tested. The remedial efforts to reduce rigidly enforced standards on students, with no options in content or in learning mode, may require a strategy of carefully designed behavior modification, including the use of peer influence. For the innovative team, the local building where the new facility exists will be the locale for much of the training activity. However, the primary-grade teacher group may attain specialized competence in diagnostic assessment of reading skills on a college campus in summer, with the help of a laboratory that is in operation there.

Relating Purpose to Principle

The four essential and different purposes to be served by in-service education require careful attention in planning programs. Operating principles can better serve as guides for planning when related to the specific purposes to be served. Just as differentiating purposes helps assure that individual needs of trainees will be better served, so relating purposes to principles assures that the latter will be applied so that form follows function. Ritualistic use of guiding principles is neither intended nor desired. Instead, careful planning is required to apply each principle to the extent that it serves well to assure the quality of in-service program in operation that produces results.

Many of the guiding principles presented here have applicability to an in-service education-planning endeavor regardless of the purpose to be served. However, certain groups or clusters of principles may require special consideration when different purposes are in focus. For instance, special competency development (purpose 3) requires much more critical consideration of principles relating to clients than is likely to be true for generic competency development (purpose 1), since the latter embraces larger portions of the total staff. On the other hand, if a crisis situation prevails timing principles becomes especially critical when remedial purposes are being served; but timing is almost always of critical importance when innovative purposes (purpose 4) are being served, because the success of the entire venture may be at stake and the various stages of implementation are sequenced rather explicitly.

Exhibit 4–5 attempts to indicate the *more* critical relationships between

Exhibit 4–5. MORE CRITICAL RELATIONSHIPS BETWEEN PRINCIPLE CLUSTERS AND IN-SERVICE PURPOSES

Principle Clusters	Purposes			
	1 Basic, Generic	*2* Remedia- tion	*3* Special- ized	*4* Innova- tions
Client Served	+	+	+	+
Timing Training		+		+
Involvement			+	+
Locale for Training		+		+
Resources		+	+	+
Locus of Control and Decision		+	+	
Scope of Planning	+			+
Systematicness of Planning		+		+
Designing for Learning	+	+	+	+
Content for Learning		+	+	+
Incentives for Participation	+	+		
Leadership		+		+
Evaluation		+		+
Policies	+	+		
Systems Interrelated	+	+		+
	6	13	6	12

clusters of principles and each type of in-service purpose. The symbol (+) is inserted to suggest that a cluster of principles might be more important to consider seriously and systematically when planning in-service programs for a particular purpose. Accordingly, the principles relating to clients — who they are, whether they are required to participate or not, and how a group is designated — are worthy of special review for program planning of any kind. In contrast, the principles relating to timing are designated as of special importance only for remediation and innovation purposes. This is not to suggest that other plans ignore work load, reimbursements, continuity, and flexibility in use of time. However, these principles may not be so clearly important when basic and specialized competency development is being served.

The principles that appear to be most clearly important to all in-service education purposes are those related to clients and design. It seems inescapable in any effort at program planning and implementation, if it is likely to be effective and efficient, that the clients and their experience be given full consideration. However, most clusters of principles may be differentially important according to purposes to be emphasized in program planning. Generic or basic and specialized competency development are shown by this analysis in Exhibit 4–5 to be somewhat less dependent upon the application of a full array of guiding principles. These purposes are quite similar in that only a few highly important clusters of principles are related to each. However, they are different, too. Basic, generic purposes are related to scope of planning, incentives, policies, and interrelatedness of systems. The more specialized purposes give importance to principles related to involvement, content, resources, and control.

Both *remediation* purposes and those related to *innovations* seem to be more fully dependent upon a full array of operating principles. Ten out of the eleven clusters of principles seem quite important for consideration when programs for remediation purposes are being considered. It may well be that since this purpose is based on a "deficient model" (66:44), has negative connotations, and is often made necessary because of prior neglect, it is an unduly sensitive operation. For quite different reasons, *innovations*-related competency development purposes also require full consideration of eight out of the eleven clusters of operating principles. These programs are *sensitive*, too. They often involve heavy commitment to major changes; they involve many unknowns; participants are often on the spot to demonstrate change; and complex systems adaptations may be related to the in-service efforts (5:26).

Certification Purposes

All of the discussion in this chapter, as well as the definition presented in Chapter I, ignores an array of points of view about purposes of in-service education. Much of the very recent literature, especially the writings of those associated with colleges and universities, is focused upon (1) continuity of preservice and in-service training (19; 44; 84), and (2) certification or recertification requirements (15; 34; 54; 76).

The concern for continuity from preservice to in-service cannot be regarded too seriously except as an endeavor by colleges, associations, and certifying authorities to extend control over in-service education for various reasons. From the point of view of responsible program development within the limits of the definition presented for in-service education, the arguments for continuity are not very forceful. The need for a clear transfer of responsibility seems self-evident. The efforts of federal legislation to create teacher centers as consortia for in-service education need to be carefully reassessed. As agencies to supplement and serve local school districts in their efforts, they may have merit under certain circumstances. As agencies vested with responsibility and authority for in-service education they seem ill advised. Howsam (36) stresses the important role of preservice teacher education as necessarily broad and encompassing much that cannot be directly job related. To attempt to diminish this educational endeavor to fit the unknown future job assignment is neither practical nor desirable. To broaden the scope of in-service education to make it a continuation of a liberal professionalization process is equally unrealistic. They are related but basically different operations that are not well served by stress on continuity.

The place of certification and recertification as a purpose of in-service education receives more careful attention in Chapter V. Recertification is being considered and adopted in some states as a requirement for continued employment (21). That such renewal could be demonstrated via in-service training stands to reason. Unfortunately, recertification plans tend to emphasize course credits, required content, uniform expectations, and rigid schedules. This trend may therefore be an unfortunate one, emphasizing regulation more than education, imposing state standards on the individual, and asking local districts to neglect their urgent needs for improving on-the-job performance in the quest for control. Time will tell whether this is indeed a continuing trend and whether the effect on the quality of in-service education is unfortunate. Perhaps neither will come to pass if new and more promising vistas can be recognized and developed.

DIRECTING AND MANAGING

The best-laid plans must be implemented before results can be assessed. The directing and managing of the implementation processes as well as the planning, designing, and evaluating require careful attention to assure quality in-service education. Schedules need to be followed, more carefully detailed, and even revised as needed. Staff need to be deployed, employed, borrowed, and relieved of other responsibilities as needed. Funds need to be allocated, dispersed, and accounted for to provide released time, materials, travel costs, consultants, and other resources according to plans. Activities need to be monitored simply to provide awareness of unanticipated problems that might require revised schedules, staff changes, or reallocation of funds.

The importance of coordination of in-service education program activities with other developmental programs — curriculum development, staffing, evaluation, and so on — has been discussed in previous sections of this chapter. Even more crucial problems of coordination must be recognized and resolved as ISE implementation intervenes upon *regular operation of schools*. The main business of schools and most colleges is the teaching of students. In-service education shares the distinction of being disruptive of the instructional program, as are other developmental services, athletics, research, and the like. Unlike athletics, developmental services have little glamour or popular appeal to support their existence. Hence, personnel assigned responsibility for directing in-service programs must constantly seek ways of delivering services with minimum disruption and maximum productivity. This is not easy to do, because the least disruption is very likely to be least productive also. After-school training sessions, for instance, are not likely to be very effective. However, releasing a teacher at 1:30 P.M for a three-hour session may well be less disruptive than a morning session or an all-day workshop.

Scheduling Events

Careful scheduling of in-service education is an important aspect of coordinated program management. Schedules need to accommodate long-range, intermediate-range, and short-range plans. Schedules need to be widely disseminated so that all who might be affected can be informed. Furthermore, schedules should provide for flexibility to avoid rigid sequencing of events that does not respond to needs or recognize unanticipated developments. Finally, schedules need to be developed at various levels with appropriate consideration of the many other demands for staff time.

Central staff personnel need not try to schedule activities for individual teachers. This is more appropriately done at the building or department level. However, workshops, demonstrations, field trips, visiting consultants, special courses, and other in-service opportunities that are being planned for multischool groups need to be scheduled well in advance (a year or more when possible) so that school principals and individual staff members can develop their schedules in coordinate fashion. Similarly, colleges, regional service centers, teacher centers, and other institutions offering in-service education opportunities on a multidistrict level should make plans and develop such schedules with even longer time frames.

Delivering units — school, project, central office, service center, and the like — should always schedule at a level well below 100 percent of capacity. Some reserve capacity is essential in responding to unexpected needs or to cover for incorrect estimates with respect to time, staff, and money to be utilized according to plans. However, an important aspect of directing and managing in-service programs involves securing a realistic balance between carefully scheduled activities that provide a structure clients and others can use while avoiding schedules that commit all resources and leave no flexibility for the processes of implementation. In coordinating delivery systems of a variety of kinds, as this author is advocating, while keeping in-service activities clearly focused on individual needs of staff members, plans must be increasingly long-range plans as they become increasingly distant from the individual consumer (client or trainee). Otherwise, competitive relationships, rather than complementary and supplementary service relationships, emerge.

To illustrate this last point, suppose a principal, team leader, or supervisor is planning with a teacher to project in-service training objectives, activities, and responsibilities for the ensuing year. It may be April or May, and summer events and all of the ensuing year might be scheduled using an individual growth-planning approach. (See Chapter VI.) If summer and fall course offerings, on and off campus, are known; if the principal's plans for special projects for the coming year are known; if central staff workshops, consultant schedules, and regional events are known for the next fifteen to eighteen months, the individual teacher can utilize or ignore these *known events* as best fits his or her needs. However, two undesirable alternatives are at hand: (1) to wait and see, and (2) to plan without consideration of such complementary or supplementary training experiences. Either of these alternatives leads to poor coordination and inefficiency and may result in conflicts and ineffectiveness as well.

Staff Assignments

"Everybody's business is nobody's business!" — at least that is widely believed. Every schedule, every projected event needs an individual or a very small team to assume responsibility for implementation. This is not to suggest autocratic arrangements. Democratic, collaborative, cooperative means of implementing in-service programs must still specify who is going to do what, when, how it will be done, and how it will be related to a larger whole. This means coordinated staff assignments, using the word "staff" to refer to any person who is willing, able, and authorized to accept a particular assignment. It may be a classroom teacher who will be the instructor for an in-service course as promoted in the Portland, Oregon, schools (54). Staff may, however, involve a teacher who is asked to make arrangements for the overhead projector for use in a particular session. It may be a principal, consultant, director, salesman, or lay person who is available to assist.

Staffing for implementation has already been discussed in relation to borrowing personnel. However, the more complex in-service education operations will need to be staffed by regular personnel whose primary job assignments are related to developmental services. Similarly, long-term programs of in-service education cannot be expected to have continuity of purpose and experience without one or more regular staff persons guiding and directing such programs over time. A common misconception about the staffing of *discontinuous* operations is that willing persons with major responsibilities for *continuous* operations can also find the time to oversee, direct, and monitor in-service education. This is a misconception for various reasons. It is most widely reflected in the recurrent efforts to make the principal of the school (or his or her assistant) the total instructional leader, directly responsible for all supervision, including in-service education, curriculum development, and evaluation.

Such expectations of a very busy full-time person with unequivocal responsibility for routine daily operational affairs are unrealistic because:

1. The maintenance responsibilities have overriding priorities.
2. The competencies needed for maintenance are strikingly different from those needed for development.
3. Change process, while characterized by *discontinuous events*, must also be characterized by *continuity* of effort.
4. Change process is more demanding of leadership, time, energy, and specialized competence than is generally realized.
5. Timing and sequencing of events are crucial to successful change, and hence they cannot afford delays while urgent affairs are given priority.

For these reasons alone, staff assignments must be carefully balanced to assure that assigned teams include the variety of staff members needed to produce results — to get the job done. The principal will often be included as an assigned member of the ISE staff, especially when implementation takes place within his or her building, or special interests or competencies are possessed by an individual. Similar criteria need to be employed in making assignments to classroom teacher, librarian, nurse, counselor, parent, or department chairperson, among others. But in-service education programs of complexity, prolonged duration, or multiunit involvement will nearly always require the sustained leadership of a central staff supervisor, project director, or other staff member who doesn't have to teach school every day or operate a regular school or program.

Funding Programs

Budget making and resource allocating are important parts of planning for in-service education. Many school districts have clearly defined, budgeted allocations of funds for in-service education, but others do not (14). Some districts attempt to meet needs for in-service education funding by using reserves, athletic funds, special projects, or even PTA contributions. Regardless of source, in-service education activities should be budgeted for, just as with any regular program. In-service programs, when properly planned, are readily amenable to program budgeting. Each program component can be costed and a budget developed reflecting the estimated cost of the training. Separate budgets need to be prepared, of course, for the overall operation of the program, including provisions for administration, logistical support, equipment, communications, and special contracts not directly associated with any specific component of the program.

Flexibility in use of certain monies is essential because many aspects of in-service education will involve responding to needs that emerge from individual teacher diagnosis. It is necessary to budget for unanticipated needs. Actually, most such needs can in fact be anticipated but may not be readily reflected in line items for specific program operations. Instead, it may be very helpful to provide each school, department, or project which is expected to respond to emerging needs of individual teachers with an allocation for miscellaneous expenditures. A reserve, budgeted under the control of the administrator in charge of the school district, is still another way of dealing with such unanticipated needs for funds.

Dollar levels of funding for in-service education range widely from district to district, state to state, and even program to program. There appears to be no fully agreed-upon standard to go by (63). Howsam (36) has suggested that 10 percent of the total school operations budget should be utilized for in-service education. This contrasts sharply with actual practice reported by Sealey and Dillon for five U.S. cities in 1976. This study reported 0.10 to 0.52 percent levels of funding reflecting from $6 to $10 per student. Florida schools have been reported to be allocating up to 6 percent of operating costs to ISE, but this appears to vary from year to year. Creekmur (14) found school systems throughout Texas to be spending varying amounts from nearly nothing to $15 per pupil, but this did *not* include staff salaries or regional education service center expenditures.

Special projects, directed toward major instructional change, usually

Exhibit 4–6.   SUMMARY OF AN IN-SERVICE EDUCATION PROJECT BUDGET

Code	Description	Sources of Funds			Total All Sources
		Title IV	*Local*	*Other*	
6100	*Payroll Costs*	$16,800	$1,200	$ 1,200	$19,200
	Project director salary	15,800	—	—	—
	Substitute teaching to provide released time	1,000	1,000		
	Other—clerical		200	1,200	
6200	*Purchased and Contracted Services*	$ 9,800	$2,000	$ 8,850	$20,650
	Computer time	1,000			
	Consultants	500			
	Regional service centers	2,000		6,000	
	Student assistants	500	500	200	
	Printing, photographic, sound services	1,400		150	
6300	*Supplies and Materials*	$ 5,650	$1,200	$ 500	$ 7,350
	Office supplies	450	650	200	
	Supplies for training materials	1,300	150	100	
	Computer supplies	1,700			
	Evaluation instruments	800			
6400	*Other Operating Expenses*	$ 2,650	$ 350	$ 450	$ 3,450
	Staff travel	650			
	Other travel	1,200	150	450	
	Communications	800	200		
Totals		$35,000	$4,750	$11,000	$50,750

Waxahachie Independent School District, Project POINT, Title IV, Part C, 1977.

demand higher levels of funding than do routine program operations. An illustration of such a special project budget is illustrated in simplified fashion in Exhibit 4–6. This project was proposed for a title IV-C grant under Public Law 93–380. The total of $50,000 for in-service education under this proposal does not include costs of regular staff who would normally be on the payroll anyway. Assuming that all staff members are served, this project budget represents approximately $10 per student, or $250 per teacher. If a total of a thousand hours of training provides for four hundred staff members, the budget represents an operating cost of $50 per hour for the project.

Exhibit 4–6 is obviously not a program budget. The dollar figures represent only rough estimates of needs of mounting a new districtwide program and include considerable money for development and evaluation purposes that might apply more to special projects than to regular program operations. However, almost all sources of promising practices suggest that in-service training will be more expensive in the future, if it is to be effective. If teachers are to be reimbursed for overtime devoted to training; if substitutes are to be employed to release trainees; if travel is recognized as often necessary; if good materials are utilized; and if outstanding consultants are used, costs mount well above the amounts currently budgeted.

An interesting comparison between in-service education expenditures in Tampa, Florida, schools ($689,669 = 0.49 percent of operating costs) and similar expenditures by the General Telephone Company in that same county is revealingly presented by Sealey and Dillon in their study (66). The telephone company program with about the same number of employees as the school system spent $4 million for training (2.10 percent of its operating budget).

Estimating Costs

It is useful to try to project estimated costs for in-service education in a variety of ways. Obviously, different kinds of training will vary in expenditure needs. Hence, program budgeting will properly show some programs as much more costly than others. The upper and lower limits of training costs might be estimated using hypothetical extremes in training units. Let's assume that the smallest unit of training likely to be effective in improving performance on the job is three hours for very simple performance objectives, highly divisible in nature, with little complexity of training requirements. Let's also assume that for truly complex, new performances involving new knowledge, skill, and practice to be effective, a minimum training sequence of twenty-one hours is required. How would the costs vary? Obviously, there must be at least a 7 to 1 ratio in costs. Accordingly, if a basic unit of the simplest training cost only $1 per trainee hour or $3 total, one could be sure that a basic unit of training of the more complex kind surely would cost $21 per trainee hour. Realistic estimates call for much higher costs when both new knowledge and skill building are involved. Furthermore, experience suggests that even the simplest training is not likely to be provided at $1 per trainee hour, even excluding the time of the participants. Suppose, for instance, that a consultant is paid $150 to conduct a three-hour seminar with twenty-five staff members with the intent that improved performance be produced. This represents a cost of $2 per participant training hour excluding costs for planning, travel, correspondence, materials, released time, and so on. A more complex unit of training involving twenty-five staff members in a series of individual, small-group, and large-group activities over a period of several months for a total of twenty-one hours of training would be much more costly, as shown in the illustrative budget in Exhibit 4–7.

This program budget illustrates the detail required for program budgeting. It also supports previous points of view expressed about reasonable costs for ISE program operations that rise above the most simplistic in

---

Exhibit 4–7. ILLUSTRATION OF A BUDGET FOR A COMPLEX UNIT OF TRAINING

Number of Participants = 25

Number of Hours (Average) of Training Activity = 22

Goal: To use an observation/analysis system for self-analysis of classroom teaching so as to produce a diagnostic profile for a recorded lesson.

A. To plan and organize the training program:
1. To identify and select participants' correspondence selection interview, etc. 35 hrs @ $10.00 $ 350.00
2. To undertake team planning in preparation for visiting consultant $ 318.00
   meetings: 3 @ 1½ hrs each with 5 persons
   travel: 3 × 3 × 10 miles @ 20¢ = $18.00*
   substitute's salary: 3 × 3½ days × $20.00 = $180.00
   staff time: 4½ hrs × 2 × $10.00 = $90.00
   conference calls to consultant(s): $30.00*
3. To finalize plans and arrangements with visiting consultant $ 330.00
   travel to visit consultant: $90.00*
   staff time with consultant: $80.88
   staff time in local arrangements: $160.00

Exhibit 4–7   continued

B. To implement the training program:

    4. To provide visiting consultant services for two
days of group activity $ 930.00
       travel: 2 trips @ $90.00 each = $180.00*
       honorarium: 2 days plus planning @
       $250.00 = $750.00*

    5. To provide for small practice group follow-up
with staff-led seminar $1,225.00
       staff time: 3 sessions, 2 hrs each = $60.00
       substitute's salary: 25 × 3 × $15.00 (1/3 day)
       = $1,125.00*
       travel for staff: 20 sessions × 10 miles × 20¢ = $40.00

    6. To provide individual consultation with local staff $ 810.00
       staff time: 75 hrs × $10.00 = $750.00
       travel: 30 trips × 10 miles × 20¢ = $60.00

    7. To provide materials for participants to use, including
observation forms, cassette tapes, and training manuals $ 250.00*
       $10.00 per participant

C. To evaluate the outcomes of the training program $2,930.00*
    Contract with university extension center for inter-
    views, observation, and group-testing sessions
    @ $10.00 per interview × 30 = $300.00
    @ $15.00 per observation × 50 = $750.00
    @ $100.00 per testing session × 2 = $200.00
    plus travel, fees, computer services, etc., $1,680.00

D. To provide logistical support in the form of typing, reproduction, use of equipment, postage, and related services $ 850.00

Total Estimated Cost of Operation $7,993.00

        Total Excess Cost* $5,553.00

Excess cost per training hour: $252.41
Excess cost per trainee hour: $ 10.10

* Excess cost excludes staff time, staff travel within the district, and all logistical support.

* Note: No costs for trainee time are included in any of the calculations in this exhibit.

design. While this illustration is by no means an extremely elaborate ISE design, the cost per trainee hour is well above $10, even excluding normal costs of local staff. An item of considerable importance in the illustration in Exhibit 4–7 is related to objective C for evaluation. Obviously, less elaborate evaluation might be employed, especially when such programs are more or less routine and their worth well known. Eliminating evaluation activities entirely or undertaking them with purely local resources would leave excess costs at $5 per trainee hour for this illustrative program.

The discussion above and the illustrations cited provide a limited basis for thinking about overall budget estimates for in-service education programs in local school settings. Applying every cost estimate to the individual trainee, the following may be useful:

average training hours per person (annual) = 50
average training hour excess cost = $3.50
average per person training allocation
   (excess cost only) = $175.00
average per pupil excess cost (at 1/25) = $7.00

Since the figures above do not consider normal costs of a staff for administration, planning, leading, and evaluating in-service education activities, such must be estimated and budgeted separately. These estimates for many medium-sized and larger school systems would likely resemble those shown in Exhibit 4–8. This illustration is for a school district of 20,000 students.

If the cost of division operations shown in the exhibit below are combined with average training costs of $7 per pupil the total budget would be approximately $485,130 or nearly $25 per student. This is not a large part of the operating budget of a school system. In fact, much leeway remains for special high-cost in-service projects within the costs projected here. A $25 per pupil cost is about 2.5 percent of the operating budget of many schools. Similar amounts spent for special innovative programs, program evaluation, curriculum development, and other staff development needs would bring the entire developmental services budget to between 10 and 15 percent of the total operating budget. Only knaves or fools would knowingly and willingly do less.

SUMMARY

Assuming that in-service education programs are primarily the responsibility of local school districts, operating policies provide direction for prioritizing, organizing, and delivering training experiences to local staff. A staff must be organized and coordinated; and it must involve a great variety of personnel, drawing upon competencies both inside and outside the local scene. A full array of operating principles is now fairly well validated to give guidance to a core staff group that must be responsible for overall

Exhibit 4-8. ILLUSTRATION OF A BUDGET FOR OPERATIONS OF ISE DIVISION

School District of 20,000 Students

Salaries (6100)			$305,000
1	Assistant superintendent or director	$ 25,000	
10	Consultants, supervisors, planners, designers, evaluators @ $20,000 each for 1% of total instructional staff	$200,000	
3	Clerical, secretarial assistants @ $10,000 each	$ 30,000	
Contracted Services (6200)			$ 8,500
	Computer services	$ 3,000	
	Printing	$ 4,250	
	Photography, graphics, equipment maintenance	$ 1,250	
Supplies and Materials (6300)			$ 15,830
	Office supplies	$ 3,450	
	Professional books and periodicals	$ 3,680	
	Consumable training materials	$ 1,500	
	Evaluation instruments	$ 1,200	
	Nonconsumable training materials	$ 3,480	
	Computer supplies	$ 600	
	Postage	$ 1,420	
	Film rentals	$ 500	
Other Expenses (6400)			$ 13,300
	Staff travel	$ 4,500	
	Communications	$ 2,500	
	Training expenses for staff	$ 1,500	
	Other travel (advisory committees, planning groups, general consultants)	$ 1,800	
	Consultants, general plans	$ 3,000	
Equipment			$ 2,500
	Total: Division Operations		$345,130

directing and managing the great variety of programs that should be provided.

Managing a complex operation that responds to both individual and institutional priorities is no simple undertaking. Long- and short-range schedules need to be developed and coordinated. Staff assignment needs to be clearly determined, and funding provided to assure that time, personnel, and other resources will be adequate.

REFERENCES

1.   Abrahamsson, Bengt. *Bureaucracy or Participation: The Logic of Organization.* Vol. 51. Sage Library of Social Research. August 1977.
2.   Barbacovi, Don R. and Richard W. Clelland. *Public Law 94–142: Special Education in Transition.* Arlington, Va.: American Association of School Administrators, n.d. [ca. 1978].
*3. Bell, Harry and John Peightel. *Teacher Centers and Inservice Education. Fastback 71.* Bloomington, Ind.: Phi Delta Kappa Educational Foundation, 1976.
4.   Berman, Paul and Milbrey Wallin McLaughlin. *Federal Programs Supporting Educational Change. Vol. 1. A Model of Educational Change.* Santa Monica, Calif.: The Rand Corporation, September 1974.
*5. Berman, Paul and Milbrey Wallin McLaughlin. *Federal Programs Supporting Educational Change, Vol. 4. The Findings in Review.* Santa Monica, Calif.: The Rand Corporation, April 1975.
6.   Berry, Keith E. "A Humanistic Approach to Main-Streaming." In *Focus on Exceptional Children* (Sally Keeney, editor). Denver: Love Publishing Company, 1974.
7.   Bola, H. S. (editor). *Literacy in Development.* A Three Monograph Series. New York: UNESCO, International Institute for Adult Literacy Methods, 1977.
8.   Bruce, William, Janet Fleischauer, David Cooper, and Jarvis Sheperd. "Harris County/Columbus College Teacher Corps Inservice Project." Chapter 4 in *Inservice Education: Criteria for and Examples of Local Programs.* (Roy A. Edelfelt, editor). Bellingham, Wash.: Western Washington State College, 1976.
*9. Burrell, David. "The Teachers Centre: A Critical Analysis." *Educational Leadership* 32, no. 6 (March 1976): 422–27.
10. Centra, John A. "Plusses and Minuses for Faculty Development." *Change* 9, no. 12 (December 1977): 47–48, 64.
11. Clearinghouse on Educational Management. "Needs Assessment." In *The Best of Eric* no. 18 (July 1976). Eugene, Oreg.: ERIC Clearinghouse on Educational Management, University of Oregon.
12. Cooper, Myrna. "Inservice Training Projects of the United Federation of Teachers." *NCSIE Inservice.* National Council of States on Inservice Education. Syracuse, N.Y.: Syracuse University, College of Education (November 1977).
13. Cooperative Educational Research Laboratory. *Leadership Role for Con-*

---

* Suggested for further reading.

tinuing Education An excerpt from the revised prospectus of "Program Alternatives." Northfield, Ill.: Cooperative Educational Research Laboratory, Inc., February 1967.

14. Creekmur, Jimmie L. "A Descriptive Analysis of Inservice Education Programs of Selected Texas School Systems Utilizing Operational Criteria." Doctoral dissertation, University of Texas at Austin, August 1977.

15. Day, Barbara D. and James W. Jenkins. "North Carolina's K-3 Staff Development Program." *Educational Leadership* 31, no. 5 (February 1975): 326–20.

16. De Kalb County Schools, *Competency Assessment/Supportive Service Project.* Decatur, Georgia: PBC/SS Project, Doraville Center, 1976.

*17. Dillon, Elizabeth A. "Staff Development: Bright Hope or Empty Promise?" *Educational Leadership* 34, no. 3 (December 1976): 165–70.

*18. Edelfelt, Roy A. (editor). *Inservice Education: Criteria for and Examples of Local Programs.* Bellingham, Wash.: Western Washington State College, 1977.

19. Edelfelt, Roy A. and Margo Johnson (editors). *Rethinking Inservice Education.* Washington, D.C.: National Education Association, 1975.

*20. Gant, Jack, Oron Smith and John H. Hansen. *Temporary Systems.* Tallahassee, Fla., 1977.

21. Geffert, H. N. et al. *State Legislation Affecting Inservice Staff Development in Public Education.* Model Legislation Project. Washington, D.C.: Lawyers' Committee for Civil Rights Under Law, March 1976.

22. General Learning Corporation. "Continuing Professional Growth for the '70s." *Instructor Development.* New York: General Learning Corporation, n.d.

*23. Goodlad, John I. *The Dynamics of Educational Change: Toward Responsive Schools.* New York: McGraw-Hill, 1975.

24. Goodlad, John I. "Schools Can Make a Difference." *Educational Leadership* 33, no. 2 (November 1975): 110–11.

25. Gourley, Mary. "Relating Inservice Education to Program Improvement: An Overview of the Portland Consortium Training Complex." Chapter 7 in *Inservice Education: Criteria for and Examples of Local Programs.* (Roy A. Edelfelt, editor). Bellingham, Wash.: Western Washington State College, 1977.

*26. Greenwood, Peter W., Dale Mann, and Milbrey Wallin McLaughlin. *Federal Programs Supporting Educational Change, Vol. 3. The Process of Change.* Santa Monica, Calif.: The Rand Corporation, April 1975.

27. Hammond, Eileen and Adelle Clewley. "Vermont R.A.P.S." In *NCSIE Inservice.* National Council of States on Inservice Education. Syracuse, N.Y.: College of Education, Syracuse University (November 1977): 1–2.

28. Hansen, John H. (editor). *Teacher Education Centers.* Tallahassee, Fla.: National Consortium of Competency-Based Education Centers, n.d.

29. Harris, Ben M. "Inservice Education." *Proceedings of the Fortieth Annual School Administrators' Conference.* Baton Rouge, La.: Bureau of Educa-

* Suggested for further reading.

tional Materials and Research, College of Education, Louisiana State University, October 19, 1973 (mimeo).

*30. Harris, Ben M. *Supervisory Behavior in Education.* 2d ed. Englewood Cliffs, N.J.: Prentice-Hall, Inc., 1975.

*31. Harris, Ben M., E. Wailand Bessent, and Kenneth E. McIntyre. *Inservice Education: A Guide to Better Practice.* Englewood Cliffs, N.J.: Prentice-Hall, Inc., 1969.

32. Harris, Ben M., Vance Littleton, Dan Long, and Kenneth McIntyre. *Personnel Administration in Education.* Boston: Allyn and Bacon, Inc., 1979.

33. Hartley, Harry J. *Educational Planning — Programming — Budgeting: A Systems Approach.* New York: Prentice-Hall, Inc., 1968.

34. Hite, Herbert. "Three Scenarios for Inservice Education." A paper prepared for the Committee on Performance-Based Teacher Education. Washington, D.C.: American Association of Colleges of Teacher Education, October 1976 (mimeo).

35. Houston Independent School District. *Handbook for Staff Development for a Large Urban School District.* Houston, Tex.: Staff Development Department, Houston Independent School District, May 1975.

36. Howsam, Robert B. "The Profession of Teaching." In *Issues in Inservice Education: State Action for Inservice.* Syracuse, New York.: National Council of States on Inservice Education, Syracuse University, College of Education, November 1977, pp. 9–13.

37. James, Barry N. "A Package for Assessing In-Service Needs of Teachers." In *Teacher Education Centers* (John H. Hansen, editor). Tallahassee, Fla.: National Consortium of Competency-Based Education Centers, n.d.

38. Joyce, Bruce R. "Structural Imagination and Professional Staff Development." In *Issues in Inservice Education: State Action for Inservice.* Syracuse, N.Y.: National Council of States on Inservice Education, Syracuse University, College of Education, November 1976, pp. 14–20.

39. Killough, Don. "A Descriptive Analysis of the Roles of Education Service Centers in Providing Inservice Training Programs for the Public School Staffs of Texas During the 1975–76 School Year." Doctoral dissertation, University of Texas at Austin, August 1977.

40. Klugman, Edgar. "Can the Teacher Education Institution Respond through the Teacher Education Center to the Changing Needs and Expectations in This Field?" Wheelock College, June 1974.

*41. Lawrence, Gordon, Dennis Baker, Patricia Elzie, and Barbara Hansen. *Patterns of Effective Inservice Education.* Prepared under contract for the State of Florida, Department of Education. Gainesville, Fla.: University of Florida, College of Education, December 1974.

42. Luke, Robert A. "Collective Bargaining and Inservice Education." *Phi Delta Kappan* 57, no. 7 (March 1976): 468–70.

43. Maryland University. "Teacher Education Center Self-Study: A Preliminary Report of and to the Partners." College Park, Md.: University of Maryland, College of Education, January 1975.

* Suggested for further reading.

44. Massanari, Karl (editor). Higher Education's Role in Inservice Education. Highlights of a Leadership Training Institute in Atlanta, Ga., December 1–3, 1976. Washington, D.C.: American Association of Colleges of Teacher Education, January 1977.

45. McLaughlin, Milbrey and Paul Berman. "Retooling Staff Development in a Period of Retrenchment." *Educational Leadership* 35, no. 3 (December 1977): 191–94.

46. McLendon, Dan P. "A Delphi Study of Agreement and Consensus Among Selected Educator Groups in Texas Regarding Principles Underlying Effective Inservice Education." Doctoral dissertation, University of Texas at Austin, August 1977.

47. Nadler, Leonard. "Learning from Non-School Staff Development Activities." *Educational Leadership* 34, no. 3 (December 1976): 201–4.

48. National Academy for School Executives. *Management by Objectives and Results*. Arlington, Va.: The Academy, 1973.

*49. National Organization of County, Intermediate and Educational Service Agencies. "Regionalism: Help in Cutting School Costs." *The School Administrator* 34, no. 10 (November 1977): 6. Arlington, Va.: American Association of School Administrators.

50. Nelson, Marilyn. "Creating Organizational Structures for the Inservice Training of Teachers." In *Cultural Pluralism and Social Change*. A collection of position papers by Richard M. Brandt et al. Report no. 5. Inservice Education Concepts Project. Palo Alto, Calif.: Stanford Center for Research and Development in Teaching, June 1976.

*51. Nicholson, Alexander M. and Bruce R. Joyce, with Donald W. Parker and Floyd T. Waterman. *The Literature on Inservice Teacher Education: An Analytic Review*. Report no. 3 of the Inservice Teacher Education Concepts Project. Palo Alto, Calif.: Stanford Center for Research and Development in Teaching, June 1976.

52. Olivero, James L. "Helping Teachers Grow Professionally." *Educational Leadership* 34, no. 3 (December 1976): 194–200.

53. Organisation for Economic Cooperation and Development. *Modernizing Our Schools: Curriculum Improvement and Educational Development*. Paris: OECD Publications, no. 21435, December 1966.

54. Perko, Laura. "Inservice Program Guidelines." Portland, Oreg.: Portland Public Schools, November 1977 (mimeo).

55. Powell, Conrad and Larry Winecoff. "The Community Development Center: A New Perspective on Meeting Program, Staff, and Community Needs." Chapter 9 in *Inservice Education: Criteria for and Examples of Local Programs* (Roy A. Edelfelt, editor). Bellingham, Wash.: Western Washington State College, 1976.

56. Project on Utilization of Inservice Education Research and Development Outcomes. *Outcomes* no. 1 (December 30, 1976). Washington, D.C.: National Education Association.

57. Reardon, Francis J. "Participant Survey of Pennsylvania Inservice." *NCSIE*

* Suggested for further reading.

Inservice. National Council of States on Inservice Education. Syracuse, N.Y. Syracuse University, College of Education (November 1977): 4, 9–10.

*58.   Rivlin, Alice M. and P. M. Timpane (editors). *Planned Variation in Education: Should We Give Up or Try Harder?* Washington, D.C.: The Brookings Institution, 1975.

59.   Round Rock Schools. "Staff Development Plan: 1976–77." Round Rock, Tex.: Round Rock Independent School District, 1976 (mimeo).

*60.   Rubin, Louis (editor). *The In-Service Education of Teachers: Trends, Processes and Prescriptions.* Boston: Allyn and Bacon, Inc., 1978.

61.   Rubin, Louis J. "A Study on the Continuing Education of Teachers." *Instructor Development.* Part II (General Learning Corporation, 1, no. 7 (April 1970): 1–6.

62.   St. Landry Parish Schools. "ESEA Title III M.B.O. Program" Opelousas, La.: St. Landry Parish School Board, February 1976.

63.   Santelli, Charles and Mike Van Ryn. "Dialogue: A State Education Agency View, and a Teacher Union View." *NCSIE Inservice* National Council of States on Inservice Education. Syracuse, N.Y.: Syracuse University, College of Education (November 1976).

64.   Schmuck, Richard A. "Developing Collaborative Decision-Making: The Importance of Trusting, Strong, and Skillful Leaders." *Educational Technology* 12, no. 12 (October 1972): 43–47.

65.   Science Research Associates. *Materials for Professional Educators, 1971.* Palo Alto, Calif.: Science Research Associates, Inc., College Division, 1970.

*66.   Sealey, Leonard and Elizabeth Dillon. "Staff Development: A Study of Six School Systems." New York: The Ford Foundation, 1976 (mimeo).

67.   Shugrue, Michael F. and Carl A. Barth. "An In-service Training Program for Teachers of English." *Illinois English Bulletin* 62 (October 1965).

*68.   Silvern, Leonard Charles. *Systems Engineering Applied to Training.* Houston, Tex.: Gulf Publishing Company, 1972.

69.   Smith, William L. "Changing Teacher Corps Programs." *NCSIE Inservice.* National Council of States on Inservice Education. Syracuse, N.Y.: Syracuse University, School of Education (February 1978): 1–3.

70.   Spears, Harold. *Curriculum Planning Through In-Service Programs.* Englewood Cliffs, N.J.: Prentice-Hall, Inc., 1957.

71.   Special Education Supervisor Training Project. *Professional Supervisory Competencies.* Austin, Tex.: University of Texas, 1974.

72.   *Starting Tomorrow: Inservice Program for Elementary School Teachers.* Cambridge, Mass.: The Ealing Corporation, 1968–69.

*73.   Stephens, E. Robert. *Regionalism: Past, Present and Future.* Executive Handbook, Series no. 10. Arlington, Va.: American Association of School Administrators, 1977.

74.   Suchman, J. Richard. "The Ortega Park Teachers Laboratory." *Instructor Development* (General Learning Corporation), 1, no. 5 (February 1970).

75.   Teacher Education Center Research and Documentation Project. "The Pos-

sibilities of Reform: Florida's Teacher Education Centers (1974–1975)." Tallahassee, Fla.: State Department of Education, December 1975.

76. Thompson, James L. and Nancy C. Johnson. "Inservice Education: New Directions for Colleges of Education." (1975) (ERIC ED 109 088).
77. Thurber, John C. "Special Report on School-Based Inservice Education and Year End Overview, 1976–77." West Palm Beach, Fla.: Department of Staff Development, the School Board of Palm Beach County, n.d.
78. Tower, M. M. "Orientation and In-service Education Practices in Ninety-One School Systems in the United States." *Educational Administration and Supervision* 42 (March 1956): 181–90.
*79. Traccy, William R. *Designing Training and Development Systems.* New York: American Management Association, 1971.
80. Van Fleet, Alanson A., S. M. Hinzer, and J. P. Lutz. "Implementing Teacher Education Centers: The Florida Experience." *Research Bulletin* 10, no. 3 (Spring 1976). Gainesville, Fla.: University of Florida, Florida Educational Research and Development Council, Inc.
81. Warner, Allen R., James M. Cooper, and W. Robert Houston. "Developing Competencies for School-Based Teacher Educators." *NCSIE Inservice.* National Council of States on Inservice Education. Syracuse, N.Y.: Syracuse University, College of Education, (November 1977): 5–11.
82. Waxahachie Independent School District. "Prescriptive Opportunities for Individual Needs Training." A staff development model, funded under title IV, part C, Public Law 93–380. Waxahachie, Tex.: Waxahachie Independent School District, 1977.
83. West Virginia State Department of Education. "Teacher Education Center Survey — Region V, West Central West Virginia." Charleston, W. Va.: The Bureau of Planning, Research and Evaluation, West Virginia State Department of Education, May 1973.
84. Yarbrough, V. Eugene. "Teacher Growth: The Field Services Cluster." *Educational Leadership* 33, no. 5 (February 1975): 335–38.
*85. Yarger, Sam. "An Exploratory Model for Program Development in Inservice Education." In *Creative Authority and Collaboration.* A collection of position papers by Sam J. Jarger et al. Report no. 4. Palo Alto, Calif.: The Inservice Teacher Education Concepts Project, June 1976, pp. 18–24.
86. Yeatts, Edward H. "Staff Development: A Teacher-Centered In-Service Design." *Educational Leadership* 34, no. 6 (March 1976): 417.
87. Zenke, Larry L. "Staff Development in Florida." *Educational Leadership* 34, 3 (December 1976): 179–83.

* Suggested for further reading.

V

Law, Policy, and Regulations

INTRODUCTION

In-service education, discussed in general terms, and like problems of design and strategic planning discussed in previous chapters, calls into operation a major set of tasks that must be guided by policy provisions. Because ISE intervenes in people's lives, it is a sensitive area of policy. Because ISE is concerned with changing the operation of schools and colleges, it is a crucial area of policy. Because ISE is costly, it cannot command resources without policy commitment.

Curiously enough, there has been little policy in most school and college settings guiding in-service education (8; 32). Supporting legal structures for ISE are present in nearly every state in the United States in one form or another; however, they tend to vary widely among states in terms of expectations (9). Certain practices and related operating structures have evolved and become established within many educational organizations, simply because of the obvious need and the freedom of action permitted by law or policy. For instance, a legal provision for "professional" leave or "leaves of absence for further education" may include no funding or operating guidelines, yet local boards may occasionally grant such leaves on the basis of individual requests as funds are available. By contrast, a college or school faculty may secure a clearly specified agreement (17:21–22; 26:6, 19; 31:30–31) calling for "professional" or "sabbatical" leaves, designating percent of faculty limitations, establishing review procedures, and designating a budget category and source of funding. In this latter instance, a *leave program* emerges because policy is formalized, and supporting structures — funds, organization, and procedural guidelines — are all in place with staff responsibilities designated.

In-service education programs, if properly supported within school and college settings as institutional as well as personal responsibilities, must be guided by law and policy that are clear and authoritative and by other supporting structures that assure policy implementation. But this statement itself highlights a variety of issues over policy and structure for in-service education. One major issue relates to *who is responsible* for the in-service education of the staff. This is one issue that has not been clearly resolved. Currently, many state laws are rather confusing, vague, or silent on this matter (32:ix). Professional associations and unions tend to act as if they had substantial responsibility for the in-service education of their members (22:31; 40:469). However, school and college officials recognize more and more the relationship of ISE to improvement of instruction in specific, organizationally unique ways (16). Hence, school officials tend to view ISE less as a personal affair and more as an organizational imperative. Historically and legally, this position is supported by requirements for some kind of program in virtually every state (9). More recent developments in a few states give still more emphasis to ISE as an institutional responsibility (5; 47; 53; 54).

ISSUES OF POLICY

A whole host of basic issues are being faced or evaded, as the case may be, by those involved in in-service education policy and law. Similarly, these issues are largely unresolved in public school and college settings at the operational levels. They tend to be issues that are not easily resolved but that are so basic that they must be attended to whenever ISE plans or improvements are contemplated. They are also basic in the sense that a given resolution of any of these issues tends to affect the kind of in-service education provided to a substantial degree.

State law or policy formulated by designated state authorities influence the way local school boards and personnel approach policy locally. However, basic issues generally remain unresolved until they are thoroughly analyzed at the local level.

Three Sets of Issues

The basic issues being referred to are shown in Exhibit 5–1. These issues are grouped as three sets. The first deals with purposes to be served. The second set of issues has to do with responsibilities. The third has to do with the character of the programs provided. From each set of issues, two sets of logical consequences seem likely to follow. For instance, if issues 1, 2, and 3 are answered in favor of the organization's purposes being served, then needs assessments focus on organizational needs and the discrepancies, if any, between those needs and staff capabilities. However, if these issues are resolved in favor of the person as a practitioner, then needs assessments focus on individual competencies, aspirations, and interests; and discrepancy analysis is directed toward in-service objectives to promote individual growth for its own sake or for general professional purposes (40:469).

As with all issues, these do not lend themselves to easy either/or solutions.* For instance, personal needs and organizational needs might be very similar, if not identical. Hopefully, in-service program activities could be so rich in multiple opportunities for learning that small differences in personnel versus organizational priorities would be inconsequential (see issue 3). Often such ideal conditions will prevail, but they often will not. It is under such conditions of *incongruence* that a position on one side or the other of an issue becomes important.

Exhibit 5–1. BASIC POLICY ISSUES

The Person vs. the Organization
1. Is in-service education (training) essentially a personal affair to be planned, directed, and controlled by the individual staff member, *or* is ISE an institutional affair with individual staff members participating, as representatives of the institution, in all appropriate ways?
2. Does in-service education include any relevant training received by staff members, *or* is in-service training to include only that which is specifically selected as relevant and part of a planned program for on-the-job improvement in performance?
3. Should urgent needs of individual staff members for ISE take precedence over all other considerations, *or* should the larger, more important needs of the institution be given priority?

* Many of these issues are adaptations of those developed by this writer in cooperation with Dr. Jim Kidd and his staff in developing state level policy for Texas schools.(65) Most of these issues are stated in terms that relate specifically to public school and college settings. Only minor variations are generally needed, however, to make each issue relate equally well to private schools and colleges.

Exhibit 5–1   continued

Shared vs. Fixed Responsibility

4. Is ISE basically a responsibility of the state, *or* of the local school district, *or* is responsibility dispersed among various agencies and shared in a variety of patterns?
5. Should funding for ISE be an integral part of the foundation program, *or* should funding be essentially a local affair with special allocations for special purposes from various sources?
6. Are time, money, and staff for ISE the full responsibility of the institution, *or* are individual and unofficial groups clearly responsible, in part, for the provision of these resources?
7. Is active participation in ISE a basic contractural obligation of all staff members, *or* is ISE a special responsibility to be negotiated or accepted as an extra duty?

Strategic vs. Logistical Programs

8. Should standards for ISE program operations be specified in terms of objective events, such as days or hours scheduled, *or* should optimum program alternatives be promoted?
9. Should ISE expectations of staff be individually planned, *or* should basic program requirements apply to *all*?
10. Should ISE be restricted to operations within local districts (campus), *or* should ISE operations be provided for in as wide an array of locations as is needed?
11. Should ISE be restricted to activities that free staff members from job responsibilities, *or* should ISE include activities that are integrated into ongoing operations?

A Set of Positions

While most of the eleven issues stated in Exhibit 5–1 could be more than two-sided, these alternative positions encompass numerous distinct differences. A position often must be chosen to guide program planning, implementation, and evaluation even though another position might be elected under special circumstances or still another alternative formulated.

In the statements that follow, a preference is expressed on each issue, and supporting arguments are presented.

1. ISE Is an Institutional Affair.   Individuals and groups of staff members at all levels in the organization are necessarily very much involved, and this involvement may well include planning, implementing, and evaluating ISE. Whenever possible, highly personalized kinds of in-service education can and should be planned with the closest possible cooperation with the individual staff member concerned. However, the expectation of growth in the individual is institutionally prescribed; the resources of the institution are appropriated for ISE purposes; and the needs of the institution are being addressed through a staff member or group. Accordingly, ISE must be viewed as no less an institutional affair than any other assigned staff responsibility or operational endeavor.

This position is in substantial disagreement with those who argue for in-service education to be a continuing responsibility of the preservice training institution (21; 25; 5:551).

Definitions of in-service education like the following are implicitly in conflict with this position:

Education that takes place concurrently with service and is job related.

Activities which provide experiences for teachers to update for new trends, skills, certification, and for personal development.

Planned services and activities specific to the needs of the client.

Each of these views of in-service education stresses the individual's personal needs and fails to give attention to the institution being served.

Similarly, the position selected on this issue conflicts with that of teachers' unions that stress the organized profession's roles and prerogatives. The National Education Association has been outspoken in some of its publications regarding the "right" (23) of organized representatives of teachers to have "decision-making power" regarding in-service education (40). This is in striking contrast to arguments for extensive teacher involvement in decision making as a part of the staff of the school, college, or district. This position has been stressed by Harris. "From initial planning to final evaluation, the staff members must be intimately involved in the activities of a program in a meaningful way" (34:9).

However, Edelfeldt (22) fairly clearly defines a different kind of relationship when he states: "Most professionals assume that when a teacher reaches a specified level of competence, the teacher and the profession (in contrast with the school or state) become the responsible parties for in-service education" (22:31). This writer rejects this latter assumption. The focus for in-service education should be on the classroom where children's needs are being served. Obviously, the personal-professional needs of the individual staff member must also be served. But legal provisions, state policy, and local school district and campus plans must all be directed toward the implementation of in-service opportunities for learning that will improve job performances of staff in important ways. The responsible agents for offering learning opportunities to staff must be local school or college officials. State, federal, regional, and private support for in-service education will be needed, but a staff member as part of the operating school or college must be the target for growth

2. ISE is planned. ISE should include only training that is selected as relevant and part of a planned program. This position does not reject the potential value of many unselected, unplanned activities. It does seem important, however, to define, delimit, and select. This assures that scarce resources (time, talent, and money) will not be dissipated, that planning will be given a prominent place, and that priorities will be more clearly assigned. It is also clear that systematic monitoring and evaluating of ISE will be aided by carefully drawn restrictions on what is and is not to be included.

3. The Urgent Needs of Individual Staff Members for ISE Should Take Precedence over All Other Considerations. This appears to be a position inconsistent with position 2. However, in humane institutions the urgent needs of individual staff members, when properly assessed as both urgent and as job-relevant needs, are in fact the urgent needs of the institution. The dangers inherent in giving precedence to the larger, less individual, institutionally impersonal needs are very grave. Such needs are often defined politically and may or may not be educationally most relevant. Such needs carry with them the power and influence of official status that give them unfair advantage when priorities are being assigned. For these reasons, the institution should always make urgent needs of individual staff members its top priority. Balance between these urgent needs and those defined in alternative ways can be maintained by assuring proper definitions of *need* and of *urgency* and appropriate procedures for assessing both with validity.

4. ISE Is Basically a Responsibility of the Local School District. ISE is not dispersed among various agencies. This follows logically from position 3. Only a clear and unequivocal responsibility at the local level can be expected to be responsive to urgent individual needs. This position does not ignore state-level responsibilities for funding, policy planning, and evaluation; nor are cooperative arrangements among districts, education service centers, colleges, and private organizations to be ignored. However, operational responsibilities for offering ISE opportunities to meet individual local staff needs should be clearly assigned to local officials. Policy provisions should clearly indicate this local locus of responsibility and delineate relationships with other authorities or agencies.

5. Funding for ISE Should Be an Integral Part of the Foundation Program of the State. If ISE is essential to school program operations offering quality educational opportunity, then it must be a part of the *founda-*

tion program, too (13:9). For practical operational and planning purposes, heavy reliance upon local and/or special funding sources creates inequities, discontinuities, and imbalances that are detrimental to good ISE programming and tend to undercut local responsibility as described in position 4. Similarly, planning tends to be ad hoc and short-range without guaranteed levels of funding with some continuity in guidelines applying to such expenditures. Staffing, too, becomes very difficult unless funds are provided as a part of the regular program allocations.

6. *Time, Money, and Staff for ISE Are Institutional Responsibilities.* Individual staff members may *elect* to contribute their personal resources; however, such contributions cannot be expected as a condition of successful employment. If ISE is important, if institutionally defined needs are to be addressed, if local school officials are to be accountable, then the resources must also be clearly allocated (40). Individual staff members make their very large contributions through cooperative involvement that assures willingness to learn.

7. *Participation in ISE Is a Basic Contractual Obligation.* This follows naturally from the essential foundational character of ISE described in position 5. Legal provisions can and should clearly define this contractual nature of ISE participation in order to justify the use of public funds. Even more basic, however, is the importance to all staff members of a contractually guaranteed opportunity for growth on the job, supported mutually by the institution and the individual. Under such circumstances morale is enhanced, misunderstandings are minimized, and the focus of planning is on what can best serve institution and individual alike.

8. *Optimum Program Alternatives Rather than Objectively Defined Standards Should Be Used to Promote ISE of High Quality.* Objective standards for program operations tend to be restricted to days, hours, official schedules, authorized agents, and so on. As such, serious limitations are introduced that rarely reflect the enormous array of needs or possible alternatives. While some few minimum standards may be necessary, a wide array of options should be sought and given official encouragement. Policy statements that designate numbers of hours of training expected should be expressed in minimum terms and avoid designating per week, month, or even annual requirements unless considerable flexibility is assured. Similarly, specifying training outcomes in terms of growth in skills or competence or other performance capabilities must be individual in nature and rarely should appear in policy statements or general regulations. Even such widely followed practices as mandating semester hours of "professional credit" (33) may deter good planning.

9. *Expectations Should Be Individually Planned.* The basic unit for ISE purposes should be the individual staff member. This is consistent with positions 1, 3, 4, and 7. This is not to suggest that all activities for all individuals must be provided in isolation from all others. It does mean that the crucial evaluation question regarding any and all ISE activities is: How is each individual staff person being served? Local responsibility, diversity of alternatives, and cooperative planning are justifiable only insofar as individuals are served. Hence, *expectations* for growth must also be individually planned. The means of meeting those expectations may or may not be individual in nature.

10. *ISE Operations Should Provide for the Use of a Wide Variety of Locations and Sources for Training.* Unlike training in basic skills, ISE sometimes involves efforts to develop extremely complex performance patterns. Such training cannot be arbitrarily located in a building, a community, or a designated agency. ISE must be responsive to a wide range of needs, and flexible opportunities to go where the best available experiences can be offered is essential.

11. *ISE Should Include Activities That Are Integrated with the Ongoing Operations.* On-the-job training that overlaps with responsibility for routine operations complicates the problem of monitoring and accounting but is essential to the flexibility defined in position 10. Just as training opportunities may be located in various places, so the *current job setting* may be one such place. The criteria for use of any setting for training, including on-the-job training, relate to preplanning, clearly selected objectives, conscious effort to learn in ways that are relevant, and probable effect in comparison with available alternatives.

Struggle for Control

The control of in-service education is a problem or concern that has rarely been raised except by teacher organizations, the National Education Association, and the American Federation of Teachers. Most state legislators have either not addressed the control of in-service education at all in any direct or specific way or have done so in ways that simply assume that the governance of education in general includes the governance of in-service education. In effect, most states operate in-service education programs as a neutral extension of other public school operations and hence treat ISE as a state function with delegated responsibilities to local boards, colleges, and regional service agencies.

Teachers' organizations, as they have grown more militant, have sought specific operations around which to negotiate contractual provisions and bargain. They seem especially entranced with in-service education as a concern of teachers (40) but also as a valuable item for bargaining. Hence, the AFT's original contract victory in New York City had only a few limited provisions, including traditional sabbatical leaves (67:32–33). However, the 1965 third contract in that city reflected an array of concerns about the character of various opportunities for in-service education. Substitutes were called for to provide released time for "professional conference(s)," "visits to other schools and to attend educational conferences" (67:33). The NEA policy by 1976 was relatively clear, however, in designating in-service education as a target for control by organized teaching groups. Luke (40) alludes to this as an NEA official by asserting that "it is imperative that teachers, *as members of their professional associations*, find the means to involve themselves in the formulation of policies [author's italics]" (40:469). He goes on to emphasize that "collective bargaining is the means by which this is done."

The issue of control has been persistently raised in recent years by strong statements from the Teacher Corps (60); the Council of States for Inservice Education; the Department of Health, Education, and Welfare (25); the NEA; and other groups (14) with specific references to involvement of teachers in decision making; policy formulation; and planning, evaluating, needs assessment, and leadership roles.

This growing expression of labor union concerns regarding governance of in-service education for school personnel has been echoed in recent years by institutions of higher education. Increasingly, these institutions have awakened to the reality that in neglecting ISE over the past decade they have also jeopardized future opportunities to exercise influence on local college programs. Hence, a reactive interest in governance and control rather than service seems to have emerged.

Control of in-service education is not, and should not be seen, as a teacher versus administrator's issue for various reasons:

1. Teachers, administrators, supervisors, librarians, counselors, aides, school secretaries, and numerous others have a direct personal interest in the quality and character, and hence control of ISE.
2. The official organizations — school district, state, school, college, and program — each have a less personal but nonetheless real interest in assuring in-service education for their respective groups of personnel.
3. Obviously, students and parents have a very large interest in in-service education opportunities offered to school personnel, as do other citizens seeking assurances of educational efficiency.

The issues regarding the proper control of in-service education tend to emerge as an array of questions about levels at which controls are exercised, mechanisms for assuring full representation of all legitimate interests, and delegation of responsibilities to individuals and groups to assure ISE that is responsive to needs and yet is efficient and effective.

One of the implicit assumptions about teacher control, often expressed in only vague ways, appears to be that "teachers know best." This is not unlike the equally naive implicit assumption of many politicians that central government knows best. Obviously, such assumptions are no more defensible than those all-too-common assumptions that administrators or local school boards know best.

The task of structuring in-service education so that controls are maintained in ways that assure a most efficient and effective service delivery system must be guided by the combined wisdom and balanced influences of all responsible parties. We must assume that both individual and organizational needs are to be met. There is much to be said for maintaining an open system in which all interests have opportunities to be expressed and to exercise influence. The steadfast avoidance of heavy concentrations of power in the hands of any one interest group seems likely to serve to assure that needs will be met. Even so, there must be clearly available avenues for redress of grievances. Responsibility for each key element in the operating system can be clearly assigned. A system of checks and balances, including systematic objective evaluation, can be provided. But clearly written policies are an essential means by which such governance can be assured (19:10).

Clarifying Relationships

Controversy, disagreement, even struggles for power are to be expected in a free society, with educators of many brands struggling to recover losses in funding, autonomy, and prestige (38). Even so, much of the current controversy stems from lack of breadth of vision. The care and feeding of the world's largest and most complex profession is inevitably multidimensional. Preservice education is not a single, simple program; it is replete with all the age-old problems of relevance — general education, specialization, professional education, theory, methodology, academic knowledge, and clinical field experience. Yet this single term represents a limited portion of the whole concept of continuing or lifelong education. Between the arbitrary limits of preservice and lifelong education is a significant variety of training needs that can be rather clearly differentiated in terms of purpose, procedure, and time. Hence, they can be distinguished and do not need to be confused with each other, nor ignored, nor in conflict (48:43).

Exhibit 5–2 attempts to show some of the relationships among various kinds of professional education over an extended period of a career. The

Exhibit 5–2. RELATIONSHIPS AMONG PRESERVICE, IN-SERVICE, AND PROFESSIONAL DEVELOPMENT

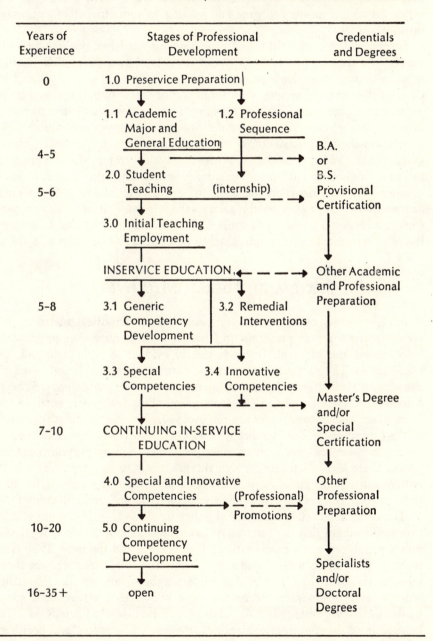

Years of Experience	Stages of Professional Development	Credentials and Degrees
0	1.0 Preservice Preparation	
	1.1 Academic Major and General Education 1.2 Professional Sequence	
4–5	2.0 Student Teaching (internship)	B.A. or B.S.
5–6	3.0 Initial Teaching Employment	Provisional Certification
	INSERVICE EDUCATION	Other Academic and Professional Preparation
5–8	3.1 Generic Competency Development 3.2 Remedial Interventions	
	3.3 Special Competencies 3.4 Innovative Competencies	Master's Degree and/or Special Certification
7–10	CONTINUING IN-SERVICE EDUCATION	
	4.0 Special and Innovative Competencies (Professional) Promotions	Other Professional Preparation
10–20	5.0 Continuing Competency Development	
16–35 +	open	Specialists and/or Doctoral Degrees

time line of this exhibit reflects rough estimates of the years that tend to transpire as preservice education comes to an end and in-service education ensues as a continuing part of professional development. Parallel certification and degree programs are also shown in this exhibit, continuing for many through a masters' degree and leading in some instances to special certification.

Formal, college- or field-based programs for academic degrees and advanced, specialized professional preparation is shown as related to, but separate from, in-service education. This point of view was expressed in Chapter I — that in-service education is only one important aspect of professional growth and lifelong learning. To the extent that ISE can contribute to other goals — degrees, certification, promotions — without distorting the on-the-job orientation of the program, so much the better. However, policies and regulations at all levels should protect the integrity of ISE as a unique and vital developmental program. To be promoted, to have another license to hang on the wall, to seek a new job, to gain a higher degree, or to gain a step on the salary schedule may all be desirable personal-professional goals. They must be justified as contributing to the on-the-job performance of the individual to be utilized as in-service education.

STATE AND FEDERAL INITIATIVES

A brief overview of numerous state and federal activities related to in-service education was presented in Chapter I. The impression of growing involvement and of commitment is clearly evident at both state and national levels. The past and present trends are highly unstable but seem reassuring in their diversity if not in their continuity or consistency. Federal activity continues largely in the form of omnibus legislation such as the Elementary and Secondary Education Act (60), the Higher Education Act, or the Education of the Handicapped Act (1), into which piecemeal provisions for in-service education or other personnel training programs are inserted. State legislation and policymaking appears to be very diverse both within and among states, with numerous provisions for general funding (29), special centers (47), special programs (64), and recertification (33).

The truth about state and federal policy in the field of in-service education is that there just isn't much. As with most school districts, legal and policy provisions are a patchwork quilt of the old and the new. They tend to be poorly conceptualized and reflect very little solid planning. For these reasons, the effort here will be limited. A number of diverse developments will be reviewed to give the reader some perspective. Suggestions for a model state law presented in Appendix F will be discussed briefly as it relates to much-needed developments at this level. The issues and positions that have been presented here will be used as a frame of reference for thinking about state and federal policy.

Federal Programs

The U.S. Congress continues to enact legislation reflecting a substantial and growing interest in in-service education. The untimely death of the Education Professions Development Program (49) signaled an end to any pretense of a federal policy on manpower development for the nation's schools and colleges. Even so, the various federal programs were reported to be budgeted for a total of some $220 million for in-service education in 1977–78. This is obviously an enormous allocation. These monies are found in Teacher Corps budgets, in vocational education funding, in Office of Economic Opportunity (OEO) manpower programs, in teacher center legislation, and in bilingual education and migrant education provisions, to name only a few.

Three recent legislative developments at the federal level are most interesting, if only because they represent policy directions that are quite different from the hodgepodge of special programs of the past. One development of note is the teacher center provisions of the Higher Education Act amendments of 1976. The second is the Teacher Corps funding of school-based in-service education (61). The third is the provision for "the development and implementation of a comprehensive system of personnel development" as part of Public Law 94–142 (1:67).

Teacher centers were originally promoted legislatively through federal grants for preservice teacher training. This stimulus has resulted in the sudden growth of a large number of very diverse centers. Coming as it did at a time when teacher shortages were disappearing and college enrollments declining, the effect of legislation was to stimulate preservice activities when a shift to in-service was more in order. The amendments to the Higher Education Act of 1976 provided for the teacher center idea to be extended to in-service education. Section 532 provides for "grants to local education agencies to plan, establish, and operate teacher centers" (25:51551). The law provides that "each teacher center must operate under the supervision of a policy board, the majority of which are representative of elementary and secondary classroom teachers" (25:51551). The curious aspects of these provisions for teacher centers for in-service education have policy implications:

1. The preservice centers were not authorized to extend their efforts into in-service delivery. On the contrary, there is no assurance that this

legislation will not create still another set of organizations providing ISE.

2. The local education agency was specified as the grant recipient. These can be defined in various ways, of course, but in many instances will be local school districts.

3. Teachers were specified as having a controlling interest in the governance of these centers.

4. No special purpose was designated to be served. The language of the act allows for nearly any kind of school-related training.

It may also be significant from a policy point of view that very little money was finally authorized for ISE teacher centers.

These four points relate clearly to positions 4 on local responsibility, 9 on institutional responsibilities, and 10 on variety of sources, presented earlier in this chapter. It seems possible that these provisions awarding federal grants for ISE teacher centers is more than a trial balloon in policy development. It may never grow and develop. But should it flourish and persist, the policy position appears to be one of support for teacher control, cooperation with institutions of higher education, a diversity of delivery systems, and local determination of purposes to be served.

Teacher Corps programs have been predominantly preservice in their orientation, too. In recent years, William Smith, the national director, has initiated a major program of in-service education. While not abandoning preservice efforts, there is an obvious effort to keep the Teacher Corps alive and growing by a shift of emphasis for the in-service development of the teaching staff. In moving into ISE, several characteristics of the new operations have policy implications (61):

1. The programs are school based with almost religious zeal for the notion that intraschool programs are best.

2. The programs are being funded for five-year periods.

3. The regulations are mandating community representation in decision making about programs.

The issues to which these developments are related include positions 2, on-the-job relationships; 4, local responsibility; 7, contractual obligation; and 10, restricted locale. The Teacher Corps is not just indicating federal recognition of in-service education as a priority. The guidelines under which Teacher Corps ISE operates represents a commitment to local programs, cooperative programs, and community-influenced programs. These efforts seem almost to argue for the maximum amount of provincialism with minimum use of outside resources beyond the local school and neighborhood. On the other hand, there can be no doubt that these programs are based clearly on the assumptions of institutional responsibility and obligatory participation.

Public Law 94–142 has been characterized as "the quiet revolution" by Dimond (20) and as the federal response "to judicial mandate" by others. It is hailed by some and feared by others. Some believe it may set in motion a new wave of litigation over the rights of states to control educational policy. The unique feature of this act, the Education of the Handicapped Act, from the point of view of in-service education, is the provision of section 613(a) (3), which clearly requires state plans for special education to include "a comprehensive system of personnel development" (1:67). Several implications of this provision relate to both federal and state policy as follows:

1. The act clearly indicates the commitment of Congress to in-service education as an essential feature of this program for educational change.
2. The requirement of a state plan for in-service education extends to *all* personnel involved with handicapped children, not just to special personnel.
3. The rationale for requiring special educational programming, the rights of the handicapped, are now linked to in-service education as well.
4. No provisions are made explicitly for training through the auspices of colleges and universities (69:477).
5. Regulations adopted implementing this act provide for "the use of incentives" (1:69).

Relating some of these features of policy reflected in P.L. 94–142 to basic issues previously presented provides strong support for the positions taken on 1, institutional reasonability; 2, planned programs; 3, urgent staff needs; 8, individual expectations; and 9, incentives. Obviously, this act gives to the federal level a commanding influence over goal setting and priorities for in-service education at the classroom level. Furthermore, the implication is clear that the state government is expected to be the agent of Congress in carrying out the federal mandate.

State Planning

There has been a genuine flurry of interest in in-service education at the state level in recent years, especially since 1975. In concert with unions, school districts, colleges, and the federal government, ISE has not been a high-priority concern with state legislatures or departments of education until recently. McCarthy's study of six southeastern state departments of education revealed a good deal about staff, functions, and expenditures in 1967, but it failed to even mention in-service education and/or staff development. Several states had taken legal actions in the 1960s to create intermediate units or other service centers, but in-service education was generally only implied or mentioned as one of several services to be provided (54:1).

Florida was truly the pioneer, it would seem, in demonstrating state-level interest in in-service education by enacting legislation for planning, program implementing, and financing in 1968 (29). Since this time, state policy and law have grown rapidly in both volume and variety. Florida has emphasized comprehensive master planning (28). New Hampshire programs have also emphasized local master plans (53). California, which had developed the County School Service Program to revitalize the county superintendent's offices in the early 1950s, enacted professional development center legislation in 1974 (4) and followed with regional school resource centers in 1977 (3). Michigan (47) by 1977 had joined a host of other states promoting professional development centers. By 1973, Georgia was in the process of formalizing a "State Plan for Staff Development" (33), and legislation in Texas authorized ten days for "inservice training and for preparation" in 1969 for the first time, clearly recognizing ISE as an integral part of the minimum foundation program of the state (24). By 1977, West Virginia was developing proposals for a "statewide program of continuing education for all educational personnel" (12:1) using a continuing education task force.

The intensive efforts of state government in behalf of in-service education during the past decade has been stimulating to both federal and local agencies as well as to colleges and professional associations. A rather diverse, unsystematic pattern of state programs seems to have emerged both among and within states. Geffert, Harper, and Schember studied all fifty states with a view to determining the status of legislation affecting in-service education (32). By 1976 they found nearly all states addressing ISE in some manner; however, rarely did they find even half of the states with similar elements in their statutes (32:ix–xi). For instance, eighteen states did "encourage" personnel to engage in educational association activities as a part of in-service education. Only thirteen states explicitly vested authority in local boards for in-service education. Curiously, while states like Utah, Vermont, West Virginia, North Dakota, and New York were still leaving in-service education as optional with school districts, thirty states had by 1976 already legally authorized negotiating or collective bargaining or both for in-service education.

In a more recent study by Collins of the policies and practices in fifty states and four territories, several interesting findings emerged (9). Most states (90 percent) formally delegate authority to local school districts.

Only 28 percent of the states require in-service education, and only 42 percent of the states derive their authority by law. Hence, it is not surprising that only 38 percent of the states report having "a state-wide policy statement," and only 30 percent have a state plan for in-service education (9:2). These are interesting findings and emphasize the still emerging character of in-service education at this level.

The view of in-service education law, policy, and program at state levels is further clarified by the heavy emphasis in many states on degree and certification programs as an integral part of in-service education. Collins reports 91 to 96 percent of all states including such programs. Carthel's review of very recent state programs in twelve selected states revealed heavy emphasis on certification and recertification in four of them (8:48). Oregon has also been persistent in seeking to tie together in-service education, professional development, and certification. These various efforts to keep certification from becoming permanent and to require continuing training are worthy. There is reason for concern, however, that the old rigidities and artificialities of licensure and degree granting may be more of a liability than an asset to program quality in these states. Some seem more intent on regulation, certification, and credit verification and control than on quality training experience.

Regionalization

A little-noticed development since the early 1950s has been the emergence of regional educational service organizations. County offices in California, boards of cooperative educational services (BOCES) in New York, regional educational service centers in Texas, the intermediate school districts in Michigan, the cooperative educational services agencies in Georgia, and many other organizations in different states represent a major trend. Even countywide or parish school districts so widely developed in the South are manifestations of regionalization. While most of these organizations are providing an array of supplementary educational services, they generally make in-service education a major service commitment. Regardless of their specific names or forms, they tend to have some characteristics in common. They are regional in the sense of serving a multidistrict area but not in the sense of extending beyond state boundaries. They tend to be creatures of the state, but they still have considerable freedom to respond to unique demands of local districts. They tend to be supplementary-service oriented, not regulatory. Furthermore, they do not normally engage directly in operating schools or programs of instruction.

The growth and development of these regional service organizations has been recognized and described in only limited ways on a nationwide basis. The rural focus of intermediate administrative units of prior years has given way to a focus on supplementary services to all schools within a region whenever such services are needed (50). Stephens (63) summarizes many of these developments in a recent booklet for school administrators, emphasizing the long history of regionalism in educational service delivery that has been too little understood in the midst of the simultaneous urbanization of our schools.

The teacher centers referred to previously are an array of efforts that are sometimes regional in nature but that tend to be distinguishable from the mainstream of supplemental service centers discussed above. Teacher centers tend to define their service area in highly idiosyncratic ways. They tend to be voluntary consortia of various institutions and vested-interest groups — colleges, districts, associations, and the like. They tend to specialize in offering preservice or in-service education but are not usually multiservice oriented. They tend to be structured for governance outside the formal channels of education. They tend to respond to individuals as individuals rather than to needs of schools, programs, and districts (70).

Initially, teacher centers were authorized in federal legislation with a focus almost entirely on preservice teacher education. With the passage of P.L. 94–482 of 1976, teacher centers were authorized specifically for in-service education purposes (25). California and Michigan are only two states that are quite obviously struggling to make federal legislation and their own programs conform to each other. This creates real problems, because the provisions of the federal law are quite poorly conceptualized from the point of view of a modern instructional improvement delivery system (57).

California's (58) school resource centers are clearly projected as regional in character with no fewer than twelve authorized by law by 1982–83. Funds stipulated are very meager, only about $100,000 per center. To facilitate integration of federal and state programs, California's law clearly follows the requirements of the U.S. Congress, establishing a governing board with a majority of teachers represented (3; 5).

Michigan's professional development centers (47) illustrate still further the efforts of states to utilize federal teacher center authorizations in their own ways. Michigan is emphasizing regionalization but on a smaller scale than many other states. The Detroit Center was the first funded in Michigan and focused primarily on the classroom teachers of that city. The Region 12 Center was funded in 1977 and includes five intermediate school districts. The Kent Center serves twenty local districts all within one intermediate school district.

These few facts about California and Michigan centers for ISE should serve to raise questions, at least, about the logic of still more teacher centers that take many forms but are seemingly not yet leading the way to any distinctive form of in-service education delivery system (57:405). Michigan's superintendent of public instruction, John W. Porter, expressed the dilemma well: "It is virtually impossible to distinguish among these" (46:1). He argues for efforts "to establish a common base around which the many diverse points of view regarding professional development . . . might emerge."

The development of regional service units to provide supplementary services to local school personnel has come about very slowly. It undoubtedly has limitations that must be dealt with. But it seems just short of irresponsible to continue the unplanned, special-purpose, uncoordinated, hodgepodge of centers that has emerged in recent years. Regional services should be supplementary to local programs. They should be multiservice organizations for various reasons of economy and efficiency. Where presently structured intermediate units have failed to demonstrate service delivery capabilities, they should not be maintained, of course. To be economical, multiservice centers must serve large regions either geographically or in terms of population. This means that in-service education services cannot be those of direct training to any large extent. But this is a blessing in disguise, because the direct training function should not be regionalized any more than is absolutely necessary. The regional service centers can be much more effective as a support service, assisting local personnel to do their own training. One regional service center staff expressed this well in asserting two goals: (1) "to assist regional schools in their efforts to provide inservice (education)," and (2) "to maximize the effectiveness and efficiency of our delivery of services" (55:2).

Need for Legal Framework

There is a growing and urgent need for a legal framework for in-service education in many states that is more comprehensive and more internally consistent than the present statutes. Those states already having a variety of provisions for funding (29), recertification (33), teacher centers (70; 47), service centers (54; 55), special in-service days (66), or accreditation (15;52) rarely deal with in-service education as a total program of major importance. The complexity and diversity of the organizational arrangements required for high-quality delivery of ISE on a continuous basis is simply neither clearly recognized nor well reflected in state statutes.

In emphasizing state law for continuing in-service education, this writer is espousing an old principle or assumption — that education is a state *function* but a *local* responsibility. We are not advocating either state or federal domination of any aspect of educational operations that directly impinge upon the personal lives of children and staff. All such operations are most appropriately left as direct responsibilities of local governmental and operational units that can interface directly with those affected.

The *function* of the state is of great importance, however. The separation of responsibilities among jurisdictions — state, regional, district, neighborhood, and personal — needs clarity in state laws and policy. The provisioning of local operations with money, staff, time, and technical support needs facilitation and direct assistance from the state level. Certain aspects of statewide prioritizing, master planning, and interfacing with federal policymaking may well require state-level control.

Suggestions for state law for continuing ISE are presented in Appendix F. An abstract of these suggestions is shown as Exhibit 5–3 to highlight the major features of the desired legislation. Suggestions for law such as these are not intended as a blueprint to be followed to the letter. They are intended, however, as an educator's conception of what might be translated into legal language and form to conform to differing practices in various states. It also would need to be carefully reviewed and adapted in terms of the provisions that already exist in any given state, since some may already be well established in law or policy while others may be conflicting with present law and necessitate repeal processes.

The purpose expressed in law by a legislature sets the tone for all provisions that follow and for policies and regulations that are later formulated for implementation purposes. In Exhibit 5–3 the emphasis is on:

equality of educational opportunity
continuous improvement
performance changes
all personnel

Any such law should give clarity to the responsibilities of the local boards and the state board. These points of emphasis tend to be very consistent with some of the major legislative developments in California (3; 4; 5) and Florida (28; 29), as previously discussed. The highly specialized provisions found in most states may speak to some of these same points. For instance, the Connecticut provisions for continuing certification have some relationship to continuous improvement. The Nebraska (52) provisions may be related to all personnel as are the Texas (18) provisions. Michigan's efforts to promote diversely organized professional development centers may relate to performance change but are not particularly helpful regarding local district responsibility. Throughout the country, the federally sponsored teacher centers are likely to add confusion rather than clarity to the issue of local responsibility.

A statement of policy should be included in legislation as an important, explicit point of view or position for any state program. At the highest levels of decision making, a clear policy position is needed. Including such a clear policy position in the basic legal framework gives it the force of

Exhibit 5–3. ABSTRACT OF SUGGESTIONS FOR STATE
LAW FOR IN-SERVICE EDUCATION *

Purpose

To assure quality educational opportunity for all children and youth by promoting continuous improvement of personnel performance on the job.

Part A: The Comprehensive State Program. Provides authority for state board policy and guidelines. Defines responsibilities of local boards of education for providing in-service education. Creates a state office for coordination and planning. Creates a state advisory council. Requires a statewide needs study within each five-year period.

Part B: Supplementary Educational Services Program. Requires the creation of regional organizations to supplement local district programs. Defines these supplementary services. Provides for diverse organizational arrangements and for democratic control.

Part C: Leadership Training and Innovations Program. Authorizes the state board of education to plan for leadership training throughout the state to assure competent personnel to implement in-service education programs. Provides for the identification, funding, dissemination, and evaluation of innovative approaches to in-service education to improve practices throughout the state.

Part D: Instructional Program Development and Improvement Fund. Creates a separate state fund for in-service education and related instructional support services. Specifies the level of funding for these services at 5 percent of the personnel costs of the schools of the state. Specifies allocations to local districts, supplementary educational service organizations, and other agencies. Defines and delimits purposes for which funds may be allocated.

---

* See Appendix F for the complete suggestions.

law, of course. In the ideas presented in Appendix F, a simple statement can have enormous implications:

> It is the declared policy of the State of _____ to provide in-service education opportunities for all personnel. . . . All personnel are contractually obligated to avail themselves of such opportunities.

The policy statement goes on to specify the essential components of the statewide effort to implement such a sweeping policy provision. This proposal contrasts sharply with that developed by Florio and Koff in a recent publication of the National Institute of Education (30) that makes in-service education primarily a new teacher responsibility. This statement clearly defines a reciprocal relationship between the institutions of the educational system and the individual person employed by those institutions. It does not preclude many other forms of professional and/or staff development as discussed here (see Exhibit 5–2), but it gives clear direction on the responsibility of the institutions to provide ISE opportunities and makes it a clear responsibility of personnel to participate. It is important to note, however, that this policy does *not* specify time for training, amount, sources, types, content, and so on. These are clearly *not* appropriate matters for state legislation.

The four parts specified in the suggestions for state law are illustrative of the appropriate *functions* of the state as distinguished from local-level responsibilities. The four parts include comprehensive state planning; creating supplementary educational service organizations; facilitating training programs and innovations; and funding local, regional, and other operations. These are hardly all inclusive possibilities for state law, but they do reflect a fairly comprehensive view of the state function that allows for leadership through initiation, coordination, facilitation, and evaluation without resorting to control as the primary element of state influence.

The program development and improvement fund proposed under part D of Exhibit 5–3 is of crucial importance for a variety of reasons. The creation of a *fund* from which in-service education programs can be financed is, of course, essential to the kind of ISE program development being advocated throughout this book. Other provisions of part D are uniquely important, too! The level of funding is expressed as 5 percent of total personnel costs rather than as a dollar amount. This has the obvious advantage of allowing for inflationary effects and for growth or decline in personnel to be served. Less obvious is the fact that such a provision eliminates the need for repeated, frequent adjustments that could threaten the entire program from time to time. Another important feature of such provisions includes flexible rather than rigid allocations, so that the purpose of equal educational opportunity can in fact be served. Still another feature is the permissive allocation of monies from this fund for curriculum development, evaluation, and other staff development in recognition that these developmental tasks must often be integrated or closely associated with each other for improvements to come about.

LOCAL DISTRICT POLICY

Local district policy regarding in-service education tends to be nonexistent or fragmentary in most school systems. This is true in spite of the widespread delegation of authority by state law or policy (32) to local school districts. In their study of six school systems of considerable diversity, Sealy and Dillon (59) found not a single one with board policy on in-service education. The absence of such policy is made more interesting by the rapid growth of teacher centers, service centers, and other quasi-legal or unofficial agencies that are in effect developing their own policies for and with local personnel. Still another development involves union contract or negotiated agreements with local boards that do in fact become local policy (35), developed to fill a vacuum or to serve as chips to be bargained away.

The Need for Policy

If in-service education is to be related to the job, is to be responsive to institutional as well as individual staff needs, is to be coordinated with other program development efforts, is to be a commitment of the school system, and is to use local resources, then local board policy is essential. Furthermore, local policy must be controlling. Effective assumption of local responsibility without policy guidelines cannot be anticipated. "Written policies are the chief means by which accountable school boards govern schools" (19:10).

The importance of local board policy that clearly reflects commitments is stressed by McLaughlin and Berman in their analysis of federal programs supporting or promoting educational change (45). They point to the "hodgepodge" that is typically staff development as a serious deterrent to change. They found "successful" projects operating as "staff development projects," and warned that "institutional support from administrators" is essential (45:191–92). But administrators cannot be expected to initiate, command resources, and give priority to in-service education in the absence of policy. Firth (27), too, emphasizes this position in concluding that "commitment by school officials" is essential (27:221). Legal pressures for well-developed policy come even from federal equal employment opportunity legislation that generates specific guidelines for training as an obligation related to affirmative action for full opportunity (44:45).

Policy Guidelines

Since little exists to guide educators or school board members in developing local policy, it might be appropriate to consider the issue statements and positions presented previously in this chapter. Some of those eleven issues speak to policy at nearly any level, but they can nonetheless be viewed from a local perspective. Certainly local policy or regulation will have to address each of the issues in some way unless state or federal controls are superimposed.

An old policy of Florida's Dade County Board of Public Instruction can be used to illustrate both a fully developed policy and a way of analyzing policy to determine how issues are addressed. Exhibit 5–4 excerpts key statements from policy 4131.3, adopted October 5, 1966 (16). Issue numbers are indicated along with explanatory notations for each one. This policy can be seen to give attention to six of the eleven issues previously discussed. Omissions include the urgent needs of the staff, uses of time, locations, and release time. These might of course be adequately dealt with through administrative regulations rather than through explicit policy statements. Except for the introductory statement in this policy, the board does not seem to be expressing commitments and intents so much as describing current practices. Hopefully, a more forceful and forward-looking policy statement has since been adopted.

Five kinds of intents need to be specified in a policy that will clearly resolve issues and still offer guidelines for implementing high-quality programs. Such intents include the following:

1. *Expectations of Improvement.* The policy must clearly indicate the expectations that all personnel will seek to improve their performance.
2. *Provision of Opportunities.* The policy must clearly indicate responsibility for providing plans and programs for personnel growth for all.
3. *Personalized Growth Process.* The policy clearly recognizes the right of personnel to personalized treatment in planning and implementation of growth activities.
4. *Allocation of Resources.* The policy clearly indicates the sources and general magnitude of resources (funds, staff, time) to be allocated for programs of personnel growth.
5. *Continuity and Flexibility in Programming.* The policy provides for the use of allocated resources in ways that assure the appropriate growth activities, offered to selected individuals, at the most opportune time, under the most suitable conditions for maximum growth.

A policy statement that is carefully drawn should make commitments to guide school administrators and others in planning and implementing programs of high quality with relatively little dissonance or misunderstanding regarding the basic issues involved. (See Appendix D).

Accreditation

Accrediting associations are among those numerous external agencies that can and do influence school policy at the local level. The Southern Association of Colleges and Schools has recently strengthened its standards on in-service education at the elementary and secondary school level. The new standards being adopted for kindergartens and early childhood programs are illustrative of provisions that local policy should consider:

Area F — School Staff

Standard 21: "All personnel shall be actively engaged in a continuing, planned program of inservice development designed to improve their effectiveness on the job." (10:5)

Exhibit 5–4. ISSUE ANALYSIS OF EXCERPTS FROM
A BOARD POLICY

	Issue No.	*Notations*
1. "The Board considers it a matter of considerable importance that complete, and up-to-date programs of in-service education shall be provided for the personnel of Dade County Schools. . . ."	1 ⠀⠀⠀⠀⠀⠀⠀⠀⠀⠀ 4	an institutional affair ⠀⠀⠀⠀⠀⠀ a local responsibility
2. ". . . both on a formal and informal basis. Formal courses are planned cooperatively with institutions of higher learning. . . ."	4	a shared responsibility
3. "The in-service credit activities are promoted and organized by the school system to meet special needs, . . . strengthening . . . competence, . . . providing special training. . . ."	2 ⠀⠀⠀⠀⠀⠀⠀⠀⠀⠀ 9	planned, selected, relevant activities ⠀⠀⠀⠀⠀⠀ individually planned expectations
4. "These credit activities are . . . geared to the needs of fully certificated personnel. . . ."	7	a basic contractural obligation
5. "[credit activities] must be limited to regularly employed personnel to justify this expenditure of funds."	6	time, money, and staff are institutional responsibilities

---

Dade County Schools policy of 1966 (16). "Staff Development in the Dade County Schools," n.d. (mimeo). Quoted by permission.

This particular standard is further elaborated to call for systemwide coordination, released time from teaching duties, and specific budgetary allocations. In short, a school system expecting to meet Southern Association standards for kindergarten accreditation has some of its policy guidelines already established.

Even some years ago, state accreditation standards such as those in South Carolina were quite explicit about in-service education expectations for elementary school personnel (15:12–13). Curiously, the evaluation criteria developed for elementary schools by the National Study of School Evaluation (51) gives very little direct attention to in-service education. No principle speaks explicitly to in-service education (51:71–72), but references are made to helping "new teachers become successful members of the faculty" (51:75) and to "Participation in inservice educational activities" and "Expanding professional competency" (51:76).

Union Contract Provisions

Collective bargaining and formal negotiating is a reality in many school systems across the nation (32). In-service education is often included in these processes, and hence contracts or agreements become school policy and regulation. In the past, traditional aspects of in-service education were of primary interest. These commonly included sabbatical leaves and released time to attend meetings of associations. Increasingly, some teachers' unions — the American Federation of Teachers and the National Education Association — have become explicit in promoting teacher control (25), organizational representation (40), and teacher involvement in all aspects of programming (2). On a more limited basis, this new interest in the proprietorship of in-service education has led to union-operated programs (14).

In many instances, formal contracts negotiated at local levels continue to reflect only limited concern for ISE. However, the fact that many states already clearly recognize in-service education as legitimate for bargaining may indicate a trend in this direction. In 1969–70 the Dearborn, Michigan, agreement between Local 681, AFT and the board included only one statement specifically on ISE in a forty-two-page document: "XXIX. In-Service Classes. Full tuition shall be paid by the Board for inservice classes" (17:36). However, there were other provisions under leaves, workshops, and organization meetings. Even so, there was no clear claim to either control or even full-scale involvement in the in-service education of these schools.

The agreement between the Hawaii Government Employees' Association (AFL-CIO), 1971–73, and the Board of Education designated "professional improvement" as a contract provision (26). This contract covers only administrators, however, and simply asserts their right to leaves to attend seminars and workshops. The Hawaii State Teachers Association agreement with the board for 1972–74 calls for "released time for various purposes including participation in meetings, conferences, and training sessions conducted by the Association or the National Education Association" (35:49). As with the Dearborn contract, no array of provisions indicate any particular interest in the in-service education of the association's members beyond the highly restrictive clause just quoted.

An agreement between Gary Teachers Union (AFT) and the Gary, Indiana, Board of School Trustees for 1976 leaves in-service education almost ignored (31). This contract does, however, illustrate provisions that relate to the issue of teacher control. An array of committees related to curriculum and materials development is identified and designated in every instance with the phrase, "non-teacher personnel shall not exceed the number of teachers" (31:8–9). An additional provision stipulates that "The union shall have the right to designate a representative to" each of these committees.

The few examples of union contracts cited here cannot be regarded as representative either of current practice or of trends. Until recently, neither the AFT, the NEA nor other organizations representing teachers (e.g., the American Association of University Professors) has taken any substantial interest in in-service education as reflected in contract provisions. Still, contracts seem to be steadily expanding those provisions that include teacher representatives on committees and governing boards. Whether in-service education will become increasingly an issue for bargaining purposes seems uncertain. What is more certain is that it could be. Furthermore, as an item in a bargaining session, it is not likely to get very imaginative treatment. Local personnel might be well advised to make every effort to provide for the fullest possible opportunities for teacher involvement in all aspects of in-service education decision making within a context of local policy.

Judicial Considerations

At local, state, and federal levels, the increasing variety of litigation relating to schools can and probably will have direct implications for in-service education law, policy, and regulation. The suit of *Peter Doe* v. *San Francisco Unified School District* (No. 653–312) was a direct challenge to the local board for allegedly allowing practices to persist that amounted to negligence, if not malpractice. The courts dismissed the case, and hence no real legal opinion or precedent was provided. However, tenure and dismissal cases are approaching the same issue from the point of view of due process. Hughes and Gordon (37) note that "irrespective of whether or not a teacher has tenure, courts may begin to insist that appropriate procedural due process be followed in dismissal or nonrenewal of contracts" (37:351).

The crucial question for school officials is whether access to in-service education will become a clear requirement of due process right along with objective evaluation. Certainly, the special interest taken in in-service education practices by the Lawyers' Committee for Civil Rights Under Law (32) seems to indicate that such interpretations may be forthcoming.

Still another judicial development of recent years that makes in-service education a more urgent policy question is the principle of "proprietary interests." "Perry v. Sindermann establishes a new kind of proprietary right, that of expectancy of employment" (37:353). In this 1972 case the U.S. Supreme Court upheld the circuit court ruling that the teacher's lack of tenure does not by itself mean that he or she cannot claim contract renewal rights. These greatly broadened rights of personnel to every consideration combine with growing public pressure for excellence in performance of public officials. If rights are fully recognized and excellence is also to be fully pursued, in-service education must become more central in policy formulation and priority funding. In effect, better in-service education may be virtually the only feasible approach to dealing positively with conflicting forces of rights and responsibilities.

SUMMARY

The legal and policy structures for in-service education are in a state of unprecedented flux, making both descriptions of current status and current trends extremely difficult to discern. With no clear federal policy, piecemeal legislation encourages reactive state programs. In the absence of clear state legal frameworks, many states are hastily putting new provisions on the lawbooks, but little consistency is reflected either within or among states. Local policy continues to be least well developed of all, even though programs are still predominantly controlled at that level.

In this chapter, a set of issues was presented and positions taken on them in an effort to suggest directions for the immediate future. Suggestions for state law and five local policy guidelines were presented to stimulate better planning at these two crucial levels.

REFERENCES

*1.　Barbacovi, Don R. and Richard W. Clelland. *Public Law 94–142. Special Education in Transition.* Arlington, Va.: Office of Minority Affairs, American Association of School Administrators, n.d.

* Suggested for further reading.

2. Bhaerman, Robert D. "Several Educators' Cure for the Common Cold and Other Things." AFT Quest Paper no. 7. Washington, D.C.: Department of Research, American Federation of Teachers, n.d.

3. California, State of. "Assembly Bill No. 551, Chapter 3.1, Section 44670 to 44680.91." *Education Code*. Approved by the Governor and Secretary of State, September 21, 1977.

4. California, State of. *Professional Development and Program Improvement Act of 1968*. ISE Evaluation. Assembly bill no. 4151, chapter 1499. (State of California, September 27, 1974). Professional Development Center Legislation.

5. California State Department of Education. "Policy on Staff Development in California Public Schools." (draft). Sacramento, Calif.: State Department of Education, State of California (ca. 1976).

6. Carroll, Donald M., Jr. "Guidelines for Approved In-Service Credit." Basic Education Circular 53–75. Harrisburg, Pa.: Pennsylvania Department of Education, revised June 1975.

7. Carroll, Donald M., Jr. "Master's Degree Equivalency Certificate," Basic Education Circular 141. Harrisburg, Pa.: Pennsylvania State Department of Education, October 10, 1974.

8. Carthel, James. "An Analysis of Documents Reporting on Selected Inservice Programs." A report to the Texas Education Agency Review Panel on Staff Development. Austin, Tex.: Texas Education Agency, 1977 (mimeo).

9. Collins, James. "Survey of State Inservice Education Practices" (preliminary draft). Syracuse, N.Y.: National Council of States on Inservice Education, Syracuse University, College of Education, April 1978 (mimeo).

*10. Commission on Elementary Schools. "Standards for Early Childhood Centers and Kindergartens." *Proceedings* 29, no. 6 (April 1977). Southern Association of Colleges and Schools, Atlanta, Georgia, p. 5.

11. Connecticut State Board of Education. "Guidelines and Procedures for the Development and Approval of Inservice Activities for Standards Certification." Hartford, Conn.: Joint Teacher Education Committee, Commission for Higher Education and the State Board of Education, August 1976.

12. Continuing Education Task Force. "A Systematic Program of Continuing Education for West Virginia." Final Report submitted to the State Superintendent of Schools. Charleston, W. Va.: West Virginia State Department of Education, May 1977 (mimeo).

13. "Continuing Professional Development: A Discussion Paper." Salem, Oreg.: Oregon Teacher Standards and Practices Commission, September 10, 1977 (mimeo).

14. Cooper, Myrna. "Inservice Training Projects of the United Federation of Teachers." *NCSIE Inservice*. National Council of States on Inservice Education. Syracuse, N.Y.: Syracuse University, College of Education (November 1977): 3, 8–9.

15. Crowley, W. B. *Standards for Accredited Elementary Schools of South*

* Suggested for further reading.

Carolina. Columbia, S.C.: State Department of Education, Division of Instruction, 1967.

16. Dade County Schools. "Staff Development in the Dade County Schools," n.d. (mimeo).

17. Dearborn Public Schools. *Agreement Between the Dearborn Board of Education and the Dearborn Federation of Teachers (Local #681, AFT).* Dearborn, Mich.: Dearborn Public Schools, 1969.

18. *Developing Inservice Education Programs in Texas — 1978.* Austin, Tex.: Department of Professional Development and Instructional Services, Texas Education Agency, June 1978.

19. Dickinson, William E. *The Process of Developing Written School Board Policies.* A paper presented at the Annual Convention of the National School Boards Association (35th Miami Beach, Florida, April 19–22, 1975). ED 105 623.

*20. Dimond, P. R. "The Constitutional Right to Education: The Quiet Revolution." *Hastings Law Journal* 24 (May 1973): 1087–1127.

21. Drummond, William H. "An Open Letter to the Dean Re Inservice Education." *NCSIE Inservice.* National Council on Inservice Education. Syracuse, N.Y.: Syracuse University, College of Education (May 1976): 5–7, 10–11.

22. Edelfeldt, Roy A. "Can Competency-Based Teacher Education Be Applied to Inservice Education? Should It Be?" A draft manuscript prepared for the Association for the Accreditation of Teacher Education, July 1976 (mimeo).

*23. Edelfeldt, Roy A. and Margo Johnson (editors). *Rethinking In-Service Education.* Washington, D.C.: National Education Association, 1975.

24. Edgar, J. W. "Notice of Proposed New Policy." A memo to the State Board of Education, November 10, 1969, Austin, Texas (mimeo).

25. "Education Amendments of 1976. Intent to Issue Regulations." *Federal Register* 41, no. 226. (November 22, 1976): 51550–52.

26. *Educational Officers' Collective Bargaining Contract.* Agreement Between Hawaii State Board of Education and Hawaii Government Employees' Association, AFSCME, Local 152, AFL-CIO. October 29, 1971 — October 28, 1973.

*27. Firth, Gerald R. "Ten Issues on Staff Development." *Educational Leadership* 35, no. 3 (December 1977): 215–21.

28. Florida State Department of Education. *Criteria for Designing, Developing and Approving a Master Plan for Inservice Education.* Tallahassee, Fla.: State Department of Education, n.d.

29. Florida State Department of Education. *Educational Improvement Expense: Plan Narrative and Statistics.* Tallahassee, Fla.: State Department of Education, October 1968.

*30. Florio, David H. and Robert H. Koff. *Model State Legislation: Continuing Professional Education for School Personnel.* Washington, D.C.: National

* Suggested for further reading.

Institute of Education, Department of Health, Education, and Welfare, December 1977.

31. Gary Schools. "Agreement Between the Board of School Trustees of the City of Gary, Indiana and Gary Teachers Union Local Number 4, AFT." *Contract with Union.* January 1, 1976 — December 31, 1976.

*32. Geffert, H. N. et al. *State Legislation Affecting Inservice Staff Development in Public Education.* Model Legislation Project. Washington, D.C.: Lawyers' Committee for Civil Rights Under Law, March 1976.

33. Georgia Department of Education. "Certification Renewal Through Staff Development." Atlanta, Ga.: Division of Program and Staff Development, Office of Instructional Services, State Superintendent of Schools, April 1976.

34. Harris, Ben M., E. Wailand Bessent, and Kenneth E. McIntyre. *Inservice Education: A Guide to Better Practice.* Englewood Cliffs, N.J.: Prentice-Hall, Inc., 1969.

35. Hawaii, Office of the Superintendent. "Agreement Between State of Hawaii, Board of Education and Hawaii State Teachers Association," February 29, 1972 — August 31, 1974. Honolulu, Hawaii: Department of Education, State of Hawaii, 1972.

36. Hite, Herbert. "Inservice Education: Perceptions, Purposes and Practices." In *Higher Education's Role in Inservice Education* (Karl Massanari, editor). Washington, D.C.: American Association of Colleges of Teacher Education, January 1977.

*37. Hughes, Larry W. and William M. Gordon. "Frontiers of the Law." Chapter 13 in *The Courts and Education* 77th Yearbook. Part I (Clifford P. Hooker, editor). Chicago: National Society for the Study of Education, 1978.

38. Iddings, Roger G. "The Memorandum." In *Higher Education's Role in Inservice Education* (Karl Massanari, editor). Washington, D.C.: American Association of Colleges for Teacher Education, January 1977, pp. 32–37.

39. Koehler, Virginia. "The California Beginning Teacher Evaluation Study: The Federal Perspective." A paper. Washington D.C.: National Institute of Education, Department of Health, Education, and Welfare, n.d. (mimeo).

*40. Luke, Robert A. "Collective Bargaining and Inservice Education." *Phi Delta Kappan* 57, no. 7 (March 1976): 468–70.

41. Maddox, Kathryn, David E. Koontz, and Phil E. Suiter. "New Dimensions in Teacher Inservice Education." *Instructor Development* 2, no. 8 (May 1971): 1, 6.

*42. Massanari, Karl (editor). *Higher Education's Role in Inservice Education.* Highlights of a Leadership Training Institute in Atlanta, Georgia, December 1–3, 1976. Washington, D.C.: American Association of Colleges of Teacher Education, January 1977.

43. McCarthy, David. "Profiles of Departments of Education and Public Instruction and Factors of Educational Environment: Alabama, Florida,

* Suggested for further reading.

Georgia, North Carolina, South Carolina, Tennessee." Atlanta, Ga.: Regional Curriculum Project, n.d.

44. McCune, Shirley and Martha Matthews. *Programs for Educational Equity Schools and Affirmative Action.* Washington, D.C.: U.S. Office of Education, Department of Health, Education, and Welfare, 1978, pp. 45–46.

*45. McLaughlin, Milbrey and Paul Berman. "Retooling Staff Development in a Period of Retrenchment," *Educational Leadership* 35, no. 3 (December 1977): 191–94.

46. Michigan Department of Education. *Professional Development for School Staffs: The Michigan Approach.* Lansing, Mich.: State Board of Education, n.d.

47. Michigan Department of Education. "State Plan for Professional Development of School Staffs." (working draft). Lansing, Mich.: Office of Professional Development, Michigan Department of Education, December 7, 1977.

*48. Mondale, Walter F. "The Next Step: Life Long Learning," *Change* 8, no. 9 (October 1976): 42–45.

49. National Advisory Council on Education Professions Development. "Leadership and the Educational Needs of the Nation." A report to the President and the Congress of the United States, October 1969.

*50. National Organization of County, Intermediate and Educational Service Agencies. "Regionalism: Help in Cutting School Costs." *The School Administrator* 34, no. 10 (November 1977): 6. Arlington, Va.: American Association of School Administrators.

51. National Study of School Evaluation. *Elementary School Evaluative Criteria.* Arlington, Va.: National Study of School Evaluation, 1973.

52. Nebraska State Board of Education. "Rule Fourteen Revised. Regulations and Procedures for Approving the Continued Legal Operation of All Schools and the Opening of New Schools." Lincoln, Nebr.: State Board of Education, August 1, 1975 (revised May 7, 1976).

53. New Hampshire State Department of Education. "Staff Development for Educational Personnel." Excerpts from Guideline Requirements in Preparation of Local Master Plans. State Board regulation adopted June, 1971. Concord, N.H.: State of New Hampshire, November 1975.

54. Pennsylvania Legislative Budget and Finance Committee. "Report on the Pennsylvania Intermediate Unit System." Harrisburg, Pa.: The Committee, Pennsylvania Senate, May 1976.

55. Region Education Service Center XIII. "Education Service Center and LEA In-Service Education: A Position Paper." Austin, Tex.: Region Education Service Center XIII, n.d. (mimeo).

*56. Rivlin, Alice M. *Systematic Thinking for Social Action.* The 1970 H. Rowan Gaither Lectures, University of California at Berkeley. Washington, D.C.: The Brookings Institution, 1971.

*57. Rogers, Vincent R. "Teachers Centers in the U.S.: An Idea Whose Time Has Come?" *Educational Leadership* 33, no. 6 (March 1976): 403–5.

* Suggested for further reading.

58. Schmitthausler, Carl M. (editor). *General Instructions: How to Apply for School Resource Center Funds.* Technical Assistance Services no. 3. Assembly bill 551, article II, Education Code sections 44670–44680.91. Sacramento, Calif.: California State Department of Education, 1978.

59. Sealy, Leonard and Elizabeth Dillon. "Staff Development: A Study of Six School Systems." A report to the Ford Foundation. New York: The Ford Foundation, 1976 (mimeo).

60. Smith, William. A presentation to representatives of State Departments of Education in a conference at Phoenix, Arizona, Del Webb Townhouse Motel, April 1978.

61. Smith, William. "Teacher Corps New ISD Guidelines." *NCSIE Inservice.* National Council of States on Inservice Education. Syracuse, N.Y.: Syracuse University, College of Education (February 1978): 1–2.

62. State of Hawaii Department of Education. "Agreement Between Hawaii State Board of Education and Hawaii Government Employees' Association, AFSCME Local 152, AFL-CIO." October 29, 1973 — October 28, 1976. Honolulu, Hawaii: Teacher Assistance Center, Office of Library Services, Department of Education, August 1973.

*63. Stephens, E. Robert. *Regionalism: Past, Present and Future.* Executive Handbook, Series no. 10. Arlington, Va.: American Association of School Administrators, 1977.

64. Texas Education Agency. "Application for Coordination of Technical Assistance in Bilingual Education by Texas Education Agency, 1977–78." Austin, Tex.: Division of Bilingual Education, Texas Education Agency, n.d.

65. Texas Education Agency. "Field Review Document on Inservice Education." A working paper. Austin, Tex.: Department of Professional Development and Instructional Services, Texas Education Agency, October 1977. (mimeo).

66. Texas, State of. *Vernon's Civil Statute.* "Education Code" section 16.055 (b), 86.

67. United Federation of Teachers. "Agreement Between the Board of Education of the City of New York and United Federation of Teachers, Local 2, American Federation of Teachers, AFL-CIO, Covering Classroom Teachers and Per Session Teachers." July 1, 1965 — June 31, 1967.

*68. Vaughan, Joseph C. "Teacher Inservice: Research and Context." Washington, D.C.: National Institute of Education, Department of Health, Education, and Welfare, October 1977 (mimeo).

*69. Warnat, Winifred I. "Inservice Education: Key to PL 94–142's Service to Handicapped Children and Youth." *Educational Leadership* 35, no. 6 (March 1978): 474–79.

70. Yeatts, E. H. "Staff Development: A Teacher-Centered Inservice Design." *Educational Leadership* 33, no. 6 (March 1976): 417–21.

* Suggested for further reading.

VI

Personalized Training

INTRODUCTION

This chapter and Chapters VII and VIII are intended to assist the in-service planner in considering the proper uses and limitations of several widely varying approaches to in-service education. Clinical supervision, independent study, peer supervision, consultation, individual growth planning, self-paced instruction, and diagnostic/prescriptive systems of in-service education are among the numerous variations emphasizing the individual staff member and the personalizing of in-service education. However, equally strong and promising developments in in-service education emphasize simulations, gaming, laboratory training, study groups, organization development, and other group approaches. These latter approaches are considered in subsequent chapters.

FOCUS ON THE INDIVIDUAL

As suggested, there are numerous ways to approach in-service education with a focus on the individual as distinguished from focusing on a problem, a program, or an institutional need. Clinical supervision, as promoted by the work of Cogan (15), Goldhammer (24), Boyan and Copeland (13), and others, has provided carefully developed and highly structured approaches to consider. In contrast, interest in independent study remains high, especially among college and university staffs where the tradition of the sabbatical and self-directed learning is strong (56). Increasingly, however, more highly structured approaches to self-directed learning have emerged in the form of learning packets (55), programmed material, computer-assisted instruction (7, 25), and individual growth planning (27).

Some of the oldest approaches to training are highly personalized and tend to be neglected even though they are among the most carefully validated approaches. Some of these include intervisitation (30:84), field trips, internships, and on-the-job training involving directed practice. Hence, when we think about personalized training for in-service staff development, it is important to consider a rather broad array of alternatives.

Learning Is Always Personal

There are strengths and limitations inherent in any approach to training. One of the most obvious realities that makes personalization so promising is a fact about learning: it is always a highly personal thing. It occurs within the individual — nowhere else. It occurs in highly individual ways with unique sequence, timing, and processes involved.

The personal nature of learning is most directly recognized, perhaps, in efforts to assess individual needs in rather precise ways. The Georgia De Kalb County Schools' efforts at elaborate assessment of competence is one illustration (17). Theodore Parsons (49) as well as Michael Evans et al. (19) and Ben M. Harris (30:292–93) have emphasized "guided self-analysis" as an obviously personalized way of assessing training needs in which the individual is not only the focus of assessment but also the primary instrument. These rigorous efforts to diagnose needs in highly personal ways need to be sharply distinguished from *opinion polls* that are so popular. Needs assessment studies often rely on opinion survey technology, but they make assumptions that extend far beyond those of the political pollsters. The use of opinionnaire data as though such responses were stable, rational, and precise, provide fragile bases upon which to make individual training decisions.

The focus on the individual and the identification of those unique learnings that need to be facilitated are greatly complicated by consideration of the person within a situational context. So long as individual needs for training are viewed egocentrically, the highly clinical approaches seem to make sense. However, Mager and Pipe (40) and Freiberg (21) are among these who stress situational factors of various kinds. Mager and Pipe emphasize motivational constraints that must be recognized. Freiberg argues for relating "teacher concerns, stated needs, and community and institutional needs" (21:58–59) in programs of in-service training. However, these may all be quite inconsistent one with another. Sergiovanni has proposed ways of looking at personal needs for in-service training by contrasting the "public" versus the "performance platform" of the individual. He points out that what teachers espouse as appropriate performance and believe that they are doing may in fact be very different from that which they can demonstrate to others.* Indeed, Hardebeck (26) demonstrated such discrepancies in his study of individualizing classroom teaching practices.

The view of learning, via in-service education, as a very personal phenomenon is not in dispute. The problem for planners of training is to avoid the overly simple conclusion that personalization equates with complete freedom — even license — to make in-service education a completely personal operation. In fact, as personal as the learning outcome must be, the inputs are social and institutional as well as personal. The same must be recognized for process. The challenge is to provide experiences for learning that are not just productive, since all experience will result in some learning. The character of the in-service education must be shaped to provide the most learning, of the most appropriate kinds, as determined by a congruence of personal and institutional needs. Exhibit 6–1 suggests ways of utilizing as many as four distinctly different perceptions that reflect both personal and institutional priorities.

The four perceived needs include two that focus on the individual and two that focus on the organization. One of each utilizes an *internal* frame of reference, and one of each employs an *external* frame of reference. Where three or four of these perceptions are congruent, an obvious priority can be presumed.

Change and the Individual

In-service education in whatever form is uniquely associated with change process. By definition, all the purposes of in-service education are related to promoting change in the individual. However, Chapter I discusses at length the importance of recognizing change process as multifaceted, and not exclusively a matter of education or training. Furthermore, in-service education in its most effective forms inevitably relates to the larger context of

---

* Based on a presentation by Thomas J. Sergiovanni at the National Curriculum Study Institute, by the Association for Supervision and Curriculum Development at Phoenix, Arizona, November 1976.

Exhibit 6–1.   NEEDS FOR IN-SERVICE EDUCATION PRIORITIZED VIA CONGRUENCE OF PERCEPTIONS

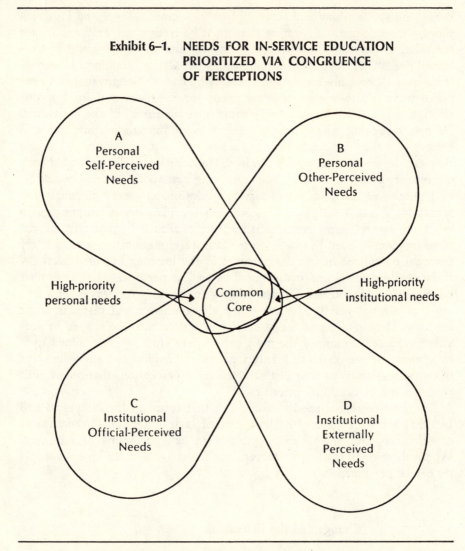

A
Personal
Self-Perceived
Needs

B
Personal
Other-Perceived
Needs

High-priority
personal needs

Common
Core

High-priority
institutional needs

C
Institutional
Official-Perceived
Needs

D
Institutional
Externally
Perceived
Needs

Based on discussions with Dr. N. Grant Tubbs and other staff members of the Virginia State Department of Education, Richmond, Virginia, September 7, 1978.

the school, college, or program in which the individual staff member performs.

The reader may wish to refer to Chapter I to the discussion of in-service education assumptions (see Exhibit 1–1) and also to Vignette 3, which describes the high school language arts team. Ann, the reading specialist, as a member of that team was off at a seminar or conference, pursuing her needs and interests in the teaching of reading. If she returns with new performance capabilities, how will she put them to work? Will her teammates encourage, discourage, or frustrate her efforts? If she is able to *change* her performance in some ways that are desirable from her *personal* point of view, will those changes be compatible with practices of others on her team? Is it possible that her learning resulting in new performance could conceivably even reduce the effectiveness or cohesion of the team?

Change process has been widely studied as an organizational phenomenon. But organizations are people, and much too little attention is given to the problem of making an array of individual personal changes add up to an innovation or improvement of substance in program. In fact, many theorists argue that educators' emphasis on the individual is misplaced. Gaynor (23:30) points out that in contrast with the views of Rogers and Shoemaker (54) and other rural sociologists, "People operating as members of organizations are simply not as free as independent entrepreneurs . . . to implement significant innovations" (23:31).

As salient as this caution is, it can easily lead to preoccupation with the organization rather than with the many individuals who give the school its character. Berman and McLaughlin (6), for instance, in a report on federal program outcomes, emphasize that "the amount of planning seemed less important than whether the quality of planning matched the needs of the project *and its participants* [italics added]" (6:19). Similarly, Fullan and Pomfret (22) review a variety of studies indicating the close relationship between amount of training and the fidelity of implementation of new programs and their effects on student learning. Carol Lukas (39) also reports that "the level of implementation varied substantially among sites implementing the same model" (39:115). However, she also reports that "most of the differences . . . are among teachers *within* sites" (39:117). In a nutshell, we have strong reason to personalize and individualize training, but we cannot lose sight of the organizational context to which the training applies as offering constraining but also as facilitating influences.

Gordon Lawrence and his colleagues at University of Florida summarize their findings from an analysis of ninety-seven separate, well-evaluated studies of in-service education (38). They found that:

1. Programs that have differentiated training experience for different teachers are more effective.
2. Programs offering teachers opportunities to choose goals and activities are more effective.
3. Self-directed training activities, while rare, tend to be successful.

However, they also found that:

4. Programs that linked the individual activities to a larger organizational effort were also more effective. (38:14–15)

Individual Designs

Several designs for personalized training are discussed in subsequent sections of this chapter. Some are highly individual oriented, and others provide for individualization even though the activities are not essentially individual in nature.

Clinical supervision programs are generally designed to be highly individual oriented. They begin with an individual and are controlled and/or guided on an individual basis. Independent study programs, study or travel leaves (14:33), intervisitations, internships, and related field study programs are often designed as highly individual undertakings. In such programs the client is an individual, the goals and objectives may be highly idiosyncratic, and the activities and sequences are tailored to the individual, with minor variations. Even the level and amount of active involvement of the client tends to be a highly personal matter.

Of the various highly individual approaches, programmed instruction in the form of programmed packets or computer-assisted instruction tend to give less freedom to the individual client. However, they remain individualistic in nature, requiring a careful match between the unique needs of the individual and the programmed objectives and activities that are designed.

Some designs for in-service programs allow for highly personalized training but do not call for isolating the individual so completely as those just discussed. Berman and Usery (5) cooperatively developed and collaboratively implemented individual growth programs that can be designed to respond to individual needs in ways that bring the individual into a variety of interactions with others. Field trips, demonstrations, field study projects, and even study leaves can be designed as group experiences in which personal needs in congruence with those of others, and in congruence with institutional priorities, can be addressed.

CLINICAL SUPERVISION

Clinical approaches to in-service education are becoming widely utilized. This type of program has its origins in some very old concepts of supervision. A single supervisor observes teaching and then sits down with the individual teacher to help with rethinking and replanning the lessons for the next day. Haskew (33) advocated a more carefully structured approach to overcome some of the abuses and inconsistencies that developed as rural programs were moved into urban settings. Goldhammer (24) and Cogan (15) were responsible for the early testing and more careful formulation of a "clinical cycle." Their work represented a synthesis of techniques drawn from nondirective counseling (53), studies of interviewing (43), microteaching (47), and analysis of instruction technologies being developed during the 1960s.

In his early work and writing about clinical supervision (16), Cogan was concerned primarily with interning teachers and the kind of supervision "master teachers" could provide. Four "levels of supervision" were distinguished as: (1) the inventory of events, (2) the anecdotal account, (3) the pattern of events, and (4) the constructive program (16:22–25). The emphasis of this approach was on observation of performance and a follow-up conference focusing on "the objective facts . . . as the base line" (16:24–25). In their later writings, both Goldhammer and Cogan formalized the clinical process while moving toward a less directive approach as far as interpersonal relationships are concerned.

The Basic Model

Various programs and plans for clinical supervision have much in common. They tend to be uniformly represented by a prescribed set of steps, stages, or processes, which are represented as follows with only minor variations in detail:

The Preobservation Conference
The Observation and Data Collection
The Analysis and Strategy Session
The Follow-up Conference
The Postconference Analysis

Various writers specify events to be included in each of these five stages somewhat differently, but each step tends to be a fairly distinct part of the total process.

The preobservation conference is a time for "negotiating" (4:4), for planning and establishing agreements on the focus of the observation (48). Morgan and Champagne (44) emphasize "agreement to focus on one or two issues" (44:2). Harty and Ritz (23) emphasize "collaboratively determined what kinds of problem will be considered." Reavis argues for the preconference as an opportunity to "establish or re-establish rapport, to get an orientation . . . , to receive information, . . . to suggest minor changes . . . , and to develop a contract, . . . an agreement" (23:361).

The observation and data-gathering process may range from rather systematic, well-instrumented procedures to relatively casual note taking. Anderson and Snyder recommend audiotape or videotape recording along with "separate notes" (4:7). Reavis suggests that the data consist only of verbatim verbal exchanges (50:361). Harty and Ritz propose that observers "make written notes" (32:18), while Cogan (16) and Berman (5:28) both argue for a more systematically sequenced set of descriptive notations. Morgan and Champagne emphasize the need to "limit" the focus to the behaviors of students and teachers that are related to preobservation agreements (44:3). Strom is one among a growing number seeking to make observations more clearly objective as well as focused to provide specific feedback on "teach intentions" in relation to actual performance (60:97–98). Acheson and Hansen (2) report rather elaborate data-gathering techniques for assuring objectivity and specificity of feedback.

The analysis and strategy stage in the commonly accepted cycle is generally not well defined by writers in this field. Obviously, the kind of data gathered will influence the analysis techniques selected. Furthermore, data and analysis procedures will greatly influence strategies that can be employed. The search for recurring patterns is stressed by Cogan in his earlier work (16), and he has urged such formal systems of analysis as those developed by Flanders (20) for use in verbal interaction analysis (50:361). When sequential narratives of events are employed, only the most demanding forms of content analysis are likely to be particularly useful.

Studies by Boyan and Copeland (13) confirm the serious difficulty still being faced with the implementation of this analytical stage of the cycle. Speaking of trainees undergoing rigorous experiences designed to assure their skill in clinical practice, the researchers conclude "that analysis of the teaching act is a complex and confounding activity" (13:29).

The follow-up conference is carefully detailed by Morgan and Champagne (44), among others, as a twelve-step process outlined below:

1. Specifying objectives.
2. Reviewing data related to objectives.
3. Selecting a focus.
4. Agreeing on the need for change.
5. Reinforcing some aspect of current practice.
6. Suggesting alternative practices.
7. Selecting an alternative practice.
8. Planning for implementing selected change.
9. Practicing new behaviors or procedures.
10. Agreeing on criteria of success for the new practice.

11. Getting feedback from the client regarding the conference.
12. Reviewing plans and commitments.*

These steps or stages provide a useful guide emphasizing the importance attached to the postobservation conference by those advocating clinical supervision. Obviously, this may be a rather protracted conference. In fact, several sessions may well be required and the "practicing" prescribed in step 9 may well occur in a different place and context from those utilized for the other conference activities. Acheson and Hansen have developed one of the most useful guides to this stage, suggesting specific techniques and cautions (2:96–115).

Postconference analysis is incorporated as step 12 in the proposals of Morgan and Champagne. Berman describes this as the "post-mortem" (5:29). It appears to be an effort to convey to the client that critical analysis of performance is appropriate for all — not just for teachers.

Recent Refinements

The clinical cycle described here has made its greatest contribution to in-service education by providing for a systematic, sequential, and logical pattern of experience for the client trainee. While much is written about rapport, nondirectiveness, acceptance, and a helping relationship in the clinical process, these do not give it a unique place among approaches to in-service education. It is the systematic sequence of events that is unique. In Cogan's words, it is "a system of supervision with enough weight to have impact and with the precision to hit the target" (15:ix).

Boyan (13), Melink and Sheehan (42), and Harris (30) have all proposed substantial variations to the more commonly accepted clinical cycle discussed above. Each of these writers has attempted to add still further to the "impact" and the "precision" of the earlier models.

The Boyan-Copeland Scheme departs very little from the traditional. Instead of five stages, eight steps are specified, however:

I. Preobservation Conference.
1. Behaviorally define area of concern.
2. Decide to obtain a base rate
    or
    Set a performance criterion.
3. Select an observation instrument.

II.   Observation.
    4.   Observe the specified behaviors.
III. Analysis and Identification of Change.
    5.   Analyze the observation results.
    6.   Identify behaviors needing maintenance or change.
IV. Postobservation Conference.
    7.   Feed back the results.
    8.   Determine strategies.
Recycle.

While this set of procedures is not basically different, it does give greater emphasis to formal observation (step 3) and tends to be more explicit about the leader's responsibility for diagnosis, based on data analysis (step 6).

Harris's three-loop clinical model emphasizes complementary activities to be related to the "basic cycle" without any effort to change the latter (30:148–50). This model proposes additional steps or stages in somewhat independent activity loops, as follows:

0.   Pre-conference planning.
1.   Teaching.
2.   Observing.
3.   Analyzing ⎯⎯⎯⟶ 3a.   Securing other related data.
4.   Feedback ⟵⎯⎯⎯ 3b.   Analyzing other data.
5.   Interpreting and diagnosing ⎯⟶ 5a.   Providing training experiences.
6.   Planning for implementing change. ⟵⎯⎯⎯
7.   Trial.
Recycle.

The inclusion of other kinds of data is advocated to provide a better basis for interpretation and diagnosis than a single observation is likely to provide. The limited reliability of any single observation makes reliance on such data unwise. However, if prior observation data, student report data, teacher self-report data, or even student achievement scores or grades have any relevance, they could be utilized to great advantage.

The other significant contribution in Harris's model may be found in the expectation that specific training experiences will be provided *in addition* to those of the clinical cycle itself. A severe limitation is imposed upon the clinical model when only conferencing activities are experienced by the client. When new skills or concepts or attitudes need to be developed, other training activities may well be essential. This is especially urgent in psychomotor learning where guided practice is very important, especially in the initial stages of learning to utilize a new technique or procedure. Furthermore, "guidance becomes more effective as task complexity is increased" (59:487). Young and Deming (62) refer to training as an integral part of the conference: "the supervisor teaches the teacher the specified behavior and how to incorporate it in his instruction" (62:14). This appears to be a needlessly restrictive view of the process.

The Teaching Improvement Process designed by Melnik and Sheehan (42) may well be the most promising of the clinical models to date. Exhibit 6–2 represents an adaptation of a sequence of events with many more options for dealing realistically with the complexities faced in improving teaching practices. As complex as the flowchart makes the process appear, it is not a fundamental departure from the basic clinical model. However, the data collection is more realistic in attending to an array of possible data sources. The design of a specific improvement plan is seen as a process that often requires inputs from consultants and others who may not have been involved previously. Steps 7a and 7b give recognition to the fact that certain improvements may well be self-initiated while others require training or guided practices.

Strengths and Weaknesses

The strengths of the clinical approaches are substantial. The focus on the individual; the use of classroom reality as a point of departure; the utilization of counseling, observing, problem-solving, and evaluating techniques in a carefully sequenced design promise a great deal of experience impact for learning. Several weaknesses include those of economy, efficiency, and effectiveness. Undoubtedly, the clinical approach in any form — old or refined — demands large amounts of time by highly skilled clinicians. Those who argue that sensitive, competent teachers with limited training can guide clinical supervision processes are engaging in wishful thinking. Because of its potential impact, it may be that the costs are not prohibitive, but they certainly must be viewed as a limitation.

The inefficiencies inherent in the traditional clinical models might be overcome, in part, by incorporating group training activities as suggested by Harris (30:148–50) and Melnik and Sheehan (42). However, it seems entirely probable that much training for changing individual practices can be quite readily accomplished in small-group situations using approaches discussed in the next two chapters without resorting to clinical modes. Such group endeavors would certainly be more efficient in many instances.

The effectiveness question still needs to be addressed. Clinical approaches have demonstrated effectiveness with young, inexperienced personnel. They undoubtedly have promise for more seasoned teachers, too. However, it would be foolish to assume that all persons or all performance

Exhibit 6–2. FLOWCHART OF THE TEACHING IMPROVEMENT PROCESS

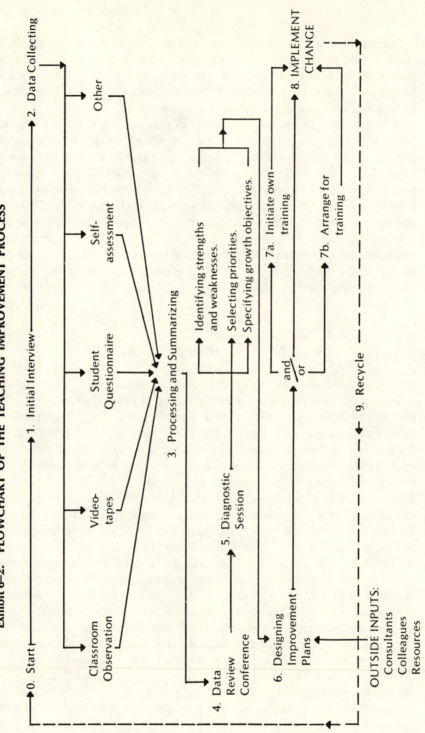

Adapted from Michael A. Melnik and Daniel S. Sheehan, "Clinic to Improve University Teaching," *Journal of Research and Development*

228

improvement needs can be effectively dealt with by this one approach. When teachers are unaware of, or unwilling to enter into, a contractual arrangement for clinical encounters, other approaches are surely required. When teachers are facing learning tasks that call for relatively unknown alternative practices — the highly innovative — it seems unlikely that clinical approaches will work.

INDIVIDUAL GROWTH PLANS

The use of collaborative diagnosis and planning models for individualizing in-service experiences has shown promise in recent years. Unlike the clinical models discussed in the last section, much more reliance is placed on independent activity, guided by a *growth plan*.

Growth-planning Sequence

The approach to individual growth planning takes various forms but can generally be described as a sequence of events as follows:

gathering of performance data
collaborative analysis and interpretation of data
identifying both strengths and weaknesses
selecting growth objectives
planning in-service experiences
implementing the plan
monitoring progress toward objectives
replanning and implementing as needed
recycling

Unique Features

The growth-planning process is highly personal and individual. It calls for close collaboration between the client and principal, supervisor, team leader, or facilitator. Performance data are also utilized. However, the learning experiences are not restricted to either the classroom setting or the conference. Classroom observation data are crucially important when the client is a teacher; however, various other kinds of data can also be utilized.

In this *individual growth-planning* model, it is not necessary to secure agreement on a problem or a need *in advance* of observing. The observation data are utilized as the basis for *collaboratively* diagnosing needs. This approach has several advantages over the clinical approach. For one thing, the entire process begins on an objective data base. Second, analysis interpretation and diagnosis are collaboratively accomplished. Diagnosis focuses on *both* strengths and weaknesses. A final advantage is found in the fact that strengths and weaknesses *both* emerge from the data rather than from opinions.

Plans for Action

The process of individual growth planning to implement a program of experiences to promote growth provides a great deal of flexibility. Specific growth objectives are selected in terms of the urgency of needs, the time available, and the resources that can be allocated. The plan of action can be as elaborate and diverse or as simple and restricted as the individual need and situation require.

The Planning Document

Appendix G includes an illustration of an individual professional growth plan as a formal planning document. The use of some kind of document has advantages over planning that relies on memory. The planning document serves to bring the data together in summary form, as the basis for the plan of action. It also clearly documents strengths and weaknesses or limitations in performances that usually extend beyond the plan of action itself. This is to say that, while strengths are not in need of in-service training, they do need to be recognized, reinforced, and documented for various reasons. Similarly, an ample array of data regarding performances will yield many needs for improvement when thoroughly analyzed. It is rarely practical to plan for improvements of many kinds simultaneously. When a few specific needs have been selected for individual growth planning, the document should provide a record of those growth needs *not* selected. This permits recycling of the growth planning process without necessarily gathering new data or engaging in new analysis and diagnosis.

Growth-planning Illustration

Remember Bill Thompson, sixth-grade "core" teacher at the end of his first year? (See Chapter I, Vignette 1) Had his principal been observing systematically in his classroom or utilizing any self-assessment or student report instruments with Bill, the *end-of-the-year* conference could have been the *beginning* of a growth plan for better teaching and more satisfaction as a teacher. Here is a scenario to depict such a process:

March 15: Principal confers with Bill Thompson on contract renewal. Bill brings his self-assessment report. The principal has already reviewed his observation records for the past three observations in Bill's classroom. The principal also has a set of student descriptions of classroom practices that match the self-assessment report.

In their conference, the main activity is *studying* the three kinds of information — looking for agreements, consistencies, patterns, and discrepancies. Prior to this, the principal has made clear to Bill his intention to recommend his reemployment; hence, that is not an issue. However, as the full range of data are shared, analyzed, interpreted, and discussed for possible *growth implications*, the principal adjourns the conference without any decision making. "Let's get school closed now. Keep all of this under your hat. I'll turn in my recommendation for reemployment on the assumption that you can do even better next year. When you get your new contract in April or May, let's sit down together again. We'll work out a *growth plan* to guide us both for the next year."

May 15: The principal sees Bill in the office and asks if his contract came through from the personnel office. Since he gets an affirmative answer, they set a date for a growth-planning conference. A sample of a well-developed growth plan is sent to Bill the next day with a note attached: "Bill: Look this over along with your notes from our previous conference. Come in and use the data in your file if you want to. Don't try to make decisions; just consider possibilities. See you four to five o'clock, June 3."

June 3, 4:00 p.m.: Bill Thompson and his principal review the data summary prepared previously. The principal has prepared two copies of the *Individual Professional Growth Plan* by Ben M. Harris (see Appendix G) through *step 2 only*. They begin to discuss step 3, "Reviewing Cumulative Data." Agreements are readily reached on "essential and desirable aspects" of teaching reflected in the data. These agreements are *recorded* very explicitly:

"Shows enthusiasm for the subject and for his work with students by frequent smiling, highly energetic presenting, and helping. Withholds negative reactions, is accepting of students' ideas, and incorporates them into the lesson."

Describing practices "most in need of modification" is more difficult (step 3b). Bill volunteers several possibilities: "I need to find better room arrangements. Also, I need to make more library assignments." The principal listens, nods, and suggests another look at the data. He asks about the fact that relatively little evidence from any source (observer, students, or self) indicates "use of a variety of activities that give students multisensory experience or active involvement opportunities." Bill agrees. "Yeh. That's a problem, all right. But, gosh! That's going to take some doing."

The principal nods. "Sure. But maybe there are some small parts of that important cluster of practices that might be worthy of attention this coming year."

"What do you suggest?" Bill asks.

"Well, what makes sense to you?" He pauses. Bill looks perplexed.

"One approach to a variety of activities involves using role playing. Another is using media — sixteen-millimeter films, tapes, and so on — especially on an individual or small-group basis. Still other possibilities include class discussions, peer-tutoring arrangements, small-group projects that are action oriented, independent study projects, and using games."

"Wow! Now I'm confused. There is so much to be learned. I need to be doing all those things, don't I!" exclaims Bill.

"Well, not necessarily, but they are a few practices many teachers have found highly useful," the principal responds.

"Let me get started on the use of media. That's concrete and practical. I think I can handle that and would like to try," Bill proposes.

"That makes sense, Bill," the principal says, encouragingly. "How do you see your growth there? Can you describe several specific practices you think you could learn to incorporate into your teaching?"

"Well, I'd start using films. I haven't made use of more than one or two this year," Bill replies.

"Are you saying your *growth* would consist of making use of more sixteen-millimeter films in the coming year?" asks the principal.

"That doesn't seem very ambitious, does it?" Bill responds in a contemplative way.

"Well, more is not necessarily better, I suspect," the principal answers. "Let me try a statement of an objective out on you, to see what you think. Let's write it out on scratch paper to consider." The principal takes a pad and writes:

1. To improve and extend the variety of audiovisual media utilized regularly in the classroom, by:
   a. Making use of at least three different kinds of AV materials.
   b. Making use of AV materials on an individual or small-group basis.
   c. Using each media item as an integral part of a lesson involving introductory activities, student participation, and follow-up activities.

"Can you visualize yourself doing these kinds of things next year, with some assistance in the form of training?" the principal asks.

Bill furrows his brow. He doesn't respond for a few seconds. Then he says, "I'd need some help. I'm not quite sure how to do some of those things." He continues to look a bit worried.

The principal smiles, leans back in his chair, and says, "Of course you'll need help! If you knew how to do these things, I'd be worried about your *not* doing them. That's what *growth planning* and in-service education are all about — to help you learn to do things better or differently is the name of the game."

Bill laughs. The principal looks at his watch. "Bill, it's getting late. You need to go home, and I do too. Let me suggest one more objective for you, and then we'll get together to review, revise, and add others if appropriate. We also need to make plans for giving you that help.

"Another objective that would be closely related to the one we are considering might be expressed as follows." The principal writes it out on the scratch paper:

2. To lead total class and small-group discussions, using an array of questioning and other leadership skills to facilitate full participation and student-to-student interaction, with a high degree of task orientation.

"Don't try to react to this one at this time. Let's both think about it and see if we can make plans that are realistic in providing you with the help you'll need. How about June 8? School will be over. We could spend nine to eleven that morning on this. Okay?"

These episodes reflect at least some of the processes and steps required to generate a fully developed individual growth plan such as the one illustrated in Appendix G. Of course, even after step 4 is completed, the review process outlined in step 5 requires still another series of conferences or interviews.

Strengths and Weaknesses

Individual growth planning has strengths not unlike those of clinical supervision. A careful sequence of events is logically prescribed. A cooperative, collaborative relationship is maintained. Objective performance, not opinions, is the focus. In addition, the individual growth-planning approach appears to have strengths in securing fuller involvement of the client in various aspects of the data analysis, interpretation, and diagnosis processes. This approach offers much flexibility in the variety and kinds of data utilized and in the training activities that can be incorporated into the plan of action.

Weaknesses include some that are shared with clinical approaches. A willingness to participate on the part of the client may not always be a reality. Heavy reliance is placed on both client and leader to be objective analysts and diagnosticians, and Boyan's (13) studies indicate that this is difficult to bring into being. The cost of this approach is still quite high in terms of staff time. Furthermore, only highly skilled consultants are likely to be very effective in this process involving data analysis, diagnostic interpretations, and detailed planning.

DIAGNOSTIC/PRESCRIPTIVE MODELS

Along with the growing interest in clinical and individual growth planning, concerns have emerged about the diagnostic processes inevitably required. A spin-off of this interest in diagnostic analysis has been the development of diagnostic/prescriptive models. Diagnosis can be separated from prescription, but linking these processes to each other logically and operationally has been an intriguing possibility. Individualized reading programs, individually prescribed programs in arithmetic, and diagnostic/prescriptive efforts for handicapped children all have given encouragement to similar approaches in in-service education. Competency-based teacher education programs have also been struggling with diagnostic/prescriptive models.

Since none of these efforts, working with relatively simple diagnosis of tasks, has been singularly successful, in-service program leaders should be cautious, at least, in employing such approaches. Furthermore, situational variables, including teacher characteristics, seem to be very influential in determining outcomes.

The several interesting diagnostic/prescriptive models developed have not been widely tested, but they have the capacity at least to suggest some logical ways of thinking about the translation of diagnosed needs into in-service training experiences.

The Mager-Pipe Model *

An elaborate logical, analytical sequence of decision alternatives has been presented by Robert Mager and Peter Pipe (40), with specific reference to determining how to deal with a "performance discrepancy" (40:61–69).

Their analytical model is especially useful in clearly designating an array of alternative approaches to any given discrepancy. Furthermore, the model includes *nontraining* alternatives, emphasizing that not all problems of non-performance or inappropriate performance are amenable to education or training.

A simplified scheme reflecting much of the thinking of Mager and Pipe is shown here. It is largely self-explanatory, consisting of a simple series of logical decisions in response to diagnostic questions.

* An abbreviated outline based on *Analyzing Performance Problems*, by Robert F. Mager and Peter Pipe. Copyright © 1970 by Fearon-Pitman Publishers, Inc., Belmont, California. Reprinted by permission.

1. Is there a performance discrepancy that has been clearly described?
   a. Yes — continue to 2   b. No — no further action!

2. Is the performance discrepancy described an important one?
   a. Yes — continue to 3   b. No — ignore it.

3. Is the discrepancy a skill deficiency?
   a. Yes — continue to 4.   b. No — skip to 7.

4. If yes, it is a skill deficiency, did the individual previously perform well?
   a. Yes — continue to 5.   b. No — continue to 6.

5. If yes, he or she used to perform well, was it used often?
   a. Yes — *then* arrange for feed-   b. No — *then* arrange for opportuni-
   back to encourage continued   ties for practice with some guid-
   use, give assurances that the   ance as needed, and then reinforce.
   performance is valued, etc.

6. If no, he or she did not perform well in the past — *then* arrange for formal
   training to provide opportunities to know, do, and apply the skill.

7. If no, the deficiency is not a skill deficiency, then consider alternative causes
   and related *non-training* courses of action:
   a. Performance is nonrewarding,   *Remove* punishment or *add* rewards.
   even punishing in its conse-
   quences?
   b. Nonperformance is more re-   *Remove* reward for nonperformance *or*
   warding?   *add* more reward for positive perform-
   ance.
   c. Does the desired performance   *Provide* feedback to reinforce desirable
   really matter? Does anyone   consequence.
   really care?
   d. Are there just too many ob-   *Remove* obstacles *or* provide assistance
   stacles in the way that inhibit   in overcoming them.
   performance?

8. If decisions reached seem too complicated, is a simpler approach needed?
   a. Yes — *then* consider simplify-   b. No — *then* proceed to 9.
   ing or changing the nature of
   the job.

9. If she or he lacks potential for responding to the solution alternatives that
   have been presented, *then* terminate employment.

10. Select best solution and implement.

The De Kalb Supportive Supervision Model

A system of diagnostic assessment of new teachers was field tested in De Kalb County Schools in Georgia as a competency-based, highly individualized effort. A three-member "assessment team" was assigned to each teacher to produce a diagnostic profile of competency levels based on the gathering and synthesizing of the data, derived from observations, tests, inventories, interviews, and the like. Once the diagnostic assessment process was completed, a new team, *the support team*, was appointed to make use of the diagnostic profile and related data and to plan and implement improvement efforts with the teacher. The support team was generally composed of the teacher's principal, a central staff supervisor, and a classroom teacher released part-time to assist with team activities.

The procedures followed by the support team varied but were essentially like those that were described for individual growth planning. The basic sequence was outlined as follows:

assessment data received
organizational conference of the support team members
preplanning conference with the teacher
developing a plan of action ("Support Plan")
implementation
postconference with teacher to evaluate support plan
recycling, if necessary

The "Support Plan" was prepared using a standard form not unlike the *Individual Professional Growth Plan* discussed earlier. The entire system is unique in only two respects: (1) a fully developed subsystem for diagnostic assessment was developed; and (2) formally organized teams were utilized to direct assessment and support activities. Berman and Usery (5:27–29) describe a similar "supervisory team" pilot study using purely clinical techniques. However, the De Kalb County program was in no way restricted to clinical techniques, but the team assessment procedures were highly developed and much more extensive than most.

Several problems emerged as a result of the first two years of piloting this approach.* One problem identified by the staff was the time lag between the readiness for "support" on the part of the teachers and the availability of a full-blown diagnostic profile. Another problem was that of coordination of a team of three busy people in their efforts to assist a single teacher. Other problems shared in common with all individual approaches to in-service education include getting clients to accept assistance, the high

* Based on discussions with project staff personnel and this author in Atlanta, Georgia, December 1976.

cost of staff, and the isolation of the individual from a peer group that might be supportive.

Despite the problems faced by the De Kalb County Schools staff in making this model operationally viable, it must be recognized for its developmental contributions. Some of the difficulties might readily be overcome with further design and testing efforts. For instance, if competency assessment even of rather elaborate kinds could become systematized as an ongoing process, then the support team might draw upon the data at any point for guidance in planning its improvement activities. A computer-based system for providing a diagnostic profile on any teacher at any point in time would surely facilitate the implementation of this model and eliminate some of the wasteful procedures weakening other models.

Platform Analysis

A set of analytical, diagnostic procedures has been suggested by Thomas Sergiovanni * in relation to his concern for discrepancies in the public versus the performance "platforms" of teachers. The basic concept is a simple one. People tend to have a set of beliefs, ideals, convictions, and perceptions about themselves as individual practitioners. When we see an individual in operation, we observe performances that permit us to infer congruence or incongruence between *belief* and *practice*. Sergiovanni and Simon argue for utilizing these discrepancies as a focus for analysis of performance using videotape analysis (57, 58). Exhibit 6–3 shows the Johari Window diagram for this kind of analysis. Four different relationships between teacher knowledge of self and supervisor knowledge of teacher are shown and designated as A — Blindness (supervisor aware but teacher is not), B — Public Sector (both are aware), C — Unknown (neither are aware), and D — Private Sector (teacher aware but supervisor is not).

Let's assume that the public sector can be approached in a straightforward way. The blindness area presents a special problem, as does the private sector. Obviously, the unknown area could be full of problems, too. Focusing on A — Blindness, the problem is defined, two alternate diagnoses are considered, and a strategy or plan of action is specified for each. Similarly, if the problem seems to be in D — Private Sector, where information is being withheld from the supervisor, a set of three alternative diagnoses and strategies can be considered.

To the extent that this way of analyzing a relationship is valid, it pro-

* Based on a presentation before the National Curriculum Study Institute (ASCD) on "Instructional Supervision" by Thomas Sergiovanni, Phoenix, Arizona, November 1976. T. J. Sergiovanni, "Reforming Teacher Evaluation: Naturalistic Alternatives, *Educational Leadership* 34, no. 8 (May 1977), also makes reference to this idea.

Exhibit 6–3.   **PLATFORM ANALYSIS AND PROBLEM DIAGNOSIS**

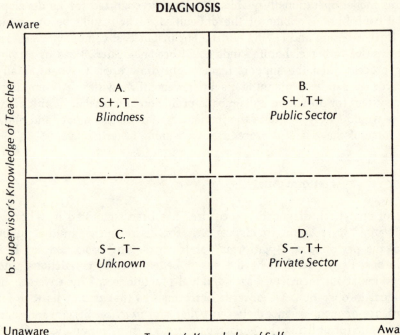

Aware

A.
S+, T−
Blindness

B.
S+, T+
Public Sector

C.
S−, T−
Unknown

D.
S−, T+
Private Sector

b. *Supervisor's Knowledge of Teacher*

Unaware   a. *Teacher's Knowledge of Self*   Aware

A.   *Blindness*
Problem: Teacher not aware of the facts of performance that others have.
Diagnoses:
1.   Feedback neglect. Teacher has no access to appropriate feedback. *Or*
2.   Communications block. Teacher ignores appropriate feedback.
Strategy:
1.   Supervisor must provide feedback.
2.   Supervisor must make information more recognizable, more easily understood, and less threatening. Clinical self-analysis, using videotapes, might be useful. Similarly, microteaching with peers analyzing performance may be useful.

D.   *Private Sector*
Problem: Teacher is aware of performance, but supervisor is not. Teacher does *not* share information. Supervisor is not fully able to understand.
Diagnoses:
1.   Concealment. Teacher feels uncomfortable, worried, anxious, and tries to cover up.
2.   Feedback neglect. Opportunities for, and provisions of, mutual sharing have not been made.

Exhibit 6–3 continued

3. Naiveté. Teacher doesn't understand the importance or relevance of the information.

Strategy:

1. Supervisor must build trust, demonstrate helpfulness. Attend to less sensitive performances while building trust.
2. Supervisor must arrange for exploratory conversations, allowing teacher more opportunities to talk. Group-sharing sessions may be useful.
3. Supervisor must arrange for teacher to consider a full array of performances that might be relevant. Intervisitation with other teachers, awareness-building laboratory sessions, and clinical self-analysis need to be provided.

---

vides leadership personnel — principal, supervisor, or others — with a basis for planning in-service training activities that are highly personalized. The anxious, worried teacher is not treated as being naive. Simple awareness needs are treated as simple feedback problems and are not overblown. Similarly, feedback neglect can be economically handled by providing opportunities for more dialogue, but serious communications blocks are not treated lightly.

CONSULTATION, CONFRONTATION, AND ADVICE

Despite the long history of independent study and self-directed learning (37), some form of intervention is nearly always associated with these efforts (60:94). The character of the interventions range widely, from text material in programmed format to various styles of interviewing and consultation. The various advocates in behalf of some human intervenor are often highly apologetic and cautiously urge "providing assistance to teachers only when . . . requested by them" (35:2). Manolakes (41) more boldly contends that "they do not require coercion or direction from outside authority" (41:52). However, an adviser role of considerable force is still proposed. Borg et al. (9) was among those in the recent past who strongly advocated self-supervision by training the individual to record, analyze, and modify his or her own behavior. Morse and Davis (45) found such self-analysis not very effective in comparison with a skilled nondirective feedback agent. Resick (51) also found that feedback from another individual is an important part of the process of improving instruction. Various studies of systematic versus unsystematic feedback indicated that the former was more influential in producing results.

These and numerous other studies that might be cited seem consistently to point toward the use of interviews, consultations, and advisory relationships in promoting individual performance changes.

The Interview as Basic Technique

The interview is most widely referred to as the *conference* in educational circles. Clinical supervision, individual growth planning, and diagnostic/prescriptive models all call upon the face-to-face interaction of the interview. Interviewing is a technique for communicating both verbally and nonverbally. The heavy influence of counseling therapy (53) on the thinking of educators has emphasized two-way interaction and nondirective techniques in interviewing.

The use of interviewing in other behavioral sciences often calls for *information-gathering* as well as *information-giving* interviews that may not be highly interactive in nature. Even when nondirective techniques are most appropriate to our purposes of in-service education, it may well be useful to recognize that Rogerian techniques were developed and tested primarily for therapeutic purposes where the content was essentially that of feelings. Substantial departures from these techniques may be quite appropriate when information sharing, analyzing objective data, describing events, planning, and decision making are in progress.

The basic skills of interviewing, regardless of the particular approach, include questioning, listening, and nonverbal interacting. Acevedo, Elliott, and Valverde (1) suggest still other techniques of special use in lesson analysis with a teacher. They suggest various responses, including *restating* an idea or question, making a *clarifying* statement, *reflecting* feelings, *summarizing*, and *suggesting*. Obviously, the problem of utilizing these various techniques in a patterned form of behavior that guides a productive interview is of special importance. Blumberg's (8) provocative study of supervisor interview behaviors from the teacher's perspective made clear the value of indirectness. Acheson and Hansen (2:97–98) suggest nine techniques for interviewers to employ, as follows:

1. Provide data.
2. Elicit feelings and opinions.
3. Ask for clarification.
4. Listen attentively.
5. Respond to substance of teacher's thoughts.
6. Avoid giving advice.
7. Provide specific reinforcement.

8. Provide for comparisons.
9. Probe for alternative explanations of ideas.

It is not suggested by these authors that this is a sequence of techniques, but it may well be useful to follow the first three in stepwise fashion.

Consultation

The term "consultation" has been widely utilized over the years in education, business, and the various social services. Generally, it has not been carefully defined but has tended to imply a broad range of assisting activities. Klopf (36) distinguishes consultation from training and counseling (36:1). He emphasizes many of the same processes found in counseling and interviewing, however: openness, clarification, listening, and so on. He argues for distinguishing consultation from dialogue, encounter, and confrontation. The unique elements of consultation appear to be in situational diagnosis, in facilitating goal and issue clarification, in making referrals for assistance, and in seeking solutions or approaches to problems out of the deliberations.

Regardless of specific roles, responsibilities, or ways of working, interest in consulting for in-service education purposes is widely expressed. Doyle (18) reports on a "faculty development" program at a large university that employs consultants as well as seminars, workshops, and design services. Borich and Sanders (10) report on effects of "consultant teams" in securing acceptance of innovative programs.

The Advisory/Helping Relationship

The "advisory system" is the term utilized by Manolakes (44) in describing the various consulting or advisory "functions." He describes the adviser as "seed planter," "technical helper," "personal support person," "expediter," and "informant and communication stimulator" (44:53–57). Beth Nelson (46) is no less ambitious in describing the responsibilities of the "helping teachers." Despite the euphemistic title, the duties are highly specific and demanding. They include a number of things: "leadership in instruction and curriculum improvement. . . . Coordinate the instructional program . . . assist in defining educational needs . . . a resource person and major contributor to staff morale. . . . Demonstrate . . . materials. . . . Establish inservice training" (46:76–77). This may well be more than a full job description. It certainly seems more like a field of endeavor than an approach, strategy, or mode of operation.

DIRECT FIELD EXPERIENCE

It would seem neglectful in any review of individualized or personalized approaches to in-service education to fail to briefly consider well-recognized field-based alternatives. Intervisitations, field trips and studies, "shadow" studies, and internships or job reassignments are all reputable though seldom-used approaches.

Intervisitations

The practice of providing opportunities for teachers and other staff members to visit other school organizations to observe others at work is one of the oldest supervisory activities. When well organized and planned to serve the specific interests and needs of an individual staff member, such visitations are apparently valuable experiences.

Harris (29) defined intervisitation with emphasis on the selection of situations, "for their close similarity to the situation of the visiting staff member" (29:543). In describing intervisitation in more complete detail in 1975, Harris emphasized distinctions between field trips and demonstrations and intervisiting. Compared with demonstrating, intervisiting is more highly individualized and more real (30:84).

While it is possible to think of intervisiting as simply a single experience that might be part of an individual growth plan, it could be much more. With a consultant making prior arrangements; observing with the visitor; leading a discussion with the staff members observed; perusing materials in use; analyzing lesson plans, schedules, and other documents, it could become a distinctive approach to guiding improved performances.

Field Trips and Studies

The field trip is usually employed for children. That is an unfortunate association, for staff members can gain from a variety of field trip experiences. The literature on the field trip as it relates to student learnings is readily available and should not need review here. However, short and extended trips into field environments different from those of the school may well be essential for certain attitudinal changes in staff personnel. They may also be essential if the knowledge base of the teacher, administrator, or curriculum specialist is to become broad enough to deal with problems of social relevance.

Trips to factories, laboratories, and mines, even if not accessible for student use, can provide science, mathematics, and vocational teachers with new concepts and knowledge for use in better teaching. Trips to a foreign country, to a black ghetto or a "barrio," and to remote village or reservation can provide teachers and other staff personnel with both insights and empathy.

The field trip is, like many approaches, suitable for both individuals and groups. However, as an unguided, passive experience it is not likely to have much value. Plans for such trips should be carefully detailed in advance, as with any other in-service program. Objectives should be specified, activities designated, and responsibilities for follow-up return clearly recognized.

Field studies are variations on field trips in that they take the form of some systematic mode of inquiry. Sometimes community opinion surveys can provide information about opinions and also provide firsthand experiences with people of different kinds. Living in with a family in another country to systematically study the language, customs, and culture can have an enormous impact on the visiting staff person.

The VISTA- and Peace Corps-type experiences suggest models for future use of field experience for in-service education that need development and testing. The impact of such extended live-in and work-with experiences has been fully recognized. The impact of modifications of these crudely designed programs, to focus on learning for participants, may be very great.

Shadowing Technique

The technique of following another person around, acting much like that person's shadow, has been usefully employed for both training and research. It has been most useful in understanding performance patterns of those staff persons who do not work in one specific observable location. While classroom teaching performance is easily studied using observation techniques, the busy principal, school social worker, nurse, supervisor, personnel director, and others move about to do their work. Their performance patterns may change drastically from one location to another. Accordingly, the "shadow" learns simply by following along, watching, recording events, and then having periodic discussions with the staff person being shadowed.

The strengths and weaknesses of this approach as in-service experience are not easily assessed. Undoubtedly, it will have greatest impact in combination with other related activities. It may well be that its utility is restricted to awareness levels of learning. Studies of the effects are needed.

Planned Reassignments

Internships and other forms of planned assignment to new job situations have long been advocated as among the most useful forms of in-service education. Unfortunately, they are not widely utilized as carefully planned training in education. When utilized, they are rarely evaluated for effect.

Internships can be distinguished from job reassignments by the circumstances that surround each. Internships are assignments to real job situations without expectation that the responsibilities of a *regular position* will be fulfilled. In contrast, job reassignments are real in the sense that the former incumbent is *not* present and the *intern* or *trainee* must assume full responsibilities.

Both internship and job reassignment approaches have the education and training of the individual as a primary purpose. The internship promotes training objectives of open-ended kinds, however. The intern can model the incumbent but can also create new roles and assignments for himself. The intern can enter into the real job situation and become deeply involved, but can also extricate himself when necessary. The intern can analyze, criticize, and make mistakes (within limits).

The reassignee on a new job for in-service training purposes enjoys few of the luxuries for learning that the intern does. However, assuming prerequisite skills and knowledges, or assistance in transferring and adapting old skills to the new situation, the trainee gains new experience, practices new or adapted skills, and develops broad understandings.

The internship is an expensive approach to training but can hardly be equaled by any other approach for effectiveness in developing complex performance patterns not previously exhibited. The internship probably is, therefore, perhaps most suitable for pretraining of those moving into new positions. Job reassignment, on the other hand, is relatively inexpensive and perhaps most effective in helping experienced staff members gain new understandings regarding the work of others and the relationships between staff assignments.

SUMMARY

Individual, personalized approaches to in-service education are numerous, currently very popular, and full of interesting potential. These same approaches are full of problems, with many unanswered questions. The problem of high cost for nearly all such in-service approaches demands careful selecting prior to use. Conversely, however, whenever approaches can demonstrate unusual experience impact for important changes in performance, cost factors should not hinder their use. Certainly, clinical supervision, growth-planning, and consultation programs under expert direction have demonstrated considerable promise.

New and more finely tuned approaches to individualized in-service education can and will be developed in the years ahead. What needs to be developed simultaneously is a better understanding of the unique and differentiated powers of each approach. Such understanding will make it possible to design programs for in-service education that incorporate a variety of individual and group approaches.

REFERENCES

*1. Acevedo, Mary A., Carol Elliott, and Leonard A. Valverde. *A Guide for Conducting an Effective Feedback Session.* Austin, Tex.: Department of Educational Administration, University of Texas, September 1976.

*2. Acheson, Keith A. and John H. Hansen. *Classroom Observations and Conferences with Teachers.* Tallahassee, Fla.: Teacher Education Project, 1973.

3. Alamo Heights Schools. *Professional Growth Planning Documents, 1975–76.* San Antonio, Tex.: Alamo Heights Independent School District, 1975.

4. Anderson, Robert H. and Karolyn J. Snyder. "Clinical Supervision Workshop." Presentation to the National Curriculum Study Institute, Arlington Park Hilton Hotel, July 11, 1978 (mimeo).

*5. Berman, Louis M. and Mary Lou Usery. *Personalized Supervision: Sources and Insights.* Washington, D.C.: Association for Supervision and Curriculum Development, National Education Association, 1966.

*6. Berman, Paul and M. W. McLaughlin. *Federal Programs Supporting Educational Change. Vol. 4. The Findings in Review.* Santa Monica, Calif.: The Rand Corporation, April 1975.

7. Bessent, E. Wailand et al. *A Computer Assisted Instruction Module. Vol. 1. Student Manual for Instructional Decision-Making.* Austin, Tex.: Special Education Supervisor Training Project, University of Texas, 1974.

8. Blumberg, Arthur, Wilford Weber, and Edmund Amidon. *Supervisor Interaction as Seen by Supervisors and Teachers.* A paper presented at the annual meeting of the American Educational Research Association, New York, February 1967. (ERIC ED 014–142).

9. Borg, Walter et al. "Videotape Feedback and Microteaching in a Teacher Training Model." Berkeley, Calif.: Far West Laboratory for Educational Research and Development, December 12, 1968 (mimeo).

10. Borich, Gary D. and J. Sanders. *The Effect of Educational Consultant Teams on the Acceptance of Innovations,* no. 2018. Austin, Tex.: Research and Development Center for Teacher Education, University of Texas, April 1972.

*11. Bosco, James J. "The Development and Evaluation of an Inservice Education Model to Develop Informal Individualized Learning." Kalamazoo,

* Suggested for further reading.

Mich.: Center for Educational Research, Western Michigan University, April 1975.

*12.   Boyan, Norman J. and Willis D. Copeland. *Instructional Supervision Training Program.* Columbus, Ohio: Charles E. Merrill, 1978.

*13.   Boyan, Norman J. and Willis D. Copeland. *A Training Program for Supervisor: Anatomy of an Educational Development.* Research Bulletin no. 2, Bureau of Educational Research and Development. Santa Barbara, Calif.: University of California, 1974.

14.   Centre for Educational Research and Innovation. *Recurrent Education: Trends and Issues.* Paris: OECD, 1975.

*15.   Cogan, Morris L. *Clinical Supervision.* Boston: Houghton Mifflin Company, 1973.

16.   Cogan, Morris L. *Supervision at the Harvard-Newton Summer School.* Cambridge, Mass.: Graduate School of Education, Harvard University, June 1961 (mimeo).

17.   De Kalb County Schools. *Performance-Based Certification Supportive Supervision Model.* Doraville, Ga.: De Kalb County Schools, 1975.

18.   Doyle, Kenneth O., Jr. "Instructional Development and Faculty Development at a Large University." A paper presented at the annual meeting of the American Educational Research Association, New York, 1977.

19.   Evans, Michael C., Ben M. Harris, and R. L. Palmer. *A Diagnostic Assessment System for Professional Supervisory Competencies.* Document no. 11. Austin, Tex.: Special Education Supervisor Training Project, University of Texas, 1975.

*20.   Flanders, Ned A. and Edmund Amidon. *The Role of the Teacher in the Classroom.* Minneapolis, Minn.: Paul S. Amidon Association, Inc., 1963.

*21.   Freiberg, H. J. "Continuing the Educational Process." *Journal of Continuing Education and Training* 3, no. 3–4 (Winter/Spring 1974): 173–78.

22.   Fullan, Michael and Allan Pomfret. "Research on Curriculum and Instruction Implementation." *Review of Educational Research* 47, no. 1 (Winter 1977): 335–97.

*23.   Gaynor, Alan K. "The Study of Change in Educational Organizations: A Review of the Literature." In *Educational Administration* by Lavern L. Cunningham, Walter G. Hack, and Raphael O. Nystrand. Berkeley, Calif.: McCutchan Publishing Company, 1977.

*24.   Goldhammer, Robert. *Clinical Supervision.* New York: Holt, Rinehart and Winston, 1969.

25.   Hall, Keith and John Knight. "Continuing Education (Inservice) for Teachers via Computer-Assisted Instruction." University Park, Pa.: Computer-Assisted Instruction Laboratory, Pennsylvania State University, June 30, 1975 (ERIC ED 11327).

26.   Hardebeck, Richard J. "A Comparison of Observed and Self-Reported Individualization of Instruction by Vocational, Academic, and Special Education Teachers in Texas." Doctoral dissertation, University of Texas at Austin, 1973.

* Suggested for further reading.

27. Harris, Ben M. *Individual Professional Growth Plan*. Austin, Tex.: Ben M. Harris Associates, October 1976.
28. Harris, Ben M. "Limits and Supplements to Formal Clinical Procedures." *Journal of Research and Development in Teacher Education* 9, no. 2 (Winter 1976): 85–87.
29. Harris, Ben M. *Supervisory Behavior in Education*. Englewood Cliffs, N.J.: Prentice-Hall, Inc., 1963.
*30. Harris, Ben M. *Supervisory Behavior in Education*. 2d ed. Englewood Cliffs, N.J.: Prentice-Hall, Inc., 1975.
31. Harris, Ben M., Vance Littleton, Dan Long, and Kenneth E. McIntyre. *Personnel Administration in Education*. Boston: Allyn and Bacon, Inc., 1979.
32. Harty, Harold and William C. Ritz. "A Non-Evaluative Helping Relationship: An Approach to Classroom-Oriented Supervision." *Educational Perspectives* 15, no. 2 (May 1976): 15–21.
33. Haskew, L. D. *The Educational Clinic*. Washington, D.C.: American Council on Education, 1949.
34. Joyce, Bruce and Marsha Weil. *Models of Teaching*. Englewood Cliffs, N.J.: Prentice-Hall, Inc., 1972.
35. Katz, Lilian G. "A Collection of Papers for Teachers." Urbana, Ill.: Institute for Research on Exceptional Children, College of Education, University of Illinois, February 1974 (mimeo).
36. Klopf, Gordon, Garda Bowman, E. Gilkeson, Robert Alfonso, and Neil Atkins. "The Processes of Consultation, Dialogue Encounter, Confrontation and Counseling." A paper developed for the Conference on New Modes of Staff Development at Denver, Colorado. Association for Supervision and Curriculum Development, January 1969 (mimeo).
*37. Knowles, Malcolm S. *Self-Directed Learning: A Guide for Learners and Teachers*. New York: Association Press, 1975.
*38. Lawrence, Gordon, Dennis Baker, Patricia Elzie, and Barbara Hansen. *Patterns of Effective Inservice Education*. Gainesville, Fla.: University of Florida, College of Education, December 1974.
39. Lukas, Carol V. "Problems in Implementing Head Start Planned Variation Models." In *Planned Variation in Education: Should We Give Up or Try Harder?* (Alice M. Rivlin and P. Michael Timpane, editors). Washington, D.C.: The Brookings Institution, 1975.
*40. Mager, Robert F. and Peter Pipe. "Is Non-Performance Rewarding?" Chapter 9 in *Analyzing Performance Problems or "You Really Oughta Wanna."* Palo Alto, Calif.: Fearon Publishers, 1970, pp. 61–69.
*41. Manolakes, Theodore. "The Advisory System and Supervision." In *Professional Supervision for Professional Teachers* (Thomas J. Sergiovanni, editor). Washington, D.C.: Association for Supervision and Curriculum Development, 1975, pp. 51–64.
*42. Melnik, Michael A. and Daniel S. Sheehan. "Clinic to Improve University Teaching." *Journal of Research and Development in Education* 9, no. 2 (1976): 68–74.

* Suggested for further reading.

43. Merton, Robert K. and P. L. Kendall. "The Focused Interview." *American Journal of Sociology* 51, no. 6 (May 1946): 541–57.
44. Morgan, John L. and David W. Champagne. "The Supervisory Conference." Pittsburgh, Pa.: University of Pittsburgh, Spring 1971 (mimeo).
45. Morse, Kevin and O. L. Davis. *The Effectiveness of Teaching Laboratory Instruction on the Questioning Behavior of Beginning Teacher Candidates.* Austin, Tex.: Research and Development Center for Teacher Education, University of Texas, 1970.
*46. Nelson, Beth. "On-Site, In-Service Training via Helping Teachers." In *Staff Development: Staff Liberation* (Charles W. Beegle and Roy A. Adelfelt, editors). Washington, D.C.: Association for Supervision and Curriculum Development, 1977.
47. Olivero, James L. *Micro-Teaching: Medium for Improving Instruction.* Columbus, Ohio: Charles E. Merrill, 1970.
48. O'Niel, Ernest. "Stages in the Clinical Supervisory Model." Austin, Tex.: Ninth Cycle Teacher Corps Project, 1975–76, University of Texas, n.d. (mimeo).
49. Parsons, Theodore. *Guided Self-Analysis Professional Development Systems. Education Series: Overview.* Berkeley, Calif.: Guided Self-Analysis Professional Development Systems, 1971.
*50. Reavis, Charles A. "Clinical Supervision: A Timely Approach." *Educational Leadership* 33, no. 5 (February 1976): 360–63.
51. Resick, Patricia A. *The Role of Feedback and Response Cost of Generalization in a Classroom.* Doctoral dissertation, University of Georgia, 1976.
*52. Robertson, Robert H. "The Individualization of Learning: Teacher-Related Problems." In *The In-Service Education of Teachers: Trends, Processes and Prescriptions* (Louis Rubin, editor). Boston: Allyn and Bacon, Inc., 1978.
53. Rogers, Carl. *Client-Centered Therapy, Its Current Practice, Implications and Theory.* Boston: Houghton Mifflin Company, 1951.
54. Rogers, Everett and F. Floyd Shoemaker. *Communications of Innovations: A Cross Cultural Approach.* 2d ed. New York: The Free Press, 1971.
55. Roueche, John E. and B. R. Herrscher (editors). *Toward Instructional Accountability: A Practical Guide to Educational Change.* Palo Alto, Calif.: Westinghouse Learning Press, 1973.
56. Scigliano, John A. and Eugene E. DuBois. "Staff Development: NOVA." *Community and Junior College Journal* 47, no. 2 (October 1976): 38–41.
57. Sergiovanni, Thomas J. "Reforming Teacher Evaluation: Naturalistic Alternatives." *Educational Leadership* 34, no. 8 (May 1977): 602–8.
58. Simon, Alan E. "Analyzing Educational Platforms: A Supervisory Strategy." *Educational Leadership* 34, no. 8 (May 1977): 580–84.
59. Singer, Robert N. "To Err or Not to Err: A Question for the Instruction of Psychomotor Skills." *Review of Educational Research* 47, no. 3 (Summer 1977): 479–98.
60. Strom, Robert D. *The Urban Teacher: Selection, Training and Supervision.* Columbus, Ohio: Charles E. Merrill, 1971.

* Suggested for further reading.

61. Watkins, Roger (editor). *Inservice Training: Structure and Content.* London: Ward Lock, 1973.
62. Young, David B. and Basil S. Deming. "Using a Systems Approach to Developing Supervisory Conference Strategies." A paper presented at the annual conference of the American Educational Research Association, April 5, 1972.

VII

Simulations, Games, and Structured Reality

INTRODUCTION

Learning by experience always implies experiences that are real or at least clearly associated with a concrete reality, in contrast with an abstraction or fragmentation only remotely related to reality. Just as beauty is in the eye of the beholder, reality is in the mind of the perceiver. What seems real, concrete, and relevant to one trainee may not be for another. Even so, much interest in recent years has been focused on real or highly realistic, simulated experience as the heart of in-service education. Accordingly, the Teacher Corps (40) emphasizes school and community involvement, almost to the neglect of on-campus training of teacher interns. The Harvard-Newton summer programs, directed by Robert Anderson for many years, were largely focused upon in-classroom experiences for in-service trainees. Butts (9) developed and tested in extensive fashion a "classroom experience model" of in-service training in implementing new American Association for the Advancement of Science teaching strategies. The micro-teaching programs initiated for preservice training at Stanford University were later utilized for in-service education by Olivero (33), along with many others (30). The extensive use of videotape in recording and analyzing classroom practices, but also the broader use of classroom observation practices for in-service purposes under the influence of Flanders (14); Amidon and Hunter (1); Simon and Boyer (39); and Harris, Bessent, and McIntryre (18:131–62) has all been based on the notion that interacting with reality in some systematic, structured way is useful for training purposes.

On-the-job training is an old and respected concept and has long been a standard practice in some nonacademic fields (44:176–77). Plumbing and electrical workers' unions have been among those utilizing apprenticeship training programs of very systematic kinds (32), even providing for in-service training of instructors to assure their being updated (32:150–53). Use of OJT programs for training of military personnel has been extensive (11). There appears to be growing interest in employee development in many fields of business and industry that emphasizes not only on-the-job methods (10:182) but also "vestibule" training (16:331) as a related kind of guided practice not unlike that advocated and described by Harris (17:86–87).

Professionals have also made extensive use of reality as experience for in-service training. The medical residency is perhaps the classic example of intensive field experience utilized for training beyond the terminal degree. Administrator and supervisor training at the University of Texas at Austin has involved a full-time semester of interning for experienced teachers since 1962. The *Summer Learning Center* (41) project in Montreal, Canada, illustrates still another of the numerous recent efforts to provide new skills for staff by direct, guided experiences with students in a school setting.

The long traditions and obvious utility of experience in real settings for training should not blind us to limitations imposed in the use of experiential learning. The layman tends to have blind faith in the worth of first-hand experience, whereas the academician disdains it for any but trivial learnings. Both are apparently in serious error. This chapter will try to suggest the promising possibilities for building on past uses of reality both for more effective and for a broader array of in-service education outcomes (36:11–12). The various ways to use *structured reality* to assure both predictable and efficient learning will be reviewed. *Simulations* as specially designed facsimiles of reality will be discussed and described to emphasize one of the most promising of the less costly approaches. *Games and gaming* will be touched upon lightly as still another cousin of experiential learning with some special promise.

SIMULATIONS AND REALITY

The term "simulation" is utilized to encompass a great variety of both training and other kinds of operations and materials (42:4). Role playing, gaming, sociodrama, laboratory training, and various computer-assisted programs are all simulations of a kind. Without serious distortion, novels, plays, case studies, scenarios, and films could be included as simulations in the way they utilize some medium for depicting reality as vividly as possible. A map or globe or any miniaturized model, diorama, or display can be thought of as simulated material in the sense that each one represents some real thing or event.

It may be useful for our purposes to recognize the rather broad concept of simulation as "an imitation or simplification of some aspect of reality," as described by Heyman (22:11). Still further, it may be useful to recognize simulation as a *process* for in-service training and to distinguish this from the various materials involved.

The Meaning of Simulation

The reference by Heyman to simulation as imitation or simplification provides a very broad and useful framework for thinking about simulations. Stadsklev (42:4–8) emphasizes "autotelic techniques" and experiential learning as the unique and important aspects of simulation. He argues for "experience in which the activities of the student are self-directed toward a meaningful end" (42:4). He also advocates the combining of the peculiar features of the game with the "social" modeling and "role-taking" of the simulation, to produce "simulation games" as the most sophisticated of forms.

Several scholars have developed schemes for analyzing simulations on a continuum from experiential or reality oriented to nonexperiential, passive or abstract. Heyman (21) suggests three levels on a continuum, with simulations, games, role playing, and mock trials at the most experiential level; placing lectures, films, and slides at the nonexperiential end of the continuum; and placing discussion at the semiexperiential level. What this arrangement does, in effect, is to focus on passive versus active involvement in much the same way that experience impact was considered in Chapter II. What is lost is the special attention to simulation as some *representation of reality* regardless of other important processes.

McCleary and McIntyre (27) defined a continuum of "methods of instruction" of greater variety, ranging from reading, lecture, and discussion on the one extreme to gaming, simulation, clinical study, team research, and internship on the other. In defining each of these methods, these authors differentiate a much larger variety of reality-oriented training alternatives. They also inadvertently demonstrate that while the medium may well dictate the character of the message (to paraphrase Marshall McLuhan), the same medium can be utilized in strikingly different ways. For instance, reading and lecture are seen as very low in reality orientation and hence are not highly associated with the simulation concept. However, a novel, scenario, or case study does call for reading, and each one can in fact be a powerful vehicle for simulation and training. Similarly, a tutorial relationship or a programmed self-instructional module may deal with such abstract content as to reflect reality not at all, but they can also reflect vividly real forms.

The essential and distinguishing feature of a simulation is its imitativeness of reality, with sufficient simplification for use in training. Obviously, the importance of involvement and other characteristics of design should not be neglected. However, only the imitative and simplifying features are unique to simulations.

Why Simulate?

If real experience has so much merit, why simulate? This is an important question because it is a reminder that simulations may be used as a fad or to add frills when real experience of greater worth for training is close at hand. The special conditions favoring the use of simulation *instead of* real experience include the following:

1. To simplify the very complex for better understanding.
2. To provide training experiences that would be too dangerous in the real situation.
3. To provide training experiences with a common situational and problem context for all.
4. To provide training experiences that would be excessively expensive in the real situation.
5. To provide training experiences with more control, structure, feedback, and related experience than is possible in a real situation.

When the reality to be studied is very complex, as it often is, a simulation can screen out the least important elements and assist the trainee in dealing with the more limited phenomenon (36:12). Hence, microteaching, utilizing a small group of children and a very short time frame for the minilesson, eliminates a vast array of complex events in the real classroom (30:146). No bells ring and no hall monitors arrive delivering messages. There is no roll call to take. Even behavior problems can be screened out if the focus is on a particular skill in questioning, discussing, or presenting.

Many real situations will not tolerate the risks of a trainee not being successful in applying new skills and concepts. The costs associated with failure may be too great (or perceived as too great) (34:21). Hence, untrained riveters are not allowed to work on high-rise beams. Unskilled counselors are not allowed to engage in therapeutic work with the severely disturbed, and inexperienced teachers are not asked to present the new grade-reporting system to a hostile parent group. When the trainee is likely to be unsuccessful and the consequences would be severe, then simulation offers the *safer* vehicle for training.

The need for a common set of situational and problem realities for training purposes has been widely neglected in many training programs that rely on group process. When trainees come together in a group, they bring a vast array of experiences with them. These experiences assure much of the prerequisite learning needed for extending in-service growth. However, the tendency of practitioners to particularize their own experiences, to see every individual's problem as essentially unique, creates serious barriers to new learning, especially in group settings. In-service programs based largely on sharing are not likely to produce either new or higher levels of understanding. Simulations present a common imaginary reality with which all trainees are asked to affiliate. In doing so, they share common experiences but differentiate their learning in transferring it to individual situations at a later point in time.

The expense of real experience can be quite excessive. The long-practiced use of the sabbatical leave represents an example of an extremely high-cost operation. Even if we are to assume that professional leave experiences are truly effective forms of in-service education (and they often are not), the cost is very great. When a person is on leave, the costs include travel, release from productive activity and from individualized supervision, plus the replacement of the trainee by another person. Any such arrangement is likely to be expensive indeed. Simulation may also be quite expensive. However, to the extent that travel costs, released time, and replacement costs are limited, simulations may be among the more economical ways of providing intensive experiences for in-service education. For example, the Dade County Immersion Laboratory (3) illustrates a foreign experience without travel costs.

The greatest advantage of simulation over real experience is most likely found in assuring a design for learning with structure, feedback, and reality orientation, giving sufficient impact and focus to produce predictable outcomes. Reality as training experience lacks structure for learning. Sequence is very difficult to impose on the real world. As trainees become immersed in the activities of a real operation, it is difficult to interrupt those events to assure the timely feedback and the critical analysis necessary for optimum learning. In the absence of such feedback, inappropriate learnings may well occur. Then, too, one has no assurance in advance that involvement in the real events will include experiences of the kinds most urgently needed. One can be sure that something will be learned, but to predict what it will be is very difficult indeed (19:10–11).

The Original War Games

Both simulation and gaming are perhaps most widely recognized as used for military training purposes. War games have been utilized in modern army, navy, and air force training to assure that skills and knowledges of individuals are learned at the application, transfer, and synthesis levels. Mock wars or battles are actually staged, and as many of the real elements of war are brought into action as possible. Such games are often *simplified* by restricting the use of real ammunition, hence reducing the anxieties associated with real casualties and reducing costs, most importantly in terms of human life, and also in terms of ammunition.

Such a simulation retains, however, as many elements of a real war as possible. Actual aggressor and defender roles and missions are assigned. Strategies are actually implemented according to plans. Planes fly and drop imitation bombs; tanks roll and shoot. Soldiers on foot are "wounded and killed" in simulated fashion. The action of the "war" may last only days or may continue for weeks, depending upon the extent of training planned. *Safe* hardships are experienced with K rations, sleeping in the rain, running out of supplies, and so on.

Obviously, there are the nonreal aspects of such a simulation. Participants receive reports on the results of their efforts from neutral officials who would not normally be involved. There are times during the "war" for pauses to analyze performances and take corrective measures. Hence, the negative consequences of reality are minimized while the opportunities for learning are maximized.

The Collective-Bargaining Simulation

A highly simplified example of a simulation is found in the collective-bargaining simulation. To a degree, this is quite comparable with war games. Trainees are divided into "labor" and "management" teams. Each individual is given a position or role. The situation is vividly described with case material, exhibits, and documents giving all trainees the appropriate information needed to engage in the bargaining activities as realistically as possible. Having studied the materials all trainees get instructions on the task at hand:

> To engage in a series of bargaining sessions to produce an agreement or contract that both sides will accept while avoiding, if at all possible, the alternatives of a *strike* or forced *arbitration*.

As the two teams get under way they argue, caucus, propose, reject, and worry. After awhile a halt is called, and trainees step out of role to discuss what has been happening (22:24–25). Questions arise on legal points that require study or access to a lawyer. Techniques are discussed and alternative strategies considered.

A recess over lunch or until the next day provides time for informal conversations among trainees, for thoughtful individual introspection, or for reading and study to be better prepared. As the training resumes, reality is simulated by taking up where the bargaining sessions ended. Roles are more expertly assumed, and participants feel more at ease but also more responsible.

Several cycles of simulation activity may be scheduled during a single day or over a prolonged period of time. Unexpected new information or new elements in the situation may be added by those in charge. For instance, a telegram or telephone call may inform bargainers that the board president has publicly threatened to jail any teacher who fails to show up for class, regardless of the progress in the bargaining sessions. The announcement of a heart attack suffered by the mother of one of the bargainers may be injected into the situation. New sources of funds may be revealed unexpectedly. Such injections of new information or new situational elements are carefully planned to retain the flavor of reality but to create demands for action by participants that will generate new learning.

The two simulations just described are both rather elaborate in several ways. Both rely heavily on lengthy, extended time frames for role taking to become fully developed. Such long hours and a sequence of episodes also assures that the many facets of the real problem situation are fully experienced. These simulations are relatively unstructured, allowing individuals and groups to be spontaneous and even creative in coming to grips with the problem situation. In the case of the war games simulations, the materials, equipment, and plans for use in the training activities are also elaborately arrayed. The collective-bargaining simulation requires much less elaborate material, equipment, and planning. However, in each instance the situational factors and the problems to be addressed are carefully prestructured.

Some simulations are more highly structured, almost programmed. In-baskets represent such structured simulations quite well. The *Shady Acres Elementary School In-Basket*, for instance, was designed by McIntyre (28) to represent the basket of memorandums, letters, phone messages, and reports on the desk of the elementary principal. This set of materials provides the full set of stimuli for trainee response. Additional structure is added in providing each trainee with rather explicit directions for proceeding through the in-basket of materials and dealing with each item. The trainee has substantial freedom in taking the role of the principal to make decisions, procrastinate, or delegate. However, at the end of a limited period of role taking, the trainees step out of role and discuss and analyze their diverse responses to a common set of problems.

Computer-assisted simulations may also be rather highly structured. Examples of these include *Exper Sim* by Dana Main (26) and an instructional decision-making module by E. Wailand Bessent (5). Both are designed to guide and direct trainees in applying rather complex technical skills. One deals with experimental designing; the other, with rational decision making. In both instances the computer programs give structure to the kind of problem, the ways of dealing with the problem, and the kind of information that is made available (8:47). The advantages of computer simulation over real problem solving of similar kinds goes beyond the structure offered to guide learning, however. The immediacy of feedback, the easy access to information, and the opportunity to gain "years of experience" in a matter of hours makes such simulations powerful training designs.

TYPES OF SIMULATION

Because simulation is such a wide-open concept of imitation and simplification of reality for training, the variety of forms is almost limitless. This variety is both a challenge and a problem for the planner of in-service training. On the one hand, an endless array of alternatives may be considered, and new creations are not to be ignored. On the other hand, how to select according to need poses a problem of overabundance.

A suitable typology for simulations does not seem readily available. Extent of structure as described in the last section is a useful way of thinking about different simulations, but the extent to which simulations provide for various kinds of experiences, the extent to which they utilize an array of media, and the group size and time allocations required may all be important, too!

Role Playing

While virtually all simulations call for role taking, the use of simple role plays or sociodramas represent one of the very simple, unstructured types of simulation (18:261–67). Any problem situation shared by two or more individuals can lead to almost spontaneous role playing. The time required can range from a few minutes upward. If a common problem is not already at hand, one can be provided by using a vignette such as those presented in Chapter I or by storytelling.

To illustrate the simple and relatively unstructured character of this type of simulation, let's assume that several of us have just read about the new principal, Ms. Jane Hunt. The group leader says, "Okay. Now let's talk about how you might have handled that situation when the irate mother arrived." The discussion will probably generate a variety of points of view. Gradually, two quite different *positions* may emerge. These positions are characterized and put into focus by the leader.

"I think I hear rather different approaches being suggested, but two strategies seem to emerge from your comments. On the one hand, I hear some of you saying in various ways, *take a firm stand*. But others of you are proposing a *conciliatory, therapeutic approach*" (pause).

"Now, why not try these out on each other? Who'd like to try the *firm stand*?" (Hands.) "Okay, let's role-play."

With just this much structure, a whole series of role plays of two to five minutes each can give trainees opportunities to become involved, to try various techniques, to feel anger and frustration, and so forth. Periodically, role playing can be interrupted and discussions interjected to assist trainees in analyzing their feelings, actions, and the consequences of these. The entire session, from reading the vignette through discussion, role playing, discussions, and summary wrap-up by the leader, might extend over a two-hour period.

Situational Simulations

A number of simulations provide a set of materials that describe situations but offer only general suggestions or guidelines for role taking. The problems are not specified but are *in context*, to be discovered and selected by trainees. The various simulations developed and distributed by the University Council for Educational Administration (UCEA) tend to be of this situational kind. A school system, a school, or a program is described, using films, simulated handbooks, policy manuals, legal documents, and cases. The task of the leader or trainer is to expose participants to the materials, discuss implications, identify problems, role-play situations, suggest courses of action, draft proposals, appear before a board, or do anything else that assures purposeful interaction with the realities of the simulated situation.

The Teaching Problems Laboratory by Donald Cruickshank and colleagues (12) was also a relatively unstructured simulation, relying primarily on stimulus materials to focus attention. However, "critical teaching problems" were presented on sound film or in written form as critical incidents. Role-playing cards were provided to suggest roles for some of the incidents. A director's guide provided background information on the "Longacre Elementary School" in which the incidents were supposed to have occurred. The guide also suggested ways in which the leader or trainer might use the material. For the most part, the simulation was unstructured, however. Lots of thought-provoking problems were presented, but their use left almost entirely to the leader and participants.

The Lemon Exercise is one of the more imaginative yet simple uses of simulation. Kenneth Lash (24) has described the exercise as utilized in perceptual training. I have seen it used in various workshops for in-service training of newly desegregated school faculties. The situation is structured very simply with a sack of lemons (one for each participant) and a series of opportunities to observe and describe. This is how the exercise is sometimes structured:

(1)   The leader brings a sack of lemons and dumps them in a pile on a table (or floor) in the middle of the room. Trainees are standing (or sitting) in a circle.

(2)   The leader invites everyone to go and take a lemon. As they do, various comments are heard: "Why?" "Are we having lemonade?" "I thought we were having in-service." The leader gives instructions as they take their lemons.

"Please return to your place in the circle with your lemon and spend a minute or two studying it. I know that seems silly, but study it carefully. Furthermore, keep in mind that everyone has his own lemon. That one is yours. You can keep it, take it with you, or do what you wish. *But* for now, don't do anything but *study* it carefully, in fine detail. In a moment I'll ask you to describe it to others."

A pause of two to three minutes is allowed. It seems like an eternity. How long can anyone stare at a lemon? Then the leader interrupts them.

"All right. Now, I want you to form triads, sets of three people, and each one introduce your lemon to the other two. Be sure to call attention to your lemon's unique features. Any little detail should be pointed out."

A pause of ten to twelve minutes results in much talk within the triads. The leader circulates and listens. She or he helps out with suggestions, if necessary, where someone is having trouble getting the idea of *detailed* descriptions. The leader encourages *personification*, such as a description that likens a blemish to a dimple or a knob to a nose.

As the three individuals "introduce" their lemons to each other, new triads are formed and the process is repeated. The leader urges them to expand on the sharing of information about their individual lemons, if possible. Since different trainees use different techniques, this second round tends to be more elaborate.

Finally, a third round is called for.

"Okay. One more time. Get into your new triad and make introductions again." When the third round is completed the leader asks, "Will you please place your lemon back on the table in a pile?"

The participants complain. They ask why. Some express a fondness for the lemon. Others complain: "You said we could keep them."

The leader reassures them. "Don't worry. You'll get yours back. But for now, just put them on the table and return to your place in the circle."

When all lemons are deposited and the participants are back in the circle, the leader comments on how much they learned about their own lemon, how detailed their observations had become, and how attached to the lemon each individual seemed to be. Then the leader says, "Okay, go get your own personal, individual lemon. Be sure you get your own."

As trainees scramble to find their own lemon, some make mistakes but most find their own quickly. Others resolve differences in a moment. When each person has his or her own lemon, the leader asks everyone to sit down. "Now let's talk about what we've learned."

The *lessons* from this can range widely from individual differences, to the place of detailed observation in teaching, to the reasons we are empathetic with some people and not with others.

This lemon exercise has a structure of sequence of activities but allows for a lot of variations and freedom of expression in its use. The lemon is an imitation person, and the studying and introducing of the lemon simulates getting to know people.

The Laboratory Approach

The science laboratory of the secondary school or college was originally a facility for simulating the work of the scientist. While much of that early concept has been lost in current practice, it has been more fully developed in other fields of training. The industrial arts or vocational shops of secondary schools are sometimes excellent simulations of their counterparts in the real world of business and industry.

Various efforts have been made over the years to adapt the basic notion of the laboratory as simulated research to the many problems of training personnel. Lull and McCarthy (25) describe a "learning laboratory" approach to in-service education that emphasizes evaluation; but it may not reflect other important features of the laboratory idea, for it must be more than active doing and concrete manipulations.

The Ealing Corporation developed a series of packages marketed under the title *Starting Tomorrow* (43) that utilized films to present models of classroom practices and provided materials designed to facilitate the teacher returning "to try out the lessons in the classroom without procurement or preparation worries." In this design, the trainees were being offered film-simulated teaching models and materials to promote trial efforts in real classroom situations. As such, it was an incomplete design for learning.

The work of Harris, Bessent, and McIntyre (18) in the 1960s resulted in the development and testing of a uniquely designed hybrid version of the simulated research laboratory. This so-called laboratory approach can be described in five general steps or "elements of design" (18:46):

1. A problem is simulated and presented for trainee consideration.
2. The trainees are guided in actively dealing with (resolving) the problem.
3. The active, problem-solving involvement of each trainee is recorded in some predetermined way.
4. The recorded information from each trainee is analyzed and feedback provided.
5. The leader guides trainees in drawing interpretations, seeing implications, and generalizing from the feedback data.

These five steps appear to be very similar to those discussed by McKibbin et al. (29) for simulations in general (29:48).

Numerous laboratory sessions are presented and discussed in detail in the volume by Harris, Bessent, and McIntyre (18). A single illustration of the five design elements follows:

EVALUATING PUPIL PERFORMANCE: LONG DIVISION

1. Introduce the *"problem"* very briefly as "How to properly evaluate student performance?"

   Distribute a sheet of paper containing a single long division *problem*, and showing the work of a student in solving the problem.

   Arithmetic Test
   Directions: Work the following problems and show your steps in arriving at the solutions:
   #1. If 3 apples cost 13¢, how much will 7 apples cost?

$$
\begin{array}{r}
4.56 \\
3\overline{\smash{)}13.00} \\
12 \\
\hline
1\,0 \\
8 \\
\hline
20
\end{array}
\qquad
\begin{array}{r}
4.56 \\
\times\,7 \\
\hline
31.92
\end{array}
$$

   Answer: 31.92

2. Give directions for *actively* evaluating the performance of the student. Emphasize that each participant should consider himself the teacher of this student. Call attention to directions to student.
3. Distribute a score sheet and ask each participant to *record* the score s/he

thinks is most appropriate for the quality of the work shown on the paper. Score sheets provide simply for assigning a single value ranging from 0 to 10.

4. Collect the score sheets. Let participants get into "buzz groups" and discuss their evaluations while scores are being tabulated. Completed tabulations tend to look as follows for a group of 28 participants.

Scores Assigned

	0	1	2	3	4	5	6	7	8	9	10	
Frequency of Scores	3	1	2	1	4	5	4	3	5	2	0	

Present the analysis as shown above to the participants on a transparency or on a wall chart.

5. *Lead participants* in the interpretation of the data. Note the following:

   a. "We are not in agreement apparently on the proper scores to assign this performance."
   b. "Some of us think it quite 'good' while others think it quite 'poor.'"
   c. "There is some tendency for a substantial number of us to agree that it is middle-range performance."
   d. "No one seems to think it is perfect performance."

Now, ask participants to explain. "How can we disagree so over a simple, objective, long-division problem? Isn't it either right or wrong?" (Smile)

Participants generally get very much involved in *explaining* their scores. Some say they scored low because of "careless errors." Some retort that "process is more important" and point out that s/he did indeed seem to know how to proceed. Others take different positions, mention different rational, logical ways of arriving at quite diverse evaluations.

Shift the discussion by asking: "What does this tell us, if anything, about our responsibilities as student evaluators?" Some probing may be needed to get participants to verbalize the implications they recognize. Put them on the board or on a transparency as they become well articulated. For instance:

1. Student evaluation tends to be subjective even when it seems objective.
2. Students have reason to be concerned about how the teacher is evaluating.
3. Teachers should be clear about their evaluative criteria and be sure students are too.

The structure imposed by the five design elements as illustrated here is not sufficient to inhibit involvement or direct thinking. However, it does assure an orderly sequence of experiences in which all participants have freedom of independent thought and response but are expected to consider the data generated in the group in drawing interpretations.

The power and impact of the laboratory approach has been most clearly demonstrated in the *Homogeneous Grouping Exercise* (18:95–106). Here the problem to be simulated is an emotionally charged one. What does homogeneous grouping accomplish? Is it effective? Participants become laboratory analysts in this exercise. They take "real data" on one hundred students and try various grouping procedures. They work in teams of two or three participants to promote discussion about each "experimental" grouping effort. They *record* the results from each grouping plan, and these are put on transparencies for discussion and interpretation. When such an exercise comes to an end, after two and one half or three hours, emotions have greatly subsided and factual concerns are much stronger. It is difficult for participants to disagree with their own findings — the data they generate themselves.

Games

Simulations become games when they are structured for competition and scoring in some form. The collective-bargaining simulation described earlier could be organized as a game if a scoring system were developed to clearly decide on a winning side of the bargaining table.

Simulations in game format have been most imaginatively developed, perhaps, by several groups concerned with training in government and politics. The *Napoli* game published by the Western Behavioral Sciences Institute (31) is one of several games that deal with problems of political-governmental affairs via the game. The Foreign Policy Association has a school services division devoted to promoting uses of games in high schools and colleges.

Napoli simulates the politics of the House of Representatives. Each member of the group is assigned a political party affiliation and a region. The group operates as a legislative body considering eleven different bills involving various social, economic, and political issues. Party platforms are described in simplified form. Survey data on public opinion are provided, region by region and issue by issue, for each party. Several sessions are conducted, and the game director scores legislators after each session, based on a formula that indicates the chances of being reelected. Each participant plays the role of a legislator as he or she desires; however, the goal is clearly that of being reelected. At the end, the director "conducts elections" to see who is reelected and who is defeated. Obviously, the excitement and struggle (and learning) are produced as individual legislators try to vote their convictions without being defeated at the polls.

Queskno * is a very simple game that illustrates the use of game format with only limited verisimilitude. Pictures are used to stimulate responses. However, teams of players role dice and select a picture at random. The player's task is to write a test question based on the picture, but one that is *also* at the appropriate level in Bloom's taxonomy of educational objectives. Hence, if a trainee rolls a one and turns up a picture of a rabbit eating lettuce in a garden patch, the question to be written would be a simple knowledge or recall question about the picture. Since several groups are working simultaneously, the competition is between groups to produce the most *points*. The higher the level of the question on the Bloom taxonomy, the more points a team earns, but only if the proper form of a question is written.

What is being simulated, in a way, is the problem of developing a test. Obviously, the features of a game tend to predominate more than the simulation of a real test design or construction situation. This illustration emphasizes that games are not always related to simulations (38:3). How much is lost in the process of emphasizing gaming at the expense of verisimilitude is not clearly known. It seems probable, however, that participants in work settings will be more responsive to the most realistic and challenging games. However, De Vries's study (13) on the effects of "non-simulation" games on elementary-age children found that *team competition* made for significant results.

A number of games are listed in Appendix A along with information about the sources from which they can be secured. Some of those listed may have value in a wide variety of in-service training situations. The *Napoli* game obviously would have little merit for many groups of school personnel, at least as far as contributing to their on-the-job performances is concerned. *Conflict*, however, is a game that deals with basic problems of human relations and might be widely useful. A rather extensive "register" of games is included in Gibbs's volume (15).

Other Simulations

The concept of simulation is sometimes best applied to in-service training needs by utilizing actual *reality* with sufficient structure to simplify rather than to imitate. This is illustrated by a device developed by the U.S. Air

---

* This description of *Queskno* is based on an unpublished paper. The game is credited to the work of Lewis B. Smith, Virginia M. Rogers, Marcella Kysilka, Caroline Gillan, and Geneva Winterrose.

Force for training B-52 crews to repair defects in the hydraulic system in flight. An *actual, working* hydraulic system of the aircraft was mounted in a room in a simulated frame of the plane. Training experiences of elaborate kinds were designed utilizing this training facility. Defects were planted in the system, and trainees were guided in locating and correcting them.

This hydraulic system training device illustrates several of the great advantages of the simulations under discussion. Although the device cost over $3 million to develop this was a small amount in terms of the lives that might be saved and of the cost of the plane that might also be saved by effective training. However, the cost of training in simulation over use of real flightline situations was very great. Furthermore, since the hydraulic system was removed from the actual plane, it was much easier to use for training purposes and greatly improved the amount and rate of learning. Finally, in a few hours this simulation provided trainees with experiences in handling problems that might take years to acquire in flight. Obviously, the risks of in-flight learning were greatly reduced.

An illustration of adapting reality to simulated use for training is provided by the classroom observation training procedures developed by Harris et al. (20). The use of an observation instrument of a comprehensive kind requires the development of an array of complex knowledges and skills. Although preliminary training can be accomplished in a laboratory context using films and videotapes, the full range of skills and knowledges is rarely developed except on application in *actual classroom* settings. Unfortunately, when observers who are unskilled go to real classrooms for training purposes, the complexities of the situation create confusion, and frustration is experienced by the trainee-observer. Abandonment rates are very high.

The simulated approach to this training problem is relatively simple and effective. The outline of procedures presented in the following list guides each in-classroom observation training session following introductory sessions in a laboratory or workshop format:

1. Arrange with the teacher to be observed.
2. Assemble as a group at the school in advance of the scheduled observation for a briefing.
3. Observe as a group in the prearranged classroom for a full period (ordinarily forty to sixty minutes).
4. Leave the classroom and reconvene immediately in a quiet place for writing and rewriting of observation reports.
5. Compute interobserver reliability coefficients (or percent of agreement) between trainees or between trainer and trainees.
6. Discuss and analyze observation procedures, evidences recorded, problems incurred, and so on.

In following these procedures the classroom reality is retained with only small variations. Arrangements with the teacher of the class are directed mainly toward reassuring him or her, and clarifying expectations. The teacher is asked to proceed as naturally as possible and to ignore observers.

The briefing of the observer-trainee group is directed toward informing them about the lesson, the students, and the location of the classroom and other facilities to be utilized.

The observation period in the classroom is a practice session, but trainees are urged to proceed just as though it were real. Using procedures and techniques previously presented, each trainee attempts to produce a full and complete observation record of the kind that could be utilized for teacher improvement purposes. Two trainers are utilized whenever possible in this classroom, along with three to seven trainees. One trainer uses all observation procedures to produce a model observation report at the end of the period. The other trainer quietly circulates among the trainees, watching their recording techniques, suggesting modifications, reassuring, and reinforcing. Hence, trainees receive some limited feedback in the midst of observing.

On leaving the classroom, all trainees and trainers assemble in a quiet work area. They delay any discussion until each individual observer completes the observation record, including any analysis of data required. Then comparisons are made between and among observers in the form of computing interobserver reliability coefficients or calculating simple percentages of agreement. Finally, careful discussion follows. The entire sequence requires approximately three hours.

SUMMARY

The design of in-service education programs is inherently related to the questions of applications to on-the-job expectations. However, realities as influences for training and learning can have even wider application. Reality should always be consciously considered in planning and implementing ISE; however, overly simplistic notions must be avoided. Experience may be the best teacher, but not without purpose. Raw experience may be frustrating or satisfying, depending on the way it is utilized. Experience may be highly meaningful or confusing, depending on the structure for interaction that is provided.

Simulations and games offer a vast array of ways of manipulating experiences for learning. When reality is too expensive, not available, too dangerous, or too unpredictable, then simulations have greater promise for ISE. Games, too, may be more or less useful. They are not necessarily simulations but are sometimes contrived for entertainment rather than for learning. When games employ reality simulation, they have a uniqueness about them that may well prove especially useful as planners become more skilled in their application to ISE program design.

REFERENCES

*1. Amidon, Edmund and Elizabeth Hunter. *Imroving Teaching: The Analyses of Classroom Verbal Interaction*. New York: Holt, Rinehart and Winston, 1966.

2. Barton, Richard F. *A Primer on Simulation and Gaming*. Englewood Cliffs, N. J.: Prentice-Hall, Inc., 1970.

3. Beebe, Von N. "Spanish Comes Alive on La Isla Caribe." *Phi Delta Kappan* 60, no. 2 (October 1978): 95–98.

*4. Bessent, E. Wailand (editor). *Designs for Inservice Education*. R&D monograph. Austin, Tex.: Research and Development Center for Teacher Education, University of Texas, February 1967.

5. Bessent, E. W., et al. *A Computer-Assisted Instruction Module*. Vol. 1. *Student Manual for Instructional Decision-Making*. Austin, Tex.: Special Education Supervisor Training Project, University of Texas, 1974.

*6. Boocock, S. J. and F. O. Schild. *Simulation Games in Learning*. Beverly Hills, Calif.: Sage Publications, 1968.

7. Broudy, H. S. "In-Service Teacher Education — Paradoxes and Potentials." In *The Inservice Education of Teachers: Trends, Processes and Prescriptions* (Louis Rubin, editor). Boston: Allyn and Bacon, Inc., 1978.

*8. Bunderson, C. Victor and Gerald W. Faust. "Programmed and Computer-Assisted Instruction." *The Psychology of Teaching Methods*. 75th Yearbook. Part I (N. L. Gage, editor). Chicago: National Society for the Study of Education, 1976.

9. Butts, David P. "The Classroom Experience Model." In *Designs for Inservice Education* (E. W. Bessent, editor). Austin, Tex.: Research and Development Center for Teacher Education monograph, University of Texas, February 1967.

10. Chruden, Herbert J. and A. W. Sherman, Jr. *Personnel Management*. 5th ed. Cincinnati, Ohio: South-Western Publishing Company, 1976.

*11. Clark, Harold F. and Harold S. Sloan. *Classrooms in the Military: An Account of Education in the Armed Forces*. Institute for Instructional Improvement. New York: Bureau of Publications, Teachers College, Columbia University, 1964.

12. Cruickshank, Donald R., Frank W. Broadbent, and Roy L. Bubb. *Teaching Problems Laboratory Simulation Director's Guide*. Chicago: Science Research Associates, Inc., 1967.

*13. De Vries, David L. "Teams—Games—Tournament: A Gaming Technique

* Suggested for further reading.

that Fosters Learning." *Simulation and Games* 7, no. 1 (March 1976): 21–33.

14. Flanders, Ned A. *Analyzing Teaching Behavior*. Reading, Mass.: Addison-Wesley, 1970.

*15. Gibbs, G. I. (editor). *Handbook of Games and Simulation Exercises*. London: E. and F. N. Spon Ltd., 1974.

16. Glueck, William F. *Personnel: A Diagnostic Approach*. Dallas, Tex.: Business Publications, Inc., 1974.

17. Harris, Ben M. *Supervisory Behavior in Education*. 2d ed. Englewood Cliffs, N.J.: Prentice-Hall, Inc., 1975.

18. Harris, Ben M., E. Wailand Bessent, and Kenneth E. McIntyre. *In-Service Education: A Guide to Better Practice*. Englewood Cliffs, N.J.: Prentice-Hall, Inc., 1969.

19. Harris, Ben M. and Jane Duckett. "Field Experiences for Instructional Leadership Development." A paper prepared for the Special Education Supervisor Training Project. Austin, Tex.: Department of Educational Administration, University of Texas, September 1974 (mimeo).

20. Harris, Ben M., Louisa Goodlett, and Cynthia Sloan. *Manual for the New Comprehensive Observation Guide*. Austin, Tex.: University of Texas, 1975 (mimeo).

*21. Heyman, Mark. "Experimental Learning: Some Thoughts About It, Leading to Categorization." *Simulation Gaming* 5, no. 1 (January–February 1978): 4–5.

22. Heyman, Mark. *Simulation Games for the Classroom*. Bloomington, Ind.: Phi Delta Kappa Educational Foundation, 1975.

23. "An Inventory of Hunches About Simulations as Educational Tools." La Jolla, Calif.: Simile II, n.d. (mimeo).

24. Lash, Kenneth. "How Basic Act of Seeing a Familiar Object Fosters Something New in Our Thinking." *Christian Science Monitor*, November 8, 1976, p. B7.

*25. Lull, F. and J. McCarthy. "Learning Laboratory: An Approach to In-Service Training." *Contemporary Education* 40, no. 3 (January 1969): 150–53.

26. Main, Dana. *Exper Sim: A System for Teaching Research Design Through Computer Simulation*. New York: Exxon Education Foundation, 1975.

27. McCleary, Lloyd E. and Kenneth E. McIntyre. "Competency Development and University Methodology: A Model and Proposal." In *Where Will They Find It?* (Thomas F. Koerner, editor). Washington, D.C.: National Association of Secondary School Principals, March 1972.

*28. McIntyre, Kenneth E., E. Wailand Bessent, Ben M. Harris, and Jack Roberts. *Shady Acres In-Basket*. Washington, D.C.: National Association of Elementary School Principals, National Education Association, 1970.

29. McKibbin, Michael, Marsha Weil, and Bruce Joyce. *Teaching and Learn-*

---

* Suggested for further reading.

ing: Demonstrations of Alternatives. Washington, D.C.: Association of Teacher Educators, 1977.

30. Meier, John. "Rationale for and Application of Microtraining to Improve Teaching." *Journal of Teacher Education* 19, no. 2 (Summer 1968): 145–57.

31. *Napoli: Participant's Manual.* La Jolla, Calif.: Western Behavioral Sciences Institute, 1965.

32. National Advisory Council on Education Professions Development. *Vocational Education: Staff Development Priorities for the 70's.* A report. Washington, D.C.: National Advisory Council, January 1973.

*33. Olivero, James L. *Micro-Teaching: Medium for Improving Instruction.* Columbus, Ohio: Charles E. Merrill, 1970.

34. Pharis, William L. *In-Service Education of Elementary School Principals.* Washington, D.C.: Department of Elementary School Principals, National Education Association, April 1966.

35. Phenix, Philip. "The Play Element in Education." *Educational Forum* 29, no. 3 (March 1965): 297–306.

36. Rubin, Louis. *Perspectives on Preservice and Inservice Education.* Syracuse, N.Y.: National Council of States on Inservice Education, Syracuse University, April 1978.

*37. Seidner, Constance J. "Teaching with Simulations and Games." *The Psychology of Teaching Method.* 75th Yearbook. Part I (N. L. Gage, editor). Chicago: National Society for the Study of Education, 1976.

*38. Shubik, Martin. *The Uses and Methods of Gaming.* New York: Elsevier Scientific Publishing Company, Inc., 1975.

39. Simon, Anita and E. Gil Boyer (editors). *Mirrors of Behavior II: An Anthology of Observation Instruments.* Vol. A. Philadelphia: Classroom Interaction Newsletter, 1970.

40. Smith, William L. "Changing Teacher Corps Programs." *NCSIE Inservice.* National Council of States on Inservice Education. Syracuse, N.Y.: Syracuse University, College of Education (February 1978).

41. Sokolyk, Dorothy. "A Report on the Summer Learning Center at St. Patrick's School: July 4–28, 1972." Montreal: Department of Educational Psychology and Sociology, McGill University, October 1972 (mimeo).

*42. Stadsklev, Ron. *Handbook of Simulation Gaming in Social Education.* Part 1. Textbook. Tuskaloosa, Ala.: Institute of Higher Education Research and Services, University of Alabama, September 1974.

43. *Starting Tomorrow: Inservice Program for Elementary School Teachers.* Cambridge, Mass.: The Ealing Corporation, 1968.

44. Swanson, J. Chester and Ernest G. Kramer. "Vocational Education Beyond High School." *Vocational Education.* 64th Yearbook (Melvin L. Barlow, editor). Chicago: National Society for the Study of Education, 1965.

45. *Urban Simulation: Monroe City Materials.* Columbus, Ohio: University Council for Educational Administration.

* Suggested for further reading.

VIII

Other Group Approaches

INTRODUCTION

The group as a unit for implementing in-service education outcomes is so universal that its critical, essential contributions can be readily taken for granted and even neglected. The era of group dynamics, group process analysis, and group relations training was at its height in the 1940s through the 1960s. The era emerged out of the urgent demands of new and unbelievably complex military undertakings. Group techniques were fostered by educators and social scientists alike as tools for developing a better, more democratic, and more humane society. The resurgence of authoritarianism was a predictable consequence of the social and political upheavals of the 1960s; but that, too, is passing, and the lessons of previous decades need renewed attention by in-service planners. Small groups continue to appear to be among the most natural of all social phenomena known to man. Hence, organizational development specialists continue their efforts to reform bureaucracies (39), and auto manufacturers search for small-group approaches to the assembly line (23).

In viewing the essential group as both natural phenomenon and working tool for in-service education, the relationship of individualization to group process needs to be considered. As interest in group techniques and processes began to wane, interest in all forms of individualization reached new heights. There is some tendency to treat these two concepts as antithetical. This writer's cautions about individualized approaches to training, as expressed in Chapter VI, are intended to seek resolutions between highly personalistic in-service education and that which is more fully anchored in group relationships (40).

It is our view that just as man lives not by bread alone, his training cannot be a solitary thing. Personal needs, like bread, are essential and must be addressed, but the group context for personalized ventures in in-service education are also essential, though not prerequisite. In the two previous chapters the focus has been on the individual as client and on reality as context and content. This chapter directs your attention to basic ways of working in groups to facilitate optimum interactions of clients with both context and content for in-service growth.

WAYS OF WORKING IN GROUPS

An enormous array of group forms are available to consider. The family is a natural and ancient small group only recently threatened by social pollutants. The hunting group is another of ancient vintage that survives to this day in many cultures, if only for social purposes. Social groups of diverse kinds are developed by various cultures. Cardplaying, prayer meetings, happy hour drinking, Sunday picnicking, and Little League baseball illustrate a few of the diverse activities and forms. Groups organized for economic, political, and production purposes are also highly diverse.

Our interest, of course, is in groups designed to promote learning and especially adult, job-relevant learning. All groups, interestingly, promote learning; and some (the family, for instance) may well be among the most powerful in influencing learning, if not directly producing specific outcomes. Learning-oriented groups include therapy groups, study groups, discussion groups, action research teams, workshop groups, and a host of other special-purpose groups (34:20–25).

A Variety of Purposes

Groups are as different in form as they vary in purpose. When groups are purely social and recreational, commonness of interests and values tends to influence their formation, and personal satisfaction and a sense of unity and allegiance among group members is important to its survival and functioning. When groups are task oriented or production groups, common interests may be very limited and a sense of satisfaction and unity may come more from recognition of differences than from the homogeneity of group members (39:54).

Learning groups have much in common with social groups, but they also are task oriented. Common interests in anticipated learning outcomes help build the unity and allegiances that may be necessary when trainees are being made uncomfortable, even threatened by insights into their own behavior. On the other hand, personal satisfaction is not an adequate reason for affiliation in a learning group. The purposes of the undertaking both reflect and contrast with individual participant needs as perceived. The inevitable diversity within the group may need to be accentuated to produce the dynamic experiences needed. The group is always client but is to a large extent simultaneously the determiner of process. A group is never a passive thing — void, vessel, or sponge.

Choice, Structure, and Variety

The various forms of learning groups give the in-service education planner a problem of choice. Without attempting to provide details regarding the more widely known group forms, some direct relationships can be suggested. For instance, *therapy* groups are intended for use in helping people learn to deal with feelings, attitudes, and values. *Discussion* groups stimulate knowledge- and opinion-level learning outcomes most readily. Higher-level cognitive learning outcomes may well be more appropriately stimulated by a *study* group format.

These distinctions among therapy, discussion, and study may not be easily maintained when a group continues in association for learning over prolonged periods of time. Hence, a workshop or intensive course extending over a period of a week or more may incorporate a broad variety of group and solitary activities. A study group may be thought of as a series of discussions focused by study materials and sequenced for learning purposes. A discussion group may become highly therapeutic from time to time.

Clear or not as these distinctions may be, they can serve to suggest differentiation in structures and leadership style, given different learning expectations (17). The emphasis in therapy groups on permissive, accepting nondirectiveness on the part of the leader calls for specialized training and self-discipline (37). On the other hand, study groups have purposes that call for setting limits, agreeing upon outcomes, and stimulating disagreements. Discussion groups employ leadership and structures that assure maximum levels of sharing and interacting (20). As such, a facilitating kind of leadership becomes essential.

The emphasis on three group forms should not cause us to neglect a larger variety of activity that groups engage in for learning purposes. We do, of course, have *viewing* groups, *listening* groups, *role-playing* groups, *manipulating* groups, *planning* groups, *analyzing* groups, and *deciding* groups. Nearly every event associated with in-service education involves group activity. Here of course we are most concerned with group activity as the primary experience for learning. Even highly structured clinical or simulated ISE involves group activity in many ways. The essence of group work, however, is making human interactions productive of learning outcomes.

A FEW ESSENTIAL ACTIVITIES

Certain activities have emerged over the years as especially stimulating and adaptable ways of working with groups regardless of purpose. Just as interviewing was stressed in a prior chapter as essential to individual approaches, so the following might be considered as essential to work with groups. *Brainstorming*, buzz sessions, discussions, and role playing were identified in previous chapters as important activities for in-service education and design. In the following pages, each of these is defined, described, illustrated, and analyzed.*

Brainstorming †

Definition.   Brainstorming is an activity in a group session in which ideas held by participants are orally expressed, with special procedures employed to avoid any discussion, criticism, or analysis. Some record or report of all ideas is maintained for later use. It is essentially an oral inventory of ideas.

Purposes

1.   To inform all participants of ideas held by others.
2.   To stimulate the development of ideas.

* These descriptions of four activities are taken from Ben M. Harris, E. Wailand Bessent, and Kenneth E. McIntyre, *Inservice Education: A Guide to Better Practice.* This was originally published by Prentice-Hall, Inc., 1969, but is now out of print. Copyright Ben M. Harris, E. W. Bessent, and K. E. McIntyre. Reprint by permission. All rights reserved. 1975.

† A. F. Osborn is generally credited with having originated this term and formalized the activity itself.

3. To provide an inventory of ideas for later use.
4. To suggest a variety of alternative approaches to problems.
5. To influence opinions or attitudes regarding the state of thinking of the group.
6. To cultivate positive attitudes toward alternative approaches to problems.

Procedure. Orientation is given to the group of participants on brainstorming. A problem, topic, or issue is selected as the focus for the brainstorming activity. The selected focus is clearly described to the group to assure unity in the frame of reference employed by each brainstormer. The ground rules or special procedures are made explicit, as follows:

1. All ideas related to the focus in any direct way are desired.
2. A maximum number of related ideas is desired.
3. One idea may be modified or adapted and expressed as another idea (sometimes called "hitchhiking" on ideas).
4. Ideas should be expressed as clearly and concisely as possible.
5. No discussion of ideas should be attempted.
6. No criticism of ideas should be attempted.

A time period is established for the brainstorming to fit the situation, type of problem in focus, size of group, and so on. Ordinarily, twenty to thirty minutes is minimal. Often, brainstorming can continue effectively for an hour or more. When ideas run out and interest seems to wane, the leader should terminate the session.

Ideas are permitted to flow without formality. In a large group, the leader may recognize individuals. In a small group, spontaneous expressions may be more desirable without formal recognition.

Each idea is recorded by a person designated as recorder. The ideas may be slightly abbreviated but should not be changed in context or terminology any more than is absolutely necessary. Ideas are recorded on a chalkboard, transparency, or large chart so that participants can refer to them during the brainstorming session.

The group leader might want to repeat ideas as expressed to indicate acceptance of each and to make sure others hear each idea. In very large groups, the leader can use a microphone on a long cord and move around among participants to assure that every contribution is heard. The leader encourages rapid-fire expression of ideas; restricts his comments; repeats ideas if necessary; and avoids any criticism by word, facial expression, or tone of voice. He receives every idea with enthusiasm and acceptance as something worthy of expression and future consideration. If ideas begin to flow that are distinctly irrelevant, the leader should briefly restate the focus and ask for ideas related to it without being critical of specific ideas.

The leader allows silence to prevail after a round of expressions. Silent periods provide time for thought. New ideas may be generating. A period of silence lasting thirty seconds seems long, but it is often essential to idea production. When silence is no longer productive of new ideas, when the same ideas are being repeated, when interest seems to wane, or when available time has been exhausted, the leader terminates the session.

A brief feedback session on the many ideas recorded should be provided to let participants see how productive they have been.

Recorded ideas, slightly edited, should be made available for whatever follow-up uses have been planned.

Suggested Follow-up Activities

1. Buzz sessions can be used for analysis and criticism of ideas.
2. Group discussion can be undertaken for analysis, criticism, assigning priorities, proposing revisions, combining ideas, and so on.
3. Committee sessions can be held for editing, revising, and suggesting ways of implementing ideas.
4. Panel discussion of ideas can be used for the purpose of suggesting combinations, challenging, or suggesting implementation procedures.

Arrangements. Group size: Two or more people can do brainstorming. Ordinarily ten or more will produce good results. A large group of sixty to seventy people tends to work quite well. When larger groups are involved, special facilities are almost essential, and two or three leaders may be needed to receive ideas simultaneously and record them as they flow from the group.

Facilities: Formal seating can be used if necessary. Chalkboard, overhead projector with transparent sheets or acetate roll, or large sheets of newsprint or butcher paper on the wall can be used for recording ideas. Microphones may be required, as the size of the group and the acoustics demand. Having a person in the audience with a microphone on a long extension cord can be very effective in securing maximum idea flow in minimum time.

Personnel: A group leader can handle all responsibilities for conducting the activity of a small group. With larger groups, recorders and assistant leaders need to be added. The leader must be able to encourage and stimulate while avoiding directiveness.

Illustration. A new videotape recorder had been purchased by the West Valley schools in connection with an in-service training project and a demonstration center. As the in-service project was nearing completion, the superintendent felt the need for ideas about future uses for the recorder. He wanted ideas for use by a planning committee, and he wanted to involve his school principals and supervisory staff as much as possible.

A dinner meeting was planned, and all principals and supervisors were invited. After dinner the superintendent briefly described his purpose in bringing the group together. He then introduced a college consultant who had been working in the West Valley schools. The consultant reviewed the procedures for brainstorming, set a time limit of forty minutes, and assured the group that follow-up on their ideas was planned by the special committee. He then asked for all ideas.

The ideas came slowly at first. The consultant used a chalkboard to record ideas himself while asking an elementary supervisor in the group to act as official recorder. Soon the ideas began to flow more rapidly:

"We should involve other grade levels."

"Can we get beyond language arts into other subject areas?"

"Let's turn attention to special education."

"Videotaping in real classroom situations would be worthwhile."

"Can you get videotape presentations of units — for example, physical education?"

"How about using tapes to inform the public of plans?"

"How much of this can be assumed by our own staff? How much additional staff are needed?"

As several of the ideas seemed somewhat irrelevant, the consultant reviewed the focus: "Remember, we're trying to get any and every idea on how we might use the videotape recorder for in-service purposes." The group resumed without further interruption:

"Let's get teachers involved in planning for demonstrations."

"Develop narrowly focused demonstrations involving specific skills."

"Homogeneous groups of observers should be tried."

"Can't we involve certain teachers according to their needs or interests?"

"Use the recorder for demonstrations of model faculty meetings."

"Let's plan for specific needs of teachers — beginning teachers as well as experienced teachers."

"Use the tapes to help the teacher see her own progress."

"Explore possibilities of bringing in specialists to demonstrate."

"A mobile unit to operate in classrooms would be helpful."

"Teachers need to have information on what to look for in demonstrations."

After the forty minutes came to an end, the consultant asked the recorder to report: "Tell us how many ideas you have listed, and read them in abbreviated form for our review." The elementary supervisor took about five minutes to read some sixty ideas. The consultant turned the meeting back to the superintendent, suggesting that he comment on next steps in making use of these very interesting ideas.

Cautions and Limitations.   Brainstorming should not be used without follow-up. Participants enjoy brainstorming, but they also expect something to be done with their ideas.

Brainstorming should not be used unless there is a real need for a look at all available ideas or the production of new ideas, or both, by a group. Obviously, this implies that the group has some knowledge about, or interest in, the topic or problem in focus. It would be useless to brainstorm with a group lacking either knowledge or interest. On the other hand, when a problem can be solved by consultation with an expert, brainstorming is hardly in order despite the group's interest. When only one or two alternative solutions are feasible, brainstorming is inappropriate.

Participants should be cautioned that not all ideas can be implemented, that critical analysis must follow, and that not all ideas should be expected to survive the process.

Summary.   Brainstorming is an activity for stimulating idea expression and production. It can be used to inform, stimulate, and develop understanding and attitudes relating to a problem and a group. The special procedures that are employed make this activity unique, and it is usable with a wide range of group sizes. Extra precautions should be observed to plan appropriate follow-up activities and to avoid use of brainstorming for inappropriate purposes.

Buzz Sessions

Definition.   The buzz session is a small-group activity in which groups are temporarily formed to discuss a specific topic with minimum structure, maximum emphasis upon interaction, and full opportunity to express ideas related to the topic. An optimum amount of critical analysis of ideas related to the topic is encouraged in a permissive topic-centered situation.

Purposes

1.   To facilitate maximum verbal interaction among participants.
2.   To promote understanding of all points of view held by participants.
3.   To determine the possibility of arriving at consensus on certain points.
4.   To identify points of view that are distinctly at issue.
5.   To stimulate interest in, and commitment to, working on a project or problem.

Procedure. A group that has focused its attention on a topic or problem issue is divided into subgroups referred to as buzz groups.

Each buzz group is assigned a specific location in which it is to work. Usually this is around a table, but in a large auditorium setting it may be simply an identified section of the available space or a cluster of chairs.

Buzz groups are asked to focus specifically upon a given topic. This topic is identified, defined, and described in advance by the leader so that all will be tuned in on it.

Buzz groups are given a definite time limit during which they are expected to discuss, analyze, and maximize their expression of ideas about the topic. Ordinarily, a minimum of ten to fifteen minutes is provided. A topic of some complexity may require forty minutes to an hour and a half.

A recorder is designated for each buzz group, with instructions to record the highlights of ideas expressed, including main points of view, agreements, disagreements, and suggestions.

Buzz groups are informed that completely free interaction with full expression of all ideas is being sought. In buzz sessions, unlike in brainstorming, participants should feel free to discuss, agree, disagree, or suggest alternatives. The interaction should be spirited, free flowing, and unrestricted. On the other hand, participants should be cautioned against making long-winded speeches or dominating the discussion.

A discussion leader is usually appointed, simply to facilitate interaction. Leaders should be selected who will not dominate or overstructure but simply encourage full, fair, and well-distributed participation. Sometimes no discussion leader is appointed, in which case the groups are clearly informed that there will be none. In such instances, each buzz group may be instructed to select its own leader, or a leaderless group discussion procedure may be followed in which each individual is expected not only to be a fully participating discussant but also to facilitate the participation of others.

Recorders should turn notes over to appropriate officials for follow-up activity planning.

Leaders should circulate among buzz groups, "eavesdropping" but not verbally participating in the interaction. This gives the leaders a feel for the quality of the thinking and of the ideas emerging. It also eliminates any notion on the part of participants that they have been abandoned by their leaders.

Suggested Follow-up Activities

1. A panel or symposium of recorders or selected participants and consultants analyze ideas expressed.

2.   Recorders' notes are analyzed, and study groups, committees, lectures, or discussion groups are organized.
3.   A tentative draft of a written document may be developed by a representative committee to synthesize ideas as a policy statement or in other appropriate form for review by all participants.

Arrangements.   Group size: It takes at least five participants to have an effective spontaneous buzz session. When total groups vary from ten to forty participants, buzz groups of five to eight persons work quite well. When large total groups are involved, buzz groups can be a bit larger to avoid the need for so many separate locations.

Facilities: A buzz group can work most effectively about a round table. A rectangular table works well if it is not too long and narrow. When tables are not available or the buzz groups are too large (tables seating more than ten persons rarely facilitate interaction), a small circle of chairs is quite satisfactory. When a circle is used, it should be as small as is consistent with the size of the group and the comfort of the participants.

No head position should be designated, neither a round table nor a circle has a head. If a rectangular table is used, the leader should avoid sitting at either end, as this is associated with the seat of authority in the minds of many persons.

Each buzz group should be separated from all others far enough to avoid interference with one another. Buzz groups can be assigned to separate rooms if any are available close at hand. If such facilities are not available, large spaces such as a library reading room, an auditorium, a cafeteria, or a gymnasium can be used by designating a corner for each buzz group.

Personnel: Leaders and recorders are needed. The recorders should be persons who can screen ideas, digest, synthesize, and analyze. They should not be stenographers. The leaders of buzz groups have only nominal leadership responsibilities. They must be coached in advance to avoid any unnecessary structuring, formal procedures, or controlling efforts. They should act as facilitators and stimulators. A brief training session is very desirable for leaders and recorders. Such a session might consist of a buzz session in which skilled personnel demonstrate how to lead and record.

Name Tags: Buzz groups work better when the participants know the names and something about the persons in the group. Name tags are advisable when even a few persons do not know each other. Color coding of name tags to show position, affiliation, or interest can help.

Illustration.   The Georgetown High School building was a shining new monument to educational progress. It was the first school building constructed in Georgetown in many years, and it served the people on "the other side of the tracks." Superintendent James Ramey took real pride in promoting this new building for the "poor kiddos." His assistant, Bill Holdsworth, had worked closely with the architect and selected staff members to be sure that instructional facilities were designed for flexibility and modern methods.

As the fall semester began in the new building, painters and electricians were still finishing their work. Trouble with the air-conditioning system caused some difficulty in September, and projection screens were still not installed in October. Despite these inconveniences, the staff members carried on as best they could. Everyone was enthusiastic about the new building. The students seemed to reflect their pride in both conduct and appearance.

By late October, Bill Holdsworth was able to turn from mechanical details to instructional concerns. He was commissioned by the superintendent to work with the high school principal and staff in developing an outstanding instructional program. Here was a fine facility, an eager and able teaching staff, and a waiting community. The new language lab could accommodate foreign language, drama, speech, and regular English classes. Some classrooms had folding walls for large-group instruction. Windowless construction made extensive use of visual aids practical. A beautiful library was available, and no study halls cluttered the facility. Bill decided to move before the holiday season to stimulate the faculty group and to get plans developed for improving instructional practices.

In consultation with the principal, Holdsworth arranged for school to be dismissed a bit early on the following Wednesday, October 27. The principal announced to his faculty that a special program-planning meeting would be held on that day, in the library, from 2:45 P.M. until 4:30 P.M. Holdsworth got in touch with a university professor who was familiar with the building and willing to serve as a consultant to the faculty. He agreed to attend this meeting and make a few introductory remarks.

As the faculty group assembled at about two forty, coffee and cookies were served. The principal called the meeting to order at two fifty, introduced the visiting consultant, and briefly stated the purpose of the meeting. Holdsworth then reviewed the plan of action.

"We want to begin thinking seriously about ways of using this building so as to provide the best possible instructional program. Superintendent Ramey has assured me that we can have just as much freedom as we need to try new ideas. We've had a couple of months now to get school started and become familiar with the building. These have been trying months for all of you, but things are now under control. We'd like to move with you in the direction of identifying promising new ways of working at teaching. If you can come up with some promising ideas, we'll work with you in developing project plans and trying these ideas this spring and next year.

"Now, to get to work today, we'd like to have you break into buzz groups. We will break into four groups of eight and nine persons each. The purpose of all of the groups will be the same. You are to concentrate on suggesting new teaching practices that might be worth trying in this school. Each group should try to identify a few practices someone in that group finds promising. Each practice suggested should be discussed and analyzed freely. When the session is over in about forty minutes, you should have one or more new teaching practices to propose in fairly well developed form. Your group does not need to agree on the value of the practice. You are not committing yourself or anyone else to adopting any practices. You are simply developing some promising ideas for further serious consideration.

"Now, are you ready to go to work?"

At this point, Holdsworth made quick buzz group assignments, getting clusters of teachers into four corners of the library where large tables had already been arranged. Group leaders were not designated, but a recorder had been assigned to each buzz group and instructed in note-taking procedures.

Holdsworth, the visiting consultant, and the principal circulated from group to group. They did not enter into the discussion. Instead, they listened for a few moments, sitting at the edge of the circle of participants. After about five minutes of "eavesdropping," the three men changed buzz groups. This was repeated at intervals until all three had listened to each group twice and had a feeling for the thinking in progress.

After thirty-five minutes, Holdsworth interrupted with an announcement. "Will you try to pull your thoughts together in the next five minutes, please? Your recorder has been taking notes. Let that person review the highlights of those notes and then spend the remaining time getting your suggestions formalized. We'll ask recorders to report suggestions of each buzz group to the total group at three forty-five."

As Bill stopped talking, the buzz of interaction reached a high pitch. Each group was now under pressure to pull its diverse ideas together. By three forty, three groups were breaking up. By three forty-five, the recorder in the last group made final notes, and Bill called for attention, directing all participants to be seated again in the center of the library. Recorders reported their suggestions after being cautioned to take only one minute each. The visiting consultant wrote brief phrases on a transparency as the recorders mentioned each major suggestion. When the reporting was over, Holdsworth asked the visiting consultant to discuss the suggestions that were made. He did so, using the visual he had prepared based on the reports. He focused attention upon similarities in suggestions, commenting on uses of facilities for implementing suggestions and emphasizing the need for attention to what was known about good teaching before any suggestions would be selected for development into project plans.

The principal concluded the meeting with a request: "I hope each of you will give some further thought to these teaching ideas in the next week. We will be asking for volunteer groups to do further planning on some of these ideas with the expectation that several new things will be in progress by early spring. Meeting adjourned."

Cautions and Limitations. Buzz sessions, like most other in-service activities, do not suffice without follow-up activities. Unlike brainstorming, buzz sessions are rarely used as introductory activities; they presume some prior events. For each session to be effective, participants must have a concern for the problem or an interest in the topic; some knowledge about the problem or topic; and opinions, attitudes, or feelings to express.

Buzz sessions should be avoided when attitudes, opinions, and feelings of the participants are not of crucial importance in approaching the problem. Teachers might appropriately engage in a buzz session when the topic is how to allocate library funds to various categories of instructional materials. A buzz session on the format of the purchase order, on the other hand, is probably not worthwhile.

Similarly, when a problem is such that expert advice is required, such advice should either precede or substitute for a buzz session. When a problem has only one feasible solution, a buzz session is inappropriate except as a way of testing the hypothesis that no other solution is feasible.

Summary. The buzz session is an activity that permits maximum face-to-face interaction in small groups even when large numbers of participants need to be involved. This activity has been used for a variety of purposes. It serves especially well when interest, stimulation, and consideration of diverse points of view are required. As temporary groups, buzz groups can be organized with maximum flexibility and can function with a minimum of structure. Lead-up activities are important to the success of a buzz session, and follow-up activities are essential.

Group Discussions

Definition. A group discussion is a small-group activity usually extending over a prolonged period of time in which systematic verbal interaction on a given topic (or problem) leads to consensus, decisions, recommendations, or clearly recognized disagreement. An extended life span assures the development of a genuine group with clearly defined group purposes, as distinguished from an aggregation of individuals sharing independent ideas.

Purposes

1. To share the knowledge of individuals with others in the group.
2. To develop understanding about complex problems.
3. To analyze proposals for dealing with problems.
4. To stimulate the development of new attitudes and opinions.
5. To arrive at carefully considered decisions for dealing with complex problems.

Procedures. Group discussion activities of a variety of kinds have been developed in recent years. The buzz session is a striking variation described in the last section. Case analysis and leaderless group discussion are briefly described as well. The procedures described here are those that apply to most discussion situations as defined. They would be modified somewhat, of course, as variations are employed.

Analyze the selected problem (or topic) to be sure that it is one that is important enough to justify the time required and is suitable for discussion as contrasted with the use of the lecture, buzz session, or other activity.

Check to see that an appropriate group of discussants is available. Discussants are appropriate when they have:

a real interest in the topic or problem
a need to discuss the topic or problem
some pertinent information, opinions, or feelings concerning the topic or problem

Select an appropriate discussion leader. It is not essential that the leader be an expert on the topic or problem in focus. In fact, expertness of that kind can complicate efforts toward efficient group action. The leader must have other characteristics, however. He should be interested in the problem, be reasonably knowledgeable about the various ramifications of the problem, have the respect of the group members, be open-minded regarding approaches to the problem, and have skill in discussion-leading techniques.

Provide training in discussion-leading techniques for the leader. Unless the person is already highly skilled, he usually welcomes an opportunity to receive training. Brief discussion sessions focusing upon vignettes of problem situations serve as effective training experiences when followed by critical analysis by a skilled discussion leader. Tape recordings of brief discussion sessions can be analyzed to help leaders employ techniques more skillfully.

Organize the initial discussion session by informing prospective discussants of the problem and the nature of the group being formed; suggest a tentative schedule and specify possible outcomes.

Conduct the initial discussion sessions with emphasis on getting acquainted, exploring the problem area, and reviewing and revising plans. It is not necessary or even desirable that procedural decisions be made at this point. Too much eagerness to "decide what to do and get it done" can lead to confusion and frustrate group cohesion.

Conduct subsequent sessions with a focus upon the identification of the basic elements or specific problems within the larger problem area. Relevant questions include: (1) What concerns participants most? (2) What is most important? (3) What may be resolved?

A group may have to wander verbally about the problem area without much direction for several sessions before basic elements or specific problems can be identified. Don't become discouraged with the group. Don't let the group become discouraged with itself. Expect some anxiety and discontent to be expressed, and accept it.

Provide resources for gaining more knowledge relevant to the problem area. This may involve use of films, books, pamphlets, visiting consultants, tape recordings, and similar resources. These should not be imposed on the group but made available and their use encouraged by individuals and the group as a whole when appropriate.

Encourage the group to make decisions or otherwise achieve bench marks of its progress by consensus. (These may be agreements, conclusions, disagreements, suggestions, and so forth.) Avoid formalities like voting or recording conclusions in very carefully worded language, but stimulate participants to consider progress and then move on.

Encourage open-mindedness in considering all ideas relevant to the basic problem or topic. Encourage participants to assume the attitude of the trial judge who withholds judgment and considers all relevant evidence before rendering a verdict. In promoting this attitude among participants, the discussion leader sets the example and uses a variety of techniques:

1. Ask open-ended questions that stimulate a variety of responses.
2. Restate unpopular points of view with the suggestion that discussants might want to react.
3. Encourage the less active discussants to express themselves.
4. Encourage discussants to search out new information and report it to the group at appropriate times.
5. Invite resource persons to share relevant information with the group at appropriate times.
6. Accept all ideas expressed as worthy of consideration by the group.
7. Avoid ignoring or criticizing ideas that seem least acceptable.
8. Avoid promoting certain ideas over others.
9. Summarize main ideas, information, or points of view relevant to a basic element in the discussion to encourage full consideration.

10. Suggest postponement of decisions when consensus has not really been achieved or information is lacking.
11. Encourage the decision to agree or to disagree when consensus does not seem possible.

Encourage the group to project its own plan and timetable for accomplishing its purposes and dissolving itself.

Arrange for the recording of group outcomes. This should not be a stenographic record but an abstract of ideas, agreements, disagreements, decisions, and plans. These notes should be maintained by one or more designated persons. The responsibility can be a rotating assignment among discussants, or an assistant to the group can serve as permanent recorder. A copy of the recorder's notes should go to each discussant prior to the session.

Case Discussion.   The case method in group discussion has been developed to provide for a more highly structured discussion situation. In this form a carefully developed case is presented to all discussants. A case is an objective report of a real situation in which many aspects of a complex problem are presented as information. This is usually a narrative description of a real situation that illustrates in very specific terms a problem or problems worthy of discussion. The case, then, not only stimulates meaningful participation but also contains much relevant information for use by discussants.

In case discussions, the basic style and most techniques of discussion leading still apply. Certain procedures are significantly different.

Since the case is not the actual problem of the participants, and available information is readily available, less time is required for analysis, and the interest span of the participants is likely to be relatively short. Such discussions are rarely extended over more than two or three sessions. Often a single two-hour session is the limit of time profitably spent.

Since the problem situation is decribed in narrative form with a minimum of irrelevant information included, discussants are led to analysis with a minimum of exploratory discussion.

A certain amount of interpretation has entered into the case writing as the writer selected information to include or omit. This places the leader in the position of being one who stimulates participants to discover the interpretations that are possible. This places him in the role of one who already knows many of the alternatives. This may or may not be true in real problem-centered discussion groups. The case discussion leader, therefore, structures the discussion to some degree. It can be quite structured when used to illustrate only a specific theory, concept, or pattern of events, but leaders should take care not to overstructure the discussion and lose spontaneity. Furthermore, a well-written case has potential for illustrating a variety of concepts, and speculation can be freely stimulated regarding the consequences that might follow from alternative events to those reported in the case. For such uses, the discussion technique must be much less structured.

Leaderless Discussion. This variation of group discussion activity calls upon participants to share the leadership responsibilities described previously. The advantage offered by having no designated leader derives from the greater feeling of responsibility and involvement on the part of the discussants. Disadvantages include the possibility that leadership responsibilities will not be adequately assumed by participants. When leadership development and group assumption of responsibility are more important outcomes than problem solving, leaderless discussions have much to offer. Leaderless group discussions tend to require the following procedures:

1. The group is oriented regarding the absence of an assigned leader and the reasons for this unless the situation requires no such explanation. Each group member is encouraged to exercise responsibilities as both discussant and leader. Formal selection of a leader is discouraged, and the group is urged to guard against letting any one person exercise leadership for an extended period.
2. Leaderless groups are carefully observed by those responsible for organizing them. Should a group completely fall apart, a skilled leader may be assigned to the group just long enough to assist discussants in analyzing progress, setting new directions, and overcoming obstacles. This technique provides each group member with an opportunity to try his hand again at exercising leadership.

Suggested Follow-up Activities. Frequently, a discussion group will have purposes that can be relatively well accomplished in the group without other follow-up activities. This is likely to be the case when development of attitudes, opinions, and understanding are the purposes selected. When decisions, suggestions, or recommendations for action come from a discussion group, the follow-up activities are important.

1. Publish a brief report on the conclusions of the group for dissemination to others interested in the same problem or topic.
2. Organize a committee or study group to formulate plans and make arrangements as suggested by the discussion group.
3. Undertake an action research or pilot project to develop and evaluate ideas generated in the group.

Arrangements. Group size: A discussion group requires a sufficient number of participants to produce a working unit as contrasted with a very small number of individuals. On the other hand, a group requires few enough participants so that full interaction involving face-to-face contact is possible. Ordinarily, a discussion group should be no smaller than seven or eight persons and no larger than fifteen.

Facilities: Discussions should be held in a quiet, comfortable room. Chairs should be arranged in a circle, or oval, or around a table. The furniture should be arranged so that each individual can easily look at each other member of the group. A head position should be avoided. The leader should be designated by his behavior rather than by his position in the circle. Chairs should be comfortable for fairly prolonged sitting.

Personnel: The need for a leader and a recorder has been discussed. Resource persons are important to the success of many discussion groups. Budgetary and other arrangements should be made for such persons to be available as needed by the group.

*Illustration.** The Austin schools, like many, were confronted with the problem of securing public acceptance and support for changes in the mathematics program under the label of "The New Math." Teacher attitudes posed a problem in some instances, too, but interest was highest in meeting the need for a program of parent information.

The mathematics supervisor developed plans for a discussion group to face this problem. Each junior and senior high school was asked to send one mathematics teacher, which made a total of fifteen teachers. Most of these people were acquainted with one another and with the supervisor.

The discussions were scheduled in the conference room of School A, a new and modern school that was centrally located in the city. In the conference room, a large round table was available to seat up to twenty people.

A series of four sessions was tentatively planned. The sessions lasted from 3:00 P.M. to 5:00 P.M., with the teachers released from teaching duties during the last period of the school day. Coffee was served at the beginning of each session, and ten to fifteen minutes were used for social interaction at this time.

Since the group was formed for a special problem, the leader initiated the first session by a brief statement of the purpose and suggested that discussants share their experiences related to the problem. Several discussants began to ask about their responsibilities as related to the problem. The leader suggested that they might be able to clarify the problem and

---

* This illustration was provided by Mr. Elgin Schilhab, Mathematics Supervisor, Austin Independent School District, Austin, Texas.

attempt to develop some recommendations for improving public relations in this field. The leader asked that each of the participants discuss the problem with his colleagues.

As a stimulus for the first discussion period, the leader used a tape recording obtained when a parent came to him for an interview. In the recording, the parent told about a back-to-school night experience with his child's math teacher. The child was taking geometry, and the teacher left the parent feeling that modern mathematics would make this course completely obsolete. Consequently, the parent felt that the child was wasting his time. The interview graphically illustrated a misunderstanding and the need for better public information. The discussion followed from this in a free and spontaneous manner, with the leader acting almost as a participant.

Sometimes group members engaged in side conversations in their eagerness to express views or feelings. These continued briefly, but the leader encouraged all members to share their thoughts with the total group when such a side conversation continued. The leader interrupted occasionally to ask for clarification of some point or to summarize briefly, and this usually stimulated still more discussion.

The discussion was scheduled to stop at 5:00 P.M., and the schedule was followed. In terminating the discussion, the supervisory leader briefly summarized major points and promised to provide a written review discussants could refer to at the beginning of the next discussion period. The leader suggested some possible next steps for the group to consider, including an attempt to identify several of the more serious public relations problems. With that the session was adjourned.

Cautions and Limitations.   Do not assume that any informed, personable, or eager person can lead a group discussion effectively. The most highly informed person may inhibit discussion, and specific skills are required for discussion leading in any case. Training of a discussion leader is essential in most situations.

Avoid a discussion group in which opinions, attitudes, and knowledge of participants are highly similar. Diversity among group members is important.

Avoid the temptation to make critical decisions for the group when consensus cannot be reached. Similarly, avoid taking a vote. If consensus has not been reached and the decision is critical, the group is not ready for decision making.

Avoid letting a discussion become a recitation in which the leader asks questions and responds to everything that is said. The leader should generally be silent, and he should make his few questions as open-ended as possible to stimulate a variety of responses.

Avoid the tendency to get everyone to participate by calling upon each participant in some systematic way. A good discussion leader gets everyone involved by stimulating free interaction, being sparing with his own remarks, and keeping others from dominating the discussion.

Do not be afraid of silence. Sometimes a group needs a chance just to sit and contemplate an idea or a problem. The silence will be broken when someone feels the need. In fact, most adults feel so uncomfortable with silence that a group discussion leader might have to encourage it occasionally.

Do not involve a discussion group in your problem unless it is also the group's problem in some significant way. Most people are too busy to deal with a problem for the time required in a discussion group unless they are interested and concerned. Leaders who organize discussion groups to make themselves feel less insecure with a problem are not likely to meet with success.

Do not organize a discussion group to support what you or some authority have already decided. Participants are very quick to sense that they are discussing a problem that the leader has already solved in his own mind. A reasonably intelligent group sees through manipulation by the leader very quickly. Even the most skilled manipulator is less than successful in that his discussion group senses that something is not quite right and hence functions inefficiently and tends to lack creativity.

Summary. The group discussion is an activity facilitating extended group interaction with focus upon a problem or idea of common interest and concern. Such an activity under skillful leadership serves well in stimulating ideas, sharing information, developing understanding, and influencing attitudes and opinions. Discussion groups are not usually action groups except in that they can make decisions, recommendations, or express consensus and disagreement. They often provide the basis of understanding upon which action groups can operate.

In several modified forms, group discussions serve special purposes. The case method of discussion provides a unique approach to stimulating thinking about complex situations. The leaderless group discussion provides for maximum involvement and is a valuable approach to leader identification and training.

Role Playing

Definition. Role playing may be defined as a spontaneous dramatization involving one or more persons assuming designated roles in relation to a specified problem in a given situation. The drama is structured by the problem and the situation but is unrehearsed and not preplanned. The objective is to encourage the fullest possible assumption of roles by the players so that they act and feel as they might in a real situation.

Purposes

1. To provide concrete examples of behavior as a basis for discussion.
2. To stimulate new attitude formation.
3. To develop skill in interviewing and questioning, or other skills needed in spontaneous verbal interaction.
4. To develop understanding of feelings and attitudes of other people.

Procedures. Role playing has been widely used to stimulate learning associated with problems of human interaction. The terms "sociodrama" and "psychodrama" have been used in describing role-playing activities of various kinds. The specific procedures vary, depending upon the purposes, the size of the group, and the extent of involvement required. Essential procedures for role playing under nearly any conditions seem to include establishing rapport, identifying a specific problem, assigning roles, adhering to roles, and terminating the activity at an appropriate time.

Participants should feel comfortable with each other if role playing is to be for real. Initial experiences with role playing are often resisted, but a group readily learns to accept this kind of activity once it comes into use. Often a group leader can begin role playing by assuming roles and inviting one or more self-assured individuals to join him. Role playing can be more comfortably experienced by some participants if two or three people are all involved and no audience is observing. Above all, leaders need to display a friendly, permissive, and constructive attitude toward all role players as they become involved for the first few times.

Role players must be directed toward a very specific problem to which all participants can relate. Roles must be played in terms of individuals interacting with others in a very concrete situation. A critical incident, a case, a lesson can be the basis for role playing, but the players must act in terms of a specific time and place as well as having the problem clearly in mind. A lesson protocol or vignette might be used for this purpose, with the role playing built upon this lesson involving this teacher, class, and period. However, each role-playing session should begin with a specific instance in the lesson with the leader suggesting, for instance, "Let's role-play that portion that starts with item number sixty-eight and see how we would try to get expressions of pupil attitudes."

Roles need to be specifically assigned so each person knows what is expected of him. It is not wise to tell participants how to act, for spontaneity is essential. However, teacher, parent, pupil, principal, and other persons involved in the specific situation should be designated in advance. When one role is not too complimentary or flattering, it may be wise to ask a very well liked participant to assume it. Roles do not need to match the people playing them. One of the characteristics that makes role playing a very useful activity is the ease with which participants can assume a role and then return to reality and discuss it objectively.

Role players should be urged to adhere to assigned roles. This is not always possible, but when roles are abandoned, the action should stop. Anxiety may cause role players to find themselves unable to adhere to the role assigned. However, participants can learn to adhere to roles with a bit of coaching and encouragement. Leaders should be alert to keep participants from getting into the habit of dropping out of a role when it becomes a bit awkward. Some self-discipline can be cultivated.

Leaders should terminate role-playing sessions at an appropriate time. Ordinarily, a few minutes of involvement in a role provides a lot of experience for discussion. If a role player remains in his role too long, he may get emotionally involved to the point of embarrassment.

Suggested Follow-up Activities

1. Ask observers to react to the role playing they saw.
2. Ask each role player to describe his or her feelings as he or she became involved.
3. Discuss alternative ways of dealing with the situation.
4. Have an observer-analyst report on his analysis of the interaction.
5. Switch roles among the role players and have the same situation played again.

Arrangements.   Group size: Role playing can be used with nearly any number of participants. Two people can role-play in a very private and personal situation. Small groups (ten to fifteen participants) facilitate optimum use of this activity since all can watch, all can discuss, and all can be role players. Large groups generally require an audience situation, and buzz groups may have to be used to get follow-up discussion.

Illustration.   Role playing is involved in most of the laboratory type sessions discussed in Chapter VII. In Chapter IX, the session on interview styles illustrates structured role playing that also serves by way of demonstration.

An interesting illustration of role playing involved Dr. Laurine Johnson, the new director of special education in the Wakeville City schools. As she met for the second time with the new screening committee, she decided to role-play a situation in which a pupil had been designated for possible placement in a special class for the brain-injured. In a previous meeting with the committee she was concerned that they seemed to want her to make the decisions for them to accept. Their discussion of the responsibilities of the committee to "review all relevant information and make the best educational placement" seemed to worry several of the committee members. One elementary school principal had said to her following the meeting, "I don't know too much about this kind of problem, but I'll go along with what you recommend." A sixth-grade teacher had asked, "Are there some materials we should read to guide our decisions?" A counselor had been overheard commenting to a supervisor during the last committee meeting, "I hope we can get a lot of new classes organized for these kids who can't make it in the seventh and eighth grades."

With these comments and questions in mind, Dr. Johnson carefully planned her second meeting of the committee as an in-service session. On their arrival, she briefly introduced her plan to have a practice session. She distributed folders containing information on a single pupil. "Now, this is not for real. We don't need to make a decision on this boy at this time. It is a real case, however, and we could well have this or another just like it at our next meeting. Let's role-play our approach to this problem. This boy is not doing at all well in school."

After this introduction, each committee member read the material carefully. Finally, when all seemed to have finished, Dr. Johnson asked, "Well, what do you think?" A discussion followed. Opinions were given; additional information was requested; suggestions were made. When specific kinds of additional information were requested, Dr. Johnson provided it, since she had a much more complete case record than had been provided for the committee members.

After nearly forty minutes, one member said, "Let's make a decision. We have other cases to review today!" Dr. Johnson said, "All right. Will you make a specific recommendation?" Another committee member volunteered, "I move we ask the parents for permission to place him in a special class for the emotionally disturbed." A flurry of discussion followed this motion. Some agreed strongly. Others were not sure. Some thought a class for minimally brain-injured would be better.

After awhile, Dr. Johnson asked, "Do we have a second to this motion for placement?" Several volunteered to second the motion. "Are we ready for a decision?" Heads nodded. "All in favor?" Most assented. "Those opposed?" One or two weak negative responses were heard.

It was now 5:05 P.M. Dr. Johnson glanced at her watch and acknowledged the lateness of the hour. "I know we must leave promptly. Before we go, however, I want to share some additional information with you about this boy and set a date for another meeting." As she talked, Dr. Johnson distributed a mimeographed sheet. "This contains physical examination data, a report from the school social worker on a home visit, and a quotation from the psychologist. Most of this is new information in the sense that you did not ask for it so I did not give it to you."

As the participants glanced at the new information, there was a flurry of comments. They saw almost immediately that some of this information might have changed their decision. Some complained, "Why didn't you give us this information, even without our asking?" Dr. Johnson replied, "I wanted to dramatize the importance of information from various sources. Also, I wanted us to realize how easily a poor decision can be made in good conscience and good faith. Would you like to meet again soon to role-play this and other cases?" Most seemed eager to do so, and a date was set.

Cautions and Limitations. Many of the cautions in using role playing have already been mentioned. Players must be encouraged to become involved for the first time and then be protected from embarrassment. Leaders must be alert to terminate role playing before emotional involvement becomes excessive.

Role playing is an activity uniquely suited for in-service education sessions designed to deal with human relations problems. The depth of involvement in simulated reality provides high experience impact for attitude and insight development as well as for building certain verbal interaction skills. While groups may need some coaching and encouragement in the use of role playing, it is readily accepted by most people in a comfortable group situation and stimulates much interest.

SUMMARY

Working in groups for in-service education is basic. Group planning, evaluating, and implementing are inescapable, even in highly personalized program operations. The natural advantages of group endeavors are enticing. Furthermore, an extensive knowledge based on the use of group processes is readily available for in-service planners to draw upon. Unfortunately, the extensive body of literature reporting on research and development in group processes is now somewhat old. It is not, however, outmoded. It should be studied and put to good use.

Much of this chapter has been devoted to a careful explication of four basic group techniques or activities. These are only four of a much larger variety. They are basic, however, in the sense that they alone can enormously enrich and diversify group experiences for in-service education. Furthermore, without the use of such basic techniques group endeavors are likely to be less fruitful than they might otherwise be.

REFERENCES

*1. Baumann, Bedrich. *Imaginative Participation: The Career of an Organizing Concept in a Multi-Disciplinary Context*. The Hague: Martinus Nijhoff, 1975.

2. Bollens, John C. and Dale R. Marshall. *A Guide to Participation: Fieldwork, Role Playing Cases and Other Forms*. Englewood Cliffs, N.J.: Prentice-Hall, Inc., 1973.

3. Bouchard, T. J., Jr., et al. "Brainstorming Procedure, Group Size and Sex as Determinants of the Problem-Solving Effectiveness of Groups and Individuals." *Journal of Applied Psychology* 59, no. 2 (April 1974): 135–38.

*4. Bradford, Leland P. and Dorothy Mial. "When Is a Group?" *Educational Leadership* 21, no. 3 (December 1973): 147–51.

*5. Cantor, Nathaniel. *Learning Through Discussion*. Buffalo, N.Y.: Human Relations for Industry, 1951.

*6. Cartwright, Dorwin and Alvin Zander (editors). *Group Dynamics: Research and Theory*. 3d ed. New York: Harper and Row, 1968.

7. Chevens, Frank. *Leading Group Discussions*. Austin, Tex.: Hogg Foundation for Mental Health, 1962.

8. Coad, Rosemary A. et al. "The Effects of an Organization Development Program on Satisfaction, Group Process, Climate, Leadership and Student Achievement." A paper presented at the annual meeting of the American Educational Research Association. San Francisco, April 19–23, 1976.

9. Coody, Betty. "A Study of the Impact of Demonstration Teaching on Experienced and Inexperienced Teachers Under Various Supervisory Conditions." Doctoral dissertation, University of Texas at Austin, 1967.

10. Cook, Lloyd and Elaine Cook. *School Problems in Human Relations*. New York: McGraw-Hill, 1957.

11. Cox, R. S. "Rewarding Instructions vs. Brainstorming on Creativity Test Scores of College Students." *Psychological Reports* 41, no. 3, part 1 (December 1977): 951–54.

12. Crowell, Laura. *Discussion: Method of Democracy*. Chicago: Scott, Foresman, 1963.

13. Day, Barbara D. and James W. Jenkins. "North Carolina's K-3 Staff Development Program." *Educational Leadership* 32, no. 5 (February 1975): 326–31.

14. Derr, Brooklyn C. "OD Won't Work in Schools." *Education and Urban Society* 8, no. 2 (February 1976): 227–41.

15. DuBois, Rachel and Mew-Soon Li. *The Art of Group Conversation: A New Breakthrough in Social Communication*. New York: Association Press, 1965.

16. Dwyer, Margaret S. "Mastering Change in Education: Involving Others in Educational Change." *Educational Technology* 16, no. 12 (December 1976): 40–41.

* Suggested for further reading.

17. Fiedler, Fred E. and Martin M. Chemers. *Leadership and Effective Management.* Glenview, Ill.: Scott, Foresman, 1974.

18. Fleming, Robert S. "Action Research for School Improvement." Chapter 6 in *Staff Development: Staff Liberation* (Charles W. Beegle and Roy A. Edelfelt, editors). Washington, D.C.: Association for Supervision and Curriculum Development, 1977.

19. Friedlander, Madeline S. *Leading Film Discussions: A Guide to Using Films for Discussion, Training Leaders, Planning Effective Programs.* New York: League of Women Voters, City of New York, 1972.

*20. Gall, Meredith D. and Joyce P. Gall. "The Discussion Method." In *The Psychology of Teaching Methods.* 75th Yearbook. Part I (N. L. Gage, editor). Chicago: National Society for the Study of Education, 1976.

21. Gibb, J. R., G. N. Platts, and L. E. Miller. *Dynamics of Participative Groups.* St. Louis, Mo.: J. S. Swift, 1961.

22. Grove, Theodore G., "Attitude Convergence in Small Groups." *Journal of Communication* 15, no. 4 (December 1965): 226–28.

23. Gyllenhammer, Pehr G. *People at Work.* Reading, Mass.: Addison-Wesley, 1976.

24. Hasling, John. *Group Discussion and Decision-Making.* New York: Thomas Y. Crowell, 1975.

25. Hawley, Robert C. *Value Exploration Through Role-Playing.* Amherst, Mass.: Education Research Associates, 1974.

26. Hill, William Fawcett. *Learning thru Discussion.* Rev. ed. Beverly Hills, Calif.: Sage Publications, 1969.

27. Johnson, Kenneth G., John J. Senatore, Mark C. Liebig, and Gene Minor. *Nothing Never Happens.* Beverly Hills, Calif.: Glencoe Press, 1974.

28. Lippitt, Ronald. "Sensitivity Training: What Is It? How Can It Help Students, Teachers, Administrators?" *Childhood Education* 46, no. 6 (March 1970): 311–13.

29. Madsen, D. B. and J. R. Finger, Jr. "Comparison of a Written Feedback Procedure, Group Brainstorming and Individual Brainstorming." *Journal of Applied Psychology* 63, no. 1 (February 1978): 120–23.

30. McLeod, Pierce H. "A New Move Toward Preservice and Inservice Teacher Education." *Educational Leadership* 32, no 5 (February 1975): 522.

31. Moffit, John Clifton. *Inservice Education for Teachers.* Washington, D.C.: Center for Applied Research in Education, 1963.

*32. Osborn, A. F. *Applied Imagination: Principles and Procedures of Creative Thinking.* New York: Charles Scribner's Sons, 1957.

33. Ostlund, Leonard A. "Case Discussion Learning in Human Relations." *Journal of Human Relations* 16 (1968): 212.

34. Pharis, William L. *In-Service Education of Elementary School Principals.* Washington, D.C.: Department of Elementary School Principals, National Education Association, 1966.

*35. Phillips, Gerald M. *Communication in the Small Group.* 2d ed. Indianapolis, Ind.: Bobbs-Merrill, 1973.

* Suggested for further reading.

36. Pinkerton, Todd. *Breaking Through Communication Barriers with Role Play*. Atlanta, Ga.: John Knox Press, 1976.

37. Rogers, Carl R. *Freedom to Learn*. Columbus, Ohio: Charles E. Merrill, 1969.

38. Rubin, Louis. *Perspectives on Preservice and Inservice Education*. Syracuse, N.Y.: National Dissemination Center, Syracuse University, April 1978.

39. Schein, Virginia E. and Larry E. Greiner. "Can Organization Development Be Fine Tuned to Bureaucracies?" *Organizational Dynamics* 5, no. 3 (Winter 1977): 48–61.

40. Schmuck, Richard A., Donald Murray, Mary Ann Smith, Mitchell Schwartz, and Margaret Runkel. *Consultation for Innovative Schools—OD for Multiunit Structure*. Eugene, Ore.: Center for Educational Policy and Management, 1975.

41. Sharan, Shlomo and Yael Sharan. *Small Group Teaching*. Englewood Cliffs, N.J.: Prentice-Hall, Inc., 1976.

42. Vescolani, Fred and Richard L. Featherstone. "Innovations in Preparation: The Externship." *UCEA Newsletter* (December 1969): 7–9.

*43. Wright, David W. *Small Group Communication: An Introduction*. Dubuque, Iowa: Kendall/Hunt, 1975.

* Suggested for further reading.

IX

Evaluation Techniques

INTRODUCTION

The evaluation of in-service education operations should not be taken lightly. As one of the most important developmental operations, ISE deserves careful, systematic evaluation. As an operation that is *sensitive* in the sense that personnel are very much concerned about the quality of in-service education, ISE should be evaluated rather closely and regularly. As an operation that can be enormously influential, yet one that is expensive and disruptive in nature, ISE deserves evaluation that is truly rigorous.

To speak of what evaluation should be as it relates to in-service education is one thing, but the mounting of evaluation efforts that are truly productive is a difficult endeavor. Limited resources must provide extensive information regarding a host of diverse facets of the operation. The intermittent nature of ISE makes timing a critical problem. The widespread involvement of personnel of all kinds makes ISE evaluation feedback an elaborate process in which findings must be in the most readily usable form.

PURPOSES OF EVALUATION

By recognizing the specific purposes that can be served and selecting from among them, evaluation efforts are made more efficient and are simplified. Obviously, evaluation is intended to improve operations (25:76). However, such improvements can be accomplished in a variety of ways (3:313). Improvements need to be sustained by providing reinforcing evidence. This is quite different from go–no go decisions that are to be made on the basis of some overall assessment. Detecting defects in a program or session is still another focus for evaluation that is essential to improving the quality of training. The clear determination of operational strengths is also important to assure their maintenance even as some revisions are undertaken.

In addition to differentiating purposes to be served, plans for evaluation have to be developed differently for programs and for sessions. Session evaluation data may be quite useful in program evaluation, if planned for. However, session evaluations should be useful in themselves, regardless of larger programmatic purposes to be served. Conversely, session evaluations can rarely be used for program evaluation purposes by simple aggregation of data. Program evaluation requires a special design and entails numerous decisions regarding the evaluation questions to be answered.

Providing Reinforcement

The people directly involved in any aspect of in-service education can profit from, and often need, the reinforcement that evaluation can offer. Traditionally, evaluation data are perceived as threatening, and they may well be. However, when people are planning well, getting results, and satisfying needs of their colleagues, they need feedback that is reassuring and supportive. Such feedback, like all evaluation outcomes, should be as clearly objective as possible. "Snow jobs" are neither ethical nor effective for reinforcement purposes. However, even the mediocre ISE program or session has some strengths, and these should not be neglected.

Evaluation efforts that are clearly useful for reinforcement purposes must be diagnostic as well as objective to assure that strengths will be detected even when many weaknesses prevail. Hence, data of different kinds, about different aspects of the operation, and from different sources need to be gathered. In the analysis of these data, the reinforcement potential must be retained by avoiding aggregates and retaining a more panoramic view. For instance, participant responses on a series of five-point scales could be reported as a mean or median for all responses of 3.1. However, reporting a range of responses from 2 to 5 is a bit more informative. Showing a frequency distribution for each of several items may be even more helpful if

Exhibit 9–1. ILLUSTRATION OF A FREQUENCY DISTRIBU-
TION OF PARTICIPANT RESPONSES TO
SEVERAL ITEMS (N = 46)

	Frequency of Responses					
Items	*1* *Slightly*	*2* *Some-* *what*	*3* *Substan-* *tially*	*4* *Highly*	*5* *Ex-* *tremely*	*Mean* *Rating*
5. How stimulating did you find the session activities?	0	1	2	8	35	4.7
7. How relevant to your job situation did you find the session content?	0	3	2	2	39	4.7
8. How useful (practical) for you was the skill or information gained in this session?	5	10	13	12	6	3.1

in fact there are substantial differences in the responses to different aspects of the session. (See Exhibit 9–1.) Finally, a scattergram showing relationships of objectives of participants to their responses may help still more to reinforce with the selectivity that guides improvements as well. (See Exhibit 9–2 for an illustration of a scattergram analysis.)

The use of carefully analyzed data in providing feedback to individuals and groups for reinforcement purposes is of course crucial. Obviously, feedback should be as rapid as possible, consistent with careful analysis of data. If those most in need of feedback can undertake the analysis process themselves, then feedback is likely to be prompt and also more meaningful. When machines or computers are utilized, turnaround time needs to be planned for the shortest possible interval, and the printout or other documents utilized for feedback purposes need to be clear, simple, and readily interpretable.

Often, feedback for reinforcement purposes is as important to the participants as it is to the officials in charge. A much-neglected use of evaluation involves giving participants information that helps them more accurately assess the worth of the ISE activities they have been a part of. Too often participants see evaluation as perfunctory — an exercise in opinion giving — but not as a systematic process for responsible assessment of an important part of school operations for which all parties *share* responsibilities and benefits.

Go–No Go Decisions

The basic program of a school or college rarely faces decision making involving the serious possibility of discontinuing an operation entirely. When such decisions are faced, the circumstances are often of an emergency kind; hence, evaluation data are not highly influential. Decisions regarding temporary systems such as ISE programs can be of the go–no go type, however. There is no rational reason to continue any particular type or form of in-service education year after year. In fact, changing circumstances nearly always make discontinuance of an ISE program worthy of consideration at some point in time.

In Chapter IV the tendency for staff groups to become associated with a program or project and to perpetuate it was discussed. This very tendency makes evaluation of the kind that can support a no go decision important. Bank and Bury (1) in studying evaluation efforts in 409 school districts throughout the United States comment that such efforts rarely involve what they call "make or break" decision-making purposes (1:24).

The emphasis on evaluation for the improvement of ongoing operations should not blind evaluators to this special purpose of informing decisions where discontinuation is a potential alternative. It is not realistic to view any ISE program as a permanent operation. Needs are so numerous that even relatively successful programs judged on the basis of the accomplishment of their own objectives may be less than top priority when judged in terms of a broad array of program alternatives for meeting other needs.

The emphasis given to needs assessment in much of the literature on planning in-service education can be seen as related to the problem of deciding to discontinue, as well as to initiate, new efforts. Unfortunately, many needs assessments approach the problem as though there were only one kind of decision to make regarding what to initiate in the way of new ISE. Such a one-sided view of the problem may well be counterproductive. Decisions to mount new programs may inadvertently force decisions in favor of discontinuing already operating programs. Instead, the evaluation efforts should be such that needs assessment data are carefully utilized in concert with other data reflecting ongoing program efforts. Under such arrangements, existing programs will be discontinued only when they are ineffective, have accomplished their purposes, or have become low in priority.

Detecting Defects

The most promising purpose of in-service education evaluation is the clear identification of operational *defects* that can be eliminated or *ameliorated*. While this purpose may seem negatively oriented, it need not be. On the contrary, recognition of the complexities surrounding ISE makes it quite logical to expect that sessions and programs will always be far from perfect. To make the best possible use of scarce resources is an urgent need because of the scarcity of such resources and also because of the important contributions to be made by ISE when it is of high quality.

Evaluation efforts directed toward identifying defects must be highly diagnostic in nature. Vague or generalized references to difficulties are not adequate for this purpose. Data gathering must assure as much validity as possible. Instrumentation should be such that reliable data are provided. But data analysis techniques must be sophisticated enough to assure that diagnostic interpretations rather than general impressions result.

EVALUATION AS PROCESS

The foregoing discussion about the various purposes of evaluation implies a data-gathering and analysis process. But evaluation is generally recognized to be much more than this process. In the past, many viewed evaluation as an act of judging something or someone (29:2), which is of course a very archaic use of the term. However, recent trends associated with technological developments in testing, measurement, and educational research have emphasized research design, data gathering, and statistical analysis to the point of creating confusion about the utility of evaluation. Evaluation is not research. The two have much in common, but the differences are extremely important (23:372–80). Some of the differences have been well expressed by experts in both fields. Thompson (25), reflects the position of Stufflebeam et al. (24) and others in defining evaluation as "the marshalling of information for the purpose of improving decisions" (25:26). Obviously, in the real world decisions are made with or without organized evaluation efforts. Hence, Thompson's stress on improving decisions is important.

Carol Weiss (29) introduces "evaluation research" as follows:

> The tools of research are pressed into service to make the judging process more accurate and objective. In its research guise, evaluation establishes clear and specific criteria for success. It collects evidence systematically . . . , and compares it with the criteria that were set. (29:1–2)

She further develops the notion of "evaluation research" being used "to measure the effects of a program against the goals it set out to accomplish" (29:4). While this concept of evaluation is consistent with those that will be presented here, it is needlessly restrictive in its focus on *effect* while ignoring possible *causes*.

Still another variant view was developed long ago and promoted by Stephen Corey as "action research":

> Basically the idea . . . is . . . to bring a little more scientific approach to the experimental efforts of teachers, and to offer a way by which teachers can work individually and/or collectively on problems encountered in their teaching—hence modifying or developing the instructional program. (18)

Although the emphasis of action research was on the classroom teacher some twenty years ago, it was characterized very much as evaluation in the modern sense of the term.

For our purposes, evaluation as defined by Stuffelbeam et al. and Thompson as clearly not encumbered by restrictions of research outcomes serves as the best basis for assessing in-service education, even though the various research methodologies and techniques are fully utilized. Accordingly, readers will want to consult the works of Cook (9), Borich (3;21), and Sonoquist and Dunkelberg (22), among others, for techniques to borrow.

A Sequence of Processes

Evaluating in-service education involves systematically implementing a set of sequenced processes, as follows:

1. *Selecting,* defining, and specifying *evaluative criteria.* What specific measurable events do we anticipate as evidence of success?
2. *Selecting,* designing, or adapting *instruments and procedures* for measuring events related to the evaluative criteria.
3. *Gathering (recording) data,* using appropriate instruments and procedures.
4. *Analyzing data* in ways that reduce and array them in relation to evaluative criteria.
5. *Interpreting results* (findings) by comparing and contrasting findings with each other, by classes, and against criteria.
6. *Valuing findings* by relating them to values and expectations of the individuals or institutions being served.
7. *Deciding* on one or more *actions* that should logically follow.
8. *Acting* on the decisions so as to improve and maintain the best of the operation.

While these eight processes are numbered in sequence and are generally followed in sequence, they may also overlap one another. Criteria are sometimes revised, refined, added, or deleted after instrumentation, data gathering, and analysis are well along, because new insights may be produced in process. Interpretation and analysis may overlap, with some new analyses being undertaken as the result of insights gained in preliminary efforts. Valuing is most dangerous out of sequence. Until analyses are thoroughly completed and thoughtful interpretations are drawn, valuing is premature and usually leads to faulty decisions.

An Illustration

This sequence of evaluation processes in simple application can be described for a single-session training program as follows:

Evaluative Criteria

1. At least twenty-five teachers will voluntarily attend.
2. Teachers attending will include at least one-third secondary and one-third elementary.
3. Participants (80 percent) will report activities as stimulating and relevant to a high degree.
4. Participants (75 percent) will estimate utility (practicality) of learning outcomes as high or extremely high.
5. Participants (90 percent) estimating utility of learning outcomes as limited will report need incongruence with objectives.

Instrumentation
    A simple questionnaire is designed to elicit postsession information as follows:

1. extent of voluntariness in attendance;
2. level of assignment—elementary or secondary;
3. extent of stimulation of activities;
4. extent of perceived relevance of content to job;
5. extent of perceived utility (practicality) of skills and knowledge;
6. a checklist of objectives to be prioritized according to perceived needs.

Data Gathering
    Present questionnaire at end of session, requesting each participant to complete it and deposit it in a basket on departing, to retain anonymity.

Analysis

1. Tabulate voluntary versus involuntary participant responses.
2. Count elementary and secondary participants. Determine percentage of each.
3. Tabulate frequency of responses on five-point scale for item on extent of stimulation.
4. Tabulate frequency of responses on five-point scale.
5. Tabulate frequency of responses of five-point scale for item on extent of utility of learned outcomes.
6. Compute mean ratings for items 3, 4, and 5 by assignment level, and voluntariness.
7. Score the checklist of objectives for each respondent giving plus and minus values to objectives as prioritized according to their relationship to those of the session. Compute a total congruence score for each participant.
8. Prepare a scattergram showing relationships between individual participant responses to items tabulated in item 5 and the congruence score computed in item 7.

Interpretation

Compare analysis 1 above (A-1) with criterion 1 (C-1).
Compare A-2 with C-2. Compare A-3 and A-4 with C-3.
Compare A-5 with C-4. Compare A-8 with C-5.
Determine whether each criterion was in fact attained.
If not, determine for which group criteria were attained by comparing and contrasting A-1 and A-2 with A-6.

Valuing

Where criteria have not been attained or exceeded, determine how serious you and others regard the discrepancy.

Deciding

For each serious discrepancy, *review factors* associated with it. What level was most clearly associated with it? To what extent was incongruence in objectives associated with discrepancies?

Specify at least two alternative actions that might relate to each discrepancy or set of discrepancies. For instance, if all criteria are far short of attainment, then:

Action Alternative 1. Scrap the entire effort. Redesign and repeat training.

Action Alternative 2. Modify training design and extend training to a sequence of sessions.

However, if only a limited number of discrepancies is detected, then other action alternatives might be in order. For instance, suppose criteria 1, 2, and 3 are fully attained, but for criterion 4 data analysis reveals only 68 percent of participants rating the session as "high" or "extremely high." Furthermore, it appears that lower-level responses are from respondents who are (1) secondary (26 percent) and (2) involuntary (22 percent). Now action alternatives of somewhat different kinds emerge:

Action Alternative 3. Confer with secondary principals and director of secondary education in an attempt to secure voluntary participation in future sessions.

Action Alternative 4. Plan another training session directed toward secondary personnel with special emphasis on voluntariness and unique needs designated in the evaluation (A-7).

Action Alternative 5. Combine alternatives 3 and 4.

Acting

Implement decisions made.

The overly simplistic illustration of the eight processes of evaluation as described here can become much more elaborate as the complexity of the session or program being evaluated varies. Also, more critical decisions require more rigorous specification of criteria, instrumentation, and data analysis. Regardless of the complexity of the evaluation required, however, the eight processes seem to remain a useful guide.

Dangers in Simplification

Both researchers and evaluators tend to offer overly simplistic approaches to evaluation that needlessly restrict their usefulness in improving in-service education. Pretest and post-test comparisons are often advocated as if controlled experimental conditions prevail, but they never do. Another common error is simply to compare objectives with outcome measures. Still another variant of such overly simple approaches is one that simply focuses on perceptions of outcomes or satisfaction by participants. Whereas any one of these approaches might be useful as a way of generating or analyzing data, none can be regarded as a useful evaluation plan or design. Furthermore, the inadequacies of these approaches remain even when sophisticated computerization statistics and language are employed.

A satisfactory evaluation design must direct our attention to at least three kinds of questions and offer some hope that answers will be forthcoming to each:

1. What kind of operation as observed (or as perceived) actually exists or existed?

All too often we evaluate an operation presuming that it has or had certain characteristics when in fact something quite different actually was implemented. When this is true, we draw faulty conclusions regardless of outcomes or pre- and post-changes. This can be illustrated by an ISE program designed to develop interpersonal skills utilizing a whole array of demonstrations, role-playing and microteaching activities. However, a controversy before the school board the night before the first session generated a great deal of spontaneous discussion among participants. This was wisely accommodated by session leaders, but as a result demonstrations were eliminated and role-playing involvement was substantially reduced in subsequent sessions. Finally, videotape equipment for use by one third of the total group did not function properly, and those participants received little feedback of this self-viewing kind.

A comparison of pretest scores with post-test scores in the case illustrated might well indicate substantial gains in knowledge but little in skill or attitude. Valid interpretations cannot be drawn regarding the relationships between discrepancies and ISE operations unless those events described are carefully documented as part of the evaluation scheme.

2. What kind of outcomes are (were) produced for what participant subgroups?

All too often we gather and analyze outcome data from an ISE session or program as though participants were a homogeneous group of sponges just waiting to absorb what is offered. Obviously, such a view is naive. Participants are a very diverse lot. Their needs, levels of experience, job assignments, learning styles, intelligence, attitudes, and so on are very different. Accordingly, if pre- or post-gain scores show limited effects or if self-reports by participants are not overwhelmingly positive, we have no clear way of interpreting these findings. Was the experience actually faulty, or was it in fact quite effective with some and not so effective with other participants? If the latter is to be determined objectively and not used simply as a basis for rationalization of results, then the evaluation plan must pro-

Exhibit 9–2. ILLUSTRATION OF A SCATTERGRAM ANALYSIS OF TWO SETS OF PARTICIPANT RESPONSES (N = 46)

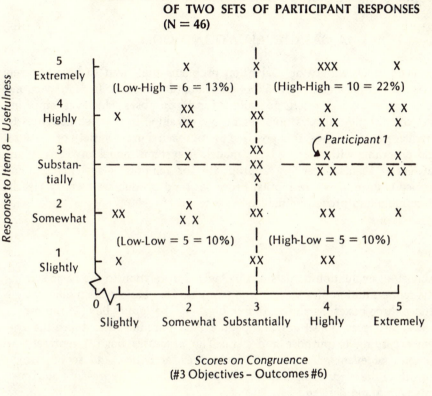

Scores on Congruence
(#3 Objectives – Outcomes #6)

vide for gathering data about participants as individuals. Exhibit 9–2 shows another way of relating individual participant characteristics to a measure of outcome.

3. What are the relationships between *controllables* — resources and procedures — and *consequences*, both planned and inadvertent?

All too often evaluation efforts concentrate on isolated sets of data rather than on relationships among them (3:328–30). For instance, in the illustrative program described the relationships between amount of skill gained and the extent of use of the videotape in microteaching should be analyzed. Such a relationship might lead to an interpretation regarding the contribution of video feedback to the growth or lack of growth shown in the data. The emphasis on relationships between those things that can be readily improved are controllable, and the outcomes produced are crucial because of the purposes discussed earlier (25:54).

A BASIC EVALUATION MODEL

The enormous variety of evaluation problems that need to be addressed does not permit a simple "cookbook" evaluation method. In fact, even one basic model or design will not suffice for all purposes. However, since in-service education always involves people engaging in planned activities to produce new learnings, it is possible to approach a great variety of sessions and programs with a single basic model. A systems model is widely advocated and seems especially appropriate for temporary systems like in-service education where inputs, processes, and products are fairly clearly discernible and predeterminable.

The Black Box

Almost all evaluation models can be viewed in relation to the basic schematic representation of a system in operation. This basic system diagram includes three boxes, as shown in Exhibit 9–3. The *inputs* box (1) represents needs, resources, objectives, and people, which are introduced into the system according to purpose and plan. The *processes* box (2) represents a complex of events, interactions, procedures, activities, and so on, which constitute the planned operation. The *products* box (3) represents outcomes anticipated and desired.

Three overly simplified evaluation plans are shown in Exhibit 9–3 in schematic form. The weaknesses in these approaches as shown have already been discussed. Each deals only with one kind of input and not that which can be readily controlled or manipulated. Furthermore, the processes are ignored in every instance. The black box is a complete mystery as far as the evaluation plan is concerned. Hence, findings in the form of answers to the three questions may be either positive or negative, but they have no consequence in either case. When needs are satisfied, the processes associated with that result are indeterminant. When objectives are not attained, no clues are provided regarding probable causes. When test score gains are large, no basis for reinforcement is provided except in a very gross way.

A Multivariate Approach

An approach to making better use of basic systems concepts in evaluating in-service education is derived from the CIPP model pioneered by Stuffle-

Exhibit 9–3. SCHEMATIC VIEW OF A SIMPLE SYSTEM WITH THREE ASSOCIATED EVALUATION PLANS

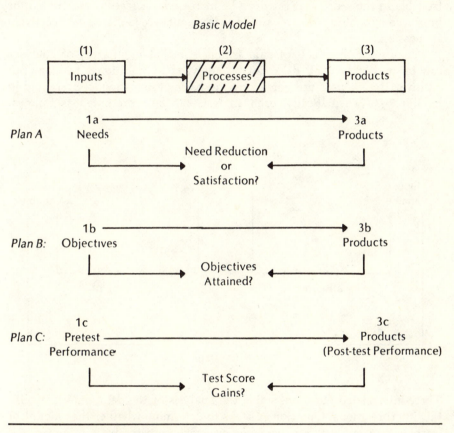

Basic Model

beam et al. (24). CIPP stands for context, input, process, product evaluation. In adapting and simplifying this model for use in in-service education, context data are treated in only informal ways while careful attention is given to input, process, and product data and the analysis of each such data set to reveal relationships that are meaningful and useful. In doing this, a limited number of selected, important, measurable products or learning outcomes are specified in advance as desired and probable. Data regarding these are sought as objectively as possible.

The evaluation plan also provides, however, for the careful selection of processes that are both important to the planned operation and are controllable in the sense that they could be increased, decreased, substituted, or changed in quality. Data regarding these processes are then sought in as objective a form as possible.

Finally, one or more inputs that are rationally and logically related to the processes of the operation are selected. These inputs must also be controllable in the sense that they can be increased, decreased, substituted, or improved in quality. Data regarding these inputs are gathered as objectively as possible.

When these three sets of data are made available, an array of analyses can be undertaken, all data can be analyzed in traditional fashion, but multivariate analyses are guided by the basic systems model presented in Exhibit 9–3. Schematically, each analysis can be represented as follows:

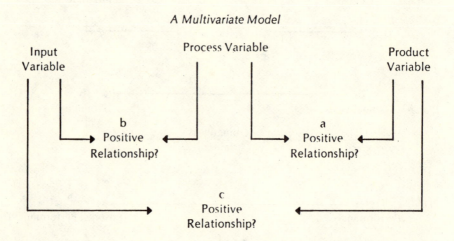

A Multivariate Model

Three interrelated questions guide the analysis of the data and also facilitate interpretations. Question A seeks to determine whether the amount of learning outcome was greater when selected processes were in ample evidence, and lower when those processes were lacking or limited. If such a relationship is found, there is a basis for deciding to maintain and/or increase those processes. If such a relationship is not found, the basis for considering the elimination or reduction in those processes is provided.

Distinguishing Variables in Analysis

But answers are not so simply found. Suppose we apply this analytical model to the illustration presented previously for a single session. Exhibit 9–1 provides a frequency distribution for three sets of data. Item 5 is *process* data indicating the extent to which processes in the session were perceived as stimulating. Similarly, item 7 may be thought of as yielding *process* data. Item 8 is product data, however. In this illustration, *input* data are provided in the form of elementary and secondary assignment levels of participants.

Relationships among these sets of data are not readily determined as shown in Exhibit 9–1. These are descriptive uses of the data, and they are interpretable only in terms of central tendencies and variations in responses. Furthermore, each set of data is analyzed as though it were unrelated to the others. In fact, we have reason to believe that relevance (item 7) might influence usefulness (item 8). Similarly, it seems logical that level of assignment might influence both relevance and usefulness. These possible relationships can be analyzed using simple paradigms or scattergrams.

The two examples that follow relate an input (assignment) to a product (usefulness), and a process (stimulation) to the same product:

	Assignment		*Stimulation*	
Usefulness	Elementary N = 30	Secondary N = 16	Extremely High N = 35	High and Lower N = 11
High* N = 17	10	7	11	6
Lower* N = 29	20	9	24	5

* High = ratings of 4 or 5; lower = ratings of 1, 2, or 3.

We can interpret this analysis as showing usefulness not consistently an outcome associated with either elementary or secondary participants but more so for secondary participants. Now, as we look at the analysis relating process (stimulation) to product (usefulness), it appears that contrary to expectation extremely high stimulation in the session is not associated with high perception of usefulness. However, we also observe that a large number of participant responses are not easily understood, since participants responding less enthusiastically about stimulation (a total of eleven) tend to perceive the session as more highly useful than other participants. Since we already have a finding regarding level of assignment being associated with product, it is possible that differences in assignment will explain these curious findings. However, still another analysis is needed to determine if this interpretation is in fact a proper one.

Decision alternatives that might emerge from this limited set of data with limited analyses completed are nonetheless fairly concrete. The findings indicate: (1) that the session needs to be redesigned in terms of its emphasis on practical usefulness, especially for elementary participants; or (2) that the participants may need to be assisted in recognizing the usefulness of the highly stimulating experiences. These two alternatives could be supported or rejected on the basis of further analysis of data relating relevance (item 7) to stimulation (item 5) to see if in fact there is little relationship between these two.

Determining Multiple Relationships

The series of two-way analyses suggested in the foregoing illustrations and discussion can be replaced to a large extent by the use of the *branching diagram analysis technique* developed by Harris (12) as a simplified application of the CIPP concepts presented by Stufflebeam et. al. (24). The branching diagrams shown in Exhibit 9–4 utilize the same sets of data analyzed in the previous section. These data have now been analyzed to reflect three-way relationships. In each diagram, input data are related to process data, which in turn are related to product data. The raw data are identical to those presented in Exhibit 9–1 as frequency distributions. However, each participant's data are treated as a set of measures, and directionality is assumed.

To interpret branching diagrams, the following logic is utilized as applied to the upper diagram:

(1) (2)   Secondary participants were predominantly extremely highly stimulated but still did not perceive the learning outcomes as highly useful products in most cases.

(7) (8)   Elementary participants were also predominantly extremely highly stimulated and also did not perceive the learning outcomes as highly useful in most cases.

(3) (4)   Less highly stimulated secondary participants perceived the learning outcomes as highly useful in most instances.

(5) (6)   Of the elementary participants who were extremely highly stimulated a majority perceived the learning outcomes as not highly useful in most instances.

A similar interpretation of the lower branching diagram produces some new, different, but not incompatible findings. (1) (2) Relevance is not highly associated with usefulness for secondary participants. The same

Exhibit 9–4. BRANCHING DIAGRAMS FOR AN ILLUSTRATIVE SESSION EVALUATION

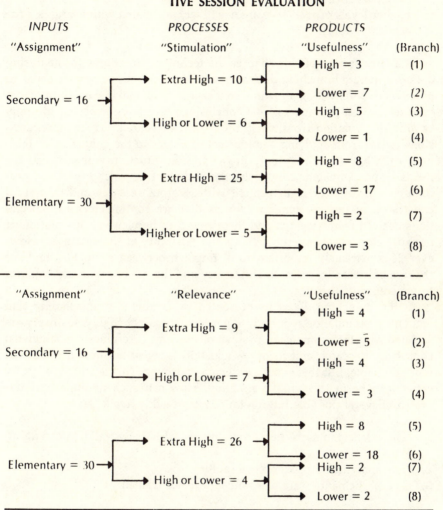

INPUTS   *PROCESSES*   *PRODUCTS*

"Assignment"   "Stimulation"   "Usefulness"   (Branch)

                                           High = 3   (1)
                    Extra High = 10
Secondary = 16   Lower = 7   (2)
                                           High = 5   (3)
                    High or Lower = 6
                                           Lower = 1   (4)

                                           High = 8   (5)
                    Extra High = 25
Elementary = 30   Lower = 17   (6)
                                           High = 2   (7)
                    Higher or Lower = 5
                                           Lower = 3   (8)

"Assignment"   "Relevance"   "Usefulness"   (Branch)

                                           High = 4   (1)
                    Extra High = 9
Secondary = 16   Lower = 5   (2)
                                           High = 4   (3)
                    High or Lower = 7
                                           Lower = 3   (4)

                                           High = 8   (5)
                    Extra High = 26
Elementary = 30   Lower = 18   (6)
                                           High = 2   (7)
                    High or Lower = 4
                                           Lower = 2   (8)

is true for elementary participants (7) (8). Extremely high levels of relevance are negatively associated with usefulness for elementary participants.

When the findings from both diagrams are brought together, we have a basis for improving this or similar ISE sessions by considering the following:

1. *Assignment* makes a difference, with high *usefulness* being more consistently associated with secondary participants.

2. *Neither* stimulation *nor* relevance is associated with *usefulness* for either secondary or elementary participants.
3. Lower levels of *stimulation* are associated with *usefulness* for secondary participants.
4. Higher levels of *relevance* are negatively associated with usefulness for elementary participants.

In a later section of this chapter the technical procedures for analyzing data to generate branching diagrams will be presented. A caution needs to be expressed regarding drawing conclusions and making decisions from such evaluation procedures. The conclusions cannot be expected to apply beyond the situation from which the data was secured. Furthermore, decisions follow from applying a unique set of values to the unique set of findings, each having validity only in the specific situation within which the ISE is being evaluated. Obviously, the findings from such evaluation procedures will often be in agreement with rigorous research and theoretical constructs. In fact, evaluation findings that are contradictory to expectations derived from research and theory need to be viewed with caution, if not suspicion, regarding the validity and reliability of the data used. However, it is extremely important to distinguish between evaluation findings that are bolstered by research and theory and the use of evaluation findings to generalize or theorize.

In the branching diagrams presented in Exhibit 9–4, the finding that amount of stimulation reported by participants is not highly positively associated with the estimates of product or outcome (usefulness) is somewhat confusing. Research and theory would both suggest a different finding as more probable. But this is not a research endeavor. This is what the reality *appears* to be *in this unique situation*. How can such findings be interpreted? Several possible interpretations are readily available:

1. The participants are not providing us with truly valid (meaningful) data.
2. The analytical procedures are faulty.
3. The participants were entertained *but* not trained.

Any of these three interpretations (others may well be possible, too) could explain the curious findings in Exhibit 9–4. Assuming assurances of anonymity, plenty of time to complete the questionnaire, nearly all participants responding, a well-designed instrument, and clear direction in administering it, we have no special reason to use the first interpretation. The second interpretation can be tested by using some alternative analytical procedures. For instance, the use of only "extremely high" responses in the upper branches of the diagrams for "stimulation" and "relevance" variables might have produced some distortions in the pattern of relationships shown. Finally, the third interpretation exists as an open possibility! It, too, can be tested by considering the nature of the specific events included in the session and by asking a small sample of the participants about this interpretation in a straightforward fashion.

INSTRUMENTATION

Instrumentation for in-service education evaluation tends to be dominated by the use of simple questionnaries. Questionnaire design can draw on well-developed survey techniques from the social and behavioral sciences. When well designed and well administered, they can provide useful data. When poorly designed, they can be useless. Furthermore, questionnaires offer only one kind of instrumentation.

Other approaches to data gathering having implications for instrumentation include interviews, observations, and tests. Each can be utilized in a variety of ways. Each calls for careful instrumentation to assure relevant and reliable data. Technical assistance with instrumentation is available in sources by Cook (9), Rattenburg and Pelletier (19), and Sonoquist and Dunkelberg (22). However, the source of the data and the kind of data gathered are both important considerations in instrument selection and design.

These four approaches or types of instrumentation are briefly described in Exhibit 9–5, along with indications of the *kinds* of data generally provided and the various sources from which such data can be secured.

Questionnaires and interviews provide much the same kind of data and utilize similar sources, unless special interview techniques are employed to produce more in-depth responses and to secure focused reactions. Obviously, the interview may have a special contribution to make where respondents cannot read and will not respond readily to a questionnaire. Interviews are costly ways of gathering data compared with questionnaires.

Tests have much in common with questionnaires but focus on securing knowledge or skill data while minimizing opinions and attitudes. Teachers seem every bit as uncomfortable with knowledge and skill tests as most other adults. In fact, considerable resistance to tests is often encountered in in-service training situations. For this reason, their use tends to be minimized despite the unique contributions they could make in evaluating ISE outcomes. Of course, tests given to students can conceivably be useful when evaluating ISE outcomes that are expected to have direct impact on student learning in rather specific ways (7). This latter use of testing has very limited utility. A more practical approach is to build the testing into the activities of the training session or program, with self-scoring, diag-

Exhibit 9–5. FOUR TYPES OF USEFUL INSTRUMENTATION
BY KIND OF DATA AND SOURCE

Type of Instrumentation	Kinds of Data	Sources of Data
Questionnaire		
Provides abbreviated, precategorized data, but also provides for a variety of kinds of responses including ratings, ranking, and open responses.	Attitudes Opinions Information	Participant Student Observer Trainer
Test		
Provides abbreviated, precategorized data.	Information Skills Concepts	Participant Student
Interview Schedule		
Provides for verbal responses to many of same kinds of questions offered by the questionnaire. Permits more in-depth data gathering.	Attitudes Opinions Information Reactions	Participant Student Observer Trainer
Observation Record		
Provides for data on observable events. Does not rely on the responses of individual. Records behaviors regardless of form.	Events Inter-relation-ships	Observer

nosis, and self-analysis provided as incentives to encourage acceptance by participants. Another technique incorporates a few test items into a questionnaire or interview schedule so that they do not generate the anxieties associated with taking a test. There are, of course, certain standardized tests that might be useful, especially as input measures. These are illustrated by the Graduate Record Examination and the National Teachers examination tests, which measure academic aptitude and knowledge with considerable reliability.

Observation records are of many kinds and varieties (13: Chaps. 7 and 14). They provide unique data, unlike those offered by any of the other instruments. Observation data can be highly reliable and valid. When classroom events — behaviors of students, teachers, or interactions among materials and people — are important kinds of data, then observations are uniquely well suited to obtaining such information. The cost of gathering observation data is, like interview data, rather high. Accordingly, observations are employed most often for the more elaborate or crucial ISE evaluation purposes.

Interestingly, carefully constructed questionnaires, designed to elicit descriptions of events *previously observed* by teachers and students, can generate unusually reliable data of the kind that observation records provide. To make effective use of a questionnaire in this way, each item must be carefully constructed to discourage opinions, attitudes, and guessing while stimulating *recall* and *estimation*. To illustrate this last point, consider and contrast these three ways of eliciting a response:

1. Did you make use of the new self-instructional materials with your students? (check one)

    ( ) yes ( ) no

2. To what extent did you use the new self-instructional materials with your students? (circle one numeral)

None	Some	Much	Constantly
0	1	2	3

3. Tell us about your use of the new self-instructional materials:
    a. Did you previously use these materials with your students? (check one option)

    ( ) no ( ) yes, some ( ) yes, a lot

    b. How much have you used the new self-instructional materials with your students *since* the workshop session? (circle one numeral)

None	Some	Quite a lot	A great deal
0	1	2	3

The first way of asking gives little information about *extent of use*. Furthermore, it encourages invalid responses, since few people like to admit that they have not followed through on training objectives. The second way of asking is little better than the first. While phrased to provide an estimation, it offers only four crudely specified response options. Since "none" is not likely to be utilized often, and "constantly" is an unrealistic estimate to be discounted if offered, the item provides little useful information. The third way of asking is more complex, of course. Part a provides the participant with a frame of reference for thinking and hopefully stimulates responses that are somewhat thoughtful. Part b provides clear guidance for the participant to estimate one of four levels of *extent of use*. The information provided by both parts 3a and 3b is useful, but a *comparison* of part 3a with part 3b provides uniquely useful information about the possible impact of the training in stimulating extent of use.

A Simple Questionnaire

Relatively simple questionnaires can provide rich sources of data for in-service education evaluation. It is not necessary, even though it might be interesting, to ask a lengthy array of questions in order to produce useful evaluative interpretations leading to decisions for improving an ISE session or program. Unfortunately, lengthy questionnaires often produce lots of data that are not very useful for various reasons. Poorly designed instruments yield poor results. But more important, data gathered must be relevant and must lead to interpretations that can guide decisions and actions. Put another way, we need to focus on the controllable or *modifiable* elements in the situation as much as possible.

The basic model discussed and illustrated in the previous section, calls for a minimum of three kinds of data, with at least one kind — input or process — subject to modification. Hence, the simplest instrument and design would call for only three bits of information, as follows:

an important bit of information about an input (age, experience, position, voluntariness, need, interest, etc.)

an important bit of information about a process (activities, group size, involvement, stimulation, work group, etc.)

an important bit of information about product or outcome (knowledge gain, intent to try, new performance, objectives achieved, enthusiasm, etc.)

A simple three-item questionnaire would generate all of this information. The participant could provide it all. A single branching diagram analysis would yield interpretations with which to consider decisions for improving the program or session.

Without trying to illustrate each variation of this simplest of all instruments, an example can serve to emphasize design considerations that are important. Suppose an instrument emerges, looking something like this:

Participant Reactionnaire

1. Your age? (circle one)
   20–30   31–40   41–50   50+
2. Your subgroup assignment? (check one)
   (   ) Group A — with teacher leader
   (   ) Group B — with principal leader
   (   ) Group C — with local supervisor leader
   (   ) Group D — with visiting consultant leader
3. How well motivated are you to try to implement the ———|———|?
   (check one that fits best)
   (   ) I am definitely going to implement.
   (   ) I am considering implementing, may try.
   (   ) I am considering implementing, have doubts.
   (   ) I am very skeptical. I may. I may not.

This instrument consists of just three items. They include an input item (age), a process item (subgroup), and a product item (intent to implement). Two of the three bits of data generated by respondents will probably be highly reliable and valid. The third item will hopefully produce data with some validity. Anonymity is assured for all respondents. Little time is consumed in data gathering. A set of traditional analyses can be undertaken, and a branching diagram might look like this:

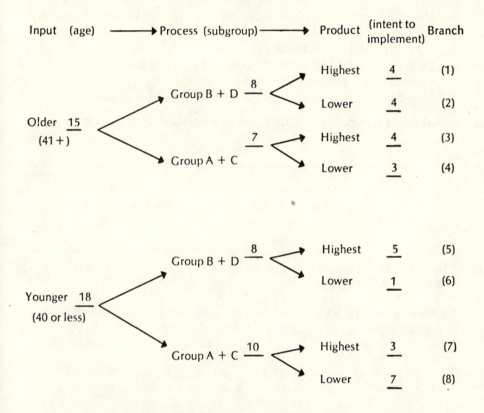

Input (age) ⟶	Process (subgroup) ⟶	Product	(intent to implement)	Branch
	Group B + D 8	Highest	4	(1)
		Lower	4	(2)
Older 15 (41 +)	Group A + C 7	Highest	4	(3)
		Lower	3	(4)
	Group B + D 8	Highest	5	(5)
		Lower	1	(6)
Younger 18 (40 or less)	Group A + C 10	Highest	3	(7)
		Lower	7	(8)

The interpretation of this branching diagram leads the evaluator to suspect that older participants, while just as willing to implement as the younger ones, were not much influenced by the high-status leaders in groups B and D. Conversely, younger teachers, no more eager to implement on the whole, were possibly influenced by being in subgroups B and D.

The age factor in this design for evaluation is not directly modifiable but is potentially controllable. It would be possible to assign participants to subgroups based on age. However, the subgroup leadership is even more subject to modification; hence, decisions can reflect these findings in future programs or sessions.

A More Elaborate Questionnaire

It is not the author's intent to urge ISE evaluators always to utilize the simplest of instruments. Just as questionnaires may not be either the best or the only instrumentation needed, so neither very simple nor very complex instruments are best. A few guidelines to consider call for the following:

1. Use the simplest, clearest, most objective instrumentation consistent with the data desired.
2. Ask only for data really needed and actually to be used.
3. Be sure each data bit is an important one, in the sense that it is relevant to the in-service effort being evaluated.
4. If in doubt, utilize more than one data source and instrument type.

Exhibit 9–6 provides an illustration of a questionnaire that utilizes only

---

Exhibit 9–6. ILLUSTRATION OF A SINGLE-SOURCE INSTRUMENT

Session Feedback Instrument

Session Topic: Using Self-Instructional Learning Packets   Date: 8/10/—
Leader: W. R. Wuthridge

1. Participant code: 1   (Do not use your name. Remain anonymous!)
2. Participant Assignment: Teacher (✓)   Other ( )
   Level: Elementary ( )   Middle School (✓)   Senior High
   ( )   Other ( )
3. Objectives: On the left check (✓) only the one, two, or three statements that *best* represent *your* needs or interests *prior* to coming to this session.

Checks (✓)	Objectives	Ranks 1 to 9
( )	To recognize the major features of a learning packet that distinguish it from a workbook.	6
(✓)	To construct test items that are highly diagnostic.	4
( )	To recall the titles of available learning packets that are appropriate to my class group.	8
( )	To estimate reading level of material using both formal and informal techniques.	7
( )	To sequence a set of activities for learning to conform to accepted principles.	2

Exhibit 9–6 (continued)

Checks ( ) *Objectives*	*Ranks 1 to 9*
( ) To schedule group work for an entire week to provide for balance and variety for students.	*3*
( ) To design a self-scoring key for use with independent study activities.	*1*
(✓) To prepare laminated materials for nonconsumable use in study packets.	*5*
( ) To recall five principles of human growth and development.	*9*

4. How did you happen to attend this session? (check *one* reason below that *best* fits you).
( ) Told to by principal (or supervisor); had no choice.
( ) Expected to; suggested by principal (or supervisor).
(✓) Decided to; it seemed to fit my interests.
( ) Agreed to; it fit with my growth plans.
( ) Convenient to attend; others going too.
( ) Had to complete requirements.
( ) Sounded exciting; promising.

5. How *stimulating* did you find this session? (check only one).
( ) Extremely stimulating.
(✓) Highly stimulating.
( ) Substantially stimulating.
( ) Somewhat stimulating.
( ) Slightly stimulating (or less).

6. Respond to the objectives listed in item 3 above again! This time, please rank from 1 to 9 the extent to which those objectives were accomplished for you! Rank 1 = most completely accomplished or gained outcome. Rank 9 = least completely accomplished.

7. How *relevant* to your job-situation did you find the contents of the session?
( ) Extremely relevant.
(✓) Highly relevant.
( ) Substantially relevant.
( ) Somewhat relevant.
( ) Slightly relevant (or less).

8. How *useful* (practical) for you was the skill or information gained in this session?
( ) Extremely useful.
( ) Highly useful.
(✓) Substantially useful.
( ) Somewhat useful.
( ) Slightly useful (or less).

a single source (the participant), generates more data than the three-item one previously presented, but still remains quite simple and easy to utilize. It is intended for use at the end of a session, but it could be modified easily for use with a program of limited duration. Items 1, 2, 3, and 4 would generally be considered input items. Items 5 and 7 might be considered process items. Items 6 and 8 are product items; however, relating responses to items 3–6 generates still another variable that can be considered a process measure. The data presented in Exhibits 9–1, 9–2, and 9–4 are derived from this instrument. Appendix H shows a full set of raw data derived from responses by forty-six participants in an ISE session.

Obviously, this instrument has serious limitations. While providing three different input items, the process items are not likely to be very useful. They both ask for perceptions that are likely to be unreliable. They are not likely to yield two quite distinct kinds of data. On the contrary, one is very likely to contaminate the other. The product item 8, in asking for an estimate of usefulness, is likely to produce data of limited validity, since it asks for opinion only. Overall, the instrument suffers from depending on a single data source. Even so, such an instrument is likely to be useful for evaluation purposes and makes practical demands on participants and planners alike.

Additional instrumentation of relatively simple kinds could be developed for use along with the *Session Feedback Instrument* presented in Exhibit 9–6. A follow-up survey of participants could offer a checklist of classroom practices to be completed providing data on self-observed events. This would supplement and make more concrete the actual usefulness of data that were sought in item 8 as merely an opinion. Of course, an observer recording in participant classrooms would provide still another way of substituting evidence of events for opinions.

Still another way of supplementing the data provided by the instrument shown in Exhibit 9–6 would be to secure more detailed information regarding the experiences of participants in the session. Regardless of the perceived stimulation from the session activities, data on verbal participation, extent of task attentiveness, and subgroup leader style could be useful for process analysis. These kinds of data are available, of course, by using an observer. In the absence of an observer who can be entirely free for such data gathering, it may be desirable to add a few items to the questionnaire to obtain participant estimates of these kinds.

Evaluative Monitoring

The emphasis on instrumentation to this point in this chapter is on evaluation process over relatively short time frames. Session evaluation or evaluation of a program that is rather limited in scope, complexity, and time lends itself to single instruments and limited analysis. Furthermore, the interpretation, decision making, and actions that result during such short-term efforts need to address some future effort. What about long-term program evaluation?

When a program is in operation over an extended time frame — months or years — new opportunities and problems of instrumentation as well as design emerge. The evaluation of such programs could still be approached as an array of discrete sessions. In doing this, each session or series of sessions is evaluated separately using the techniques that have been suggested. However, this approach may have serious limitations. For instance, suppose all sessions are suffering from involuntariness as an input problem. That problem might be identified early and decisions made to prevent its reoccurrence. But to do so may require focusing specifically on that input variable across the entire program. "Piecework" evaluation suffers also from too much concern for product at an early point in a sequence of training, when products are unrealistic. Similarly, exclusive concern for small fragments of product without attending to the larger end results that are desired leads to evaluation findings that are inconsequential.

Monitoring efforts can be related to program evaluation in ways that assure that necessary data will be gathered, used to monitor and guide the program in progress, and still be utilized later for more comprehensive evaluation purposes. In approaching instrumentation from this perspective, *input*, process, and product instrumentation are distinct and separate.

Input data are gathered early in the implementation phase of the program. The specifications for desired or necessary inputs are clearly defined in advance. Checklists, observation instruments, and questionnaires are designed to provide feedback to program managers on each input variable. Are qualified leaders designated for every session and/or component? Are leaders being designated well in advance? Are plans and preparations for every activity in order in advance? Are objectives clearly specified, realistic, and relevant? Do participants get advance information? Are principals encouraging voluntary participation and avoiding compulsion? Is space adequate? Is equipment in working order? Are group sizes realistic and functional?

Process data are gathered even while feedback from input data analysis is generating changes in the program. These data clearly focus on objective activity relationships and basic design considerations. Observers and interviewers are used to supplement information gathered from participants via the questionnaire. Sampling procedures are utilized, since it is not necessary to have data on all sessions or from all participants in a session in order to give program managers feedback and alert them to major problems. Data gathered focus on a variety of process questions. Do participants know the objectives? Are activities related to objectives? Are activities multisensory? Are activities highly involving? Are materials available, well developed, and useful for follow-up? Are interpersonal relations of high quality maintained? Is continuity between sessions provided for? Are individual differences recognized, accepted, and accommodated?

Product data for a continuing program of in-service education must be gathered in terms of *formative* as well as *summative* outcomes. It is inappropriate to instrument for measuring terminal outcomes until a reasonable series of training sessions has been completed. Hence, those terminal product expectations need to be specified and data gathering delayed. On the other hand, it is unwise to wait until the end of a program to gather product data. A well-conceived program should produce results in steps or stages. These should be used as the focus for instrumentation and data gathering in progress. For instance, the program for training in individualization of instruction described in Appendix E suggests several points at which specific outcomes are essential to steady progress in the total program. A specific illustration involves conducting interobserver reliability tests at the end of a specified sequence in observation training. If reliabilities were not rather high, additional training would be needed promptly, since subsequent training activities and planned operations of other kinds would depend on these observation skills being demonstrated at a high level of reliability.

Self-Evaluation

Self-reported data can be utilized from the trainers and planners of in-service education programs just as they are utilized from participants. Of special value is self-evaluation that focuses on preplanning rather than on actual operations. Many problems can be avoided by preevaluation of the plans and arrangements themselves. Instruments for use in evaluating plans were discussed in Chapters II and III and are illustrated in Exhibits 2–5 and 3–3. One of these instruments focuses on session planning; the other applies to program plans. Both make explicit the kinds of provisions that are likely to be essential for operations to be implemented successfully. They focus heavily on input specifications. If these checklists are utilized systematically prior to finalizing plans and actual implementation, fewer problems of routine kinds emerge to frustrate initial efforts at implementation. Preoperational evaluation of plans followed by replanning assures that evaluative feedback on inputs are likely to be largely positive and reinforcing in early stages of the program operation. Furthermore, evaluation efforts can focus more quickly and thoroughly on *process* evaluation.

The planning documents discussed in considerable detail in Chapter III are still another kind of instrument for evaluation and monitoring. To the extent that the *plans* themselves have been well documented, they serve as guides to monitoring the operation as a basic reference for instrumentation. If schedules call for certain events on certain dates, these schedules should be used to monitor events. The Gantt chart discussed in Chapter III most clearly illustrates this use of plans/operations comparisons as a way of monitoring. However, discrepancies observed in the process of monitoring should become the focus for more detailed data gathering. Why are events behind schedule? What can be done with resources saved? How does one delay affect another event?

GRAPHIC ANALYSIS AND DISPLAYS

In previous chapters and in the illustrations given in this chapter, a number of analysis and data display techniques have been shown. There is, of course, an enormous array of options available for *both* analyzing and displaying data in forms that assist with interpretations and decision making. The use of simple frequency distributions and scattergrams is widespread. They are useful and generally easily interpretable. Bar graphs and line graphs are also in widespread use in education, business, and government. The branching diagram analysis technique illustrated earlier is one that we think deserves more attention because it is multivariate and not well known. Others, of course, need to be utilized when needed.

Scattergrams

The two-dimensional analysis of scattergrams is illustrated in Exhibit 9–2. Any two sets of data that can be paired can be displayed in scattergram form. To be meaningful, the two kinds of data need to be logically related to each other. In effect, the scattergram is a graphic way of looking at correlations between two sets of events. Correlations often occur by chance or because each of the two sets of data are related to a third. Hence, it is foolish to simply correlate all sets of data with each other (as statisticians are inclined to do).

In Exhibit 9–2 the *relevance* rating of the session as perceived by each participant is related (correlated) to (with) the congruence score for that same participant. Using Appendix H, these values are shown for participant 1 to be 4 and 3, respectively. Accordingly, these two values are plotted as shown as an X, which is identified on the exhibit. This scattergram has interpretive value because it addresses the relationship of congruence between priority objectives of the participant and his or her learning to his or her perception of usefulness. It seems logical to hope that a session will be more *useful* to those who see their *needs* being fulfilled. In the scattergram presented in Exhibit 9–2, this relationship holds strongly for 32 percent of the participants and not at all well for the others.

The interpretative potential of the scattergram is illustrated more fully by looking at the number of participants who are graphically represented by X's plotted in each quadrant of the exhibit. Six participants fall in the upper left hand quadrant. They reported highly useful outcomes but little congruence with their needs. As such, this is a *bonus outcome*. The participants report usefulness even though not related to their highest priorities. If we add these seven participants to those ten that fall in the upper right-hand quadrant, we can presume "successful" outcomes for both groups. In the lower left-hand quadrant, five participants report both low usefulness and low congruence. This identifies a defect, and it is clearly one of inadequate response to needs. The five participants in the lower right-hand quadrant also are not served well in terms of *usefulness*. The defect for them appears to derive from some source other than failure to respond to need, however.

Bar and Line Graphs

Perhaps the least complicated graphic display is the bar graph. The line graph can also be used with few complications. Both permit easy interpretation and comparisons among an array of data. The set of responses from a single questionnaire item can be seen at a glance for example, as shown below:

6. "This was a good way to exchange information about new teaching techniques and ideas."

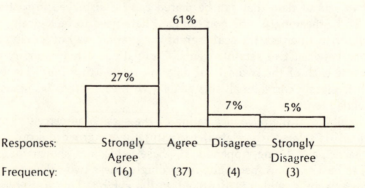

From Janie Williams, "Junior High Mathematics Staff Development Evaluation Results." Paper for the Department of Educational Administration, University of Texas at Austin, March 2, 1978.

Such a graphic display is more readily understood by some, provides the numerical detail of a tabular display, and also adds visual comparisons.

Evaluation results for an entire program utilizing an array of criteria is another format for using bar graphs (21:23). This can be illustrated with the scores produced in applying the twenty criteria of the *Descriptive Observation Record for In-service Sessions* (13:415–22). (See Exhibit 9–7.)

This summary profile of a two-day workshop for teachers in an elementary school combines observer ratings on twenty descriptors, clustering them to form only four bars (19:17). This permits easy comparisons and

Exhibit 9–7. SUMMARY PROFILE FOR A WORKSHOP

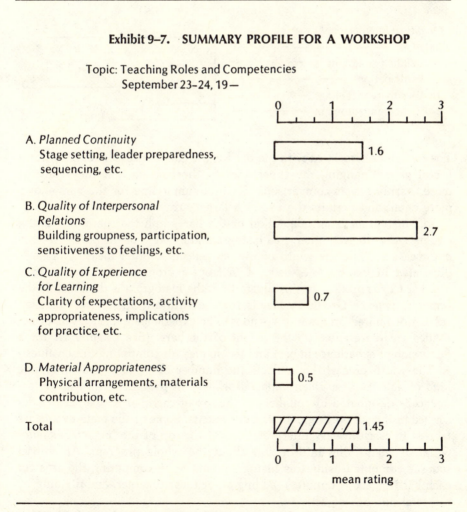

Topic: Teaching Roles and Competencies
September 23–24, 19—

A. *Planned Continuity*
Stage setting, leader preparedness, sequencing, etc.   1.6

B. *Quality of Interpersonal Relations*
Building groupness, participation, sensitiveness to feelings, etc.   2.7

C. *Quality of Experience for Learning*
Clarity of expectations, activity appropriateness, implications for practice, etc.   0.7

D. *Material Appropriateness*
Physical arrangements, materials contribution, etc.   0.5

Total   1.45

mean rating

reveals at least two clusters of the operations that are distinctly weak, according to these criteria.

A limitation of the bar graph is recognized when one attempts a display with many bars. The five bars shown in Exhibit 9–7 are readily accommodated by the technique. If all twenty descriptor scores were shown, much of the graphic advantage would be lost. A technique for accommodating more bars and providing more detail involves the use of a set of lines for each type of data that provides somewhat different but related information. For instance, cluster "B. Quality of Interpersonal Relations" can be displayed in more detail as shown below:

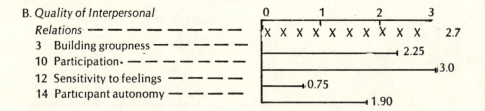

B. *Quality of Interpersonal*
  Relations
  3 Building groupness
  10 Participation
  12 Sensitivity to feelings
  14 Participant autonomy

The four lines associated with the bar for the cluster provide diagnostically useful data. Changing the appearance of the bars so that they contrast more sharply assists comparisons. Using a simple line for the bars shows more detail and permits the use of a larger array without loss of clarity.

The histogram is an adaptation of the bar graph that permits relating two measures to each other. In a histogram, the height of the bar represents one measure while the width of the bar reflects another measure. This is illustrated in Exhibit 9–8, using data from a program of activities in a Teacher Corps project. In this illustration, the histogram is designed as the *Impact/Sequence Graph* by Harris for use with any in-service education session or limited program of sessions. The experience impact levels of activities are represented by the height of the bars. (See Chapter III for a discussion of experience impact and techniques for computing these values.)

The width of each bar reflects the number of minutes that a specific kind of activity at a *given impact level* was in progress. The activity sequence is designated by numbers at the top of each bar and is further described in the supporting planning documents. Some of the main events are labeled to assist in easy interpretation. At the top of the *Impact/Sequence Graph* is identifying information about the whole program. An impact score is computed using this histogram simply by computing the area for each bar (impact × minutes), adding all of these together, and dividing by the total minutes of activity.

Line graphs do much the same simple graphic display job that bar

**Exhibit 9–8. RELATING EXPERIENCE IMPACT TO
TRAINING ACTIVITY SEQUENCE**

The IMPACT/SEQUENCE GRAPH ©
Session or Program: "Roles and Competencies in Teaching"
Date(s:) 9/23–24/—
Client Group: Elementary school teachers and aides. N = 38
Place/Sponsor: Allison Elementary School/Teacher Corps
Leaders: Dr. Rubin Olivarez and Teacher Corps team

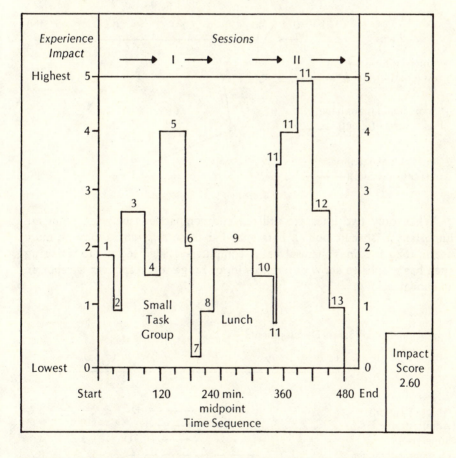

graphs do. A line graph can substitute for any simple bar graph. Line graphs have special value, however, when two or more sets of related data need to be compared. Pre- and post-inventory data can be displayed nicely by a pair of line graphs, as illustrated in a program offered by the Riverside, California schools (6). A series of seminars was utilized to deal with desegregation problems and attitudes. Objectives related to improving acceptance of certain concepts were assessed, using an inventory or test before and after the seminar series. Examples of their findings are displayed as line graphs below (6:44):

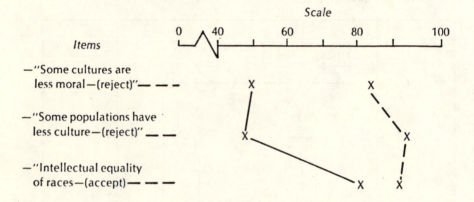

When only two lines are utilized and comparisons between them are important at specific points, bars showing these *differences* may be more useful than the lines themselves. A computer-assisted technique for using such bar graphs to show differences in, or ranges of, responses is reported as shown below:

1. Individualized Program Development.

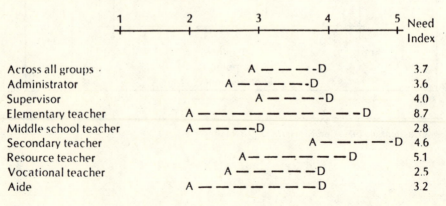

Two lines connecting all points labeled A and D would be less easily interpreted than this series of bars.

Line graphs have their greatest value when several related sets of data are being displayed and their *slopes* and *relationships* are both important. For instance, experience impact scores, attendance rates, or effectiveness measures for different projects or consultants over time can be analyzed and displayed with a series of lines. Exhibit 9–9 presents hypothetical data

Exhibit 9–9. SATISFACTION LEVEL OF TEACHERS BY PROJECT COMPONENT 1974–76

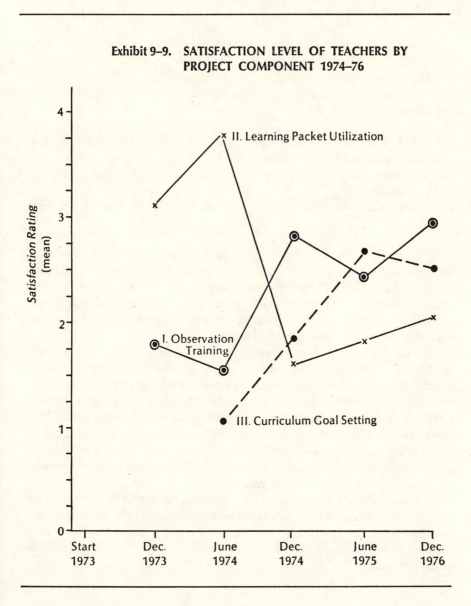

on participant satisfaction levels over a two-and-one-half year period. The lines show both ups and downs in three of the various components of the program for individualization presented in Appendix E and discussed previously in Chapter III. Such a graphic display provides a retrospective view of satisfaction levels. However, it suggests trends that are generally encouraging for all components shown.

Branching Diagrams

In previous sections of this chapter, branching diagram analysis has been illustrated. Its importance has been stressed as a multivariate analysis technique that does not depend upon statistics but that is useful in guiding decisions for improving programs. The essential features of this analytical and display technique include:

three clearly different measures of importance to the in-service operation and independent of each other

a logical basis for interpreting each measure as an input, process, or product measure

a common source or other linkage between each bit of data of the three kinds

In an earlier section of this chapter, data were used from a single questionnaire so that the same person was supplying input, process, and product data. Each of the three different questionnaire items were designed to reflect input (e.g., age), process (e.g., involvement), and product (objectives gained). Assuming that the three questionnaire items do elicit valid information, then the three essential features are present.

In a study of an ongoing program for the in-service training of teachers in the use of the *Taba Teaching Strategies* for elementary social studies, Carthel (7) utilized questionnaire data from teachers about the "voluntary vs. involuntary" nature of their participation to secure a single "voluntariness" score for each teacher as an *input* measure. Then he utilized attendance records, observation records, and a questionnaire to produce an index of extent of "involvement" as a *process* measure. Finally, he used observation reports and student responses combined to generate an estimate of "extent of use" as a *product* measure. Each of these three sets of data came from different instruments and sources. However, they were related to each other because they were concerned only with voluntary participation and involvement in Taba training and the use of those strategies. Each bit of data was linked to relate bits by focusing on the individual teacher in each instance.

Data in its preanalyzed form that illustrates branching diagram analysis
is shown below:

Teacher	Input Voluntariness	Process Involvement	Product Extent of Use
a	1 Low	2 Low	1 Low
b	4 High	2 Low	3 High
c	1 Low	4 High	2 Low
d	2 Low	3 High	3 High
e	4 High	4 High	4 High
f	3 High	4 High	4 High
g	2 Low	1 Low	2 Low
h	3 High	2 Low	3 High

The three scores for each individual teacher are shown side by side. Each
score is designated as high or low using either a split-half technique or a
natural break in the distribution.

Plotting scores on the branching diagram simply involves inserting a
frequency tally for each teacher on three branches as shown below:

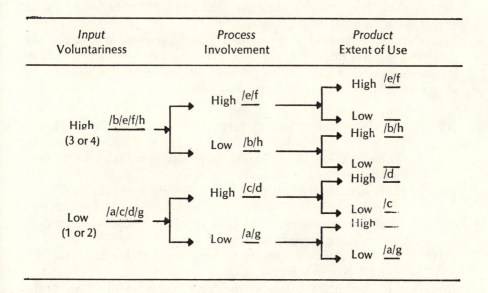

Each tally mark carries an identifying superscript to assist the reader in
following the *plotting* of the data from the table of scores by teachers to

the diagram. When such plotting has been completed, a full diagram may look like the one below:

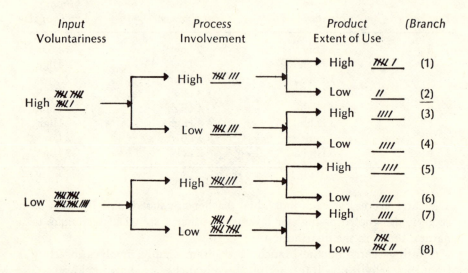

As a final display, the tally marks are replaced with arabic numerals, as shown in earlier branching diagrams.

Interpreting branching diagrams is a thoughtful exercise in logic. The procedure involves interpreting each branch separately and then interrelating these separate interpretations to draw one or more conclusions. The diagram just shown can be interpreted as follows:

(1) (2)* Highly voluntary teacher participants (sixteen individuals) who were *also* highly involved in the in-service training program, made more extensive use of Taba strategies in their classrooms in six out of eight instances.

(7) (8) Less voluntary teacher participants (twenty-four individuals) who were also *not* highly involved in the in-service training program, made *less* extensive use of Taba strategies in their classrooms in twelve out of sixteen instances.

(3) (4) Highly voluntary teachers who were *not* highly involved were equally split in extent of use.

(5) (6) Less voluntary teachers who *were* highly involved were also equally split in extent of use.

* Numbers in parentheses refer to branches being interpreted.

Conclusions: Voluntariness is highly and consistently associated with extent of use. Involvement is also highly associated with extent of use.

(1) (3) Highly voluntary teachers make more extensive use of Taba strategies in ten out of sixteen instances.
(5) (7) Less voluntary teachers make more extensive use of Taba strategies in eight out of twenty-four instances.

However:

(1) (5) Highly involved teachers make more extensive use of Taba strategies in ten out of sixteen instances.
(3) (7) Less involved teachers make more extensive use of Taba strategies in eight out of twenty-four instances.

Therefore: Both voluntariness *and* involvement are associated with extent of use.

Decision: Both voluntariness and high levels should be promoted in in-service program plans and implementing procedures, if extent of use of strategies is to be maximized.

The illustration presented here was simplified to provide the reader with an easy-to-understand example. Exhibit 9–10 shows still another illustration using data from three different self-assessment instruments. This was a retreat-type institute extending over a two-week period involving over one hundred hours of training. Preassessment data were utilized from a competency assessment instrument. Process data were collected daily using a simple reactionnaire. Product data constituted a self-report prepared *following* the institute after returning to the job situation. It consisted of indicating the extent to which institute objectives had been achieved for each participant.

A detailed interpretation of this branching diagram would reveal that prior competence (self-perceived) was strongly associated with success in attaining the objectives, and yet highly stimulated participants tended to be successful regardless of initial competence.

Appendix H includes a set of data and a branching diagram analysis of three sets of measures where interpretations are not so clear and clean. For instance, this particular diagram (Appendix H) reveals neither elementary nor secondary teacher participants in a training session particularly positive about the outcomes *despite very positive* reports on the activities (process). The best conclusion for this set of interpretations is that participants were entertained but not trained.

Other Analyses

Numerous analytical techniques of tabular and graphic kinds have much promise. Statistical methods also have merit when circumstances, time, and

**Exhibit 9–10. BRANCHING DIAGRAM ANALYSIS OF A
TWO-WEEK LEADERSHIP TRAINING INSTITUTE**

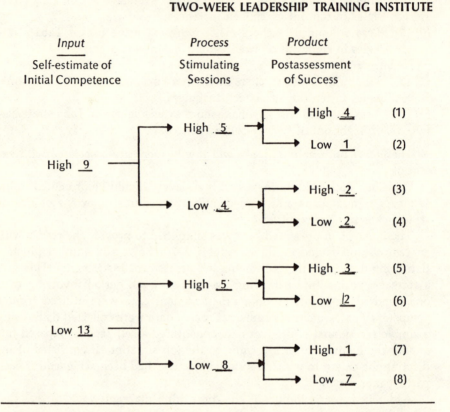

Input	Process	Product
Self-estimate of Initial Competence	Stimulating Sessions	Postassessment of Success

Based on "An Evaluative Report on the Leadership Training Institute for Administrators and Supervisors of Schools for Children Who Are Deaf" by Ben M. Harris, Institute Director at Camp Trail, Hunt, Texas, July 1974, p. 39.

available resources warrant. Sanders and Cunningham (20) discuss such techniques as Q-sort (20:284), task analysis (20:286), and Delphi (20:292). More than one analytical technique is nearly always desirable both because new insights can emerge and because different formats appeal to different users.

The circle graph can be useful whenever a circle can appropriately represent 100 percent of something and the data lend themselves to displaying and comparing parts of the whole. Hence, all the time utilized in a training program can be shown as pie slices, each representing a different kind of training activity.

Various tabular displays have been shown here but not discussed in detail. Obviously, tables are nearly always utilized. When large displays of detailed data need to be presented, tables are essential. Furthermore, summarizing and comparing a few selected pieces of data can often be displayed in tabular form with great advantage.

Data analysis and display should facilitate interpretation, valuing, and decision making (25:26). The techniques chosen should be dictated by the kinds of interpretations, values or orientations, and decisions that are appropriate to the situation. Above all else, however, analyses must promote communications. We cannot interpret what we do not understand. Hence, multiple approaches, graphic displays, and systems-related techniques are likely to be most valuable.

SUMMARY

Evaluation of in-service education has only been introduced here. The science and art of program evaluation is in its infancy (5). New tools of evaluation are at our disposal. In-service education demands evaluations of the most rigorous kinds because it is such a sensitive and important aspect of the school and college operation.

This writer sees little to be gained by continuing to adopt and adapt research methods to evaluation of in-service education in most day-to-day operations. Practitioners should borrow from the experiences and techniques of researchers but forge their own methodologies. The work of Stufflebeam et al. (24) is certainly the most promising to date for use as a start in developing specific procedures.

This chapter has tried to provide a beginning for those who want practical approaches to evaluation. New and promising alternatives are being developed and should not be ignored. The "adversary evaluation" model being explored by Thurston (26) illustrates an effort to borrow from an entirely different profession in approaching educational evaluation. Whatever our approaches are, they should be rigorous, objective, systematic, and open-ended. The problem is one of constantly better understanding what the in-service efforts are and acting on that growing understanding to make them better. The problem is *not* one of finding the correct answers.

REFERENCES

1. Bank, Adrianne and James Burry. "Directions in Testing and Evaluation: CSE, 1978." *Evaluation Comment* 5, no. 3 (July 1978), UCLA Center for the Study of Evaluation, pp. 1–9.

*2. Bishop, Leslee J. *Staff Development and Instructional Improvement: Plans and Procedures.* Boston: Allyn and Bacon, Inc., 1976.

*3. Borich, Gary D. (editor). *Evaluating Educational Programs and Products.* Englewood Cliffs, N.J.: Educational Technology Publications, 1974.

*4. Borich, Gary D. and Susan K. Madden. *Evaluating Classroom Instruction: A Source Book of Instruments.* Reading, Mass.: Addison-Wesley, 1977.

5. Brandt, Ronald. "On Evaluation: An Interview with Daniel Stufflebeam." *Educational Leadership* 35, no. 4 (January 1978): 248–54.

6. Carter, Thomas P. and C. Ray Fowler. "Preliminary Report and Evaluation of the Riverside In-service Institute." Study of desegregation in the Riverside, California Public Schools, August 26, 1966 (mimeo).

7. Carthel, James T. "An Application of a Systems Analysis Model to the Evaluation of an Instructional Improvement Program." Doctoral dissertation, University of Texas at Austin, 1973.

8. Coker, Homer and Joan G. Coker. "A Competency Based Certification System." A paper presented at a national invitation Conference on Research on Teacher Effects: An Examination by Policy Makers and Researchers. Austin, Tex.: University of Texas at Austin, November 1975.

*9. Cook, Stuart W. *Research Methods in Social Relations.* 3d ed. New York: Holt, Rinehart and Winston, 1976.

*10. Franklin, Jack L. and Jean H. Thrasher. *An Introduction to Program Evaluation.* New York: John Wiley, 1976.

11. Hagen, Nancy J. "A Computer-Assisted Approach to Evaluation to In-service Education." A paper prepared for the Superintendency Program, University of Texas at Austin, May 10, 1978 (mimeo).

12. Harris, Ben M. "Constructing and Interpreting Branching Diagrams for Evaluation of Instruction." Austin, Tex.: University of Texas, December 1974.

*13. Harris, Ben M. *Supervisory Behavior in Education.* 2d ed. Englewood Cliffs, N.J.: Prentice-Hall, Inc., 1975.

14. Jones, V. M. "Trouble-Shooting Social Studies In-service Programs." *Social Education* 32, no. 7 (November 1968): 709–11.

15. Lasell, Warren L. "Product Evaluation as a Way of Thinking." *American Vocational Journal* 49, no. 1 (January 1974): 25–26.

16. McDonald, Frederick. "Criteria and Methods for Evaluating Inservice Training Programs." In *Issues in Inservice Education: State Action for Inservice.* Syracuse, N.Y.: National Council of States on Inservice Education, Syracuse University, College of Education, 1977, pp. 68–73.

17. Miller, William C. "Unobtrusive Measures Can Help in Assessing Growth." *Educational Leadership* 35, no. 4 (January 1978): 264–69.

18. Ogletree, James R. "Current Techniques for Improvement of Instructional Programs." *Person-Centered In-Service Education—Why Not? Bulletin of the Bureau of School Service* 30, no. 1 (September 1957). Lexington, Ky., pp. 9–18.

*19. Rattenburg, Judith and Paula Pelletier. *Data Processing in Social Sciences*

* Suggested for further reading.

with OSIRIS. Ann Arbor, Mich.: Survey Research Center, Institute for Social Research, University of Michigan, 1974.

*20. Sanders, James R. and Donald J. Cunningham. "Formative Evaluation: Selecting Techniques and Procedures." In *Evaluating Educational Programs and Products* (Gary D. Borich, editor). Englewood Cliffs, N.J.: Educational Technology Publications, 1974.

*21. Scriven, Michael. "Standards for the Evaluation of Educational Programs and Products." In *Evaluating Educational Programs and Products* (Gary D. Borich, editor). Englewood Cliffs, N.J.: Educational Technology Publications, 1974, pp. 15–24.

*22. Sonoquist, John A. and William C. Dunkelberg. *Survey and Opinion Research: Procedures for Processing and Analysis.* Englewood Cliffs, N.J.: Prentice-Hall, Inc., 1977.

*23. Stake, Robert E. and Terry Denny. "Needed Concepts and Techniques for Utilizing More Fully the Potential of Evaluation." Chapter 16 in *Educational Evaluation: New Roles, New Means.* 68th Yearbook. Part II (Ralph W. Tyler, editor). Chicago: National Society for the Study of Education, 1969.

*24. Stufflebeam, Daniel L. et al. *Educational Evaluation and Decision Making.* Phi Delta Kappa Study Committee on Evaluation. Itasca, Ill.: F. E. Peacock Publishers, 1971.

25. Thompson, Mark S. *Evaluation for Decision in Social Programmers.* Lexington, Mass.: Lexington Books, D. C. Heath, 1975.

26. Thurston, Paul. "Revitalizing Adversary Evaluation: Deep, Dark Deficits or Muddled Mistaken Musings." *Educational Researcher* 7, no. 7 (July–August 1978): 3–8.

27. Tyler, Ralph W. (editor). *Educational Evaluation: New Roles, New Means.* 68th Yearbook. Part II. Chicago: National Society for the Study of Education, 1969.

28. Van Fleet, Alanson A., Suzanne M. Kinzer, and J. P. Lutz. *Implementing Teacher Education Centers: The Florida Experience.* Gainesville, Fla.: Florida Educational Research and Development Council, Spring 1976.

*29. Weiss, Carol H. *Evaluation Research: Methods for Assessing Program Effectiveness.* Englewood Cliffs, N.J.: Prentice-Hall, Inc., 1972.

30. Williams, Janie. "Junior High Mathematics Staff Development Evaluation Results." Paper for the Department of Educational Administration, University of Texas at Austin, March 2, 1978.

* Suggested for further reading.

Appendix

A

List of Training Materials and Sources

The materials and sources listed here are only a few selected examples of the great variety of ready-made training aids that are available. The publisher of a specific kit, game, or program may also have other materials available.

Analyzing and Sequencing Learning Behaviors
Teacher Competency Development System
Prentice-Hall, Inc., P.O. Box 132
West Nyack, New York 10994
    Programmed material   Individual   1 hour

In this program, techniques of task analysis are applied to instructional objectives. Practice is provided so that an operational objective can be

Many of these descriptions of materials were taken from Corine Martinez and Ben M. Harris (editors), *A Directory of Competency-guided Supervisory Training Materials for Independent Study*, Document No. 9 (Austin, Tex.: University of Texas, Special Education Superviser Training Project, 1975).

analyzed into subareas designated as either entry or en route skills. Use of a particular strategy is advocated in which instruction is approached in terms of learners' responses rather than teacher presentation.

Analyzing Sets of Curricular Objectives
Far West Laboratory for Educational
   Research and Development
1855 Folsom Street
San Francisco, California 94103
   Programmed material   Individual   2–3 hours

The purpose of this text is to acquaint the participant with the analysis techniques they will use in the Terrabella High simulation (Part Two of this module). General familiarity with the ideas and concepts will be developed. Contents include: sets of curricular objectives; what makes an adequate set of curricular objectives; appropriate representation of cognitive behaviors; appropriate representation of affective behaviors; adequacy of subject matter coverage; internal consistency.

Basic Skills in Communication
by American Management Association
Didactic Systems, Inc.
P.O. Box 457
Cranford, New Jersey 07016
   Programmed material   Individual   20 hours

This program shows the learner how to get his message across — the most immediate, urgent, and practical part of communication. It is designed to enable the manager to improve the quality of his messages, to align the meaning of the message to the sender with the meaning of the message to the receiver, and to master communication as dynamic, creative interaction between sender and receiver. It is a self-contained course, which any individual may take on his own time with much profit.

The CSE Elementary School Evaluation Kit (Needs Assessment)
by Ralph Hoepfner et al.
Allyn and Bacon, Inc.
Longwood Division
470 Atlantic Avenue
Boston, Massachusetts 02210
   Kit   Individual   Extended time period

A package of materials for use by the principal in tapping various sources of information, including those of the community, for use in identifying critical needs for a school program.

Current Conceptions of Educational Evaluation
Teacher Competency Development System
Prentice-Hall, Inc., P.O. Box 132
West Nyack, New York 10994
Programmed material   Individual   1 hour

The goal of this program is to make the reader aware of the following:
measure versus evaluation
formative evaluation versus summative evaluation
employment of process criteria versus employment of product criteria
evaluation as an assessment of merit versus evaluation as an aid to decision makers

Deciding on Defensible Goals via Educational Needs Assessment
Teacher Competency Development System
Prentice-Hall, Inc., P.O. Box 132
West Nyack, New York 10994
Programmed material   Individual   1 hour

This program deals with a specific procedure that may be employed by educators to more judiciously select their educational goals. The strategy examined in the program is usually referred to as an educational needs assessment and has been used with increasing frequency during recent years at local and statewide levels.

Determining Instructional Purposes
by Joyce P. Gall, Charles L. Jenks et al.
Far West Laboratory for Educational
    Research and Development
1855 Folsom Street
San Francisco, California 94103
Kit   3–5 persons   Extended time period

Participants are led through a complete training process focused on an important skill in instructional purposing. Generally, each module includes a statement of the learning objectives, reading assignments, and self-tests; suggested responses to the self-tests; additional input information; which participants use for particular training tasks, work sheets, and feedback in the form of suggested responses by the developers or evaluations of their work by other teams.

Developing Job Descriptions
by Kenneth E. McIntyre and Gwen Carter
Special Education Supervisor Training Project
Department of Educational Administration
The University of Texas, Austin, Texas 78712
    Self-Instructional module   Individual   3–5 hours

    A structured sequence of materials and directions is provided to develop skill in actually producing a well-designed job description.

Early Warning Kit on the Evaluation of Teachers
Instruction and Professional Development Division
National Education Association
1201 16th Street, N.W.
Washington, D.C. 20036
    Kit   5–6 persons   2 hours

    The purpose of this kit is to assist members of the United Teaching Profession to examine the ways in which they are being or may be evaluated, to assess the appropriateness of instruments being used to measure their performance, to assure that they are held accountable only for those activities that may be expected of a professional, to guarantee due process for teachers, and to assure that information will be used appropriately in designing in-service teacher education.

Edventure II
by Ray Glazier and Ezra Gottheil
ABT Associates Inc., 55 Wheeler Street
Cambridge, Massachusetts 02138
    Game   Individuals or small group   2–3 hours

    A career guidance game designed to demonstrate educational options, lifelong learning, types of educational offerings, and so on. The game simulates a 1981–2000 educational market for continuing education.

Effective Interviewing for the Supervisor
by American Management Association
Didactic Systems
P.O. Box 457
Cranford, New Jersey 07016
    Programmed material   Individual   15 hours

    This course concentrates on interviewing as an exchange of information and on those techniques of effective communication that will produce such an exchange. Also, because it is likely that the supervisor is competent in the usual question-and-answer technique of interviewing, the course gives considerable attention to the more difficult nondirective approach, to encourage the interviewee to talk freely and spontaneously as a way of eliciting full and reliable information about him. Three units of PRIME VII cover the use of the nondirective techniques. One introductory unit deals with the basics of effective communication, and another gives general guidelines that can be applied to all interviews.

Experience Teaches Kit #4: Puzzles and Mazes Teach
by Ted Ward
Learning Systems Institute
Michigan State University
    Kit   Any number of persons   Variable time

Puzzles and Mazes Teach is an intriguing series of six problem-solving exercises in which the participants are encouraged to look at themselves and to clarify their approach to dealing with problems involving unknown solutions. Instructions are given on the cassette tape in the kit.

The 5:01 Deadline
Training House, Inc.
120 East 30th Street
New York, New York 10016
    Self-instructional   Small groups   3 hours (2hours in advance
    materials   plus 1-hour group session)

A set of materials designed to provide training in planning a series of activities with parallel scheduling and PERT.

The Game of Time Management
Training House, Inc.
120 East 30th Street
New York, New York 10016
    In-basket   Small groups   3 hours

An exercise designed to produce insights into one's own methods of establishing priorities, delegating, and organizing work. An in-basket device is utilized.

Generation Gap
by Erling O. Schild and S. S. Boocock
The Bobbs-Merrill Company, Inc.
4300 West 62d Street
Indianapolis, Indiana 46268

Game   Six players   3–4 hours

A simulation game that involves players in conflict situations. A parent and teenager work out problems.

The Greening of Students
by Scottie Littleton and Jim Miller
Education Service Center XIII
Austin, Texas
    Kit (multimedia)   Individual and small group   10 hours

A kit of materials for facilitator and individual participant use as self-instructional, self-paced exercises. Four modules focus on student self-concept, positive reinforcement techniques, classroom interaction, and analyzing verbal interaction. Readings, cassettes, and filmstrips are provided as well as pre- and post-tests and work sheets.

Experience Teaches Kit #7: Simulations Teach
by Ted Ward
Learning Systems Institute
Michigan State University
    Game   Teams, 3–5 persons   Variable time

The Sequencing Game is an active group exercise simulating the processes of analyzing a task in order to conduct an orderly accomplishment of the task. The simulation is culminated in a competitive game.

Ghetto
by Dove Toll
The Bobbs-Merrill Company, Inc.
4300 West 62d Street
Indianapolis, Indiana 46268
    Game   10 persons   Extended time period

The ten people in the game represent people in one neighborhood. Each player is given a descriptive profile of a different poor person and tries to improve that person's life. The game lasts from eight to ten rounds. In each round a player is given hour chips, depending on his family situation. The hour chips represent the number of hours per day he has available to invest in improving his living standard. The player allocates his time among the alternatives available to him. He can invest in school or work; spend his time in relaxation and recreation; go on welfare; take up neighborhood improvement activities; or take up hustling, which is defined as any illegal activity. Players are awarded with points for the investment of time. The points represent a combination of financial rewards and the intrinsic satisfaction of the activity.

Handling Conflict in Management: III
by Erwin Rausch and Wallace Wohlking
Didactic Game Company
Educational Services Division
Westbury, New York 11590
    Game   5 persons   2–3 hours

This is the third in a series of three didactic games designed to provide an opportunity for managers and managerial trainees to improve their conflict resolution skills. The purpose of these games is to create a framework for practice and for the exchange of ideas on how potential conflict situations can be turned into productive channels. The participants are encouraged to discuss the defensive and other emotional reactions that arise: how to recognize them, how to deal with them, and how to turn them toward constructive problem solving.

Information
by Gail M. Fennessey and Erling O. Schild
Academic Games Associates, Inc.
430 East 33d Street
Baltimore, Maryland 21218
    Game   8 or more persons   1–1 1/2 hours

The game is designed to create a healthy blend of competition and cooperation in small groups; its rules provide a carefully structured set of activities and scoring procedures so that players' success in answering questions about some particular topic can be encouraged and recorded. Information can be used to teach, drill, or review any body of information.

In-Service Training Design Simulation (ED 051 091)
by Massachusetts University (Amherst), School of Education
ERIC Document Reproduction Service
4827 Rugby Avenue
Bethesda, Maryland 20014
    Simulation   3–10 persons   10 hours

This exercise simulates the process of planning for in-service training. It requires that a planning group formulate a plan for the sixty-five staff members of an elementary school, given the constraints of an in-service training budget, a school calendar, and a limited amount of consultant help. Recommendations are to be developed for an in-service training program for a school year that will prepare the school staff to implement differentiated staffing in the next school year.

Interaction Analysis Training Kit — Level I
by Edmund J. Amidon and Peggy Amidon
Association for Productive Teaching, Inc.
5408 Chicago Avenue South
Minneapolis, Minnesota 55417
    Kit   2–5 persons   15–20 hours

The purpose of this kit is to provide the participants with practice in tallying classroom interaction and develop their experience in building matrices from the resulting data. There are four sessions: three dealing with short exercises depicting verbal behavior and one that is a diagnostic exercise.

Interaction Analysis Training Kit — Level II
by Edmund J. Amidon and Peggy Amidon
Association for Productive Teaching, Inc.
1040 Plymouth Building
Minneapolis, Minnesota 55402
    Kit   Any number of persons   20–30 hours

This kit provides an opportunity for the participant to understand and interpret classroom interaction. It specifically provides insight into teaching patterns that can be identified through interpretation and analysis of the matrices utilized in the system of interaction analysis.

Leading Groups to Better Decisions
by Erwin Rausch and George Rausch
Didactic Systems
P.O. Box 457
Cranford, New Jersey 07016
    Game   5 persons   2–3 hours

This game is designed specifically to help managers and executives improve their skills as effective conference leaders in problem-solving and decision-making situations, irrespective of their relative position of authority with respect to the other members of the problem-solving group.

PERT for CAA Planning — A Programmed Course of Instruction in PERT
Office of Economic Opportunity
Washington, D.C. 20506
    Programmed material   Individual   4–7 hours

This booklet offers the program evaluation and review technique in the form of programmed instruction for the student.

Policy Negotiations
by Frederic L. Goodman
Urbex Affiliates, Inc.
474 Thurston Road
Rochester, New York 14619
    Game   6 persons   3 hours

This game involves policy negotiations between teachers and the school board. A gaming process of three distinct but overlapping phases develop during the use of the game: initial introduction to, and play of, the priming game; creation of a new game through modification of the original game to meet the needs and/or interests of the players; play of the revised version of the game.

Selecto
by Sandra K. Bolan
Rocky Mountain Special Education Instructional Materials Center
The University of Northern Colorado
Greeley, Colorado 80631
    Game   3–5 persons   2–3 hours

This game was designed primarily for teachers of the learning disabled or retarded but is capable of adaptation to the needs of teachers of children with other disabling conditions. The game is also adaptable to the needs of the regular class teacher who has special problems in his class. The game presents the task of selecting and evaluating instructional materials for a hypothetical classroom and can be repeated more than once and still be of value due to the variety of possible situations arising from drawing Go-Cards that set different problems and constraints.

Teaching Problems Laboratory
by D. R. Cruickshank, F. W. Broadbent, and Roy L. Bubb
Science Research Associates, Inc.
259 East Erie Street
Chicago, Illinois 60611
    Simulation   Any number of persons   Extended time period

The materials are presented in two units. The Instructional Unit of the program includes filmstrip and long-playing record, films, role-playing cards, the simulation director's guide, a set of spirit masters of the critical teaching incident, and a sample Participant Unit. The Participant Unit is intended for use by each person attending the training session. Simulation technique regarding the nature of the critical teaching problems presented within each unit of instruction is discussed.

Team-Kit
Human Development Institute
20 Executive Park West, N.E.
Atlanta, Georgia 30329
    Kit (programmed)   Small group   6 hours

A series of training sessions is guided by materials to explore human relationships. Cassettes guide group and individual activities in role-playing, viewing, and discussing activities.

Test Questions
by Grant E. Barton and Andrew S. Gibbons
Young House
Brigham Young University Press
Provo, Utah 84602
    Programmed material   Individual   1–2 hours

Principles that will be helpful in discriminating between technically adequate and technically inadequate test questions are presented in this booklet. In the proficiency examination at the end of the booklet, two or three sample test questions are given of each of six test types: true-false, multiple-choice, completion, short answer, matching, and essay. Respondents are asked to identify which, if any, of the principles of test construction listed in the booklet are violated in the sample questions.

Transactional Analysis: Social and Communication Training
by David S. Abbey and R. H. T. Owston
Human Development Institute
166 East Superior Street
Chicago, Illinois 60611
    Programmed material   9–15 persons   3 hours

A programmed text offering procedures for a group to follow as they explore concepts of transactional analysis in relation to their own lives. Sets of illustrative figures included for use by subgroups.

Union Organizing Game
Labor Relations Associates, Inc.
3 Greenway Plaza "E"
Houston, Texas 77046
    Game   Small groups   4–6 hours

An elaborate set of simulation materials designed for use by nonunion participants. Objectives are specified in terms of learning about union organizing tactics, strategies for management, and employees' concerns.

B

Harris's Estimates of Experience Impact Potential for 28 Activities by Characteristics

Activity	1 Senses Involved	2 Multiple Interactions	3 Experience Control	4 Focus	5 Activeness	6 Originality	7 Reality	Total
1. Analyzing and calculating	2	2	2	3	3	1	1	16
2. Brainstorming	1	1	3	2	1	2	2	12
3. Buzz session	2	3	2	1	2	2	2	14
4. Demonstrating	1	1	3	1	1	2	3	12
5. Discussing, leaderless	2	2	1	1	1	1	2	10
6. Discussing, leader facilitated	2	2	1	2	1	1	2	11
7. Film, TV, filmstrip viewing	2	1	1	2	1	1	2	10
8. Firsthand experience	3	3	3	3	3	3	3	21
9. Group therapy	2	3	1	2	2	3	3	16
10. Guided practice	3	3	3	2	3	2	3	19
11. Interviewing, informative	1	2	2	1	1	1	1	9
12. Interviewing, problem solving	2	3	2	2	2	2	2	15
13. Interviewing, therapeutic	2	3	2	2	2	3	3	17
14. Lecturing	1	1	1	1	1	1	1	7

	1 Senses Involved	2 Multiple Interactions	3 Experience Control	4 Focus	5 Activeness	6 Originality	7 Reality	Total
Activity								
15. Material, equipment viewing	3	2	1	1	2	2	1	12
16. Meditating	1	1	1	2	2	3	2	12
17. Microteaching	3	2	2	3	3	2	3	18
18. Observing systematically in classroom	2	2	1	1	2	2	3	13
19. Panel presenting	2	1	1	1	1	1	1	8
20. Reading	1	2	3	3	2	1	2	14
21. Role playing, spontaneous	2	2	1	2	3	3	3	16
22. Role playing, structured	2	2	3	3	3	2	3	18
23. Social interaction	3	2	1	1	2	3	1	13
24. Tape, radio, record listening	1	1	1	1	1	1	1	7
25. Testing	2	2	3	3	1	1	1	16
26. Videotaping or photographing	3	2	1	2	3	2	3	16
27. Visualizing	2	1	1	2	1	1	1	9
28. Writing or drawing	2	1	1	2	3	2	1	12

C

Illustration of a Planning Document for an ISE Session

INTRODUCTION TO CLASSROOM OBSERVATION

Corpus Christi Schools   Spring 19 —

Phase II—Sessions 1 and 2 Wednesday, January 15, 19—

Goal A-1

"To promote the development of new administrative staff members as instructional leaders."
To develop skilled observer-analysts.

Objectives

A-1.1   To observe and record in live classroom situations with objectivity
        and reliability.
        a.   To recognize objectively recorded evidence given samples from

observation records showing ratings, feelings, opinions, etc., as well as descriptions of objects and events.

b. To record evidence in a live classroom situation (or filmed), given a structured comprehensive observation guide, for a period of 35 to 45 minutes, so that no opinions, judgments, or conclusions are expressed.

c. To record evidence in a live classroom as in (b) so that 80 percent of the entries are substantively the same as those produced by an experienced observer.

d. To record evidence in a live classroom as in (b) so that the teacher reading the edited record would object to no item as evidence of fact and would have only a few items of evidence to add.

General Information

Place: Administrative Building, 1305 Leopard Street
Group Size: 20–25
Contact Person: W. Davis

Phone: 939-5811
Participants: New administrators and supervisors. Mostly assistant principals.

Sequence of Events—Session 1, "Introduction to Classroom Observation"

Time	Activities	Materials	Leaders
8:30 A.M.	*Introductions* of visiting consultants, etc. Brief orientation to project.	Scratch pads	Williams Davis
8:45 A.M.	*Getting Acquainted.* Name plaques, code numbers, positions, etc.	Session-rating sheets, colored paper (8½ × 11), envelopes (9 × 4), flow pens, pencils.	Harris
9:00 A.M.	*Overview of the Day.* Review time schedule. Indicate sequence: 1. Learning about observation techniques. 2. Learning about one observation instrument. 3. Learning to use one observation instrument.	Chalkboard outline Time schedule	Harris
9:15 A.M.	*Introducing the Observational Problems* Relevance, objectivity, reliability. Brief reference to the need for observations that we can trust to base efforts at improvement of instruction. Brief reference to three problems. Introduce film-viewing activity. Show sixth-grade film with observation guide. Give quiz of objective evidence. Self-score quiz. Lead discussion of the teaching observed and problems in answering. Prepare transparencies.	16 mm film 16 mm projector Answer sheet Sixth-grade test Quiz key transparency	McIntyre
10:00 A.M.	*Coffee Break*		

Sequence of Events (cont.)

Time	Activities	Materials	Leaders

10:20 A.M.	*Feedback on Test Results*
	Present lecturette on implications
	1. Unstructure; observations lack reliability, accuracy, or details. We seek too little, do not remember enough, and draw conclusions that might be faulty. Different individuals see quite different things.
	2. The problem is this:
	   a. There is too much to see, so we select.
	   b. We value different things to select.
	   c. We cannot remember details, so we generalize.
	   d. We get preoccupied with certain events and ignore others.
		Feedback transparencies	Harris

10:30 A.M.	*Presentation of Comprehensive Observation Guide (COG)* Brief lecturette visualized to show basic features of the COG. 1. There are four main sections to focus observer attention on sequentially. 2. "I. The Classroom." 3. "II. The Teacher." 4. "III. The Pupils." 5. "IV. The Lesson." 6. Under each section is a series of very specific questions (examples). 7. The observer simply describes what he sees in response to each question as he constantly scans the events and objects of the classroom.	Transparencies of NEWCOG format Overhead projector and screen Flow pens, pointer, three-prong adapter, blank transparencies	Harris

Time	Activity	Materials	Presenter
10:45 A.M.	*Distribute and Scan NEWCOG* Allow time for all participants to scan material. Brief participants on several key points by calling attention to examples. 1. Notice that events are described. No value judgments, opinions, or ratings are called for. Questions ask for *evidence!* 2. Notice that some questions are blank. 3. Notice that evidence is described as vividly as possible to convey meaning for one who was not an observer. 4. Notice that the absence of events that might be expected is objective "negative evidence." *Present Procedures for Using NEWCOG* 1. Write while in classroom. 2. Read every item sequentially from front to back and record all that is observable. 3. Use shorthand note-taking procedures. 4. Avoid getting too engrossed in a portion of the lesson—keep attention roving. 5. When all items have been used initially, use time to concentrate on "IV. The Lesson" and other new events that arise. 6. Go back to all blank items and try to add evidence.	NEWCOG Sample showing actual recording	McIntyre
11:00 A.M.		Handout—Four Problems in Recording Evidence	Harris
11:05 A.M.	*Questions*		
11:20 A.M.	*Discuss plans* for final briefing on observation practice after lunch. Give directions on reassembling at school where observation practice sessions are planned.	Maps	Davis
11:30 A.M.	*Adjourn*		

D

Illustration of a Local District ISE Policy

STAFF DEVELOPMENT

A. In-Service Education for All Personnel

The continuous efforts to improve instruction for all students shall be promoted by a program of in-service education (ISE).

1. Definition. In-service education includes planned learning opportunities provided under the direction of the staff for improving performance in already held or assigned positions.
2. All personnel are entitled to, and responsible for, participating in in-service education throughout the period of tenure with the district.
3. The administration shall provide for an ISE program or programs that assure: (a) attention to the most urgent needs of the district for improving its operations, and (b) attention to the specific needs of individual staff members for improving performance on the job.
4. The administration shall develop a long-range plan for the ISE of personnel and shall update it annually.

5. All affected personnel will be provided opportunities to influence the character of the ISE program(s) by direct or representative participation in planning, evaluating, and implementing.
6. Training opportunities developed by colleges, teacher centers, professional associations, and other agencies may be utilized for ISE purposes so long as they are coordinated with, and guided by, the ISE program plans of the district.
7. All required ISE activities shall be on time specified under the contract of the personnel involved. Activities necessitating overtime or out-of-contract time periods (summer or holidays) shall be authorized under mutual agreements for extra pay or compensatory time exchanges.

E

A Comprehensive Plan
for Individualizing
Instruction

Rock Meadows Public Schools
*Part A: The In-Service Education Plan.**
1980 to 1985

CONTENTS

* Other parts of the complete plan include: Part B—Curriculum and Materials Development and Acquisition Plan; Part C—Facilities and Equipment Plan; and Part D—Community Involvement Plan.

IV. Plan A Overview: In-Service Education
     Components. Phasing. Staffing and coordinating responsibilities.
     Released time. Visiting consultants.
 V. Objectives for Components
     Objectives for component I: Observing and analyzing classroom
     practices. (others not shown)
VI. Descriptions of Operations
     Component I: Observing and analyzing classroom practices.
     (others not shown)
VII. Staff Assignments (not shown)
VIII. Budget
     Program budget summary. Component I: cost analysis, 1975–
     77. Activities anticipated. Explanation of expense items.
Exhibits

I. THE LONG-RANGE GOAL

By the end of the instructional year, in June 1985, all classroom teachers
will be making full, high-quality use of five approaches to individualization
of instruction in their classrooms and laboratories. Sixty percent of all instructional time will evidence some form of individualization in operation.
Eighty percent of the high-priority goals and objectives of the curriculum
will provide for individualization in three or more ways.

Other evidences that a truly high-quality, full-scale program of individualization is in operation will be the following:

1. Learning resource centers will be in full operation, staffed and regularly used by students, teachers, and aides.
2. Learning activity packets will be in evidence in use and available in all
   content areas at all levels.
3. Observations will report a full range of individualizing practices in
   evidence.
4. Teacher self-reports will indicate growing use of all five approaches.
5. Student descriptions of their instructional life will report use of individualization consistent with observations.

II. OVERVIEW OF THE PROGRAM

Rationale

Students are very different one from another. They differ in interests; prior
experiences; prerequisite learnings; and physical, social, and emotional
development.

Learning expectations and modes of instruction should be different for every student. Differences should be those that are needed to create optimum conditions for the maximum amount of the most relevant learning for each individual.

Teachers are very different in their interests, competencies, and ways of working with students. These differences should be utilized to provide all students with the most suitable kind of instruction and also to assist all teachers to become more versatile and more fully competent.

Materials, assignments, tests, time limits, grades, and grouping arrangements should all reflect the best interests of the individual learner.

The Program Plans

Four separate but related plans for individualizing instruction are to be implemented.

A.   The In-Service Education Plan
B.   The Curriculum and Materials Development Plan
C.   The Facilities and Equipment Remodeling Plan
D.   The Community Development Plan

All plans will be implemented during the period from August 1980 through July 1985. Since all plans are related to the single, long-range superordinate goal of individualizing instruction for all students, specific objectives and all activities of each plan will be related to this single goal.

Since individualizing of instruction comes about primarily through the efforts of classroom teachers as they work with students, the *In-Service Education Plan* will be the *core* around which the entire program is to operate. The in-service education plan (A) will be utilized to guide and direct curriculum and materials development rather than vice versa. That is to say, when teacher skills and knowledges are such that they request new materials, then they will become the focus of other developmental endeavors. Similar responses to in-service education outcomes are provided for in plans C and D.

III. COMPREHENSIVE PROGRAM GOALS

A.   *In-Service Education*
  1.   To develop a comprehensive understanding of the meaning of individualization of instruction (II) among all staff personnel.
  2.   To become skillful in utilizing five different approaches to II in the classroom for all teaching personnel.

    3. To become analytical in the use of observations and other data sources for diagnosing growth needs of all teaching personnel.

B. *Curriculum and Materials Development*
    1. To develop a selected set of high priority goals and objectives for student learning for each content area on an ungraded basis.
    2. To produce, test, and provide for the distribution of self-instructional learning activity packets for each priority goal and objective.
    3. To select and purchase a collection of multimedia instructional aids for use in relation to each priority goal.
    4. To organize and make operational one or more learning resource centers for purposes of storing, cataloguing, distributing, and using a full array of instructional materials and equipment to facilitate individualization of instruction.

C. *Facilities and Equipment*
    1. To select, purchase, and arrange for the storing and maintenance of instructional equipment to assure ready access to multimedia by both students and teachers.
    2. To remodel at least one area in every school for special use as a learning resource center for multimedia utilization.
    3. To remodel up to 60 percent of all classrooms to facilitate their use for individualization of instruction.

D. *Community Involvement*
    1. Same as A–1 for a broadly representative group of parents and other citizens.
    2. To secure acceptance of four out of five major approaches to individualization of instruction by 70 percent of parents and 80 percent of students.
    3. To secure active involvement of a representative group of citizens as aides, tutors, visiting specialists, and advisory committee members.

IV. PLAN A OVERVIEW: IN-SERVICE EDUCATION

Components

The in-service education program will include four fairly distinct, though related, operational components, as follows:

Component I. *Observing and Analyzing Classroom Practices*
    The entire staff will develop skill in using a systematic set of classroom observation procedures with a focus on specific individualization practices. Furthermore, teachers will provide feedback to other teachers on observed events. Self-reports on practices will be developed.

Component II. *Using Learning Activity Packets (LAPs)*
    The teachers will learn to make selected use of LAPs with individuals and small groups.
Component III. *Individual Growth Planning*
    Teachers in consultation with principals and consultants will learn to develop diagnostic analyses of teaching performance patterns and develop growth plans to guide improvement efforts on an individual basis. Cooperative implementation of growth plan activities will be provided.
Component IV. *Learning Resource Center Utilization*
    (See Exhibit 3–7 for a flowchart for component I.)
Exhibit E–1 displays goals and activity descriptions for each program component.

Phasing

Components I and II will get top priority during 1980 and 1981 with learning resource center utilization, Component IV becoming more of a priority by the summer of 1982, and into the 1982–83 school years. Component III will get little attention until 1983–84.

Staffing and Coordinating Responsibilities

Each of the four components will have an individual acting as coordinator throughout the school district. Similarly, a coordinating committee for each component will have a teacher representative from each school and program level as well as a principal, consultant, or assistant principal on each committee.

The superintendent will serve as chairman of the districtwide council for the program, which will have an administrative and teacher representative from each school. (Attachments for staff assignments for 1980–81 and for Guidelines for Committees and Councils not shown here.)

Released Time

To the fullest possible extent teachers will be released from regular classroom duties to allow for the activities of the program that are scheduled during the instructional day. Released time will be planned by: (1) arranging for aides, student assistants, principals, counselors, librarians, and duty-free teachers to assist; (2) employing substitute teachers; and (3) releasing students from classes for all or portions of the instructional day. (See attachment for suggestions on Released Time Planning, not shown here.)

Exhibit E–1.   IN-SERVICE EDUCATION: GOAL/COMPONENT RELATIONSHIPS

*In-Service Components**

Goals	I Observing and Analyzing Classroom Practices	II Using Learning Activity Packets	III Individual Growth Planning	IV Learning Resource Center Utilization
1. To develop comprehensive understanding of the meaning of individualization of instruction.	Observers gain a variety of insights into the kinds of practices already in operation.	Users gain experience with diagnostic techniques for assigning appropriate packets.	(Not necessarily related.)	Teacher gains new respect for students' ability to direct own learning. Teacher develops appreciation of, and knowledge about, a great variety of materials for instruction.
2. To become skillful in utilizing five different approaches to individualizing instruction in the classroom.	Observers compare and contrast their practices with others. Feedback provided assists in refining practices.	Users learn about both values and limitations of packets, and other approaches that need to be used in relation to packets.		Teacher develops skill as organizer and coordinator of diverse learning activities.
3. To become analytical in the use of observations and other data sources for diagnosing growth needs.	Observers become fully aware of specific events associated with each approach and gain ability to be explicit about improvements to be sought.	(Not necessarily related.)		(Not necessarily related.)

* See Exhibit 3–8 for a Gantt Chart for In-Service Education showing component I and II events for 1975–76.

A substantial amount of the activity planned for components II, III, and IV can and will be concurrent with teaching activities. After-school hours will be utilized as needed, and selected teachers will be given opportunities for overtime contracts when serving on the program on Saturdays and during vacation periods.

Time requirements for the program are presented in great detail in Attachment C (not shown here). On the average, thirty to fifty hours per teacher per year are estimated to be required during the life of the program.

Visiting Consultants

A general consultant will be selected to serve for all aspects of the program. This person will be a distinguished scholar serving with a major university who can contract for a minimum of two days per month on-site. A team of visiting consultants will be selected and organized to work with the local staff in implementing the various components. It is anticipated that the *team* of visiting consultants will vary from three to five persons serving fifty to sixty days a year.

V. OBJECTIVES FOR COMPONENTS

Objectives for Component I:
Observing and Analyzing Classroom Practices

The staff will learn:

1.0. To develop a comprehensive understanding of II by:
  1.1. Identifying at least twenty specific practices that can be observed in classrooms that relate to individualization of instruction.
  1.2. Categorizing an array of thirty specific practices within a set of five approaches or modes of individualization.
  1.3. Identifying specific events in classrooms that are clearly evidence of individualization.
  1.4. Recording descriptively and scaling objectively the extent of individualization observed in any classroom.
2.0. To become skillful in utilizing five approaches to II by:
  2.1. Identifying similarities and differences between the array of practices observed and those in one's own classroom.
  2.2. Using feedback provided by observer reports for making specific changes in practices.

3.0. To become analytical in the use of observations and other data sources for diagnosing growth needs by:

    3.1. Analyzing a series of observation reports over time to identify recurrent events that suggest improvement needs.

    3.2. Comparing and contrasting self-reports with observation reports to detect discrepancies between perceptions.

    3.3. To translate an identified need into a vividly descriptive statement of improved performances that are desired.

Objectives for Component II:
Learning Activity Packets

(Not shown.)

Objectives for Component III:
Individual Growth Planning

(Not shown.)

Objectives for Component IV:
Learning Resource Center Utilization

(Not shown.)

VI. DESCRIPTIONS OF OPERATIONS

As has been indicated, the four components of the in-service education program plan will parallel the developmental efforts outlined in plans B, C, and D. All in-service education will be directed toward goals and objectives specified.

Component I:
Observing and Analyzing Classroom Practices

a. The entire faculty will have an opportunity to become familiar with the purposes to be served by classroom observations, the instruments to be utilized, and the training and other procedures planned. A general faculty meeting will be planned. This will be followed by school-level discussions.

b. A coordinating committee for component I will be organized. Each building and grade level will have an elected teacher representative on the committee. Each building will have an administrative representative. The central staff will be represented by an instructional supervisor from each of the elementary and secondary divisions, and the superintendent will serve as chairman at least for the first year.

c. A local training team will be organized and trained as observation trainers in each building. Most if not all of these trainers will also be members of the Coordinating Committee. At least three trainers in each building will be selected, provided with released time, and trained in the use of systematic classroom observation techniques. They will also be given training in the use of standardized training procedures and provided with consulting services from a visiting consultant.

d. As training teams are ready, they will proceed to work with one fourth of the faculty in each building to train them in the use of classroom observation procedures.

e–h–j. As each group of the faculty gains skill in the use of observation techniques, interobserver reliability checks will be scheduled to secure agreements of high order. Training will be conducted in workshop settings but quickly move to classrooms, where small groups will practice on each other.

i. A visiting consultant will be holding regular conferences with training team leaders (trainers) to discuss problems, reactions, and concerns they may be encountering.

k. Demonstrations will be planned and presented to provide opportunities for observers to see specific practices under high-quality conditions. If necessary, some of these demonstrations will be scheduled in schools in other districts to assure only top-quality displays of practices.

f. As trainers certify a substantial portion of the faculty as qualified observers, routine observations with individual feedback will be scheduled. Observations will provide each faculty member no less than five feedback reports by five different observers, one for each of an array of lessons.

n. Principals will have debriefing sessions with small faculty groups to determine concerns and problems and obtain suggestions for revisions in procedures during the following year.

Procedures for subsequent years will be much like those described here, with only a few exceptions: (1) new teachers will be trained as soon as possible; (2) rechecking of reliability levels will be provided; (3) growth planning will be related to observation and feedback processes beginning early in the second year as a part of Component III.

Component II:
Using Learning Activity Packets

(Not shown.)

Component III:
Individual Growth Planning

(Not shown.)

Component IV:
Learning Resource Center Utilization
(Not shown.)

VII. STAFF ASSIGNMENTS
(Not shown.)

VIII. BUDGET

Program Budget Summary
Plan A: In-Service Education for   *Date: February 10, 1980*
Individualizing Instruction

		Budget Classification			
Component	6100 Payroll	6200 Central Services	6300 Supplies/ Materials	6400 Other	Total All Classifications
I. Observation and Analysis of Classroom					
1980–81	$26,100	$ 6,300	$ 900	$270	$ 33,570
1981–82	12,050	3,450	400	155	16,055
Est., 1982–85	36,000	17,500	1,100	400	55,000
Total—5 years	$74,150	$27,250	$2,400	$825	$104,625

II. *Use of LAPs*
1980–81
1981–82

(Not calculated or shown)

Est. 1982–85
Total—5 years

III. *Individual Growth Plan*
1980–81

(Not calculated or shown)

1981–82

IV. (Not shown)

Component I: Cost Analysis, 1980–85 *

Activities Anticipated.   Local personnel will be trained in using classroom observation techniques. All trained instructional personnel will be scheduled periodically to observe in all classrooms. Related conferences for pre-

---

* Based on suggestions and materials developed by Dr. Edward Manigold, Division of Planning Projects, Texas Education Agency.

planning and feedback will be scheduled. Workshops, field trips, and demonstrations will be related.

Operations (See Gantt Chart, Exhibit 3–5)	Expense Items	Budget Classifi-cation	Amount 1980–81	Estimated 1981–82
A. Orientation and Organization		—	($ 2,120)	($ 1,605)
(1) Selecting consultant(s)	Communications (letters, telephone)	6400	$ 20	$ 5
	Trip(s) for staff to discuss project	6400	250	150
(2) Briefing consultant(s)	Trip for consultant(s) to site	6200	500	300
	Released time for Coordinating Committee	6100	100	100
(3) Orientation session for entire staff	Consultant(s) services	6200	500	500
	Materials production	6300	400	200
	No released time—use ISE day as authorized			
(4) Organization of Coordinating Committee	Consultant services	6200	350	350
B. Observation Training		—	($11,850)	($ 2,400)
(5) Training local trainers	Consultant services	6200	$ 350	$ 350
	Released time for teachers	6100	1,000	250
(6) Training of total staff	Materials for observations	6300	400	100
	Released time for teachers	6100	9,600	1,200
	Clerical assistance	6100	500	500
C. Reliability Checks				
(7) Training for procedures for reliability check	Consultant services	6200	500	350
(8) Periodic checks	Released time for teachers to administer check	6100	1,000	200

Operations (See Gantt Chart, Exhibit 3–5)	Expense Items	Budget Classification	Amount 1980–81	Estimated 1981–82
D. Full-scale Observations and Feedback	Clerical assistance	6100	500 ($13,600)	— ($10,850)
(9) Develop schedules for spring observations	Released time	6100	$ 400	$ 400
(10) Observations	Computer services	6200	3,000	1,000
	Released time	6100	6,000	6,000
	Materials	6300	100	100
	Clerical assistance	6100	3,000	3,000
(11) Debriefing sessions with faculty groups	No released time	—	—	—
	Consultant services	6200	600	350
E. Pre- and Post-Conferences			($4,500)	($650)
(12) Training in conference and feedback procedures	Consultant services	6200	500	250
	Released time	6100	4,000	400
Totals—Component I			$33,570	$16,055
6100: Payroll			$26,100	$12,050
6200: Contracted Services			$ 6,300	$ 3,450
6300: Supplies and Materials			$ 900	$ 400
6400: Other Expenses			$ 270	$ 155
Total for Two-year Operation 1980–82			$49,625	

Explanation of Expense Items

Generally applicable bases for estimating expenses:
      200 staff members involved
      20 new staff members for 1981–82
      2 consultants involved some of the time

$20 per day or fractional part of a day utilized as *average* released-time cost

10 teachers included among the trainer group, plus administrators, supervisors, etc.

B (6)   Training time of 21 hours × 200 staff trainees = 3 days × 80% released time = 480 days @ $20 each = $9,600 for 1980–81. Same formula for 1981–82 with only 20 *new* staff trainees.

D (10)   Observations involve 3 × 200 teachers = 600 observations × ½ day for each set of 2 observations = 300 half days of released time @ $20 = $6,000.

D (11)   Debriefing can utilize after school or off periods on various campuses.

E (12)   Conference training involves a single workshop for each of several groups for 3 hours. Hence, 200 staff × ½ day @ $20 = $4,000.

F

Suggestions for State Law
for In-Service Education

Purpose

It should be the intent of the legislature to assure the quality of educational opportunity for all children and youth by promoting the continuous improvement in on-the-job performance of all personnel [1] serving regularly in the free public elementary and secondary schools of the State of_____.
It is further the intent that continuous improvement in on-the-job performance should be promoted for personnel regardless of prior training or experience. It is essential to the welfare of children and youth and to the people of the state that all personnel continue to improve job performance throughout their careers in the public schools.

It should be the intent of the legislature that: (1) local school districts provide opportunities for in-service education for all personnel; (2) the State Board of Education provide guidelines and support for a statewide

---

[1] *Personnel* can be defined broadly as "all employees." However, the strongest rationale is found, perhaps, by a definition of personnel that includes all with direct influence on students or the instructional program.

plan for in-service education; (3) the statewide program be regularly evaluated and updated.

Legislation Should Specify as Purpose: To promote the continuous [2] provision of quality opportunities for in-service education for each individual included on the staff of every local school district and other education agencies.[3]

Legal Provisions

An act might be referred to as the "In-Service Education Opportunities Act of 19   ."

a. Part A should be known as the "Comprehensive State In-Service Education Program."
b. Part B should be known as the "Supplementary Educational Services Program."
c. Part C should be known as the "Leadership Training and Innovations Program."
d. Part D should be known as the "Instructional Program Development and Improvement Fund."

Statement of Policy

It should be the declared policy of the State of ———— to provide in-service education opportunities for all personnel of the public elementary and secondary schools.[4] The law should provide authorization for the State Board of Education to develop a comprehensive statewide plan to assist local school districts in providing in-service education programs of high quality for all personnel. In pursuit of this policy, four provisions should be considered:

a. A comprehensive statewide plan for in-service education: (1) setting forth policies, regulations, and guidelines for local districts; (2) estab-

[2] "Continuous" refers to continuing throughout every individual's career and being provided for at various times throughout every school or calendar year. "Continuous" should not be construed as requiring continuous opportunities for education at any and all times, nor requiring continuous involvement by every individual.

[3] "Other education agencies" includes supplementary service organizations, state education agencies, and other organizations officially serving the public schools.

[4] This provision restricting the application of the provisions of the act to elementary and secondary schools could be modified to include colleges, vocational schools, and other educational institutions where other legal provisions make such modifications compatible.

lishing a state office for coordination and planning; and (3) creating a statewide advisory council.

b. Creation of supplementary educational service organizations to offer in-service education and other instructional services to local school districts.

c. Leadership training and innovative in-service education to stimulate and facilitate improved quality of in-service education.

d. Creation of an Instructional Program Development and Improvement Fund and appropriating (authorizing) specific amounts of money for in-service education purposes.

Definitions Might Include:

a. In-service education. Any planned learning opportunities provided to personnel of the local district or other authorized agency for purposes of improving the performance of such personnel in already held or assigned positions.

b. Personnel. Any full-time or part-time employee of the local school district, supplementary educational service organization, or state education agency.

c. Local school districts. Any public local education agency authorized by law to provide elementary and secondary or *(other)* education under the policies of the State Board of Education.

d. Supplementary education services. Any approved regional organization providing in-service education and other instructional support service to local school districts.

e. Leadership training. Training and/or education specifically designed to improve performances of personnel in assignments involving planning, designing, organizing, staffing, implementing, or evaluating in-service education activities.

f. Instructional program development. Any planned efforts to improve the quality of instruction available to children and youth through curriculum and materials development, in-service education, improved staffing, and instructional evaluation.

g. Innovative in-service education. Any activity, plan, procedure, technique, material, or delivery system for in-service purposes that is not widely utilized.

PART A: THE COMPREHENSIVE STATE PROGRAM

The State Board should adopt policies and guidelines that promote the delivery of in-service education services for all school personnel.

1. Each board of each local education agency should develop its own policies and programs for the delivery of in-service education of local personnel.
2. An office for coordination and statewide planning of in-service education should be established.
3. An advisory council representing both professional and lay interests should be created.
4. (Other.)

A study of needs for in-service education should be undertaken no less frequently than every five years.

1. The needs of teachers and other types of personnel should be assessed on the basis of objective individual performance data.
2. The needs of schools and local communities should also be assessed.
3. Priorities should be established on the basis of needs defined for individuals, schools, districts, and programs.

PART B: SUPPLEMENTARY EDUCATIONAL SERVICES PROGRAM

Supplementary educational service organizations (SESOs) of regional character should be created to advise and cooperate and collaborate with local school districts and other agencies in providing for in-service education for school personnel.[5]

1. The number of SESOs should be _____.
2. No school district should be denied an opportunity to be included in the SESO serving the region.
3. The services provided by each SESO in each region of the state should include in-service education for personnel but should not be restricted from providing other services.
4. Each SESO may represent a consortium of various agencies and institutions but should include not less than two school districts.
5. Each SESO should be approved by the State Board of Education for funding by the Instructional Program Development and Improvement Fund.

---

[5] Numerous prototypes for such organizations are already in existence. Regional educational service centers are well developed in such states as New York, Wisconsin, Texas, and Pennsylvania. County school service organizations in California and some teacher centers in various parts of the nation offer promising patterns to be considered.

6. A governing board of parents, classroom teachers, and school officials should be elected for each SESO.

PART C: LEADERSHIP TRAINING AND INNOVATIONS PROGRAM

The State Board of Education should adopt a plan for the continuing training of leadership personnel directing and implementing in-service education programs.

1. The training plans should provide training in modern techniques for planning, designing, implementing, organizing, and evaluating in-service education programs.
2. Training opportunities should be available to staff personnel currently assigned to positions of responsibility for in-service education at state, regional, and local levels.
3. Training opportunities should be provided to assure that classroom teachers, visiting consultants, and others assuming leadership responsibilities for in-service education have appropriate competencies.
4. The training plans should include cooperative efforts among schools, universities, and other agencies to stimulate the development and/or upgrading of graduate programs for the preparation of leadership personnel for in-service education.
5. Training program plans should provide for the coordination of leadership training provided by all agencies and institutions.
6. (Other.)

The State Board of Education should adopt a plan for initiating innovative programs of in-service education.

1. Promising in-service training programs and practices should be selected for funding and evaluation as pilot projects.
2. Dissemination of information about most promising innovations in in-service education should be provided for.
3. Pilot projects that prove to be most promising should be selected as demonstration centers for use in promoting adoptions by local school districts.
4. (Other.)

PART D: INSTRUCTIONAL PROGRAM DEVELOPMENT AND IMPROVEMENT FUND

An Instructional Program Development and Improvement Fund (IPDIF) should be established to provide for continuous and flexible funding for all aspects of in-service education in the state.

1. Not less than an amount equal to 5 percent of the total allocation for salaries of school personnel throughout the state should be designated for the IPDIF annually.
2. The State Board of Education should allocate all monies from the IPDIF with the advice of the State Advisory Council on In-Service Education according to the Comprehensive State Plan.
3. Allocations should not be rigidly controlled by formula but should reflect local, regional, and statewide needs. Funds allocations should reflect the following percentages for aggregate expenditure over each five-year period beginning ———— ———— 198   :

   (Month)   (date)

   a. Seventy percent to local school districts.
   b. Twenty percent to Supplementary Educational Service Organizations
   c. Ten percent to any agency for purposes specified above at the discretion of the State Board with advice from the State Advisory Council for In-Service Education.
4. The State Board of Education should cause a comprehensive evaluation of in-service education throughout the state to be completed at least every fifth year from the date of implementation of Part D of this Act.
5. Nothing in this Act should be construed as prohibiting or restricting the use of additional personnel, funds, facilities, time, or services for purposes herein designated.
6. Allocations from the Instructional Program Development and Improvement Fund should be made for curriculum and materials development, instructional and personnel evaluation, and other staff development [6] so long as such expenditures are directly related to in-service education program plans and do not exceed 35 percent of total allocations or more than 45 percent of the allocations to any agency or program.
7. Administration of in-service education programs with the exception of periodic evaluations, training activities, and other specific provisions for planning and coordination should not be approved for IPDIF funding in excess of 3 percent of the fund expenditures. State education agency allocations for purposes of administering this Act should not exceed 1 percent of the fund allocations.

---

[6] "Other staff development" refers to manpower planning; career ladder training; and improving selection, recruitment, and assignment of personnel.

G

Case Illustration of an Individual Professional Growth Plan

Name: *Ms. M. L. Wiggins*   Date: *11/19/78*
Position: *Teacher – 8th Eng, Soc. Stud.* School/Office/Dept.: *Rolf Jr. H. School*

Directions: In collaboration with your immediate supervisors, this plan for your continuing growth on the job should be developed as soon as possible once reliable observations of your performance have been completed. The following steps are involved:

(1) Two or more observations of your performance should be completed by assigned personnel (step 1).
(2) A self-report describing your performance should be completed (step 2).
(3) Preliminary interviews should be completed with your immediate supervisor or other assigned personnel for the purpose of reviewing observation and self-report data (step 2).

(4)   A planning interview should be completed for the purpose of completing this growth plan (steps 3 and 4).
(5)   A review interview should be scheduled for discussing progress toward growth plan objectives (step 5).

This five-step process should be repeated every six to twenty months depending upon the practical realities of each situation.

Multiple copies of step 4 are provided to facilitate revised planning and follow-up planning using the same set of observation data.

STEP 1 SUMMARY OF OPERATIONS

Instrument(s) Used	Date/Observer-Analyst	(Describe specific events, scores, etc.)
Descriptive Observation Record for Individualization of Instruction and Individualization of Instruction Inventory	9/16/78 C.L.M. Principal	Total score 68. Subscores Intraclass Grouping – 17 – High Pupil Autonomy – 15 – Med. High Variety of Material – 12 – Low Differentiated Assign. – 14 – Med. Tutoring – 10 – ?
(Ditto)	9/24/78 L.T.V. Teacher	Total Score 64 – Same Pattern as above. Material tends to be worksheets text, and a sample kit.
(Ditto)	10/21/78 C.L.M. Principal	Total score – 77 I.C. Grouping – 20 P. Autonomy – 16 Variety of Matl. – 13 Different Assign. – 17 Tutoring – 11

STEP 2 SUMMARY OF SELF-REPORT

Instrument(s) Used	Date	FINDINGS	COMPARISONS (Similarities and Differences between Steps 1 and 2)
Individualization of Instruction Inventory only.	9/12/78	Total = 88 – High by 11 to 24 points Grouping = 22 – High by 2 to 5 points P. Autom. = 17 – Only slightly high Var. Matl. = 18 – High by 5 to 6 points Diff. Assign. = 18 – High by 1 to 4 points Tutoring = 13 – High by 2 to 3 points	Largest discrepancies in use of a Variety of materials.

STEP 3   REVIEWING CUMULATIVE DATA
Based on a careful review and discussion of the data on the previous page:

A. *Describe*, in performance terms, the professional practices that are recurrent
   and appear to be essential and desirable aspects of your "style" or way of working.

-uses intraclass groups rather systematically and in most content areas.
- Pupil autonomy, while not exceptionally strong, is consistently promoted via freedom of movement in the classroom, encouraging students in aiding each other, and leading group activities with students' activities.

B. *Describe*, in performance terms, those selected practices that are recurrent and
   appear to be most in need of modification as aspects of the teacher's way of
   working.

1- Materials in use restricted largely to texts, work-books, and ditto sheets.
2- Tutoring is limited to that done by teachers with no involvement of pupils, parents, resource persons.
3- Tutoring by teacher is unplanned, reactive to situations that arise, and rarely are well distributed among students. They are usually only fleeting moments of personal attention.

C. The above review and interpretation was collaboratively completed on:

_____11/19/78_____   by:

Name: M. L. Wiggins   Position: Teacher, 8th Engl./Soc. Studies
      (Signature)

Name: Harold Le Shin   Position: Coord. of Instruction
      (Signature)

STEP 4   GROWTH PLAN DECISIONS

Based on specific practices to be modified as described in Step 3B, define a plan of action as follows:

Objective(s) for Change (specific behaviors)	Activities to Be Undertaken (describe what will be done)	Responsible Person	Target for Completion (date)
3B-1- The teacher will demonstrate the use of at least three different types of materials during the same lesson with no students being restricted to a single material.	1(a) A visit to a classroom where multimedia activities are common will be arranged.	C.L.M.	12/1/78
	1(b) A planning session will be scheduled following the visit above with coordinator.	M.L.W. and H.LeS.	12/5/78
	1(c) A planning session with the media coordinator will be arranged.	H.LeS.	12/7/78
	1(d) The principal and teacher will review a series of lesson plans for multimaterial utilization.	C.L.M. and M.L.W.	12/10/78
	1(e) Observations in classrooms will be scheduled to observe new lessons.	M.L.W. H.LeS. C.L.M.	1/20/79
3B-2- Not included in plan at this time — — — — — — — — — — — — — — —			
3B-3- The teacher will tutor at least three selected students each day with pre-planned purpose for at least three minutes.	3(a) Tutoring techniques will be tried in roleplaying situations.	H.LeS.	1/3/79
	3(b) Tutoring plans will be developed and reviewed.	M.L.W. H.LeS.	1/5/79

The plan above is agreed to on ___11/20/78___ by:

Name ___M. L. Wiggins___   Name ___Harold Le Shier___
      (Signature)   (Signature)

STEP 5   REVIEWING PROGRESS AND REPLANNING

a. *Progress Report* on improvement plan in operation (refer to Step 4)
   (1) Which objectives have been accomplished?   3B-1 ,_____ ,_____
   (2) Which objectives are in progress?   3B-3 ,_____ ,_____
   (3) What changes (revisions, additions, substitutions) are needed?
   Need to revise objective 3B-3 and to arrange
   added activities.

b. *Growth Plan Revisions*

(1) Objectives for Change	(2) Activities	(3) Responsible Person	Target Date
3B-3 Tutor at least one selected student each day according to preplanning for at least 5 minutes.	3(c) Visit with and observe another teacher who utilizes tutoring.	H. Le S.	1/5/79
	3(b) Tutoring plans.	M.L.W. H. Le S.	1/10/79

c. *Next Steps*
   (1) Continue to implement plan until __2/1/79__ (including changes above).
   or (2) Revise improvement plan on _____ (refer to Targets for Completion, above).
   or (3) Initiate new growth plan by _____

Approved by:
Signature: __M. L. Wiggins__   __Harold Le Shier__
Title: ____teacher____   ____Coord. of Instruction____
Date: ____12/12/78____   ____12/12/78____

H

Illustrative Data
from 46 Participants
in a Training Session

1	2	4	5	7	8	3–6
Partici-pant	Assign-ment Level *	Volun-tariness	Stimu-lating	Rele-vance	Useful-ness	Objective Congruence
1	S	3	4	4	3	3
2	E	2	5	5	1	3
3	E	3	2	3	2	2
4	S	2	5	5	4	1
5	E	2	5	5	3	3
6	E	4	5	4	3	4
7	E	0	4	5	1	1
8	S	4	4	5	5	5
9	E	3	5	5	4	2
10	S	2	4	4	4	3
11	E	3	5	5	5	4
12	S	5	3	2	5	4
13	E	4	5	5	2	3

* E refers to elementary level; S refers to secondary level.

1	2	4	5	7	8	3–6
Partici-pant	Assign-ment Level *	Volun-tariness	Stimu-lating	Rele-vance	Useful-ness	Objective Congruence
14	E	0	4	5	3	2
15	S	5	5	5	4	5
16	E	3	5	5	3	4
17	E	2	5	5	2	3
18	S	4	5	4	3	3
19	E	1	3	2	4	2
20	E	0	4	5	2	1
21	S	5	4	4	4	4
22	E	0	5	5	4	2
23	S	3	5	4	2	4
24	E	4	5	5	2	5
25	S	4	5	4	3	5
26	E	3	5	4	3	3
27	E	2	5	5	3	3
28	S	1	5	4	2	2
29	E	4	5	5	4	5
30	E	5	5	5	5	4
31	E	5	5	4	1	4
32	S	4	5	5	4	3
33	E	0	5	5	2	1
34	E	4	5	4	4	5
35	S	4	4	2	4	2
36	E	3	5	5	5	3
37	E	1	5	5	2	2
38	E	4	5	4	3	5
39	S	4	5	5	3	4
40	E	0	5	4	3	1
41	E	3	5	4	2	4
42	E	4	5	4	1	3
43	E	5	5	5	4	4
44	E	3	4	3	5	2
45	S	5	5	5	3	5
46	S	5	5	5	1	4

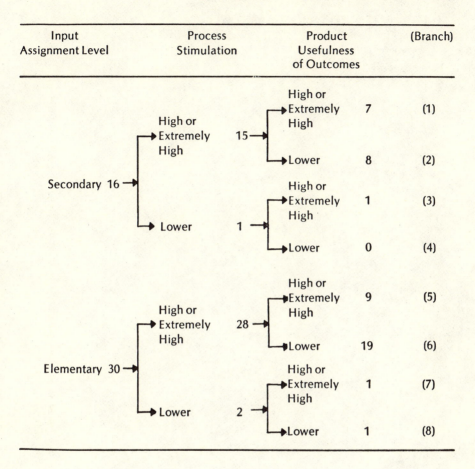

Input Assignment Level	Process Stimulation	Product Usefulness of Outcomes		(Branch)
Secondary 16	High or Extremely High 15	High or Extremely High	7	(1)
		Lower	8	(2)
	Lower 1	High or Extremely High	1	(3)
		Lower	0	(4)
Elementary 30	High or Extremely High 28	High or Extremely High	9	(5)
		Lower	19	(6)
	Lower 2	High or Extremely High	1	(7)
		Lower	1	(8)

Index